Psychological Research

METHODS FOR DISCOVERY AND VALIDATION

Psychological Research

METHODS FOR DISCOVERY AND VALIDATION

❖

Arlene C. Vadum
Assumption College

Neil O. Rankin
Assumption College

Boston, Massachusetts   Burr Ridge, Illinois   Dubuque, Iowa
Madison, Wisconsin   New York, New York   San Francisco, California   St. Louis, Missouri

Irwin/McGraw-Hill

A Division of The **McGraw·Hill** *Companies*

1 2 3 4 5 7 8 9 0 DOC/DOC 9 0 9 8 7

ISBN 0-07-066787-X

Editorial director: *Jane Vaicunas*
Sponsoring editor: *Sharon Geary/Joseph Terry*
Senior project manager: *Denise Santor-Mitzit*
Production supervisor: *Karen Thigpen*
Designer: *Matthew Baldwin*
Photo research coordinator: *Keri Johnson*
Compositor: *Shepherd Incorporated*
Typeface: *10/12 Palatino*
Printer: *R. R. Donnelley & Sons Company*

Library of Congress Cataloging-in-Publication Data

Vadum, Arlene C.
   Psychological research : methods for discovery and validation /
  Arlene C. Vadum, Neil O. Rankin.
     p. cm.
   Includes bibliographical references and index.
   ISBN 0-07-066787-X (alk. paper)
   1. Psychology--Research--Methodology.   I. Rankin, Neil O.
  II. Title.
  BF76.5.V33   1998   97-29579
  150'.72--dc21

http://www.mhhe.com

To Marjorie Rankin, and to the memory
of James Rankin and Marie Josephine Vadum

Preface

———— ❖ ————

This textbook, written for undergraduate courses in research methods, covers basic issues, advanced topics, and practical concerns in designing and conducting research. Our treatment of these issues is comprehensive, using classical and up-to-date examples of research to illustrate the methods discussed.

The first section of the book presents the fundamentals: scientific method, a classification of research designs, experimental control, measurement, correlation, randomized experimental designs, and ethics. The second section considers more advanced topics: factorial designs, single-case experimental designs, and field research, including quasi-experimental designs, observational techniques, and survey research. The last three chapters focus on practical concerns: finding a research problem, planning the study, and writing a research report in the APA style.

What distinguishes our text from others is how we present this material. In our book we tell the stories of how modern research methods, ethical principles, and procedures for communicating research developed and led to later advances. This approach highlights the logic of the methods and the kinds of research questions to which they apply, helping students to get the "big picture" of research methods in an understandable and memorable way. Explaining the context in which the methods developed naturally stresses their novel features, separating important ideas from less important ones. Because the innovators were fascinating people with brilliant ideas about how to do research, their stories also give students a sense of the challenges and excitement of science.

Our narrative, contextual approach allows us to use the originators' own words and examples to explain the methods. Their presentations are clear and compelling. When students are introduced to the ingenious logic of randomization as Fisher presented it (see Chapter 6), they can understand why his work revolutionized experimental design. When they learn how Galton developed the concepts of correlation and norm-based measurement (Chapters 4, 5), they can see why these methods are indispensable in modern psychology. When they read about the empirical studies that led to the Nuremberg Code and the Belmont Report (Chapter 7), they can appreciate the need for the ethical code and research review procedures used in psychology today. When students learn how scientists became a global community through shared writing in scientific journals, they can better appreciate the noble tradition they are joining when they write their own reports.

We have tried to organize the book to allow instructors flexibility in assigning the readings. Because later chapters build on ideas presented in earlier ones, the first six chapters are best read in order. The chapter on ethics, seventh in the book, does not have to be assigned in this position. We chose to present ethics in the middle of the book so that students would have an understanding of the basics of research design before reading it. We think this helps them to better understand the ethical dilemmas facing researchers. We also find that discussing ethics at mid-semester provides a welcome break from focusing on the more technical aspects of research. The sections of Chapter 12 on debriefing, applying to the IRB, and writing consent forms can be read in conjunction with the chapter on ethics, as can Chapter 13's discussion of the ethics of analyzing data and reporting results. The Belmont Report, which the federal government states researchers and members of IRBs should consider as a required reference work, is reprinted in its entirety in Appendix A.

Each of the advanced chapters can stand alone, so instructors can assign all of them or select from among them. Chapter 8, Factorial Designs and Interactions, is an extension of the material in Chapter 6, Randomized Designs. If both Chapters 9 and 10 are used, we recommend assigning them in order. The discussion of n = 1 designs (Chapter 9) introduces the notation used in Chapter 10's discussion of quasi-experimental designs. There also is overlap between the n = 1 designs and time series quasi-experimental designs, discussed in Chapter 10.

Students can read the three chapters on practical concerns, Chapters 11, 12, and 13, at any time during the course. We recommend that they study Chapter 11, Finding a Research Problem, early in the semester. The chapter is filled with examples of research illustrating strategies that students can use to come up with ideas for projects. The chapter also teaches students the how-tos of doing library research, including the use of tools like *PsycINFO* and *PsycLIT*. Chapter 12, Planning the Study, and Chapter 13, Communicating Research, can be assigned whenever students need to know the particulars of doing research and writing the report. Chapter 12 offers practical advice on recruiting participants, randomly assigning them to groups, finding or developing measures, dealing with demand characteristics and experimenter expectancies, applying to the IRB, and debriefing participants. Chapter 13, which instructs students on the basics of writing APA style research reports, includes examples of leads, rationales, and closes to serve as models for students in their writing. As a further guide for students, we have included a published research paper, reprinted in APA manuscript form, in Appendix B.

In addition to these pedagogical features of the book, many of the chapters include boxes presenting concrete illustrations or extensions of ideas discussed in the narrative. The boxes contain documents, ethical codes, information on how to do computerized searches of the literature, computer programs for randomization, formats for questions, APA style rules, etc. As a further aid to students, important ideas are reviewed at the end of each chapter in a section on key concepts, key people, and review questions.

We also have set up a Website
(http://www.assumption.edu/html/academic/users/avadum/index.html)
that can be used with the text. The site has programs for randomly assigning subjects to groups, random sampling, and doing basic statistical calculations, such as the mean, standard deviation, and *t*-tests. These statistical ap-
plets, written in Java, can be run online from any computer with an Internet
connection and a Web browser compatible with Java 1.0, such as Netscape
Navigator 3.0. The Website also links to the Websites discussed in the text
(e.g., APA and Buros Institute).

A complete statistical program, *Student Statistician*, and its manual
(Rankin, 1986) also can be downloaded from our Website. *Student Statistician*
runs on IBM compatible computers using the MS-DOS or Windows operating
systems. This program does all the basic statistical tests usually encountered
in student research (nonparametric and parametric through two-way analysis
of variance), and it has an easy-to-learn graphical interface. Instructors using
this text may distribute the program and manual to their students without
charge, so students can take copies home to run on their own computers.

ACKNOWLEDGEMENTS

Many people at Assumption College assisted us with this project. Regina Edmonds, Charles Estus, and George Scarlett read various chapters in development and shared references and ideas that improved them. Terry Shelton informed us about the Belmont Report and the federal regulations for human subjects research. Wayne Rollins gave us information on the universality of the golden rule. Angela Dorenkamp provided articles on interpretation and linguistic analysis that shaped our discussion of case studies. Charles Flynn, John McClymer, and Daniel Mahoney were interested in and enthusiastic about the work.

The able assistance of Priscilla Berthiaume, Jean Hayes, Kathleen Hobin, Carol Maksian, Amanda Nelson, Larry Spongberg, Harvey Varnet, and Janice Wilbur, librarians at Assumption College, rescued us at critical points in the project. We thank the members of the Sabbatical Review Committee, the Faculty Development Committee, past Provost Richard Lamoureux, former Academic Vice-President Richard Oehling, and President Joseph Hagan for supporting the project financially.

The undergraduate and graduate students in Experimental Psychology and Research Seminar at Assumption College, who for many years read photocopies of chapters rather than a "real book," deserve our special thanks. They complained hardly at all and gave us much appreciated positive feedback. Thanks also to Chris Brouillard who managed the distribution of the chapters to them.

There also are many people off campus who helped us in various ways. Jesse Rankin, University of California, Berkeley, wrote our computer programs in Java for the Internet and designed our Website. Susan Vogel, University of Massachusetts Medical School, read and discussed chapters with us, and wrote many times in support of the project. Mary Moynihan, University of New Hampshire, gave us valuable feedback on one chapter. Marsha Dutton sent us handouts on writing that she created for her English classes at Hanover College. Tiffany Field of the Touch Research Institute, University of Miami Medical School, allowed us to reprint her manuscript on massage therapy as a model of a research report.

Casey Rankin helped debug *Student Statistician* and shared his expert knowledge of how to navigate in cyberspace. Hal Kiess and Doug Bloomquist, both at Framington State College, tested *Student Statistician* in their classes, making the program easier for students to use. Kamal K. Mittal and others at the Office for Protection from Research Risks (OPRR), National Institutes of Health, offered us valuable advice and educational materials on the ethics of doing research with human and animal subjects. Carolyn Gosling of *PsycINFO* User Services, APA, generously read and corrected our discussion of *PsycINFO, PsycLIT,* and *Psychological Abstracts.* The friendship of Laura Menides and Leena Osteraas encouraged us during the many years we worked on this project.

The insightful comments and helpful suggestions of the following reviewers improved the book immeasurably: Bernard C. Beins, Ithaca College; Terry L. Davidson, Purdue University; Dana S. Dunn, Moravian College; Susan E. Dutch, Westfield State College; Rosemary T. Hornak, Meredith College; Harold O. Kiess, Framingham State College; Rosanne Lorden, Eastern Kentucky University; and Linda M. Noble, Kennesaw State College.

Finally, we wish to acknowledge the gracious, professional people at McGraw-Hill with whom it has been our great pleasure to be associated. We thank Jane Vaicunas, our editorial director, and Brian McKean, our former sponsoring editor, for their faith in our project and in us as authors. Art Levine initiated our contact with McGraw-Hill and kept us informed of the status of our project prior to its acceptance for publication. Sharon Geary took over as editor toward the end of the writing when we had to face the daunting task of seeking permissions and readying the book for production. She made the transition and the tasks enjoyable. Joe Terry, a recent arrival at McGraw-Hill, helped us with last-minute decision making. Matt Baldwin designed an extraordinary cover. Keri Johnson, senior photo research coordinator, and Alexandra Truitt and Jerry Marshall did an incredible job of acquiring photos. Denise Santor-Mitzit, senior project manager, and Karen Thigpen, production supervisor, oversaw the production of the text and worked with Shepherd Incorporated to turn our manuscript into a book of which we are proud.

Brief Contents

BASIC ISSUES

CHAPTER 1   SCIENTIFIC METHOD   1

CHAPTER 2   CLASSIFYING RESEARCH   29

CHAPTER 3   CONTROL IN EXPERIMENTATION   57

CHAPTER 4   MEASUREMENT   83

CHAPTER 5   CORRELATION   108

CHAPTER 6   RANDOMIZED EXPERIMENTAL DESIGNS   128

CHAPTER 7   ETHICS OF RESEARCH   156

ADVANCED TOPICS

CHAPTER 8   FACTORIAL DESIGNS AND INTERACTIONS   182

CHAPTER 9   SINGLE-CASE EXPERIMENTAL DESIGNS   203

CHAPTER 10   FIELD RESEARCH   228

PRACTICAL CONCERNS

CHAPTER 11   FINDING A RESEARCH PROBLEM   260

CHAPTER 12   PLANNING THE STUDY   287

CHAPTER 13   COMMUNICATING RESEARCH   317

APPENDIX A   353

APPENDIX B   367

REFERENCES   393

ACKNOWLEDGMENTS AND PHOTO CREDITS   401

NAME INDEX   407

SUBJECT INDEX   411

Contents

———— ❖ ————

CHAPTER 1   SCIENTIFIC METHOD   1

THE APPEAL OF SCIENCE   2
DISTINGUISHING FEATURES OF SCIENCE   3
    Appeal to Evidence   3
    Rules of Evidence   4
    Cycles of Discovery and Validation   5
    Progress   6
THE PROCESS OF SCIENTIFIC RESEARCH   6
    Identifying a Research Problem   6
    From Observation to Explanation   6
    Hypotheses   9
    Designing a Test of the Hypothesis   10
    Drawing Conclusions   16
    Evaluation by the Scientific Community   17
A CASE STUDY IN PSYCHOLOGICAL RESEARCH   18
    The Cycle of Discovery: Mesmer and Animal Magnetism   18
    The Cycle of Validation: King Louis XVI's Royal Commission   21
KEY TERMS   27
KEY PEOPLE   27
REVIEW QUESTIONS   27

CHAPTER 2   CLASSIFYING RESEARCH   29

THE EXTENT OF RESEARCHER MANIPULATION
  OF ANTECEDENT CONDITIONS   33
    Stage of the Inquiry   33
    Laboratory versus Field Research   34
    Research Interests of Psychologists   35
THE EXTENT TO WHICH THE RESEARCHER LIMITS RESPONSE
  ALTERNATIVES   41
    Surveys   41
    Archival Research   42

Participant Observation   43
Phenomenological Research   46
NATURALISTIC RESEARCH DEFINED   47
IDIOGRAPHIC VERSUS NOMOTHETIC RESEARCH   49
The Single-Case Experiment   51
The Case Study   51
Psychobiography and Life Narratives   53
THE VALUE OF DIVERSITY   54
KEY TERMS   55
KEY PEOPLE   55
REVIEW QUESTIONS 55

CHAPTER 3   CONTROL IN EXPERIMENTATION   57

A LIFE DEVOTED TO EMPIRICISM   58
A BOLD EXPERIMENT   59
MILL'S METHODS: A DEFINITION OF CONTROL   60
Two Steps of Research   61
Method of Difference   62
Method of Concomitant Variation   65
Method of Agreement   69
THE LANGUAGE OF VARIABLES   71
Independent and Dependent Variables   71
Quantitative and Qualitative Variables   71
LIMITATIONS OF MILL'S EXPERIMENTAL METHOD   72
Internal Validity   72
External Validity   73
Construct Validity   74
APPLYING THE METHODS   75
Within-Subjects Design   76
Between-Subjects Design   77
APPROACHES TO DEALING WITH UNCONTROLLED VARIABLES   79
The Within-Subjects Design with Virtually Total Control   79
*Statistical Control: Measure the Uncontrolled Variables and Remove
Their Effects   80*
Randomized Experiments   80
KEY TERMS   81
KEY PEOPLE   81
REVIEW QUESTIONS   81

CHAPTER 4   MEASUREMENT   83

THE VARIETY OF MEASURES IN PSYCHOLOGICAL RESEARCH   84
SCALES OF MEASUREMENT   87
STANDARD AND NORM-BASED SCALES   90

THE BEGINNINGS OF NORM-BASED MEASUREMENT   91
DESCRIBING INDIVIDUAL DIFFERENCES   93
    Percentiles   93
    The Normal Distribution   95
    Percentiles and the Normal Curve   98
    Why the Normal Distribution Is So Common   99
    Galton's Scaling Method   100
NORMAL OR NON-NORMAL? THE LOGIC OF STATISTICAL TESTS   101
KEY TERMS   106
KEY PEOPLE   106
REVIEW QUESTIONS   106

CHAPTER 5   CORRELATION   108

THE DISCOVERY OF REGRESSION   109
    The Concept of Regression   110
    The Regression Coefficient   111
THE SCATTERPLOT: THE GRAPH OF CORRELATION   112
THE CORRELATION COEFFICIENT   115
    The Independence of Variables   115
    z Scores   116
    r, an Index of Correlation   117
    Calculating r   118
    r and the Reliability and Validity of Measures   118
CORRELATION AND PREDICTION: THE METHOD OF LEAST SQUARES   119
    Nonlinear Relationships   120
    Statistical Control   121
CORRELATION'S BAD REPUTATION   122
    Causal Relationships   123
    Noncausal Relationships   124
KEY TERMS   126
KEY PEOPLE   126
REVIEW QUESTIONS   127

CHAPTER 6   RANDOMIZED EXPERIMENTAL DESIGNS   128

A MEASURE OF ERROR   130
THE RANDOMIZED BLOCKS DESIGN   133
    Replication   133
    Random Assignment   133
    Determining the Measure of Error   134
    The Null Hypothesis   135
    The Significance Probability, p   136
    Interpreting p   136
    The t Test   137

COMPLETELY RANDOMIZED DESIGN AND THE LATIN
   SQUARE DESIGN   138
FISHER'S DESIGNS IN PSYCHOLOGY   140
        Completely Randomized Design: Evaluating Cognitive Therapy   143
        Randomized Blocks Design: Stimuli Necessary
          for Perceptual Development   144
        Latin Square: High Sugar Diet for Children   145
POWER ANALYSIS: DECIDING ON THE NUMBER
   OF SUBJECTS   146
        Type I and Type II Errors   146
        The Treatment Effect Size   148
        How to Estimate the Effect Size in Your Own Research   150
        Other Strategies to Increase Power   150
STATISTICAL CONCLUSION VALIDITY   152
        Low Statistical Power   153
        Violation of Assumptions   153
        Error Rate Problem   153
        Instability   153
FINAL COMMENT   154
KEY TERMS   154
KEY PEOPLE   155
REVIEW QUESTIONS   155

CHAPTER 7   ETHICS OF RESEARCH   156

THE NUREMBERG CODE   159
        Informed Consent   162
        Risk/Benefit Analysis   163
THE NEED FOR LEGISLATIVE CHANGE   165
THE BELMONT REPORT   166
        Respect   167
        Beneficence   167
        Justice   167
CODE OF FEDERAL REGULATIONS FOR THE PROTECTION
   OF HUMAN SUBJECTS   168
AMERICAN PSYCHOLOGICAL ASSOCIATION (APA) CODE OF CONDUCT
   FOR RESEARCH   170
ETHICS IN ANIMAL RESEARCH   175
        Animal Welfare Act of 1985   176
        APA Code of Conduct: Care and Use of Animals in Research   177
FINAL COMMENTS   179
KEY TERMS   180
KEY PEOPLE   180
REVIEW QUESTIONS   180

CHAPTER 8   FACTORIAL DESIGNS AND INTERACTIONS   182

THE FACTORIAL DESIGN   185
 Assigning Subjects to Treatments   186
 Comparisons between Conditions   187
 The Interaction between Factors A and B   187
 Main Effect of Factor A   189
 Main Effect of Factor B   189
 The Analysis of Variance   190
VARIATIONS IN FACTORIAL DESIGNS   190
 Between-Subjects Factors   191
 Within-Subjects Factors   193
 Subject Factors   194
 The Number of Factors   198
ADVANTAGES OF THE FACTORIAL DESIGN   199
 Efficiency   199
 Comprehensiveness   200
 External Validity   200
THE GENERAL LINEAR MODEL   200
KEY TERMS   201
KEY PEOPLE   201
REVIEW QUESTIONS   201

CHAPTER 9   SINGLE-CASE EXPERIMENTAL DESIGNS   203

THE O X O SINGLE-CASE DESIGN   206
LIMITATIONS OF RANDOMIZED CONTROL GROUP DESIGNS   208
 Getting Enough Subjects   208
 Misleading Summary Statistics   208
 Relevance   211
SKINNER'S BASIC EXPERIMENTAL DESIGN   211
REPLICATION IN MODERN SINGLE-CASE DESIGNS   215
 Sequential Replication Designs   216
 Illustration of the ATD Design: Temporal Discrimination in Goldfish   217
 Simultaneous Replication Designs   219
 Illustration of the Multiple Baseline Design: Behavioral Treatment
  of Depressive Behaviors   221
PRINCIPLES OF DESIGN AND ANALYSIS   223
 Choice of Design   223
 The Size of the Study   224
 Handling Threats to Internal and External Validity   224
 Data Analysis   225
KEY TERMS   226
KEY PEOPLE   226
REVIEW QUESTIONS   226

CHAPTER 10   FIELD RESEARCH   228

THE DESIGN OF FIELD EXPERIMENTS (QUASI-EXPERIMENTS)   230
        Pretest-Posttest One-Group Design: O X O   230
        Replicating the O X O Design with Different Measures
            and Subgroups   232
        Replicating the O X O Design with Repeated Measures,
            Time-Series Designs   232
        Nonequivalent Control Groups   235
NATURALISTIC OBSERVATION   237
        Deciding on Behavioral Units   239
        Reducing Observer Bias   242
        Observer Reliability   244
        Reducing Subject Reactivity   244
SURVEY RESEARCH   249
        Probability Sampling   250
        Measuring Error   252
        Modes of Administering the Survey   253
        The Wording of Questions   255
FINAL COMMENTS   256
KEY TERMS   257
KEY PEOPLE   258
REVIEW QUESTIONS   258

CHAPTER 11   FINDING A RESEARCH PROBLEM   260

PREPARING THE MIND   262
        The Literature Search   263
        Collecting Your Own Observations   268
EUREKA!—DISCOVERING IDEAS   273
        Use Theory to Generate Ideas   273
        Explore Analogies and Metaphors   274
        Keep Alert for Anomalies   275
        Look for Gaps in Knowledge   276
        Turn Assumptions on Their Heads   278
        Look for Patterns in Findings   278
        Try to Resolve Discrepancies   279
        Develop Skepticism about Findings, Methods, and Interpretations   280
        Improve Apparatus, Measures, and Procedures   280
        Focus on Practical Problems   282
FINAL THOUGHTS   283
KEY TERMS   284
KEY PEOPLE   284
REVIEW QUESTIONS   285

CHAPTER 12   PLANNING THE STUDY   287

RECRUITING PARTICIPANTS   288
    Probability Sampling   289
    Convenience Sampling   289
ASSIGNING SUBJECTS TO GROUPS   290
DECIDING ON APPARATUS AND MEASURING INSTRUMENTS   290
    Instruments   290
    Self-report Measures   292
CONSTRUCTING YOUR OWN QUESTIONNAIRE   295
    Open versus Closed Questions   295
    Closed Item Formats   296
    Use Standard English—Define Your Terms   300
EVALUATING PSYCHOLOGICAL MEASURES   301
    Reliability   301
    Validity   302
EVALUATING OBSERVATIONAL MEASURES   303
SPECIAL PROBLEMS OF CONTROL WITH HUMAN PARTICIPANTS   305
    The Hawthorne Effect   305
    Demand Characteristics and Experimenter Expectancies   307
    Controlling for Suggestion and Reactivity   309
DEBRIEFING   310
APPLYING TO THE INSTITUTIONAL REVIEW BOARD   311
    Recruitment Procedures   311
    The Consent Form   312
    Procedures Involved in the Research   314
    Confidentiality   314
FINAL COMMENTS   314
KEY TERMS   315
KEY PEOPLE   315
REVIEW QUESTIONS   315

CHAPTER 13   COMMUNICATING RESEARCH   317

THE LANGUAGE OF SCIENCE   320
CONTENTS AND ORGANIZATION OF PSYCHOLOGICAL RESEARCH
  REPORTS   321
    Title Page   322
    Abstract   323
    Introduction   323
    Method   328
    Results   329
    Discussion   336
    References   341
    Appendix, Author Note, Footnotes, Tables, and Figures   342

CONTENTS

APA EDITORIAL STYLE   342
WRITING WITH "STYLE"   345
ORAL PRESENTATIONS   347
THE ETHICS OF SCIENTIFIC COMMUNICATION   348
FINAL THOUGHTS   350
KEY TERMS   351
KEY PEOPLE   351
REVIEW QUESTIONS   351

APPENDIX A THE BELMONT REPORT   353
APPENDIX B MODEL MANUSCRIPT   367
REFERENCES   393
ACKNOWLEDGMENTS AND PHOTO CREDITS   401
NAME INDEX   407
SUBJECT INDEX   411

Psychological Research

METHODS FOR DISCOVERY
AND VALIDATION

1

Scientific Method

———— ❖ ————

Science as something existing and complete is the most objective thing known to man. But, science in the making, science as an end to be pursued is as subjective and psychologically conditioned as any other branch of human endeavor.

ALBERT EINSTEIN

———— ❖ ————

THE APPEAL OF SCIENCE
DISTINGUISHING FEATURES OF SCIENCE
    Appeal to Evidence
    Rules of Evidence
    Cycles of Discovery and Validation
    Progress
THE PROCESS OF SCIENTIFIC RESEARCH
    Identifying a Research Problem
    From Observation to Explanation
    Hypotheses
    Designing a Test of the Hypothesis
        Subjects
        Research design
        Apparatus, procedures, and measures
    Drawing Conclusions
    Evaluation by the Scientific Community
A CASE STUDY IN PSYCHOLOGICAL RESEARCH
    The Cycle of Discovery: Mesmer and Animal Magnetism
        A theory invented
        Mesmer's observational and experimental
          research

The Cycle of Validation: King Louis XVI's
Royal Commission
The research problem: assessing
animal magnetism
Hypothesis
Test implications of the hypothesis
Drawing conclusions
Evaluation by the scientific community
KEY TERMS, KEY PEOPLE, REVIEW QUESTIONS

THE APPEAL OF SCIENCE

The mission of the *Starship Enterprise* in the popular television series *Star Trek: The Next Generation* was "To boldly go where no one has gone before," a phrase which also aptly describes the mission of people who dedicate their lives to science. Some scientists, like those on the *Enterprise,* explore "strange, new worlds" at the farthest reaches of the universe; most chart new territories closer to home.

Psychologists, the scientists we focus on in this book, try to understand the world of the child (a world we once lived in but no longer know), or study how people organize the "blooming, buzzing, confusion" that surrounds us, or work to piece together a picture of what life is like for the animals that share the world with us. Because psychology is a relatively new science, there are many frontiers to explore.

Antoinette and John Lilly explored one such uncharted region in their pioneering research on communication in dolphins and whales. Their reports of the experience convey a sense of the excitement and challenge that attract people to science and keep them involved in it. In the following quotation, Antoinette Lilly describes the thrill of her first close encounter with a whale:

> The joy of the next few minutes can only be described as absurd. . . . This whale's invitation to share her world gave me a glimpse through a cosmic crack between species . . . a oneness of all living beings as we will know them someday in the future . . . a place we have been before and will return to again . . . a peaceful promise . . . *the* "peaceable kingdom." (Lilly, in Ferrucci, 1990, p. 239)

John Lilly tells of the apprehension that also accompanied them on their foray into that unknown world:

> This opening of our minds was a subtle and yet a painful process. We began to have feelings which I believe are best described by the word "weirdness." The feeling was that we were up against the edge of a vast uncharted region in which we were about to embark with a good deal of mistrust in the appropriateness of our equipment. (Lilly, in Ferrucci, 1990, p. 238)

The recollections of these pioneers give us some sense of the intense and even uncanny emotions that accompany research on the frontiers of science. They also demonstrate that, despite popular stereotypes, scientists are not a special breed of people set apart from others by their superhuman rationality and robotlike detachment; and science is anything but the dull, methodical enterprise it is often assumed to be. Quite the contrary is true. Scientists are passionate people and scientific work is ignited and fueled by passion; otherwise it would not be possible for scientists to give so much of themselves to it.

For some scientists, inspiration comes from the promise science holds out of answering age-old questions of the meaning of life and/or our place in creation. Jean Piaget, the psychologist whose pioneering research revolutionized our understanding of children's thought, is one example:

> I recall one evening of profound revelation. The identification of God with life itself was an idea that stirred me almost to ecstasy because it now enabled me to see in biology the explanation of all things and of the mind itself. The problem of knowledge . . . suddenly appeared to me in an entirely new perspective and as an absorbing topic of study. It made me decide to consecrate my life to the biological explanation of knowledge. (Piaget, 1952, p. 240)

For others, science offers an opportunity to make one's life meaningful by doing work that makes a difference, and the potential of achieving a type of immortality—the chance to leave one's mark on the world. According to Thomas Kuhn:

> What . . . challenges [the scientist] is the conviction that, if only he is skillful enough, he will succeed in solving a puzzle that no one before has solved or solved so well. (Kuhn, 1970, p. 38)

Yet the possibility of making a contribution is not the only inspiration to scientific work. It's not just solving the puzzle that excites the scientist, it's finding just the right puzzle, and working on the puzzle too. George Kneller, a historian of science, puts it this way:

> The scientist studies nature not simply because it is useful but because he delights in it. He sees beauty in the harmony of nature's parts which his mind is able to grasp. "Intellectual beauty," wrote Henri Poincaré, "is sufficient unto itself, and it is for its sake, more perhaps than the future good of humanity, that the scientist devotes himself to long and difficult labors." (Kneller, 1978, p. 151)

DISTINGUISHING FEATURES OF SCIENCE

Appeal to Evidence

Scientists work at discovering facts and inventing theories to explain them. A basic assumption underlying their efforts is that it is indeed possible to make sense of the events being considered. Science involves a continuous interplay between collecting observations and thinking about them; the aim is to develop formal principles to explain what has been observed.

Much of a scientist's time is spent carefully observing events, asking questions, formulating answers, and checking them by observing again. When things go well, explanatory principles and theories to account for their own and others' observations are the result. These explanatory principles and theories, in turn, lead to predictions, which are tested by making more observations.

The essence of the scientific method is the acquisition of facts and the testing of ideas by *appealing to the evidence.* No matter how much the scientist may want the results to turn out a particular way, a rule of scientific procedure is that judgment must be suspended until the evidence is in. This approach to acquiring knowledge—through observation and experimentation—is called *empirical.* All sciences that involve research are *empirical sciences.*

In England, in the middle of the 17th century, a group of thinkers committed to the empirical method refused to accept established truths that were backed up only by the authority of the church and state. These skeptics formed a society of revolutionists who vowed to "listen to the answers experiments give us and no other answers!" (de Kruif, 1926, p. 5). The society, called *The Invisible College,* met secretly to avoid the death penalty that would have been imposed on them if they had been discovered in their heretical activities. Robert Boyle, the chemist and physicist, and Isaac Newton, the physicist, were members of this group of scientists that later became the prestigious Royal Society of London (de Kruif, 1926, p. 7).

In the spirit of *The Invisible College,* scientists today are trained to be skeptical and to accept nothing on authority. Whereas the nonscientist may believe an idea to be true just because it feels right, because it seems logically correct, because it has always been believed, or because an authority claims it to be so, these bases for beliefs are unacceptable in science. The scientific community accepts as valid knowledge only those statements about events that are supported by convincing evidence.

In science, statements about events must be backed up by empirical evidence.

Scientists aim to produce error-free results, the kind of evidence that will be convincing to themselves and other scientists. One way to reduce the likelihood of drawing conclusions based on accidental, one-time happenings is to systematically repeat one's observations and calculations. When researchers get a given result over and over, that is, when results can be *replicated,* the likelihood of error produced through accident is reduced.

In science, errors in observing or in drawing conclusions must be avoided by systematically checking and repeating one's observations.

Rules of Evidence

Scientists are acutely aware of errors that can result from group and personal biases (from cultural assumptions, desires, values), readily acknowledging that their passion can foster blindness and self-deception. Antoine Lavoisier, the founder of modern chemistry, cautioned scientists against seeing and recording only evidence that fits their preconceptions (Ferrucci, 1990, p. 207). Charles Darwin, the naturalist who developed the theory of evolution, systematically wrote down observations that contradicted his ideas; he knew he would forget these most easily (Ferrucci, 1990, p. 207).

It is to counteract such sources of error that scientists have developed a community standard for testing and evaluating the truth of their assertions. To be accepted in science, research must meet agreed upon criteria for objectivity and precision. Only certain types of questions—those that are potentially answerable by collecting observations—qualify as scientific questions. Measures and procedures—instruments, research design, and data analysis—must comply with accepted practice in the field. Original methods and procedures have to be fully explained and justified.

Cycles of Discovery and Validation

So far, we have discussed the scientist as an individual collecting observations and formulating and testing principles for making sense out of those observations; but the great strength of science is that it is a *collective enterprise.*

Kneller (1978) has distinguished two phases in scientific work. The first he calls the *cycle of discovery.* In this phase, investigators work alone or in a team, collecting observations, formulating and testing tentative understandings. It is this activity that most people envision when they think of science, and it is this phase of scientific work that we have discussed so far in this chapter. But the image of science as solitary is misleading. For even in their solitary activities, scientists are mindful of the second phase of research, what Kneller calls the *cycle of validation*—the review of the work by other scientists.

In the cycle of validation, the scientist reports the research to scientific peers. In addition to carefully evaluating the merits of the work, these scientists may do research to replicate its findings or to test rival explanations of its results. Science depends on both types of activity—on committed researchers discovering and testing ideas, and on a community of scientists ready to question evidence and interpretations, and offer alternative interpretations and the evidence to support them.

The aim in science is to eliminate insights or observations that are available only to particular persons and to accept only knowledge that has been verified by others in the scientific community. In science, evidence must be public.

Any trained scientist using the same methods must be able to reproduce the results.

When other scientists can repeat a procedure and replicate its results, the likelihood that false ideas will be detected and corrected is increased.

The requirement that results be reproducible is an important check on systematic error produced by bias in observers, inadequacies in measuring instruments, or other peculiarities of the testing situation.

Progress

A scientist from just a century ago would surely be amazed at the great strides we have made in our understanding of human behavior—the facts are now different and antique theories have given way to new understandings. We no longer think you can read character in the bumps of the skull or in facial features. Modern psychologists no longer treat mental disorders by applying magnets to the body or by administering the "bath of surprise" (throwing a blindfolded patient into a river or lake).

The success of science in establishing new facts and developing theories to explain known facts is responsible, in part, for the respect we give to scientific work and to those who devote their lives to it. As a result of such advances, science has earned a reputation as perhaps our most trustworthy source of knowledge.

A scientist from the past would marvel not just at the knowledge we now have but also at the advances we've made in understanding how to answer questions in science, and the scientist would view these advances as anything but trivial. For scientists know that it's not their brilliance as a group (though many are) nor their superiority as observers (though many are) that makes science such a reliable source of knowledge. It is its methods.

THE PROCESS OF SCIENTIFIC RESEARCH

Identifying a Research Problem

Empirical research begins with a research problem. This is true both in original research on a problem and in research conducted to assess the validity of that work. The problem is usually phrased in the form of a question. In psychology, we ask: What kinds of learning are animals capable of? Is intelligence inherited? How often do people dream? How does empathy develop in children? How should mental disturbances be classified? To be suitable for science, the question that is posed must be potentially answerable by the appeal to evidence.

From Observation to Explanation

Research in a new field, or on a new problem, or on previously unexamined phenomena, is likely to focus more on "getting the facts" than on testing a theory. At an early stage of the research, one's theories may even be seen as biases, untested assumptions and prejudices, that could "get in the way" of really seeing what is going on. For this reason, researchers sometimes try to set their preconceptions aside and let the data "speak for themselves."

However, some philosophers of science question whether there really can be anything like pure fact-finding. They believe that the way we structure the events we encounter is colored by our basic assumptions and preconceptions, our theories about the world. Carl Hempel (1966) concluded that all research is guided by theory. He reasoned that whenever we are advanced enough in our thinking to select a particular set of events to relate, we are testing a theory, albeit an informal and perhaps poorly articulated one.

B. F. Skinner, whose pioneering research led to the principles of operant conditioning, disagreed. Skinner did not think that he had been guided in his research by theory, especially in the beginning. Skinner described his discovery of "curves of extinction" as primarily a result of a fortunate accident. When his apparatus for delivering food pellets broke down, the rats in his experiment failed to receive a pellet for each correct response they made. The observations Skinner then made led to his famous "curves of extinction" of learned responses.

> I am not saying that I would not have got around to extinction curves without a breakdown in the apparatus; Pavlov had given too strong a lead in that direction. But it is still no exaggeration to say that some of the most interesting and surprising results have turned up first because of similar accidents. (Skinner, 1959, p. 367)

Whether we use the term "theory" or not, it's clear that in research on a new problem, the first observations are guided only by the vaguest expectations. But once the basic observations are in, they become the "raw material" used in formulating a generalization to account for what is observed. Skinner thought of this process as a matter of being in the right place, at the right time, when the right things happened. But philosophers of science, whose job it is to reflect on the process of scientific activity, use more formal terms, taken from logic, to describe this process. They call this type of reasoning *induction*.

> *Induction* refers to the process of reasoning from particular facts or individual cases to a general conclusion.

Whenever researchers observe particular events and then formulate a generalization to explain them, or make particular observations and draw general conclusions from them, they are using induction or inductive reasoning. Induction is involved in every research study; scientists make only certain observations yet draw general conclusions from them. Induction also is involved in all theory building.

The process of induction is mysterious. Studying the results of exploratory observations, the scientist hopes for the "flash of insight," the eureka experience, that will explain and systematize them. Unfortunately, no one knows the precise set of ingredients that leads to useful generalizations or hypotheses. To quote Hempel:

> Scientific hypotheses and theories are not *derived* from observed facts, but *invented* in order to account for them. They constitute guesses at the connections that might

obtain between the phenomena under study, at uniformities and patterns that might underlie their occurrence. "Happy guesses" of this kind require great ingenuity, especially if they involve a radical departure from current modes of scientific thinking. (Hempel, 1966, p. 15)

But we do know some of the ingredients. Happy guesses do not come completely out of the blue. Skinner knew that he was onto an important principle of learning because he had been prepared for the discovery of extinction curves by studying the work of the famous Russian physiologist Ivan Pavlov. The prepared mind can see meanings and possibilities in events when other minds, less prepared, cannot.

Happy guesses also seem to require total absorption, sometimes even obsession, with solving the problem. Thomas Edison was so involved in his experiments that he forgot to attend his own wedding. Marie Curie reported that while she and her husband were engaged in the work that led to the discovery of radium, they lived "with a single preoccupation, as if in a dream" (Ferrucci, 1990, p. 226). Happy guesses sometimes emerge only after months or years of hard work. For this reason, scientists must be able to endure uncertainty, even confusion, over long periods of time.

Historians of science point to other ingredients that are important in this creative process. Thomas Kuhn (1970) concluded that revolutionary ideas in science come most often from people new to a field or from young people, whose backgrounds and academic training allow them to see things in a fresh way. Jean Piaget is a good example.

Piaget earned his doctorate in zoology before becoming a developmental psychologist. Right from the beginning, Piaget (1952) asked different questions about intelligence than were standard in the field. Piaget's first job as a psychologist required him to test schoolchildren's intelligence. The standard procedure was to count the number of correct responses on an intelligence test. But Piaget was curious about the reasoning behind the children's answers; so he went beyond the usual practice, asking the children to explain each of the answers that they gave. Piaget also was able to use the observation skills that he had acquired in studying sparrows and mollusks to make systematic observations of his own children's behaviors in infancy and childhood. These methodological innovations led eventually to a revolutionary theory of intellectual development.

Piaget is only one of many innovators in psychology who came from other disciplines. Indeed, many of the pioneers in research methods that we discuss in this book were trained in fields other than those in which they made their major contributions.

Paul Feyerabend (1975) provides a thought-provoking explanation for why newcomers so often make important innovations in science. Feyerabend believes that scientific revolutions result from criticism of the basic prejudices and assumptions of a discipline. This can't happen, he says, from within the discipline because "prejudices are found by contrast, not by analysis" (Feyerabend, 1975, p. 31). He asks:

> How can we possibly examine something we are using all the time? How can we analyze the terms in which we habitually express our most simple and straightforward observations and reveal their presuppositions? How can we discover the kind of world we presuppose when proceeding as we do? The answer is clear: we cannot discover it from the inside. We need an external standard of criticism, we need a set of alternative assumptions or, . . . an entire alternative world, we need a dream-world in order to discover the features of the real world we think we inhabit. (Feyerabend, 1975, pp. 31–32)

Kuhn's and Feyerabend's observations suggest that a nonconforming personality may be an asset in science. Indeed, Frank Sulloway (1996), a historian of science, found that great theoretical advances often are made by the youngest child in a family, the last born, the family rebel.

Hypotheses

Early in this century, psychologists offered competing answers to the question "How do animals learn?" One influential theorist, Edward Thorndike, thought that animals learned only by blind, trial-and-error. In Thorndike's view, unintelligent stimulus-response connections were blindly "stamped-in" whenever an animal's response led to satisfaction. Wolfgang Köhler, a proponent of the Gestalt theory of learning, thought that animals were more intelligent than Thorndike gave them credit for. He thought animals responded to "gestalts," that is, to the whole character of situations, to the relationships between stimuli rather than to the absolute properties of stimuli, as Thorndike's theory asserted.

These ideas of Thorndike and Köhler are tentative answers to research questions. Philosophers of science call such ideas *hypotheses* when the focus is on using the idea as a guide to empirical research. Hempel offers the following definition of a hypothesis:

> [The *hypothesis* is] whatever statement is under test, no matter whether it purports to describe some particular fact or event or to express a general law or some other, more complex proposition. (Hempel, 1966, p. 19)

It is the hypothesis, the tentative answer to the research question, not the question itself, that determines which observations to make in a study (Kneller, 1978). Research that is guided by a hypothesis is said to involve *hypothesis testing*. Most of the research published in psychology journals tests hypotheses.

So far, we have discussed how hypotheses are developed inductively. Both Thorndike's and Köhler's hypotheses about animal learning came about in this way—by observing what animals do and trying to make sense of it. But this picture of hypothesis formation is incomplete. Hypotheses also are derived from theories and suggest themselves in the process of research. A theory, like Köhler's Gestalt psychology, leads to many specific hypotheses. Unexpected findings in research prompt the refinement of working hypotheses and the replacement of older hypotheses by newer ones.

Early in a program of research, hypotheses are more likely to be rough guesses at how the events of interest might be related. The researcher might wonder, for example, how sensory deprivation affects critical thinking or whether the self-esteem of introverts is different from that of extroverts. As the research progresses and more is learned about the phenomena being studied, hypotheses become more specific.

Designing a Test of the Hypothesis

Thorndike developed his hypothesis, that animals form stimulus-response connections, by watching chickens learn to escape from an enclosure. Köhler came up with his hypothesis, that animals take account of the relationships between stimuli they encounter, by watching apes and other animals in a variety of problem-solving situations. All Thorndike and Köhler could observe were animals making particular responses. The processes they hypothesized to underlie these responses could not be observed; Thorndike saw no "stimulus-response connections," nor Köhler any "gestalts." These hypothetical processes were invented to make sense out of the concrete behaviors they did observe.

The difference between explanatory concepts and the events they explain becomes important in hypothesis testing. To test a hypothesis, the researcher must make inferences about what will be observed in a concrete test situation. Hempel called such predictions the *test implications* of a hypothesis.

> The *test implications* of a hypothesis are if . . . then statements based on the assumption that the hypothesis is true.

They are predictions that if certain conditions hold true, certain other events also will hold true.

The logical process used to derive test implications is called *deduction* by philosophers of science:

> *Deduction* refers to the process of reasoning from a premise to a logical conclusion or from a general principle to specific observed events.

When researchers derive a particular hypothesis from a theory, or predict what will happen in a particular test situation on the basis of a previously established principle, they are using deductive reasoning.

One of Köhler's subjects discovers how to stack
boxes to retrieve a banana.

To test his hypothesis, Köhler had to devise a concrete test situation that
would demonstrate that his animals had learned by perceiving gestalts and
not by forming stimulus-response connections. He first had to reframe his hypothesis as an if . . . then statement of the sort: Given that animals learn by
perceiving the relationships between stimuli, if they are placed in this type of
learning situation, they will behave as follows.

Köhler (1925, in Heidbreder, 1961) decided to test hens in a discrimination
learning experiment. In the preparatory phase of his experiment, grain was
placed on two pieces of paper of different shades of gray.

When the hens pecked at grain on the darker of the two papers, they were
allowed to eat it; when they pecked at grain on the lighter gray paper, they
were shooed away. After several hundred trials, the hens pecked quite consistently at the darker paper, only rarely pecking at the lighter one.

Then came the test of the hypothesis. Grain was once again spread on papers of two shades of gray. But in this test, the stimuli were "transposed"; the
previously rewarded "dark gray" paper was now the lighter of two papers,
being paired with a paper of an even darker gray.

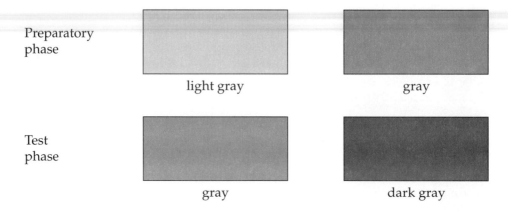

The question was whether the hens would now peck the paper of the same gray they had learned to peck in the preliminary training (as Thorndike's hypothesis would predict), or whether they would peck now at the darker paper, supporting Köhler's hypothesis that the hens had learned to respond to the darker of two stimuli. In most cases, the hens pecked at the darker paper, supporting Köhler's hypothesis.

Köhler was able to devise a test situation in which his theory and Thorndike's led to different predictions. Philosophers of science (Hempel, 1966) call such tests *crucial experiments*:

> In a *crucial experiment*, a test situation is envisioned in which two well-established hypotheses derived from two competing theories predict mutually exclusive outcomes. The single test then simultaneously provides support for one of the hypotheses and lack of support for the other.

We can use Köhler's experiment, considered a classic experiment on learning, to illustrate the decision making that goes into devising a test of the hypothesis. Decisions have to be made about subjects, the research design, as well as the study's apparatus, procedures, and measures.

Finding just the right test of a hypothesis requires ingenuity. Researchers must anticipate that other scientists, working with other theories, will scrutinize every aspect of the study and be all too ready to suggest alternative explanations for its results. Every effort must be made, therefore, to set up the test situation so that if the hypothesis is true, the evidence supporting it will be unambiguous.

Subjects. Researchers must decide whether to test animal or human subjects, what age the subjects should be, and how many should be studied. We use the term *subjects* in psychology to point to the distinction between psychology's subject matter, the behavior, thoughts, and feelings of living beings (subjects, not objects), and the nonliving subject matter of physical science. In written reports, whenever possible, psychologists replace this impersonal term with more specific terms that describe the subjects or capture their role in the research more precisely—for example, "participants, individuals, college students, children, or respondents" (American Psychological Association, 1994, p. 49). Although only certain subjects can be tested in a study, researchers hope to be able to draw conclusions that will *generalize* (that is, apply) to animals or people other than those used in the research.

Köhler used apes in much of his research. He most likely tested chickens in the "transposition" experiment because Thorndike had formulated his stimulus-response hypothesis observing these birds. By testing chickens himself, Köhler was able to show that his results, showing more complex learning processes than Thorndike's, applied to the very animals that Thorndike studied.

In addition to the question of generalization, subject selection depends on the hypothesis being tested. Hypotheses about children require the researcher to test children; hypotheses predicting differences in the behaviors of men and women require testing these groups.

In later chapters, we present a variety of research designs that offers researchers the option of studying individuals or groups of subjects. We also discuss strategies for deciding how many subjects to test.

Research design. Researchers also must decide on a *research design*.

A *research design* is a general strategy for collecting observations in research.

There are two general types of designs to choose from: *experiments* and *observational studies* (also called *passive-observational studies*). The main difference between them is the amount of control the researcher can exercise over the test conditions.

In an *experiment,* the researcher manipulates the test situation so as to create the precise conditions required for testing the hypothesis. Potential rival explanations of the results are eliminated by holding conditions associated with them constant.

It was possible for Köhler to devise an experimental test of his hypothesis, but many questions of interest to psychologists cannot be studied experimentally. Sometimes the concepts referred to in the hypothesis cannot be created (we cannot change a person's body build, temperament, or birth order); sometimes ethical considerations prevent it (it is not ethically permissible to cause phobias or depression in people, for example).

The researcher can do an *observational study* when the conditions required for testing the hypothesis cannot be created or when the research question or hypothesis demands it.

[In a *passive-observational study*] the hypothesis must be tested nonexperimentally, by seeking out, or waiting for, cases where the specified conditions are realized by nature, and then checking whether [the event] does indeed occur. (Hempel, 1966, p. 20)

Observational studies are common in psychology. For example, Piaget (1954) used this type of design to establish the stages of intellectual development in children.

In designing a study, researchers must anticipate what will happen in the cycle of validation, studying the planned research to see whether holes could be poked in the evidence it will yield. They must ask, for example, whether there are events or conditions, other than those specified by the hypothesis, that vary in such a way that a critic might argue that these, rather than the hypothesized events or conditions, led to the results.

> To the extent possible, potential rival explanations of the results should be eliminated by holding the conditions associated with them constant. This strategy is called *controlling for rival hypotheses.*

The more familiar researchers are with the conditions or events that influence the behavior under study, the greater the likelihood that potential rival explanations will be identified and eliminated by appropriate controls.

Köhler anticipated that if he did not vary the positions of the gray papers that the chickens pecked, his results would be open to a rival explanation. A critic might argue that the chickens had learned to peck at a particular location, rather than at the darker of two stimuli. This argument would be tenable, for example, if the darker paper was always on the right or left side. To control for position, Köhler kept the percent of trials on which the darker paper was in the two positions equal throughout the learning trials. By this means, he eliminated position as a potential rival explanation of his results.

Researchers do not create the test conditions in an observational study, but select for them or wait for them to occur. Because events in nature occur in combinations, it is not always possible to control for potential rival explanations of results in observational studies. For this reason, the conclusions drawn from such studies often are less clear-cut than those from experiments. Whenever feasible, therefore, experiments are preferred over observational studies for testing hypotheses.

Apparatus, procedures, and measures. Decisions also must be made on the particulars of the test situation—where to test subjects, with what apparatus, instructions, manipulations, and measures. Such choices will depend on the hypothesis being tested and on the available technology and traditions in a particular area of research. You can increase your likelihood of finding just the right situation for testing a hypothesis by reading the published studies on the problem.

To test a hypothesis, its theoretical terms must be translated into specific procedures. For some concepts, this will mean manipulating conditions or events in a particular way (like Köhler did); for others, it will mean finding the right measuring technique. Developing precise procedures for manipulating and measuring theoretical concepts in research is called *operationally defining* them. Operational definitions are part of a movement in science called *operationism.*

Operationism is the demand that all theoretical terms in science—that is, those that do not refer to something directly observable—be given operational definitions. (Leahey, 1994, p. 519)

The term *operational definition* was coined by the physicist Percy Bridgeman in 1927 and introduced to psychology in 1935 by S. S. Stevens, a psychologist whose work we discuss in Chapter 4, Measurement.

The goal in operationally defining concepts is to specify them with sufficient precision so that others trained in the field can understand and use them in their own research. In this way, it is hoped that subjective, individual understandings of concepts will be eliminated and objective public procedures and measures put in their place. When precise operational definitions are used, scientists can think clearly about problems, and other researchers can understand and replicate the defined features of studies.

To illustrate, Skinner (1938) operationally defined "hunger" in his experimental subjects by varying the number of hours of food deprivation they experienced prior to testing. His rats were allowed "to feed freely once a day for a definite length of time. . . . After about a week of this procedure a high and essentially constant degree of hunger is reached each day just before the time of feeding" (Skinner, 1938, p. 56). With such an operational definition, there is little misunderstanding of what is meant by hunger.

To take another example, intelligence might be operationally defined as the score a person achieves on a standard intelligence test, like the Stanford-Binet or Wechsler Intelligence Test; a different operational definition of intelligence would be needed to study intelligence in newborns or chimpanzees.

The researcher tries to create a manipulation that is self-evident (like Skinner's), or, if the events must be measured rather than created, the best measure possible. When the phenomena of interest can be observed directly (for example, which paper the hens pecked in Köhler's experiment), and when physical measurements are used, this is relatively easy. In such cases, demonstrating the adequacy of the measure is a matter of showing that the instruments are accurate.

The clock used to assess the number of hours of food deprivation would be certified to be accurate to + or − a certain number of seconds per year. Measurements of height or weight would be made with instruments calibrated to match standard measures kept at the Bureau of Standards in Washington, DC. Within the limits of measurement error of the instrument, which normally would be small, height as measured would correspond to height as understood by others.

Researchers face a more difficult task in establishing the accuracy of psychological measures. Investigators who purchase an intelligence test, for example, would find no mention of its accuracy in the test manual, discovering instead a discussion of the test's *reliability* and *validity*.

The *reliability* of a measuring instrument is a numerical index of the extent to which it yields consistent results from one occasion to the next. To quote Anne Anastasi, a specialist in measurement:

Reliability refers to the consistency of scores obtained by the same persons when re-examined with the same test on different occasions, or with different sets of equivalent items, or under other variable examining conditions. (Anastasi, 1988, p. 109)

A metal ruler would yield a highly reliable measure of a person's height, since repeated measurement would yield the same results. A less reliable measure would fail to produce comparable results with replication. Adequate reliability is a minimum requirement for a measuring instrument.

Intelligence tests are highly reliable but there is concern about their validity. The *validity* of a measure has to do with whether it measures what it is supposed to measure. Again, quoting from Anastasi:

The *validity* of a test concerns *what* the test measures and *how well* it does so. It tells us what can be inferred from test scores. . . . The validity of a test cannot be reported in general terms. No test can be said to have "high" or "low" validity in the abstract. Its validity must be established with reference to the particular use for which the test is being considered. (Anastasi, 1988, p. 139)

To establish the validity of an intelligence test, its developer might compare how similar the results of the new test are to those obtained using established intelligence tests, or, alternatively, how scores on the new test relate to grade point average or other behaviors thought to be related to intelligence.

Usually a great deal of research must be done to establish the validity of a measuring instrument in psychology. For this reason, whenever possible, psychological researchers use measures with established validity rather than developing their own measures; the validity of a new test must be documented before it is considered acceptable for research. The reliability and validity of psychological measures are discussed more fully in Chapter 12, Planning the Study.

Drawing Conclusions

Once a research design and the details of procedure have been worked out, the planned observations are collected and analyzed. The observations must be recorded in some symbolic form—as words, frequencies of particular behaviors, or numerical scores (e.g., time, scores on a test). Scientists use the term *data* (plural) to refer to the recorded observations that are analyzed to reach conclusions in a study. The term *results* refers to the outcome of the analysis of the data.

Researchers must be concerned with what conclusions to draw from their observations. In research involving hypothesis testing, the question is whether the data support or refute the hypothesis; if the results turn out as predicted, the hypothesis gains credibility. If the results are not in line with predictions, the hypothesis, and ultimately the theory from which it derives, are rendered less credible. In the words of the famous statistician, R. A. Fisher:

The severest test of a theory is to build upon it a system of inferences, for if any rigorously logical inference is found to be untrue the theory fails. If, on the contrary, facts previously unsuspected are inferred from the theory, and found on trial to be true, the theory is undoubtedly strengthened. (Fisher, in Box, 1978, p. 216)

The credibility of a hypothesis is increased with each successful test, especially when the same result is achieved by many researchers testing the hypothesis under different circumstances. The credibility of a hypothesis, however, does not depend only on confirming predictions; it also depends on how well potential rival hypotheses have been controlled.

Although good researchers take pains to avoid drawing incorrect conclusions, the possibility of error can never be eliminated. Even if the results support the hypothesis consistently, we never can know for sure that future tests will yield the same consistent results. For example, Köhler's study did not resolve the issue of whether animals respond to the absolute properties of stimuli or to the relationship between them. For a discussion of subsequent studies, see Klein (1996). No matter how exacting the methods, scientific conclusions are not without fault.

When the results are uniform, all pointing in the same direction, it is relatively easy to reach conclusions. But such results are rare in psychology. Usually some observations argue for one conclusion, others for the opposite conclusion. Various strategies to help researchers draw conclusions in such cases, including a variety of statistical tests, are considered in later chapters of this book.

Evaluation by the Scientific Community

Scientists form a community bound together by shared knowledge and agreed-upon rules of operation and standards of evaluation. In the second phase of research, the cycle of validation, researchers communicate their findings to other scientists through informal discussion, presentations at conferences, and publication in professional journals. To be accepted for presentation at conferences or for publication in journals, research papers must meet the standards of referees and editors qualified to evaluate the work.

Referees judge the importance of the research problem addressed (does the paper add substantively to scientific knowledge?), the appropriateness of its arguments and analyses, and the adequacy of the evidence on which its conclusions are based. In psychology, the subjects, measures and manipulations, and research design would receive careful scrutiny.

Research papers must be written according to an accepted format and give appropriate credit to other scientists. The American Psychological Association's publication manual (1994) specifies the content, organization, and style that is now standard in the field (see Chapter 13, Communicating Research).

Once published or presented at a conference, the research is subjected to a second wave of evaluation. Scientists who attend the conference or read the journal evaluate the research as the referees did; but their judgments may be quite different. They may write papers criticizing the research or conduct studies challenging its hypotheses and testing rival theories. If the findings are validated in this cycle, they slowly become established knowledge in the field.

A CASE STUDY IN PSYCHOLOGICAL RESEARCH

So far in this chapter, we have discussed the vocabulary and procedures shared by psychologists. We now turn to a case study of research, the story of how a scientific theory and a form of treatment based on that theory were invented and evaluated, to illustrate how these terms are applied.

The experiments that follow, perhaps the first ever performed in clinical psychology, evaluated a popular and controversial theory—that obstructions in the flow of an invisible fluid, "animal magnetism," in people's bodies caused pain and other symptoms.

The Cycle of Discovery: Mesmer and Animal Magnetism

A theory invented. Anton Mesmer, inventor of the theory of animal magnetism, was a wealthy Viennese physician who studied philosophy, theology, and law before settling on a career in medicine. Mesmer introduced the idea of animal magnetism in 1765 in the thesis he submitted to obtain his medical degree.

In this thesis, Mesmer hypothesized the existence of a universal force of nature that penetrated and surrounded all things. In the physical world, Mesmer believed, this force took the form of mineral magnetism, gravity, and electricity; in human beings, it took the form of animal gravity or, as he came to call it, animal magnetism. Animal magnetism was a "subtle fluid," which could not be seen or felt but could be shown to exist only through its effects.

It is not possible to say exactly where Mesmer's theory came from. No doubt its invention involved a complex interplay of induction and deduction. Discoveries in other branches of science certainly set the stage for Mesmer's thinking. To quote John Darnton, a historian:

> Science had captivated Mesmer's contemporaries by revealing to them that they were surrounded by wonderful, invisible forces: Newton's gravity, made intelligible by Voltaire; Franklin's electricity, popularized by a fad for lightning rods and by demonstrations in the fashionable lyceums and museums of Paris; and the miraculous gases of the Charlières and Montgolfières that astonished Europe by lifting man into the air for the first time in 1783. Mesmer's invisible fluid seemed no more miraculous. (Darnton, 1968, p. 10)

Mesmer was particularly impressed with Newton's theory of gravity, especially his discussion of how the moon's gravitational pull caused the tides. Drawing an analogy between the physical and animal "machines," Mesmer *deduced* the *hypothesis* that the heavenly bodies influence not only the oceans but human bodies as well:

There is almost no change which happens in the heavenly bodies without its influencing the fluids and solids of our earth in agreement. Then, who would deny that the animal machine would, in these circumstances, be agitated to a certain degree by the same causes? The animal is a part of the earth and is composed of fluids and solids, and when the proportion and the equilibrium of these fluids and solids are modified to a certain degree, very perceptible effects will occur from this. (Mesmer, in Bloch, 1980, p. 13)

Once Mesmer developed the idea of animal magnetism, he went on to explore its importance to health. Knowing that his ideas would carry no weight with the medical faculty without support, Mesmer searched the literature for *evidence* that the human body was affected, like the oceans, by the positions of the heavenly bodies. He was not disappointed.

The medical literature contained many reported cases of pain, fever, hemorrhages, epileptic seizures, madness, and nervous disorders becoming worse during the new and full moon. Mesmer even found evidence of people's faces being disfigured, as though by a tidal pull, during certain phases of the moon:

A curious case published by Kerkring is worth mentioning; that of a French woman endowed with a very pretty fat-cheeked face during full moon, but whose eyes, nose, and mouth would turn to one side during the decreasing of the moon. She was then turned so ugly that she could not go out into the world until the full moon returned and she regained the beauty of her face. (Mesmer, in Bloch, 1980, pp. 15–16)

Satisfied that his observations justified the theorized links between the state of the human body and the positions of the sun and moon (the process of *induction*), Mesmer encouraged his readers to consider the medical applications of these ideas. He promised to dedicate himself to finding out how the medium for such effects, animal magnetism, could be used to restore health and vitality.

Mesmer's observational and experimental research. Some years later, the opportunity arose for Mesmer to test his theory empirically. The *subject* was a Fräulein Oesterline, a 29-year-old woman who suffered from an incredible array of disabling problems:

[The patient] had undergone terrible convulsive attacks since the age of two. She had an hysterical fever to which was joined, periodically, persistent vomiting, inflammation of various visceral organs, retention of urine, excessive toothaches, earaches, melancholic deleriums, *opisthotonos, lypothymia,* blindness, suffocation, and several days of paralysis and other irregularities. (Mesmer, in Bloch, 1980, p. 26)

Since Mesmer had tried all the standard procedures, to no avail, the possibility of a treatment based on his thesis suggested itself. But Mesmer first wanted to determine whether his patient's symptoms were affected by the positions of the heavenly bodies, as his thesis predicted. This first investigation would have to be an *observational study,* since Mesmer could not control the positions of the heavenly bodies. To *test* his *hypothesis,* Mesmer systematically recorded his patient's symptoms and the positions of the sun and moon over several months. As in all *hypothesis testing*, this study involved *deduction;* a hypothesis was used to predict what would occur when specific observations were made.

Mesmer's findings were encouraging. He reported that as the study progressed he began to see regularity in Fräulein Oesterline's symptoms; gradually, by taking account of the positions of the sun and moon, he could foresee his patient's relapses and even predict how long they would last.

His observations led to refinements in his thinking about the causes of illness. He now hypothesized that obstructions in the flow of animal magnetism led to disease. Formulating the *test implications* of this hypothesis, Mesmer reasoned that *if* he placed magnets at strategic points on his patient's body, *then* her symptoms would be washed away. He wrote:

> Magnetic matter, by virtue of its extreme subtlety and its similarity to nervous fluid, disturbs the movement of the fluid in such a way that it causes all to return to the natural order, which I call the harmony of the nerves. (Mesmer, in Bloch, 1980, p. 29)

Mesmer applied the magnets to his patient's chest and feet and waited for the *results*. Almost immediately, she reported "a burning and piercing pain" in her body, accompanied by sweating on the side of her body that had been paralyzed. Shortly thereafter, she had a convulsion and was freed of her symptoms. The next day, some symptoms returned, so Mesmer *replicated* the treat-

The magnetic treatment.

ment, producing the same breathtaking support for his hypothesis. Although Fräulein Oesterline had several relapses, she finally was cured. She later married Mesmer's stepson and bore several children.

Excited and inspired by these results, Mesmer conducted other experiments to discover the principles of animal magnetism and the extent of its power. Based on his experiments, Mesmer concluded that magnetic fluid acted very much like electricity. Bottles could be filled with it, just like Leyden jars could be filled with electricity. Like electricity, the fluid could be magnified to produce painful jolts. Anything that could be touched could be magnetized— paper, bread, wool, stones, glass, porcelain cups, water, dogs, people.

Mesmer also concluded that people could be magnetized from a distance. This observation led him to modify his theory. Although he believed that magnets conducted the fluid, he no longer saw them as necessary for the cure. Instead Mesmer now thought that magnetic effects were caused by the diffusion of animal magnetism from the magnetist, where it was highly concentrated, to the patient, where it was depleted. The rush of animal magnetism produced the convulsions, or "crises," which produced the cure.

The Cycle of Validation: King Louis XVI's Royal Commission

By 1784, animal magnetism had become the rage in Paris. Parisians talked of little besides magnetism and flocked to the salons where Mesmer "operated" on them. Many great philosophers and scientists saw magnetism as a medical breakthrough, a means of curing illnesses that no one before had treated successfully. To them, animal magnetism offered a wonderful alternative to traditional treatments, which often left patients worse off for having seen a physician than they would have been without.

But there were skeptics as well. Many scientists saw animal magnetism as a figment of Mesmer's overactive imagination and Mesmer as an unfortunate victim of self-deception. Others, less charitable, believed that Mesmer was a charlatan, a fraud, interested less in relieving people of their illnesses than in relieving them of their money.

The research problem: assessing animal magnetism. Fortunately, there was a way to settle this difference of opinion. French law required that all new medical treatments be evaluated by the government, in the same way that we require that drugs be tested and approved before they are prescribed. Animal magnetism was to go on trial, and the trial, by special commission, was to decide whether animal magnetism was real and useful.

The Royal Commission, established by King Louis XVI, included France's most prominent physicians and scientists. Benjamin Franklin, ambassador to France from the United States and the world's leading expert on electricity, headed it. J. S. Bailly, the famous astronomer; Antoine Lavoisier, the founder of modern chemistry; and J. I. Guillotin, for whom the "humane" instrument of death used during the French Revolution was named, were among the commissioners.

A public session at Mesmer's salon. Patients, seated around the *baquet,* a wooden tub containing iron filings and magnetized water, use its iron rods and ropes to conduct magnetic fluid to afflicted parts of their bodies. A smaller *baquet* in the back room is for less well-to-do patrons. Mesmer, in the left foreground, assists a patient in crisis (Tatar, 1978).

The commission's report is a most unusual scientific document, which provides a rare glimpse into the step-by-step thinking of a distinguished group of scientists. The report describes how the commissioners gathered facts regarding animal magnetism, formulated hypotheses to explain its workings, decided on research procedures, gathered data, and arrived at conclusions.

Hypothesis. Although the commissioners had been charged with finding out whether Mesmer's magnetic fluid was real and useful, they chose to concentrate on the question of magnetism's reality.

> The question of its existence is first in order; that of its utility it were idle to examine, till the other shall have been fully resolved. The animal magnetism may indeed exist without being useful, but it cannot be useful if it do not exist. (Report, 1785, p. 29)

As they made their fact-finding *observations*, the commissioners grew more and more doubtful of the existence of animal magnetism and increasingly confident that animal magnetism's effects resulted from suggestion rather than from an invisible fluid. Mesmer's experimental design, they believed, left open the possibility that it was his patients' faith in the magnetic treatment alone that produced the odd sensations and the relief from symptoms that they experienced.

Test implications of the hypothesis. But deciding on the reality of the magnetic fluid was no easy task. Given the invisibility and intangibleness of the fluid, the commissioners concluded that the only way it could be studied was to follow Mesmer's lead—the treatment had to be studied through its effects. But what sorts of effects should they examine and using what kind of testing situation?

One way to evaluate the magnetic treatment would be to assess its effectiveness in curing patients. To do this, the commissioners would have to administer the treatment repeatedly over an extended period of time. They rejected this option on methodological grounds. Given enough time, they reasoned, nature cured many diseases; so if patients recovered following a course of magnetic treatment, it would be impossible to decide whether their cures resulted from the treatment or from a spontaneous recovery, occasioned only by the passage of time.

Because the commissioners wanted their experiments to be "decisive and unanswerable," they chose to study the immediate sensory and behavioral effects of the magnetic treatment—the pain and other sensations, and especially the convulsions, or crises, which Mesmer claimed brought about the cures.

The commissioners also had to decide who to test. People varied in their susceptibility to magnetism. Some exhibited early and extreme "crises"; others, like the commissioners, experienced nothing. Since the commissioners were interested in explaining the cause of these convulsions, they decided to test patients who were known to respond to the magnetic treatment by exhibiting them.

When magnetism was put on trial in France, Mesmer wanted no part in it. Instead, his most celebrated student and protégé, Charles Deslon, opened his salon so that the commissioners could learn firsthand what went on in the public sessions that had become so popular in Paris's high society. The commissioners decided against using the public sessions as a setting for their research, because too many events were happening all at once to allow for accurate observations. They reasoned that if their research was to be decisive, they would have to isolate subjects and create precisely the right conditions for testing their hypothesis. They therefore chose *experiments* over *observational studies*.

The designs that the commissioners selected were brilliant, anticipating alternative ways of interpreting and explaining results and eliminating them as possibilities by means of *experimental controls*. They hoped to design a series of *crucial experiments* that would enable them to decide conclusively between two *hypotheses:* their own hypothesis, that the effects of the magnetic treatment were due to suggestion, and Mesmer's hypothesis, that the effects were caused by the invisible fluid.

Their first step was to translate their hypothesis into *test implications,* as follows: *If* magnetism is applied without a subject's awareness, *then* there will be no effects; conversely, *if* a subject believes that magnetism is being applied when it is not, *then* there will be effects. Mesmer's hypothesis would predict the opposite results.

The commissioners conducted many experiments using different subjects. Although the procedural details varied, their research design was always the same—individual subjects were given several different treatments, and their responses to them were compared. Sometimes the magnetic treatment was given without the subject's awareness; sometimes the subject was led to believe that magnetism was being applied when it was not. The commissioners recorded the presence or absence of convulsions under each condition.

We will look at only two of the many experiments they conducted.

Experiment 1 The first experiment took place in two rooms separated by a doorway that was covered by paper. The subject, a seamstress, and Deslon's patient, was led to one of the rooms where she joined a commissioner and a woman who supposedly wanted some sewing done for her. Both people were seated already when the patient arrived, leaving only one chair, located right in front of the doorway, for her.

Once seated and involved in conversation, a different commissioner then magnetized her through the paper for 30 minutes from a distance of 18 inches. Since Mesmer claimed that magnetic fluid could pass through doors and walls, the paper over the doorway would be no obstacle to its flow. The patient, unaware that she was being magnetized, experienced no special effects; on the contrary, she appeared cheerful and reported that she felt fine. The magnetic treatment produced no effects under this condition.

Next, the commissioner who had just magnetized the patient through the door came in and asked her if she would agree to be magnetized. Once she agreed, he did so, again from 18 inches, the same distance as in the previous test; but there was one additional wrinkle. Although the subject thought that she was being magnetized in the standard fashion, the commissioner actually performed the magnetism in a way that Mesmer's theory would predict would lead to no effects. Nevertheless, the patient went into convulsions, once again supporting the commissioners' psychological hypothesis.

Experiment 2 The second experiment, done with a different subject, involved some porcelain cups. It was well known that convulsions resulted if people who were susceptible to magnetism came close to or touched magnetized porcelain cups. In the experiment, several cups, none of which actually was magnetized, were presented to the subject. The first cup produced no unusual sensations, but the second cup did; by the time the patient touched the fourth cup, she went into full-blown convulsions. Since none of the cups was magnetized, these results supported the hypothesis that the convulsions were due to suggestion; magnetism couldn't have produced the convulsions because they occurred in its absence.

Once the convulsions stopped, the patient asked for water, giving the commissioners an opportunity to test for the effects of magnetism in the absence of suggestion. Without her awareness, the commissioners put the water in a magnetized porcelain cup. According to Mesmer's theory, the patient should have had convulsions, or some other unusual symptoms, as she held the cup and drank. But just the opposite occurred; contrary to the theory, the water appeared to soothe her, supporting the hypothesis that magnetism, without suggestion, had no effects.

Drawing conclusions. The commissioners believed that their experiments were conclusive. In every replication, and in every separate condition of their experiments, the results supported the commissioners' explanation and failed to support Mesmer's hypothesis. The commissioners concluded:

> Having demonstrated by decisive experiments, that the imagination without the magnetism produces convulsions, and that the magnetism without the imagination produces nothing; they [the commissioners] have concluded with an unanimous voice respecting the existence and the utility of the magnetism, that the existence of the fluid is absolutely destitute of proof. (Report, 1785, pp. 105–6)

Evaluation by the scientific community. Despite the attempts of the magnetists to save their theory by offering alternative explanations of the commission's findings, the commissioners' report was the beginning of the end of animal magnetism. The popularity of the treatment waned after the report and its use all but died out during the French Revolution.

The research design used by the commissioners, in which a single subject is exposed consecutively to different treatments, became standard practice in psychology until the early 20th century, when it was supplemented by other research designs. In addition, the commissioners laid the groundwork for a methodologically important procedure, the *placebo,* that still is used in modern medical and psychological experiments.

> In a *placebo treatment,* subjects are given a treatment that appears the same as the experimental treatment but lacks its "active" ingredient.

Without this methodological advance, like Mesmer, we would be unable to sort out the effects of suggestion, or faith in the treatment, from the effects of the treatment itself.

By demonstrating the powerful effects of suggestion, the commission's investigation of animal magnetism also ultimately led to psychological explanations of nervous disorders. We now believe that many of Mesmer's patients suffered from conversion disorder, a psychological condition characterized by dramatic bodily symptoms with no anatomical basis (paralysis without injury, blindness with no damage to the eye).

Le Magnétisme dévoilé

Political cartoon showing magnetists fleeing at the sight of the Royal Commission's report. Benjamin Franklin is holding the report. The magnetists are shown as asses, the symbol of the quack.

Although Mesmer's theory was discredited, he deserves an important place in the history of psychology. Mesmer's bold theory helped make sense, in a logical way, of many medical "facts" of his day that were not accounted for by any other theories. In addition, the theory he invented accomplished dramatic cures of symptoms that had resisted other forms of treatment. Mesmer's work set the stage for revolutionary changes in the treatment of psychological problems, first by suggestion and hypnosis and eventually with modern psychotherapies.

Many people would conclude that Mesmer's theory and research deserve only to be forgotten, and as quickly as possible. But in the introduction to their report, the thoughtful men of science who made up the commission disagreed, offering the following compelling argument why ideas like Mesmer's warrant our continuing attention:

> Perhaps the history of the errors of mankind, all things considered, is more valuable and interesting than that of their discoveries. Truth is uniform and narrow; it constantly exists, and does not seem to require so much an active energy, as a passive aptitude of soul in order to encounter it. But error is endlessly diversified; it has no reality, but is the pure and simple creation of the mind that invents it. In this field the soul has room enough to expand herself, to display all her boundless faculties, and all her beautiful and interesting extravagancies and absurdities. (Report, 1785, pp. xvii–xviii)

KEY TERMS

Evidence
Empirical sciences
The Invisible College
Replicated results
Cycle of discovery vs. cycle of
  validation
Induction vs. deduction
Research problem
Hypothesis
Hypothesis testing research
Test implications of a hypothesis
Crucial experiment
Subjects

Generalizable results
Research design
Experiments vs. observational studies
  (passive-observational studies)
Controlling for rival hypotheses
Apparatus, manipulations, and
  measures
Operational definition
Operationism
Reliability
Validity
Data, results, observations
Placebo treatment

KEY PEOPLE

Antoinette and John Lilly
Jean Piaget
George Kneller
Charles Darwin
B. F. Skinner
Ivan Pavlov
Wolfgang Köhler

Edward Thorndike
Percy Bridgeman
S. S. Stevens
Anne Anastasi
Anton Mesmer
Benjamin Franklin

REVIEW QUESTIONS

1. Identify and discuss four distinguishing features of science.

2. Why is it important to replicate the results of a study?

3. Identify and discuss the two phases of scientific work that Kneller distinguished.

4. What general steps are involved in scientific research?

5. What did Hempel see as the role of theory in research?

6. Why did Skinner think that his research was not guided by theory?

7. Distinguish between induction and deduction, the two processes of reasoning used in scientific work.

8. How do philosophers and historians of science explain why newcomers to a field often make important innovations?

9. What is the difference between the hypothesis and the test implications of the hypothesis?

10. Describe Köhler's experiment testing his Gestalt hypothesis of how animals learn against Thorndike's stimulus-response hypothesis.

11. Distinguish between experiments and passive-observational studies.

12. How did Skinner operationally define hunger in his experiments with rats?

13. Distinguish between the reliability and the validity of a measure.

14. What did R. A. Fisher think was the severest test of a theory?

15. What is the purpose of publishing research in scientific journals that require articles to be evaluated by referees and editors?

16. Describe the evidence Mesmer used in developing his theory of animal magnetism.

17. Describe one of the experiments that Franklin's commission did to evaluate Mesmer's theory.

18. What happened to Mesmer's animal magnetic cure for illness in the years following the commission's report?

2

Classifying Research

❖

The goal of research is to answer a question in such a way that it
is convincing and can be defended with cogent arguments.
Methods are to be developed as responses to specific questions.

DONALD POLKINGHORNE

❖

THE EXTENT OF RESEARCHER MANIPULATION
   OF ANTECEDENT CONDITIONS
      Stage of the Inquiry
      Laboratory versus Field Research
      Research Interests of Psychologists
         Testing causal hypotheses
         Studying coexistence
         Testing hypotheses about sequence
THE EXTENT TO WHICH THE RESEARCHER LIMITS
   RESPONSE ALTERNATIVES
      Surveys
      Archival Research
      Participant Observation
      Phenomenological Research
NATURALISTIC RESEARCH DEFINED
IDIOGRAPHIC VERSUS NOMOTHETIC RESEARCH
      The Single-Case Experiment
      The Case Study
      Psychobiography and Life Narratives
THE VALUE OF DIVERSITY
KEY TERMS, KEY PEOPLE, REVIEW QUESTIONS

When Jane Goodall was just one year old, her mother gave her a large, hairy, toy chimpanzee named Jubilee, after the first chimpanzee born in captivity at the London zoo. Perhaps it was Jubilee that helped to inspire Goodall's life-long fascination with studying animals. Whatever the origin, this interest was evident from very early on. At four years of age, Jane hid in a stuffy hen-house for hours to see how hens lay eggs. By the time she was eight, she had decided that when she grew up she would move to Africa and live among the wild animals.

In her late teens, this dream came true. Soon after moving to Kenya at the invitation of a friend, Goodall met Louis Leakey, the curator of the National Museum of Natural History in Nairobi and a renowned physical anthropologist. Leakey told Goodall about a group of chimpanzees living on the shores of Lake Tanganyika. Studying them, he believed, "might shed light on the behavior of our stone age ancestors" (van Lawick-Goodall, 1971, p. 6). When Leakey asked her if she would be "willing to tackle the job," Goodall enthusiastically agreed. Much of her life since has been spent in the forests of Gombe observing that group of chimpanzees—collecting the observations needed "to piece together bit by bit, the overall pattern of chimpanzee life" (Goodall, 1986, p. 51).

At first, Goodall's observations were made from a rocky peak, which offered her a good site for watching some happenings in chimpanzee life. Later she began to shadow individual chimpanzees (all assigned names, like David, Graybeard, Hugo, and Fifi!) for hours on end, meticulously recording every event that caught her eye. The stories that Goodall tells have transformed our understanding of these primates and shattered many widely accepted myths as well.

Contrary to accepted knowledge, Goodall discovered that chimpanzees, formerly thought to be strictly vegetarian and invariably peaceful, eat meat, use weapons, and engage in gang attacks on other chimpanzees. Like people, they have individual personalities, spend much of their youth at play, use tools, establish close family ties, and display generosity. Because of observations such as these, the U.S. government's guidelines regulating the care and treatment of animal subjects in research now require researchers to make efforts to promote the psychological well-being of their primate charges (see Chapter 7, Ethics of Research).

Ronald Kessler and his colleagues (1994) at the Institute of Social Research at the University of Michigan used very different data collection strategies from Goodall's. Kessler directed the National Comorbidity Survey (NCS), "a congressionally mandated survey designed to study the comorbidity of substance abuse disorders and nonsubstance psychiatric disorders in the United States" (Kessler et al., 1994, p. 8). (*Comorbidity* is the presence of two or more illnesses or abnormal conditions in the same person.) According to Kessler and his coauthors, "The NCS is the first survey to administer a structured psychiatric interview to a representative national sample in the United States" (Kessler et al., 1994, p. 8).

Jane Goodall and a chimp at the Gombe Stream Research Center in Nigeria in 1972.

Kessler's group had responded to a congressional mandate calling for information on the prevalence of psychiatric disorders in the United States. To collect such data, needed for national health care planning, an interview procedure had to be developed that would allow nonclinical interviewers to reliably diagnose the psychiatric disorders of members of the general public. Kessler et al.'s state-of-the-art structured diagnostic interview, the Composite International Diagnostic Interview, was designed to do this.

Using this instrument, eight thousand people, representing all 15- to 54-year-olds in the civilian noninstitutionalized population of the United States, were diagnosed according to which, if any, psychiatric disorders they had experienced in the previous year, or at some point in their lives. The diagnoses were based on the *DSM-III-R (Diagnostic and Statistical Manual III—Revised)* of the American Psychiatric Association. Although this manual has since been revised, at the time this diagnostic system was the accepted standard among mental health practitioners.

Like Goodall's findings, the results of this ground-breaking survey were unexpected. Almost half of those interviewed, both male and female, had had a major psychiatric disorder sometime during their lives. About a third had experienced a psychiatric disorder in the 12 months prior to the interview. In addition, the "results show that while a history of some psychiatric disorder is quite common among persons aged 15 to 54 years in the United States, the major burden of psychiatric disorder in this sector of our society is concentrated in a group of highly comorbid people who constitute about one sixth of the population" (Kessler et al., 1994, p. 11). Data on the incidence and nature of psychiatric disorders, according to sex, race, socioeconomic, and other factors, are reported later in this chapter.

Although scientists as a group share an allegiance to scientific method—to the goals, practices, and rules of evidence that we discussed in Chapter 1, Goodall's and Kessler's studies, combined with the research we discussed in Chapter 1, illustrate that what psychologists actually do in their research is anything but uniform. Because the kinds of questions that investigators hope to answer are so varied, the methods they use also must be. Research does not take place in the abstract. Deciding on the particulars of a study is a complex process that is guided in large measure by the questions the researcher hopes to answer. The research designs used by psychologists, that is, their general strategies for collecting observations, reflect the diversity in research questions they pose and the other choices they make as they translate their abstract ideas into concrete actions.

In this chapter, we present several dimensions for classifying the research designs used by psychologists today. We describe the essential features of the basic designs and the kinds of questions they are most suited to answering. Most of the research strategies we outline in this chapter are discussed more fully later in the book. There you will learn how the designs were developed, their strengths and limitations, as well as improvements that have been made in them since they first were introduced.

Our presentation of research designs is organized using a classification scheme developed by Edwin P. Willems (1969). Willems's classification focuses on differences in what psychologists do in conducting studies, assigning these activities to a position in a "two-dimensional descriptive space." The first dimension describes "the degree of the investigator's influence upon, or manipulation of, the antecedent conditions of the behavior studied." The second "describes the degree to which units are imposed by the investigator upon the behavior studied" (Willems, 1969, p. 46).

*T*HE EXTENT OF RESEARCHER MANIPULATION OF ANTECEDENT CONDITIONS

Willems's first dimension is one that most psychologists would use to classify research designs, one that we introduced in the last chapter: the distinction between experiments and observational studies. In experiments, the researcher manipulates the test situation to create the precise conditions needed to test the hypothesis. In observational studies, hypotheses are tested by "seeking out, or waiting for cases where the specified conditions are realized by nature, and then checking whether [the event] does indeed occur" (Hempel, 1966, p. 20). According to Willems, research studies can be roughly arranged according to the degree —from high to low—of the investigator's manipulation of antecedent conditions.

Experiments would be at the high end of this dimension; passive observational studies would be low because their observations are selected rather than manipulated. But at the lowest point on this dimension, we would place research like Jane Goodall's *naturalistic observation*. Naturalistic observers try to observe the pattern of events in a given situation without pinpointing any particular antecedents as being of special interest.

When Mesmer wanted to test the effects of magnets in relieving Fräulein Oesterline's symptoms, he did an *experiment*. When he wanted to see how the waxing and waning of the moon influenced her, a *passive-observational* study was the order of the day. When the commissioners were trying to learn as much as they could about the magnetic treatment, they went to the public sessions and observed, watching everything that went on (*naturalistic observation*). Later they experimented to test their suspicion that suggestion played an important role in the effects attributed to magnetism. Decisions like these about whether to use an experimental or observational approach, depend on what already is known about the behavior under study, on the setting where the research will take place, and on the type of question the researcher hopes to answer.

Stage of the Inquiry

Research on previously unexamined behaviors usually begins with relatively unstructured fact-finding. Such *exploratory research* is intended to chart new frontiers of knowledge by observing and identifying regularities in the phenomena of interest. Early in an inquiry, the researcher often is unprepared to select particular events to observe and tries instead to discover what is important by observing the full range of behaviors that emerges, interfering as little as possible with ongoing events.

When researchers begin to note patterns in the phenomena being studied, to observe that certain events regularly occur together or that one phenomenon regularly precedes another, and to classify phenomena according to similarities and differences, the researcher moves from pure description to *analysis*. At this point, new research designs, which allow the researcher to assess the nature and extent of relationships, become appropriate. Finally, when theories to account for relationships suggest themselves, still other designs are needed to test them.

With few exceptions, *experiments* are concerned with testing hypotheses. Köhler was testing a hypothesis about animal learning derived from Gestalt theory against Thorndike's stimulus-response theory. The experiments on animal magnetism tested the commissioners' suggestion theory against Mesmer's physical one. *Observational studies* are a necessary alternative to experimentation for hypothesis testing when the antecedents of interest cannot be manipulated for practical reasons (Mesmer could not create the phases of the moon) or for reasons of morality (we cannot abuse children to study the effects on them).

One type of hypothesis of special interest to scientists is cause–effect. Causal hypotheses assert that particular antecedent conditions lead to particular consequents. The logic of how to establish clear-cut cause–effect relationships by controlling for rival hypotheses was first formally presented by John Stuart Mill in the 19th century. Mill's methods are the focus of Chapter 3, Control in Experimentation.

When conditions permit the use of experiments, it is generally conceded that they, rather than observational studies, are the method of choice for testing hypotheses of causation. In the words of Lee J. Cronbach:

> The well-known virtue of the experimental method is that it brings situational variables under tight control. It thus permits rigorous tests of hypotheses and confident statements about causation. (Cronbach, 1957, p. 672)

Although experimentation has this advantage over observational designs, it would be a mistake to consider the observational design only as a poor substitute for experimentation. As we will see, cause–effect is not the only type of relationship of interest to psychologists, and the experiment often is not the best method for research.

Laboratory versus Field Research

Psychologists also label research according to where it takes place.

> *Laboratory research,* as its name implies, is conducted in the laboratory, where antecedent conditions can be strictly controlled.

Willems's analysis reminds us that the degree to which the antecedents can be controlled in research is a continuum rather than an either-or matter. Precise control over antecedent conditions can be achieved in the laboratory, somewhat less in places like zoos, prisons, schools, or hospitals, and least of all when studying animals in the wild, or people as they go about their daily activities.

Field research takes place in settings located outside the laboratory, like clinics, schools, or industry, where it is more difficult to control the antecedents experienced by subjects. Collectively, such settings are called *the field*.

Both experiments and observational studies can be conducted in laboratory or field settings. Experiments done outside the laboratory are called *field experiments;* observational studies in such settings are called *field studies.* When nature creates the kinds of variations in events that might be sought in laboratory research, the resulting study is called a *natural experiment.* Chapter 10, Field Research, discusses the contributions and special challenges of field research.

Some critics of psychological research believe that we ought to do research in field settings before plunging into laboratory experimentation. They base their conclusions on discrepancies between the findings of laboratory and field research. The following example shows how field studies provide an important check on laboratory findings.

Henry K. Beecher (1959, 1960), a medical researcher, was interested in studying the effectiveness of narcotics, like morphine and other analgesics, in relieving people's pain. He found that small doses of these drugs were remarkably effective in relieving the chronic pain of malignant disease and the acute pain caused by surgical wounds. Increasing doses produced comparable increases in pain relief for both types of pain. Placebos also proved to be effective in relieving pain from these sources.

But Beecher found that drugs and placebos do not work this way when the pain is created artificially in the laboratory, as it is in many experiments. In his trials, even large doses of the drugs were ineffective in controlling experimentally induced pain, as were placebos. In Beecher's view, these results may stem from the fact that fear or anxiety usually accompanies the pain of disease or injury, whereas this is not the case with experimental pain. Beecher's findings remind us to be cautious in generalizing results from the laboratory to the field.

Research Interests of Psychologists

In 1952, the Policy and Planning Board of the American Psychological Association (APA) began a project of considerable scope, involving the collection of empirical data from psychologists throughout the country. The project had two goals. Project A was intended to assess the status of psychological science—its methodology, its theories, and its empirical knowledge. Project B looked at professional relations in psychology by collecting and analyzing empirical data from a variety of sources, including practicing psychologists.

Sigmund Koch, a psychologist at Duke University, was put in charge of Project A. Koch asked the country's leading psychologists to write chapters discussing their work. The results were published in six volumes, edited by Koch, which provided psychologists of the day with a summation of what was known to scientific psychology. These books now are considered classics in the field (Koch, 1959–1963).

Project B, directed by Kenneth E. Clark, a psychologist at the University of Minnesota, was empirical. It required a central research staff, the assistance of committees of the APA and its divisions, as well as the cooperation of psychologists across the country, who served as subjects in the research (APA, 1952, p. 566). Once funding for Project B was received from the National Science Foundation, the committees set to work to decide how to learn more about psychology as a profession. Robert L. Thorndike, a member of one committee, had a promising idea about how to study the professional values of psychologists. If psychologists were given the names of important figures in the discipline's history and asked to rate the value of their contributions, he reasoned, their judgments would be shaped by their values. He was given the go-ahead, and the project was under way.

Thorndike first prepared a list of psychologists who were judged by colleagues, students, and himself to have made important contributions to the field. To know the names of these psychologists is to know a great deal about the history of our discipline and the diversity of interests and methods of those who have been a part of it. Thorndike organized the names of the psychologists into groups of three, each representing equally significant contributions but varying as much as possible in the nature of those contributions. The triads were put together in an inventory that was sent to two hundred Fellows of the APA for their ratings. They were asked to rank the three psychologists in each triad in order of the importance of their contributions.

One hundred and twenty-five inventories that were returned in usable shape were analyzed. Thorndike's classification of research contributions and his findings on the preferences of psychologists were published in the *American Psychologist,* the journal of the APA (Thorndike, 1954). Most important for our purposes is Thorndike's finding that the evaluations given to the psychologists depended on the type of work done by the psychologists rating them. In a nutshell, experimental psychologists preferred experiments conducted in the laboratory. Clinicians and psychologists in other applied fields saw nonexperimental contributions as most valuable.

Because Thorndike's data were obtained from a diverse group of psychologists from across the United States, Lee J. Cronbach, then president of the APA, concluded that its results provided a clear picture of how the research interests of psychologists differ. In his presidential address to the APA membership, Cronbach (1957) argued on the basis of these data for the existence of "two historic streams of method, thought, and affiliation which run through the last century of our science. . . . Psychology continues to this day," he went on, "to be limited by the dedication of its investigators to one or the other method of inquiry rather than to scientific psychology as a whole" (Cronbach, 1957, p. 671). For this reason, Cronbach titled his speech "The Two Disciplines of Scientific Psychology."

According to Cronbach, psychologists fall into two groups—"experimenters" and "correlators," distinguished according to whether they most value experimental or observational (also called correlational) research methods. Experimenters and correlators differ in their goals and in their standard operating procedures. Correlators use the design we have called passive-observational and often use a statistic called the correlation coefficient, which we discuss in Chapter 5, Correlation.

Experimenters want to vary environmental events and control differences between subjects. To experimenters, individual differences between subjects are "an annoyance rather than a challenge" and they take pains to avoid them. Experimenters standardize the heredity and other life experiences of their animal subjects and select their human subjects "from a narrow subculture." (College sophomores are used so frequently in psychological experiments, for example, that they have been called "psychology's fruit flies"!)

Correlators are interested in studying the very differences between subjects that experimenters try to eliminate. Correlators want to keep environmental conditions constant and study the effects of individual differences between subjects. They want to know how "already existing variation between individuals, social groups, and species" that results from biology or social circumstances influences their adaptation. "What present characteristics of the organism determine its mode and degree of adaptation?" is the question that correlators seek to answer (Cronbach, 1957, pp. 671, 674).

From our discussion in Chapter 1, you already are familiar with the work of a number of experimenters—Köhler, Skinner, and the commissioners are good examples—so we will now turn to some examples of research done by psychologists who fit Cronbach's criteria for correlators. In the remainder of this section, we will look at examples of correlational research testing, respectively, hypotheses of causation, coexistence, and sequence.

Testing causal hypotheses. Thomas Elbert and his colleagues (1995) studied the impact of musical experience on the cerebral cortex (the part of the brain associated with higher functions) of stringed instrument players (a cause–effect hypothesis). The study compared the cortical functioning of musicians (six violinists, two cellists, and one guitarist) and nonmusicians, to learn whether years of musical practice would affect brain functioning. Previous experimental research on monkeys had revealed that prolonged tactile stimulation of the fingers results in increased cortical representation for the portion of the fingers stimulated. String players were chosen for the study on humans because playing stringed instruments requires continuous fingering by the left hand with much less finger movement and tactile stimulation for the right hand.

The subjects were all between 21 and 27 years of age, and the musicians had been playing from 7 to 17 years. If experimental manipulation of stringed instrument playing had been used in the research, it would have been impossible to study the impact of such prolonged experience. In the testing session, light pressure was applied to the subjects' first digit or fifth digit of either hand in separate trials, and records were made of their cortical functioning by means of magnetic source imaging. The results showed "that the cerebral cortices of string players are different from the cortices of [nonmusicians] in that the representation of the digits of the left hand is substantially enlarged in the cortices of string players" (Elbert, Pantev, Wienbruch, Rockstroh, & Taub, 1995, p. 305).

Building a brain for music.

Figure 1, from the published report of this research, shows that the extent of the enlargement depends upon the age at which the musician first began to play. This result is something that would not have been detected without a correlational design. Although alternative interpretations of the results might be offered, the authors concluded, based on this and their experimental work with animals, that playing a stringed instrument leads to an increase in the cortical representation of the digits of the left hand.

Studying coexistence. Correlational interests also prompted the data collection and analysis done by Kessler and his colleagues (1994). They wanted to find out the nature and extent of psychiatric disorders in various subgroups of their national sample—males versus females, urban versus rural residents, lower versus higher socioeconomic status, and blacks versus whites. They were interested in learning which types of people had which disorders so that planned mental health services would meet actual needs. Note that this hypothesis is not about cause and effect.

Kessler and his colleagues found that women experienced more affective disorders (except mania, for which there were no differences) and anxiety disorders; men, on the other hand, had higher rates of substance use and antisocial personality disorders. In general, the results showed that rates of psychiatric disorders decrease proportionately with increasing income and education (two indexes of socioeconomic status).

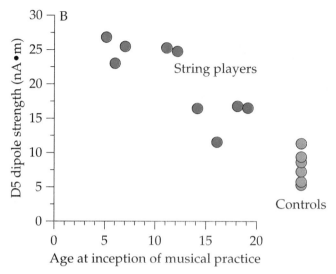

FIGURE 1
The size of cortical representation as a function of the age when musical practice begins (Elbert, T., Pantev, C., Wienbruch, C., Rockstroh, B., & Taub, E. (1995). Increased cortical representation of the fingers of the left hand in string players. *Science, 270,* 305–7.)

For the most part, differences between city and rural residents were not significant, and blacks were found to have significantly lower rates of affective disorders, substance use disorders, and lifetime comorbidity than whites. The authors found these last two findings particularly intriguing; residents of rural areas have lower income than urban dwellers, and blacks experience both financial difficulties and lower education, both factors that put people at risk for psychiatric disorder. For this reason, "future analyses of the NCS data will explore these patterns in more depth with the expectation that some as yet unknown resources protect rural people and blacks from the adverse psychiatric effects that we would otherwise expect to be associated with their stressful lives" (Kessler et al., 1994, p. 18).

Testing hypotheses about sequence. Developmental psychologists are interested in charting the course of psychological development—in studying, for example, when and how particular cognitive abilities emerge and what problems typify different epochs of life. Although there are noncorrelational designs that can be used to learn about the sequencing of events, developmental psychologists frequently use one of two types of correlational design to study changes that occur over time.

> *Longitudinal studies* collect observations on the same subjects on at least two separate occasions. *Cross-sectional studies* collect observations on subjects of different ages at one point in time.

The distinctive feature of the longitudinal design is that the same subjects are tracked over time. Such tracking allows the researcher to study the stability and change of particular behaviors in a given subject and can yield information on the impact of early events on later development. Jane Goodall (1986) observed individual chimpanzees throughout their lives to learn how events that took place in their infancy and youth led to individual differences in the chimpanzees later in life. Jean Piaget (1954) also used a longitudinal design when he assessed changes in his children's cognitive abilities as they developed. Lewis Terman tested and retested a group of intellectually gifted children, his "Termanites," over many decades to learn how their extraordinary early intellectual achievement was related to their accomplishments later in life (Terman & Oden, 1947, 1959).

In a cross-sectional design, groups of subjects of different ages are tested to discover how age relates to the behaviors of interest. Recall that Kessler et al.'s survey sampled the 15- to 54-year-old civilian noninstitutionalized population of the United States. When the authors broke down the incidence of psychiatric disorders according to age, they found the highest prevalences among people 25 to 34 years of age, and declining prevalences at later ages.

The advantage of the cross-sectional design over the longitudinal design is the savings in time required to conduct the research. Longitudinal studies require a lengthy time commitment of both the subjects and the researchers; the researcher is likely to stick with it, the subjects may not. Subjects are less likely to drop out of cross-sectional studies, since they participate only once. This advantage must be weighed against a major disadvantage of the design; namely, that the subjects in the different age groups differ from one another in many ways other than age. The effects of individual differences in personality and life experience are not a problem in longitudinal studies because the same subjects are tested at the different ages.

Our brief survey of correlational studies should convince you of the importance of correlational designs in the research of psychologists. Indeed, in the years since Cronbach wrote his classic paper dividing psychologists into "experimenters" and "correlators," the value of multiple methods in psychological research has been increasingly recognized. But back in 1957, Cronbach, a correlator himself, felt the need to passionately defend his method against the criticisms of those in the other camp—the experimenters. Calling for a "true federation of the disciplines," Cronbach wrote:

> The correlational method, for its part, can study what man has not learned to control or can never hope to control. Nature has been experimenting since the beginning of time, with a boldness and complexity far beyond the resources of science. The correlator's mission is to observe and organize the data from Nature's experiments. As a minimum outcome, such correlations improve immediate decisions and guide experimentation. At the best, a Newton, a Lyell, or a Darwin can align the correlations into a substantial theory. (Cronbach, 1957, p. 672)

*T*HE EXTENT TO WHICH THE RESEARCHER LIMITS RESPONSE ALTERNATIVES

To illustrate his second dimension, Willems (1969) described a study he conducted to find out what attracted high school students to five extracurricular activities. He varied the way participants in his study were allowed to respond. In the first procedure, an interview, the students simply were asked, "What, if any, were for you real reasons for or pulls toward attending this activity?" In the second, the students were required to sort cards, on each of which was a particular reason for attending. They sorted the cards into two piles—those that applied to them and those that did not. The third procedure was a checklist on which the students were asked to check all of the reasons that applied to them. Willems found that "the interview method, the technique with the least restriction of response alternatives and lowest on [his second] dimension" yielded the best predictions (Willems, 1969, p. 48).

Willems's second dimension, then, has to do with "the degree to which units are imposed by the investigator on the behavior being studied" (Willems, 1969, p. 46). Such imposition occurs when the researcher *restricts* the subjects' behavior so that they can respond only in certain ways, as was done in the study described above, and when the researcher *records* only limited aspects of the subjects' behaviors. In studying conversations, for example, the researcher might record only the number of nouns and verbs spoken rather than the entire discussion. This dimension refers to restrictions imposed by the researcher during the data collection, not to any structuring of subjects' responses later for the purpose of analysis. As we will see in the discussion that follows, this dimension also proves useful for classifying psychology's research designs.

Surveys

The *survey* is a method of systematically collecting data from people about their behaviors, attitudes and beliefs. Subjects for surveys are carefully selected to represent the group of people about whom the investigator intends to draw conclusions.

Although variations have been built into the questions of some surveys as experimental manipulations, for the most part, surveys are passive-observational studies. Survey researchers compare the responses of groups of subjects sorted according to particular attributes or past experiences. Kessler et al.'s study of psychiatric disorders, with which we began this chapter, is a good example of a survey.

The subjects in a survey can be interviewed in person, as they were in Kessler's study, or on the telephone; or they might complete a self-administered paper-and-pencil or computerized questionnaire. Whatever the mode of data collection, the questions in a survey are carefully constructed to yield the precise information that the investigator is seeking. Usually surveys require respondents to choose between response alternatives that are supplied by the researchers; so most surveys would fall at the highly structured end of Willems's second dimension. The exception would be surveys that use open-ended questions, comparable to essay questions on an exam.

Subject selection procedures in survey research have become highly sophisticated, ensuring that the characteristics of the subjects studied (called the *sample*) match closely with those of the larger group (the *population*) to which the researcher plans to generalize. Subjects are selected so that the various groups that compose the population of interest are represented, and in their correct proportions, and that there is no systematic bias in selecting participants from the groups. In the Kessler et al. study, for example, the subjects were selected so that they represented the 15- to 54-year-old, civilian, noninstitutionalized population of the United States.

As we will discuss more fully in Chapter 10, Field Research, the procedure used to eliminate bias in selecting subjects for research is *probability sampling*. In such sampling, subjects are selected from a particular population by chance; and because the research is anonymous and nonpainful, often a high proportion of those selected agree to participate.

The state-of-the-art in generalizing results precisely from a sample to a known population has been reached in public opinion research, where the intent frequently is to predict responses to events that have not yet happened—to forecast election results or to assess responses to proposals for social change, for example. In such research, it is particularly embarrassing, and obvious, when the poll fails to predict the event accurately.

Surveys are useful for collecting data on stable forms of behavior that subjects can answer questions about. Although the survey's structured response alternatives yield precise, quantifiable data on the behaviors, attitudes, and opinions of interest to the researchers, this structure also limits the usefulness of surveys for uncovering unanticipated possibilities. In this respect, the survey is very different from some of the other methods we consider later in this chapter.

Archival Research

The questions and results of some comprehensive national surveys are published so that other researchers, not involved in the study, can conduct their own analyses of the data. Results published in this manner are said to be *archived*, and research using these results is called *archival research*.

> *Archival research* uses existing records, gathered originally for some other purpose, as data. An archival study might examine census figures; birth records; scores on tests administered in schools, clinics or businesses; criminal records; or personal documents, such as diaries or letters.

TABLE 1 HOME TEAM WINNING PERCENTAGE DEPENDS ON THE DIRECTION OF VISITOR'S TRANSCONTINENTAL TRAVEL (FROM RECHT ET AL., 1995)

Visitor's direction of travel	No. of games	Games won	Winning %
No travel	712	385	54.1
East→west	194	109	56.2
West→east	175	110	62.9
Totals	1,081	604	55.9

To illustrate this method, let's look at an ingenious study that used archival data to study the impact of jet lag on the wins and losses of major league baseball teams. Lawrence Recht and his colleagues (1995) examined the records of 19 North American major league baseball teams, based in the Eastern and Pacific time zones, over three complete seasons (1991–1993). They were interested in studying whether the "home field" advantage (54% wins at home; 46% away) might be due to jet lag, a physiological condition known to affect physical strength and endurance, and which is worse when traveling east than west.

To test their hypothesis, the researchers looked at the statistical records for the two games before and after a transcontinental trip (jet lag lasts about one day for each time zone traversed). They found that the overall records of the Eastern and Pacific teams were the same, but the probability of winning home games depended on whether the visiting team had just traveled east. Their archival data, presented in Table 1, show that home teams won a higher percent of their games than usual when the visitor had just traveled east; only western teams "face the double handicap of playing their away games after eastern trips" (Recht, Lew, & Schwartz, 1995, p. 583).

Archival research can fall anywhere on Willems's two-dimensional classification. Archives can record data as diverse as the results of experiments in which strict control of antecedents and subject responses are possible, to material over which researchers have exercised no control at all, like someone's personal papers or the artifacts of an ancient civilization. The baseball study would be classified as low both on control of antecedents and restrictions of subjects' behavior, since the researchers controlled neither the games nor the recorded behaviors of the participants.

Participant Observation

The term "participant observer" was coined by Eduard Lindeman (1924), a University of Chicago sociologist, to refer to "individuals who belong to a group and report on that group to investigators" (Easthope, 1974, p. 90). Today the term still is used, but now it refers to a researcher who interacts with group members for the purpose of studying them.

The extent of participant observers' involvement with their subjects varies from study to study, as do the means they use to gain entry into their subjects' worlds. Researchers may spend extended periods of time with the people they study, sharing many life experiences with them, or the data may be gathered over a relatively short time by means of one or a few intensive interviews. Some investigators have gained access to groups deceptively, by passing themselves off as regular group members. Others identify themselves as researchers from the outset, hoping that those they plan to study will grant them access to information usually reserved for insiders.

> Participant observers try to learn as much as possible about how the people they study understand and give meaning to the events in their lives, by sharing "as intimately as possible" in their lives and activities. (Denzin, 1970, p. 187)

Researchers using this approach try to understand their subjects' worlds by walking a mile in their shoes, so to speak. Their data may be collected by means of open-ended interviews, questionnaires, examining artifacts and stored information, overhearing conversations, as well as observing ongoing events. Participant observers usually keep detailed field notes. When anthropologists use the method, it is called *ethnography*, which "literally means 'a portrait of a people'" (Ward, 1996, p. XI).

Participant observers collect facts related to the questions of interest to them, trying to develop explanations and understandings to account for the data they have collected. The result might be an analysis of the stages in the "career" of a mental patient, an explanation of what life is like for a ballet dancer, an attempt to understand the causes of rape by studying how rapists see themselves and their victims, or a description of the lives of teenage boys, as in the following study.

Jay MacLeod (1995), a participant observer, came to the Clarendon Heights public housing project as one of three university students starting a youth enrichment program for 11- to 13-year-old boys. While working with the youth program, MacLeod noticed the failure of the boys to aspire to middle-class jobs. Puzzled by their low aspirations, MacLeod decided to study their older brothers for clues about possible contributing factors. Gradually this interest developed into a plan for a research project that would be the basis for MacLeod's senior honors thesis.

As we have noted, one problem faced by participant observers is how to gain access to the worlds of those they want to study. As Denzin, an expert on the method, noted, participant observers must work "to carve out a role for themselves in the ongoing interaction of which they are a part" (Denzin, 1970, p. 188). This was less of a problem for MacLeod than it might have been. His work with the youth program helped to earn him the respect of the Clarendon Heights community, including its teenagers. Another big step toward entering the world of The Brothers and The Hallway Hangers, the groups MacLeod studied, was gaining the trust of respected members of these groups and sharing in activities valued by group members. MacLeod, a very good athlete, spent hours playing basketball with the boys.

At first, MacLeod observed what went on unobtrusively. Later he told the boys about his research project and asked them to help him out by being interviewed. As he hung out with the boys and spent hours interviewing them, MacLeod reflected on what he was learning, trying, as all participant observers must, to formulate generalizations, which would be tested and retested as the participant observation continued. As MacLeod described this:

> If my own experience is at all typical, insight comes from an immersion in the data, a sifting and resifting of the evidence until a pattern makes itself known. (MacLeod, 1995, p. 270)

> Fieldwork is an organic process that should include a nearly continuous analysis and reorganization of the material into patterns and models that in turn guide the fieldwork in new directions. (MacLeod, 1995, p. 283)

Incredibly, MacLeod's senior paper was published as a book, *Ain't No Makin' It* (1995), which describes the lifestyles of the two groups of teenage boys in the Clarendon Heights project—The Hallway Hangers, a group of predominantly white boys who had given up hope of achievement through legitimate pursuits; and The Brothers, predominantly black youths, who still believed that hard work and success in school would get them good jobs. The book provides a firsthand glimpse into the worlds of these boys, revealing not only their aspirations but why they saw things as they did.

MacLeod's book also gives his firsthand observations on some of the joys and difficulties of participant observation. Besides the pleasures of coming to know the boys, MacLeod faced some difficult decisions, like whether to violate the law to fit in with The Hallway Hangers. He also found himself unconsciously adopting the style and mannerisms of the boys he was studying:

> My speech became rough and punctuated more often with obscenities; I began to carry myself with an air of cocky nonchalance and, I fear, machismo; and I found myself walking in a slow, shuffling gait that admitted a slight swagger. These were not, on the conscious level at least, mere affectations but were rather the unstudied products of my increasing involvement with The Hallway Hangers. (MacLeod, 1995, p. 278)

Losing one's outsider's perspective is one of the pitfalls of participant observation.

Participant observation is a method of collecting observations that is low on Willems's second dimension, the imposition of restrictions on subjects' response alternatives. Participant observers may simply observe happenings as they take part in group activities or they may conduct open-ended intensive interviews. Whatever the particulars, the participant observer begins collecting data uncertain of what will be discovered, and this lack of structure yields both benefits and problems. One benefit is the richness of the descriptive material that the method yields. Participant observation is particularly useful for uncovering the "how" and "why" of behavior, for developing an understanding of sequences of happenings and forms of interaction that are in flux, and for discovery.

A disadvantage of the method is that it is very time-consuming. In addition, the method takes a kind of courage not required of researchers using more structured approaches. Participant observers must face the constant stress of having to generate insights and revise hypotheses throughout the study.

Phenomenological Research

The phenomenological method shares many features with participant observation, including its low position on Willems's second dimension. A major difference between the methods is what is being studied. Rather than focusing on the "why" of behavior—how people explain what they think and do—the phenomenological researcher looks at the nature of human experience itself.

Researchers using this method systematically collect descriptions of a particular experience, for example, the experience of "really feeling understood," "being angry," or grieving over the loss of a child, from people who have had it. Once gathered, they analyze the descriptions to "come to a grasp of the constituents or common elements that make the experience what it is" (Polkinghorne, 1989, p. 46). The aim of phenomenological research is to enable those who read its results to "come away with the feeling that 'I understand better what it is like for someone to experience that'" (Polkinghorne, 1989, p. 46).

After reading the best psychological writers on human relationships, Ruthellen Josselson (1992), a clinical psychologist, used the phenomenological method to discover how people view their relationships—"What are the dimensions of a relationship as they appear from the inside? What do people mean to others? How do we make use of others in our own development?" (Josselson, 1992, p. xii) .

Because the phenomenological method sets out only general guidelines for research, investigators must devise their own particular strategies for generating the kinds of descriptions they need. The success of the method depends upon investigators collecting accurate and full descriptions of experience. Josselson's starting point was to ask her subjects to draw a "relational space," using circles to indicate the important people in their lives—first at age 5, then at 5-year intervals thereafter. Figure 2 shows one such relational space, for Tom at age 5.

Josselson then conducted 3 to 5 hour in-depth interviews with 55 people to help her understand their "lived experience" of important relationships. The people she interviewed ranged in age from 11 to 93 and represented a variety of cultural backgrounds, so that she would have data on the full range of variations of the experience. The interviews focused on the atmosphere of the relationships, important moments, and their changing nature. Josselson's "aim was to offer myself as a nonjudgmental and interested other. . . . I did not listen as an expert. I was a student, trying to learn how people make others important to them" (Josselson, 1992, p. xiii).

Josselson analyzed the descriptions she collected to yield eight basic dimensions that she believes capture the essentials of the experience of relation-

Tom Age 5

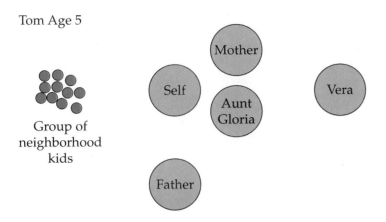

Group of
neighborhood
kids

FIGURE 2
Sample relational map. (From Josselson, 1992.)

ship with others: The dimensions include the experience of being held by the other, "finding ourselves in the other's eyes," and caring for and being cared for by others. The eight dimensions are discussed in separate chapters of Josselson's book *The Space Between Us.*

Since the ideal of the phenomenological method is to arrive at an accurate and complete picture of experiences, the results of phenomenological research are judged by their clarity. When results of a phenomenological study are published, it is assumed that others will evaluate its analysis against their own experiences. As a further check, investigators often compare their findings to the descriptions of other researchers, as Josselson did.

NATURALISTIC RESEARCH DEFINED

One of the reasons why Willems developed his classification scheme was to enable him to provide a clear definition of naturalistic research, the type of research that he does himself. To understand his definition, we first must review how studies are assigned to a particular position in Willems's two-dimensional space. To assign a study requires that we decide both whether it is low, medium, or high on the manipulation of antecedent conditions, and whether it is low, medium, or high on the imposition of units on subjects' responses. Figure 3 gives an overview of Willems's two-dimensional space for describing research activities and locates the studies we have discussed so far in this and the previous chapter. To illustrate the assignment, let's look at Skinner's experiments on operant conditioning and Goodall's observations of chimpanzees in the wild.

B. F. Skinner (1938) wanted to learn how varying environmental events shape particular behaviors of animals in a laboratory setting. In his experiments, a pigeon or rat was placed in the apparatus, an experimental environment that

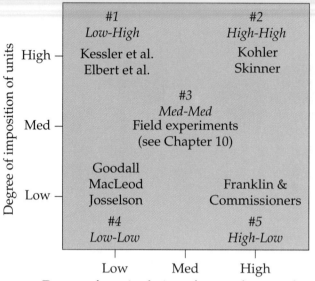

FIGURE 3
Two-dimensional space for describing research studies. (From Willems, 1969.)

limited the animal's response alternatives and allowed Skinner to deliver food pellets automatically on a predetermined schedule. Skinner recorded only the frequency of highly selected, specifically defined behaviors (e.g., the pigeon's pecking at a stimulus or the rat's bar pressing). The type of design that Skinner used, the single-case experiment, which is discussed later in this chapter and in Chapter 9, is high on Willems's first dimension, the manipulation of antecedents (e.g., schedules of reinforcement), and also high on his second dimension, the imposition of units on the subject's responses. We therefore would place Skinner's research at the high-high position in Figure 3.

Jane Goodall (1986), by contrast, did everything in her power not to manipulate her subjects' behaviors, remaining as unobtrusive and inconspicuous as possible. Instead, she attempted to capture the patterns of chimpanzee life as accurately and completely as possible in her written field notes. Goodall's study is an example of *naturalistic research*.

Willems defines research studies that are low-low in his two-dimensional space (position #4), like Goodall's, as naturalistic. Using Willems's definition, Recht, Lew and Schwartz's baseball study, MacLeod's participant observation study, and Josselson's phenomenological investigation also would be examples of *naturalistic research*.

> Research is *naturalistic* to the extent that it allows subjects' behaviors to unfold without investigator manipulation of antecedent conditions and without restricting the response alternatives of subjects.

Such naturalistic methods generally are recognized as useful in the early stages of research, because they allow researchers to get to know the subjects they are studying. But there are other advantages of naturalistic research. In Willems's (1969) opinion, a naturalistic study is the method of choice when researchers want to study people's everyday behavioral achievements, document the distributions of various behaviors in nature, describe and classify behavior, assess the range of behaviors in a person or animal's repertoire, and when ethical considerations do not permit the manipulation of subjects' behaviors. Naturalistic methods also provide important checks on the generality of the results of laboratory research, since most naturalistic studies are done outside the laboratory, in field settings.

*I*DIOGRAPHIC VERSUS NOMOTHETIC RESEARCH

Although Willems's classification allows us to think clearly about many differences between research designs, an additional dimension is needed to distinguish between studies focused on the individual case and other types of research. Gordon Allport (1937) introduced the distinction between *idiographic* and *nomothetic research* into the language of psychology to meet this need. According to Allport:

> Research is *nomothetic* if it focuses on discovering general principles of behavior; it is *idiographic* if it focuses on understanding the behavior of a particular subject.

To illustrate this distinction, let us look at two very different attempts to map the structure of personality. The first, like most research in personality, is nomothetic; the second, done by Allport himself, is idiographic.

A recent report on the achievements of basic behavioral science research listed the discovery of "the fundamental structure of individual differences in personality" among them (Bower & Kilhstrom, 1995, p. 487). This breakthrough in psychologists' understanding of personality was the result of systematic research on personality done by many researchers committed to nomothetic goals.

Over the past decades, psychological researchers have conducted studies aimed at learning the number of dimensions needed to account for individual differences in personality. In such research, large numbers of subjects complete questionnaires about their behaviors, thoughts, and feelings. The results then are analyzed statistically using a complex procedure called *factor analysis* (a correlational technique) to determine the basic traits (or factors) that describe personality. A consensus is emerging from such nomothetic research that five basic dimensions—the Big Five (Goldberg, 1981, 1993) or the five-factor model (McCrae & John, 1992)—are needed to describe the structure of personality: neuroticism, extraversion, openness to experience, agreeableness, and conscientiousness (Pervin, 1996, p. 43).

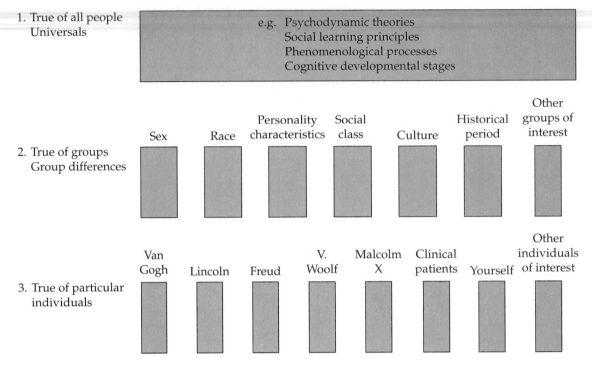

FIGURE 4
Runyan's levels of generality in the study of lives. (From Runyan, 1983.)

Gordon Allport's (1965) analysis of Jenny Gove Masterson's personality is an example of idiographic research. Jenny's son was Allport's roommate in college (Winter, 1996) and Jenny wrote 301 letters to Allport over a span of 12 years. According to Allport, these letters "tell the story of a mother-son relationship and track the course of a life beset by frustration and defeat" (Allport, 1965, p. v). Allport's analysis of the traits that made Jenny the unique person she was is reported in his book *Letters from Jenny.*

Figure 4 shows how William Runyan (1983), a personality psychologist, illustrated the distinction between the nomothetic and idiographic approaches to the study of lives. Although most research in psychology focuses on nomothetic goals, that is, on understanding people in general (level 1 in Figure 4) or categories of people (level 2), personality psychologists, like Runyan, increasingly are recognizing the importance of idiographic research (level 3), which aims at "the indepth understanding of individual lives" (Runyan, 1983, p. 417). In Runyan's view, such understanding is attainable only through idiographic methods, such as

"searching for the individual's reasons for acting in a particular way, through collecting as much information as possible about the individual and looking for idiographic patterns within it, and through organizing information about the case into an intelligible narrative." (Runyan, 1983, p. 418)

In the remainder of this chapter, we present several idiographic approaches to research. The first, the single-case experiment, is a quantitative method; the other two methods, the case study and psychobiography, are examples of the kind of natural language descriptions that Runyan advocates.

The Single-Case Experiment

Until early in this century, behavioral science research often involved observing single subjects under a variety of circumstances. Mesmer and the commissioners tested individual people in their experiments on animal magnetism. Hermann Ebbinghaus (1885/1964) also used this method in his classic studies of memory. Ebbinghaus studied forgetting by repeatedly testing his own recall of variously constructed lists of nonsense syllables. The research to which we now turn illustrates how modern clinical psychologists use this same design, now called the single-case experiment, to study the impact of treatments on their patients.

George Morelli (1983) evaluated a cognitive-behavioral treatment for the compulsive behavior of an adolescent with this design. The subject was a 13-year-old boy with a history of compulsive tapping in threes. He would tap parts of his body, or other things, using his arms, legs, and head for tapping. He would bounce in threes as he moved around in his environment. These behaviors were not only interfering with his own functioning; they were driving his mother and sister to distraction.

In the first phase of the experiment, the boy's mother was taught cognitive strategies so that she could control her own angry outbursts at her son's behavior. Next she was asked to record his compulsive behavior for 7 days (the baseline), then to begin applying a behavioral technique that she had been taught. Every time the mother saw her son behaving compulsively she was to ask him unemotionally to retrace his steps substituting an appropriate response. Figure 5 shows that this treatment quickly reduced the compulsive behavior, and the gains were maintained at a 9-month follow-up.

Morelli's experiment illustrates how a well-planned single-case experiment, conducted in a controlled setting, can result in a convincing demonstration of a clinical treatment. The single-case design used in this experiment, which is the focus of Chapter 9, also can be used nomothetically to assess the impact of treatments on groups of subjects (see Chapter 10, Field Research).

The Case Study

The best known of the idiographic methods is the case study, a favorite research method of clinical psychologists and the medical profession. The clinician uses this design to identify and describe psychological problems and to test practical strategies for solving them. But the case study is not restricted to problem behaviors. Many popular personality and developmental theories justify their assertions using material gathered through case studies. Case studies also are used to shed light on rare conditions and exemplary talents, like creativity, leadership, and musical or artistic ability.

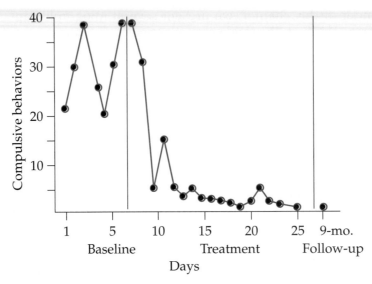

FIGURE 5
Frequency of compulsive behaviors in different phases of
Morelli's experiment (Reproduced with permission of author and pub-
lisher from: Morelli, G. Adolescent compulsion: a case study involving
cognitive-behavioral treatment. *Psychological Reports,* 1983, 53, 519–22.
Psychological Reports.)

D.B. Bromley defines the *case study* as follows:

A case study is a reconstruction and interpretation, based on the best evidence
available, *of part of the story of a person's life.* (Bromley, in Runyan, 1982, p. 443)

The evidence used in case studies can come from many different sources—
interviews, observations, test results, archival data, experiments, reports of others, or "any other method capable of producing relevant information" (Runyan,
1982, p. 443). The following case study of a "wild child" found in California answered some questions about language and intelligence but raised even more.

When she was discovered by social workers at age 13, Genie weighed only
59 pounds. She could not straighten her arms or legs and did not know how to
chew. But what intrigued psychologists, neurologists, and linguists most was
her odd silence; Genie didn't speak. Her only sounds were occasional whim-
pers. Gradually it was learned that Genie had spent most of her life, from age
20 months to the time of her liberation, restrained, and in almost total isolation. She was the unfortunate child of a tyrannical father who could not stand
the noises of children and of a mother who was too frightened of him to op-
pose his dictates.

Linguists saw in this rare case an opportunity to test theories that argue for
a critical period in language development. According to one such theory, unless
language is acquired between age 2 and puberty, it will not develop at all. Genie

was tested extensively after she was discovered, and was exposed to the best language instruction to help her learn to speak. She eventually learned some words and phrases, discrediting one aspect of critical stage theory. Despite all her training, however, Genie never achieved the kind of grammatical structure that linguists believe distinguishes human language from that of animals. This finding supported the theory that there is a critical period in language development beyond which normal language cannot be acquired (Pines, 1981).

This case study illustrates the power of the method—the research answered questions about language and about the future possibilities of a little girl, Genie, that would not have been answered otherwise, as well as some of its problems. These include: 1) the possibility of alternative hypotheses to explain the same data, and 2) the fact that the validity of the interpretations reached through case study depends on the completeness and accuracy of the data on which they are based. Genie's father restrained and isolated her because he believed that she was intellectually subnormal, suggesting an alternative explanation to the critical period hypothesis to explain her failure to acquire normal language. Or perhaps Genie's education just was not equal to the task. If more complete information were available on Genie's development prior to her enforced isolation and deprivation, we might be able to decide between these possibilities.

In Bromley's view, the ultimate test of a hypothesis is its acceptance "by competent investigators working independently of one another" (Bromley, 1986, p. 37). To increase the likelihood of such acceptance, Bromley advises case study researchers, like attorneys in a court of law, to anticipate opposition to their interpretations and prepare for it. They should ask themselves whether the evidence on which their interpretation is based is solid; whether they have established clear links between the evidence and the conclusions they have drawn from it; whether there are gaps in the argument or evidence; whether alternative interpretations of the data might be raised; and whether predictions based on the interpretation have been substantiated.

Psychobiography and Life Narratives

Psychobiographical methods are a special case of the case study method. Sigmund Freud's *Leonard da Vinci and a Memory of His Childhood* (1910/1957) is identified by experts as the first use of the psychobiographical method in psychology. McAdams defines *psychobiography* as follows:

> Psychobiography is *the systematic use of psychological (especially personality) theory to transform a life into a coherent and illuminating story.* In psychobiography, the life to be so transformed is usually that of a famous, enigmatic, or paradigmatic figure; and the storied rendering of the life is communicated to the public in written form. (McAdams, 1988, p. 2)

Unlike the case study, psychobiography focuses on understanding and interpreting the entire life of a given person rather than on understanding only some aspect of it. The goal of psychobiography is to formulate "the central, organizing, animating story of that person's life" (McAdams, 1988, p. 2). Usually the person is someone of historical interest.

Alice Miller (1984), a psychoanalyst, studied Adolph Hitler's childhood to test her theory that human destructiveness is a reaction to being demeaned and humiliated in childhood rather than something innate, the result of what Sigmund Freud called "the death instinct." By studying biographies of Hitler, Miller was able to "imagine and feel what it must have been like for a child to grow up in the Hitler household" (Miller, 1984, p. 144).

Miller believes that when parents simultaneously abuse and demand respect from their offspring, the children must repress the hate engendered by such mistreatment in order to survive. Nevertheless, the history of abuse is "stored up somewhere" in the child, she believes, to appear later in disguised form, in destructive behavior toward others. Miller used Hitler's own writings and speeches, the testimony of witnesses, and the facts of his life to reveal parallels between his mistreatment as a child and his political acts of destruction.

The *life narrative* approach had its roots in the early 20th century, when sociologists used it to solicit the life stories of various marginal members of society.

> Like psychobiography, *life narrative research* attempts to illuminate the central organizing themes of a human life, but it uses as its data first person accounts of lives written by people in their own words.

This method declined in popularity after World War II, but interest in the method is reviving among psychologists. In the future, we are likely to see more research based on people's own accounts of their life experiences and many more methodological discussions of this approach.

THE VALUE OF DIVERSITY

Donald Polkinghorne (1983), the psychologist we quoted at the beginning of this chapter, studied the etymological roots of the word *method* and discovered that its Greek roots are *meta,* which means "from or after," and *hodos,* meaning "journey." Scientific methods, then, are means of "going-after" or "pursuing" knowledge. Research designs are the roadways on this scientific journey.

Scientists seek answers to many different kinds of questions, and the routes they take reflect this diversity. Our aim in this chapter has been to introduce you to the full range of research methods available to psychologists. We hope that we have been successful in showing that no one design is most useful for answering all the questions posed by modern psychologists.

As the quote with which we began this chapter reminds us, the goal of research is to answer questions as convincingly as possible. This task is not easy. Doing research that leads to clear-cut conclusions about animal and human behavior presents many challenges and pitfalls. Fortunately for us, many innovative researchers, pioneers in research methods, have preceded us on this journey. As you will come to see in the chapters that follow, we can learn much from the tales they tell us of their adventures along the way and from the detailed maps they have left behind.

KEY TERMS

Willems's two-dimensional
  descriptive space
Experiments vs. passive
  observational studies
Naturalistic observation
Exploratory research
Field experiments vs. field studies
Natural experiment
"The Two Disciplines of Scientific
  Psychology"
Longitudinal vs. cross-sectional
  studies
Surveys

Sample vs. population
Probability sampling
Archival research
Participant observation
Ethnography
Phenomenological research
Naturalistic research
Idiographic vs. nomothetic research
Five-factor model
Single-case experiment
Case study
Psychobiography
Life narrative

KEY PEOPLE

Jane Goodall
Ronald Kessler
Edwin Willems
Lee Cronbach
Henry Beecher
Kenneth Clark
Robert Thorndike
Thomas Elbert
Lewis Terman
Lawrence Recht

Jay MacLeod
Ruthellen Josselson
B. F. Skinner
Gordon Allport
William Runyan
Hermann Ebbinghaus
George Morelli
Sigmund Freud
Alice Miller

REVIEW QUESTIONS

1. What research method did Jane Goodall use in observing chimpanzees in the wild? What did she discover?

2. Describe the purpose, general approach, and some of the unexpected findings of Kessler et al.'s survey.

3. What is the first dimension of Willems's two-dimensional classification of research designs? Give examples of at least one study at the high and low ends of the dimension.

4. Where on Willems's first dimension would exploratory research typically fall? Explain your answer.

5. According to Cronbach, what is the well-known virtue of the experimental method?

6. Explain the difference between laboratory and field research.

7. Describe Beecher's research on pain. What important general lesson about methods can be drawn from this research?

8. Explain the steps in Robert Thorndike's study of the professional values of psychologists. What were the results of Thorndike's study?

9. What conclusions about the methods, thoughts, and affiliations of psychologists did Cronbach draw from Thorndike's results?

10. Identify three types of hypotheses that can be tested in correlational research. Give an example of a study testing each type of hypothesis.

11. Explain the difference between a longitudinal and cross-sectional study. Give an example of each type of study.

12. What is the second dimension of Willems's two-dimensional classification of research designs? Give examples of studies at different positions (high and low) on this dimension.

13. Identify the distinguishing characteristics of the types of research listed below. For each, give an example of the research and explain where it would be classified on Willems's two dimensions.
    surveys
    archival research
    participant observation research
    phenomenological research

14. How does Willems define naturalistic research using his two-dimensional classification scheme?

15. For what kinds of research questions and situations is naturalistic research the method of choice, according to Willems?

16. Explain the difference between idiographic and nomothetic research. Give an example of each type of study.

17. Distinguish between a single-case experiment and a case study. Give an example of each of these idiographic approaches to research.

18. How do psychobiography and life-narratives differ from standard case studies? Give an example of psychobiography.

3

Control in Experimentation

———— ❖ ————

The only thing that I believe I am really fit for, is the investigation of abstract truth, & the more abstract the better. If there is any science which I am capable of promoting, I think it is the science of science itself, the science of investigation—of method.

JOHN STUART MILL

———— ❖ ————

A LIFE DEVOTED TO EMPIRICISM
A BOLD EXPERIMENT
MILL'S METHODS: A DEFINITION OF CONTROL
    Two Steps of Research
        Step 1: The event analysis
        Step 2: The research design
    Method of Difference
        Case: The magnetized seamstress
        General research design
        Definition of control
        Control using a placebo
    Method of Concomitant Variation
        Case: The dancing bees
        General research design
    Method of Agreement
        Case: A mysterious disease
        General research design
THE LANGUAGE OF VARIABLES
    Independent and Dependent Variables
    Quantitative and Qualitative Variables
LIMITATIONS OF MILL'S EXPERIMENTAL METHOD
    Internal Validity
    External Validity
    Construct Validity

APPLYING THE METHODS
    Within-Subjects Design
        History and maturation
        Testing and instrumentation
        Carryover effects
    Between-Subjects Design
        Selection and Mortality
APPROACHES TO DEALING WITH UNCONTROLLED
    VARIABLES
        The Within-Subjects Design with Virtually Total Control
        Statistical Control: Measure the Uncontrolled Variables
            and Remove Their Effects
        Randomized Experiments
KEY TERMS, KEY PEOPLE, REVIEW QUESTIONS

The studies by Franklin's commission that falsified Mesmer's theory of animal magnetism were models of clarity of thought. Presented with a bewildering set of observations and theoretical claims, the commissioners were able to cut to the heart of the matter and develop a critical test of Mesmer's ideas. Using simple techniques to *control for rival hypotheses,* they demonstrated that Mesmer's magnetic treatment on its own had no effect and that the effects attributed to it were due to suggestion; and they conducted these elegant and compelling experiments half century before formal models for achieving control over rival hypotheses in research were even developed.

The job of formalizing principles for scientific data collection was done by John Stuart Mill. In his book *A System of Logic* (1843), Mill presented a set of abstract rules, "analogous to the rules of the syllogism," for researchers to use in reaching valid conclusions about cause and effect. If scientists follow these rules, Mill believed, their research yields conclusive results; otherwise, it does not. The rules Mill specified still set the standard of excellence in evaluating experiments and observational studies.

This chapter focuses on these rules, now known as *Mill's methods,* and illustrates how they are applied in psychological research. As we will see, modern research methods retain the logic of Mill's methods but introduce new techniques to overcome limitations in applying them.

A LIFE DEVOTED TO EMPIRICISM

John Stuart Mill described himself as a student of "the science of science itself, the science of investigation—of method" (Mill, in Robson, 1973, p. xlix). With his work on scientific methods, Mill hoped to undermine the influence of intuitive philosophy, which held "that truths external to the mind may be known

John Stuart Mill, philosopher of science

by intuition or consciousness, independently of observation and experience" (Stillinger, 1969, p. 134). He wanted to strengthen the case for empiricism, the only approach he found acceptable for verifying laws of nature.

Mill planned to identify and describe all possible procedures for discovering and verifying scientific truths by studying the methods used by great scientists like Sir Isaac Newton, Johann Kepler, and Pierre Laplace. He thought that presenting scientists with formal methods for doing research would be a marvelous accomplishment. Not only would the availability of the methods lead to faster progress in science (future scientists would have only to select the right procedure from an exhaustive list of possibilities), but the methods would further the aims of utilitarianism, the philosophy that had shaped the entire course of Mill's life. As we shall see, although John Stuart Mill was not a scientist himself, he had been intimately involved with a program of research from his earliest years.

A BOLD EXPERIMENT

In the early 1800s, James Mill, John Stuart's father, a historian and writer, and Jeremy Bentham, a jurist, invented a new moral theory, which Bentham called utilitarianism. It was aimed at improving the lot of humanity through innovative educational and economic programs and new laws extending the vote to working men and women. In true scientific spirit, utilitarians held that it was not enough to judge programs on their intent, or by a rational analysis of their content, or by citing the opinions of authorities. Rather, they believed that the value of a program could be determined only by appealing to the evidence— by changing the circumstances of people's lives and observing the consequences. The best programs and laws would be those with the greatest utility, that is, those producing the "greatest good for the greatest number."

But Mill and Bentham didn't just write these ideas, they lived them. When John Stuart Mill, James's eldest son, was a toddler, his father and Jeremy Bentham devised a unique social experiment, based on utilitarian principles, with John as its subject. In utilitarianism, all differences in the character and abilities of people are thought to result from differences in their lives. The birth of John Stuart afforded these men an opportunity to test this assumption. If they could give John Stuart the right kind of education, they reasoned, they could shape him into a child prodigy, an independent thinker, a world-class philosopher, and a champion of utilitarianism. John's life thereafter was given over to this idea.

To produce such clear-cut results, John's education would have to start early and be thorough and rigorous. Since James Mill worked at home writing, he became John's tutor, devoting three or four hours a day to the task. John's daily routine began with studies at six in the morning. He would stop for breakfast at nine, then study five hours more. Late in the afternoon, he and his father would walk and discuss the books that John was reading. After dinner, lessons in mathematics began. John had no holidays, and when not studying himself, he taught his eight younger brothers and sisters.

Given John's early training, steeped in utilitarian philosophy and the empirical method, it is understandable that his writings would focus on empirical procedures for evaluating the impact of environmental changes. After all, this idea was central to utilitarianism. Also, John had been fed a daily diet of empiricism ever since he could remember—in the books he was given to read, in the conversations that took place in his home, and in the aim of his educational regime. And given the restrictions of his childhood, his fascination with ideas of control comes as little surprise. Moment by moment, day by day, year by year, John's life had been regulated according to the precise specifications of his father's experimental design.

Despite the toll of this regime on John (he had no normal childhood and in his adult life suffered from depression), James Mill probably judged the experiment a success. John was a child prodigy. He studied Greek at 3, Latin at 8, and read extensively in these languages by the time he was 12. By 12, he also had studied mathematics through differential calculus. Although John never attended college (sending him to Cambridge was considered but dismissed by his father as a waste of time), he later became the great philosopher and proponent of utilitarianism that James Mill and Bentham had envisioned at the start of their bold experiment.

MILL'S METHODS: A DEFINITION OF CONTROL

John Stuart Mill was an empiricist. In true scientific spirit, he looked to experience as the final authority for beliefs. Mill was interested in developing rules of procedure that would allow scientists to establish proof of cause-effect relationships in nature. The four methods he devised were, in his view, methods for discovering and proving laws of causation. They specify the precise observations that must be collected in order to reach a clear-cut conclusion that one event, event A, is the cause of another event, X. In Mill's terminology:

> Laws of causation specify an inevitable sequence between two different events, the antecedent and consequent events—the cause and the effect.

As we will see, Mill's methods are ingenious strategies for testing predictions from the hypothesis that event A causes event X, while *controlling for rival hypotheses,* for example, the hypothesis that event B or C is really the cause of X.

In Chapter 1, we discussed several phases in the research process, from selecting a research problem to drawing conclusions from results. In Mill's analysis, the process of discovering and verifying causation was broken down into two general steps: looking for patterns and verifying relationships. We will discuss each of these in turn.

Two Steps of Research

Step 1: The event analysis. In Mill's view, the process of discovering and verifying causal relationships begins with relatively unstructured observation of the phenomena of interest, a process that today would be called naturalistic observation. At first, no patterns are discernible—no links between antecedents and consequences are evident. Instead, as Mill wrote:

> The order of nature, as perceived at a first glance, presents at every instant a chaos followed by another chaos. We must decompose each chaos into single facts. We must learn to see in the chaotic antecedent a multitude of distinct antecedents, in the chaotic consequent a multitude of distinct consequents (Mill, 1843/1973, p. 379).

Mill called the analysis of a situation into its component parts the *event analysis*. In his opinion, general rules for the event analysis could not be specified, since the nature and extent of the analysis would depend on the problem being investigated. The only preparation for this phase, in his view, would be a general preparation of the mind, "for putting it into the state in which it will be most fitted to observe, or most likely to invent" (Mill, 1843/1973, p. 380). Mill believed that the event analysis was complete when the researcher could select from the chaos particular antecedents to relate to particu-lar consequents.

Franklin's commissioners, for example, began their work by observing the public magnetism sessions and developing some ideas of the elements that were involved. They decided to discontinue observing the public sessions when it became apparent that "too many things are seen at once for any one of them to be seen well" (Report, 1784, p. 25). At that point, they isolated individual subjects and selected the antecedents and consequents they would study. After considerable thought, they decided to investigate only the immediate effects of the magnetic treatment, administered with and without suggestion; they would look at the patients' reports of their sensations and any unusual behaviors on their part, such as vomiting, convulsions, or fainting. They were not interested in their subjects' personalities, intellectual abilities, or styles of dress.

This first step in research is important. If any part of the event analysis is incorrect or incomplete, important antecedents or consequences can be overlooked. Analyzing the events in a complex situation and deciding on a fruitful hypothesis to test remain part of the creative challenge of doing research. Since any research situation is extremely complex, Mill was well aware of how difficult the event analysis can be; he believed "to do this well is a rare talent" (Mill, 1843/1973, p. 380). Yet skill in observing and analyzing can be acquired. In part, such skill comes through training in one's discipline; in part, by becoming familiar with the analyses of past researchers working on similar problems. Reading the published research is an invaluable aid to clearly identifying the important elements to consider in a particular area of research.

Step 2: The research design. In Mill's second step, the researcher finds out which antecedents are connected to which consequents, either selecting a particular antecedent and observing what follows it or selecting a particular consequent and determining what precedes it. Mill called this step "varying the circumstances." Varying the circumstances means observing the phenomena you are studying under varying conditions.

The varying observations could be made in either of two general ways: either *by finding* naturally occurring variations or *by making* the variations by artificial arrangements. Recall that these are the two general types of research design discussed in Chapters 1 and 2: the *observational study* is based on naturally occurring events, the *experiment* on artificial arrangements. Mill saw no logical difference between the results of research using these two approaches—"as the uses of money are the same whether it is inherited or acquired" (Mill, 1843/1973, p. 381). (Today, we make a sharp distinction between these two approaches; see Chapters 5 and 6.)

Mill believed that, for the study to lead to conclusive results, the variations in circumstances that we find or make should follow the form of one of four methods: the *method of difference, concomitant variation, agreement,* or *residues*. In Mill's view, all research strategies for determining cause–effect relationships can be reduced to these four. Which method to apply depends on the particular problem being studied and how much is known about it. Since the method of residues is rare in psychological research, we will skip this one and discuss the other three, starting with the method of difference, the one that Mill considered the best.

Method of Difference

Case: The magnetized seamstress. One of Franklin's experiments fits the method of difference so well that we will use it as an illustration. Remember the case of the magnetized seamstress, Experiment 1 in the first chapter. The subject was a patient of Deslon, who was known to have convulsions when exposed to the standard magnetic treatment. When she knew she was being magnetized, she regularly had convulsions. When the commissioners gave her the magnetic treatment without her awareness by magnetizing her through a paper screen, she had no convulsions. From these two observations, that the standard treatment given with the woman's awareness caused convulsions, and that the treatment given without awareness did not cause convulsions, the commissioners were able to conclude that suggestion rather than the magnetic treatment caused the convulsions.

Because the *only difference* in antecedents for these two observations was the suggestion to the subject that she was being treated, the only explanation for the convulsions occurring in the first observation but not in the second is suggestion. It couldn't be the magnetic treatment that caused the convulsions because the patient was treated in the second observation but no convulsions occurred.

General research design. This experiment allowed the researchers to reach a clear-cut conclusion because of its design, which contrasts two observations differing only in a *single* antecedent. The general form of this design, called the method of difference, can be clearly stated using a diagram.

Let "X" indicate the occurrence of the consequent event under investigation, and "no X" its absence. Also, let the letters "A," "B," "C," and so on indicate different antecedent events and "no A," "no B," and so on, the absence of these events. With this notation, we can state the method of difference as follows:

Method of Difference

If we can find or make two observations that have the following form:

    Obs 1: no A + B + C + no D + etc. $\longrightarrow$ no X

    Obs 2: A + B + C + no D + etc. $\longrightarrow$ X

Then we can conclude that antecedent event A is the cause of consequent event X.

The diagram shows one observation where X occurs and one where X does not occur. The only difference in antecedents is that event A is absent in Obs 1 and present in Obs 2. Since no other antecedent changes from Obs 1 to Obs 2, we can conclude that event A causes event X.

According to the method of difference, we can prove A to be the cause of X if our observations are:

1. *consistent* with A being the cause of X and

2. *inconsistent* with *any other event* causing X.

If we can rule out *every possible cause other than A*, then, by elimination, A is the cause of X.

The observations in the diagram are consistent with A causing X. In Obs 1, A is absent and X does not occur, and in Obs 2, A is present and X occurs. The

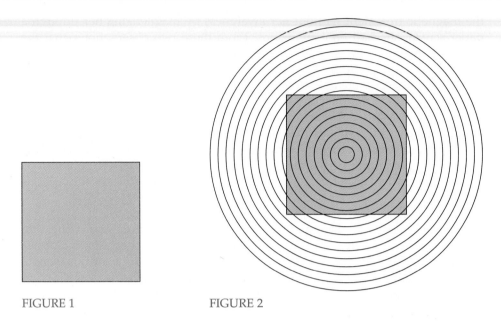

FIGURE 1   FIGURE 2

observations also are inconsistent with any other event causing X. Take B, for example. Could B be the cause of X? In Obs 1, B occurs but X does not occur, so B does not cause X.

To understand the method of difference better, consider the following experiment on visual perception. Look at the square in Figure 1. Now look at Figure 2. The sides of the rectangular figure bow inwards. But the bowing of the sides is an illusion! The figure actually is square; if you are not convinced, place a straight edge next to the lines in Figure 2. The only difference between the drawings in Figures 1 and 2 is the background of circles added to Figure 2. This single difference, then, in accord with the method of difference, is the cause of the visual illusion.

Definition of control. Mill's method of difference is the source of an important principle of research design that we presented in Chapter 1:

> To the extent possible, the researcher tries to eliminate potential rival explanations of the results by holding the conditions associated with them constant. This strategy is called *controlling for rival hypotheses*.

Mill's method provides us with a definition of *control* in a study. The events B, C, D, etc. in the diagram of the method are said to be controlled. If an event is held constant, it cannot cause changes in other events and thereby influence the results of the study. With good controls, the study leads to clear-cut conclusions.

> In a *well-controlled study*, or a study having *good controls*, the experimenter succeeds in controlling for rival hypotheses.

A study which fails to control for critical events is said to be *confounded*.

> In a *confounded study*, the effects of the antecedent of interest are mixed up or confused with uncontrolled events, allowing for rival explanations of its results.

Mesmer's demonstrations of cures through magnetic treatment are good examples of confounding. Mesmer saw his cures as the best evidence in favor of his theory of animal magnetism. But the possibilities of spontaneous cures or cures through suggestion could not be ruled out; they were confounded with the magnetic treatment.

Control using a placebo. Spontaneous cures and the effects of suggestion are still major concerns in experiments evaluating the effectiveness of treatments for illness, and researchers still use Franklin's strategy of giving the patient a placebo treatment. Studies evaluating new drug treatments, for example, compare observations of patients who receive the drug with observations of patients who receive a *placebo*. The placebo looks like, tastes like, and even has the same side effects as the experimental drug, but it is missing the drug's active ingredient. Since all patients receive a dose of something, all receive the suggestion that they are being treated. In this design, spontaneous cures should occur equally in both conditions and thus not favor the active treatment.

The most sophisticated version of this experiment is a *double blind study*.

> In a *double blind study*, neither the patients nor the observers know until the end of the study which patients got the placebo and which the active drug.

The patients are kept unaware to avoid the effects of suggestion and the observers in order to eliminate any possible influence of their expectations either on the observations they make or on their treatment of the subjects. Logically, then, any difference in the improvement rates of the groups can be attributed only to the active ingredient given to one of the groups, since this is the only antecedent that differs between them.

Method of Concomitant Variation

The method of difference is particularly well suited for designing experiments in the laboratory where the experimenter has control over relevant aspects of the situation. The method of difference assesses the effects of the *presence* or *absence* of an antecedent on the presence or absence of a consequent event: A subject is magnetized or not magnetized; she either does or does not have convulsions.

In some investigations, however, the experimenter cannot control the antecedent events, and sometimes the consequent events are not either/or events, as required by the method of difference. Mesmer started his investigations by wondering what effect the moon had on his patient's symptoms.

Karl von Frisch observing bees in his garden.

He certainly could not study the influence of the moon by presenting and removing it. But he could study how variations in the position of the moon would be associated with variations in his patient's symptoms. He wanted to look not only at the presence or absence of the consequent events, his patient's symptoms, but at their intensity and any other qualitative changes in them. Mill introduced the method of concomitant variation to cover this type of situation.

Case: The dancing bees. A study on bees by Karl von Frisch (1950) provides a good illustration of the method of concomitant variation. As in Mesmer's study, the antecedent and consequences of interest to von Frisch were not the either/or events required by the method of difference.

Von Frisch observed that soon after a honey bee discovers food and returns to its hive, hundreds more bees from the hive arrive at the newly found food. Von Frisch wanted to know how the bees so quickly found food, which was sometimes very far from the hive. He hypothesized that the first bee communicated the location of the food to the other bees. To test this hypothesis, von Frisch decided to study what a returning bee did and how the other bees responded. He designed special observation hives and developed an ingenious system for applying dabs of paint to individual bees so that he could identify each bee in a hive.

Von Frisch found that when the bee who discovered food got back to the hive, she transferred the food from her stomach to other bees and then performed a dance. Von Frisch was able to distinguish two variations in the dance: in the "round dance" the bee was "whirling around in a narrow circle, constantly changing direction"; in the "wagging dance" there was "very striking, rapid wagging of the bee's abdomen" during one part of the dance. Von Frisch also observed that the wagging was done at different rates, from about 8 to 36 wags per minute. After the dance was performed, the other bees became excited, and soon after many of the bees would arrive at the distant food source.

Von Frisch first ruled out the possibility that the new bees simply followed the leader. Then he came up with the hypothesis that the type of dance the bees did communicated the distance of the food to the other bees. The method of difference, which calls for variation in the presence or absence of the antecedent, was not appropriate to test his idea. Instead, von Frisch chose to vary the *distance of the food* from the hive to see if the *dance* varied systematically with the change in distance. This type of variation of events, in degree or in kind, is the focus of Mill's method of concomitant variation.

General research design. The diagram below shows that this method is similar in its logic to the method of difference; the difference is that the presence and absence of events is replaced here with variations in degree or changes in quality, as indicated in the diagram by the subscripts. Following the logic of the method of difference, the observations in the diagram are consistent with the conclusion that the variation in A causes the variation in X. Other explanations of the change in X are ruled out because only A changes between observations 1 and 2; all other events are controlled.

Method of Concomitant Variation

If we can find or make two observations that have the following form:

$$\text{Obs 1: } A_1 + B + C_1 + \text{not } D + \text{etc.} \longrightarrow X_1$$
$$\text{Obs 2: } A_2 + B + C_1 + \text{not } D + \text{etc.} \longrightarrow X_2$$

Then we can conclude that the *variation* in event A, from A_1 to A_2, is the cause of the *variation* in event X, from X_1 to X_2.

Applying the logic of the method of concomitant variation, von Frisch systematically changed the distance of the food source from the hive and observed the effect on the dance. He found that when the food was less than 50 meters from the hive the returning bee did the round dance. Between 50 and 100 meters from the hive, the round dance changed into a rapid wagging dance. Then from 100 up to 6,000 meters (3.7 miles), the rate of the wagging decreased systematically with the distance of the food from the hive. A slower

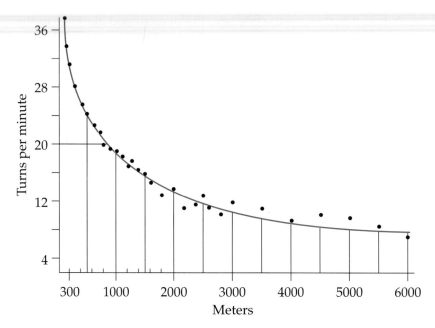

FIGURE 3
The distance of the feeding place is indicated by the number of turns of the wagging dance within a given time (adapted from von Frisch, 1950).

rate of wagging was associated with a greater distance. The graph below shows von Frisch's remarkable results for 3,885 observed dances of bees returning from food sources from 100 to 6,000 meters from the hive. The graph plots the turns per minute versus the distance of the food from the hive in meters.

From these results von Frisch concluded that in the language of the bees the round dance means food very close to the hive and that a decreasing tempo of the wagging dance indicates food progressively farther away, up to a distance of almost 4 miles! In additional experiments, von Frisch discovered how bees communicate the direction of food from the hive; they do their dances at different angles to the sun!

In terms of the diagram of the method, the antecedent event (A) that was varied in this experiment was the distance of the food from the hive. Numerous locations, $A_1 - A_n$, were used in the experiment. As far as we know, all conditions other than the distance from the hive of the nectar (e.g., the type of feeding dish, sugar concentration, scent of the nectar, etc.) were kept constant. The consequent event (X) was the type of dance the bees performed; the dances varied depending on changes in A. The observations were consistent with the hypothesis that varying the distance of the food resulted in the different dances. Because the bees who saw the dances were able to find the food, von Frisch concluded that the dance variations communicated the distance of the food. Other rival explanations of the results could be ruled out because conditions other than A were controlled.

These plants grown under identical conditions —
Except for the plant food

Control (no fertilizer added).
Same water, same soil, same growing
conditions except no fertilizer was added.

This plant fed with the
leading dry granular fertilizer.
All other conditions were identical.

This plant fed with
Miracle-Gro® Plant Food.
All other conditions were identical.

FIGURE 4
Advertisement relying on the Method of Concomitant Variation

The method of concomitant variation is a basic tool in modern research. Many modern studies are concerned with the effects of variations in degree and kind. Studies of perception show that differences in the wavelength of light result in different colors being perceived; drug studies investigate how types of side effects are related to the doses of drugs; developmental psychologists study how different styles of thinking are typical of different stages of development.

The logic of the method of concomitant variation has become so familiar that it is now part of our popular culture. The advertisement in Figure 4 uses the method to demonstrate how plant growth is related to the type of fertilizer used in cultivation.

Method of Agreement

Case: A mysterious disease. The methods of difference and concomitant variation are suited to research where the experimenter tests a well formulated hypothesis about the effect of a particular antecedent. Sometimes, though, the experimenter is faced with an effect and needs to discover its cause rather than to test whether a hypothesized event is the cause. A dramatic illustration occurred in Philadelphia in July 1976, when an unknown disease suddenly struck down a number of people. Health officials needed to discover its cause immediately to prevent further outbreaks and to help in finding a cure. The methods of difference and concomitant variation were of no help because the antecedent (A) of the disease (X) was unknown.

General research design. The health officials began at once to apply Mill's method of agreement. All known cases in whom the symptoms (X) occurred were examined to determine whether they shared any antecedents in common. According to the method of agreement, the *single* antecedent common to the cases is the cause of the consequent, X.

Method of Agreement

If we can find or make observations that have the following form:

$$\text{Obs 1: A +} \quad \text{B + no C + no D + etc.} \longrightarrow X$$
$$\text{Obs 2: A + no B +} \quad \text{C +} \quad \text{D + etc.} \longrightarrow X$$

Then we can conclude that antecedent event A is the cause of consequent event X.

X occurs in both observations and the observations have only one antecedent in common, A. Since the observations are consistent with A being the cause of X and inconsistent with any other antecedent causing X, A must be the cause of X.

When the health officials interviewed the victims, as you might expect, they found many personal and background characteristics that were not common to the group (e.g., their occupations, home towns, where they ate, their contact with pigs—the officials suspected swine flu), and the general condition of their health; these characteristics were eliminated as potential causes of the disease. The investigators discovered, though, that many of the victims were attending an American Legion convention and staying at the same hotel, the Bellevue Stratford, or had walked past the hotel. The hotel then became the focus of an intense investigation. An examination of the premises uncovered no known agent, no virus, bacteria, or toxin, that could be the cause. Nevertheless, the hotel soon closed due to poor business.

Biological work in the laboratory finally revealed an unknown microorganism in blood specimens taken from the victims. Additional tests on the blood samples yielded results that were consistent with the conclusion that the microorganism caused the disease. The bacterium, later named legionella, apparently grew in the water towers on the roof of the hotel. Water vapor containing it had infected passersby on the street below, and fans had blown the vapor into the hotel (Astor, 1983).

This case illustrates how the method of agreement is used in the initial stages of research to find common antecedents to a phenomenon of unknown origin. These antecedents suggest hypotheses that can then be put to more rigorous tests using the methods of difference or concomitant variation. The method is commonly used in just this way to identify the causes of disease and the toxic agent in cases of food poisoning. For example, it led to the discovery that several persons who died suddenly in Chicago in the fall of 1992 had all been poisoned by cyanide-laced Tylenol capsules. Recently, researchers used the method to suggest a specific genetic basis for homosexuality by showing that several sets of homosexual brothers shared genetic material on the X chromosome (Pool, 1993).

THE LANGUAGE OF VARIABLES

In Mill's methods, the required observations are specified in terms of events being absent or present, or present to a certain degree. Researchers now speak of *variables* rather than events.

A *variable* is a classification or measure of the properties of people, animals, objects, or events, (e.g., height, temperature, sex, intelligence, anxiety, etc.).

Independent and Dependent Variables

Instead of referring to antecedent and consequent events, we now refer to *independent and dependent variables*. The modern terms were borrowed from mathematics. In a mathematical formula, such as $y = 2x + 7$, the variable y is called the *dependent variable*, because its value *depends* upon the value of x. For example, if $x = 1$, then $y = 9$; or if $x = 2$, then $y = 11$. The value of x, by contrast, can be set to any value *independent* of the variable y.

In an experiment, the situation is analogous to that in mathematics. The experimenter sets the values of the independent variable, either by creating special conditions or selecting the conditions in nature, and then observes whether or not the variation on the dependent variable is related to the variation on the independent variable.

For example, in his study of bees, von Frisch placed food at several distances from the hive and watched the dance the bees did when returning from the food. He observed that the type of dance done by the returning bees, the dependent variable, depended upon the distance of the food from the hive, the independent variable. In Franklin's study of the magnetized seamstress, the independent variable was the presence or absence of suggestion, and the dependent variable was the presence or absence of convulsions.

In general terms:

An *independent variable* is a variable that underlies the creation or selection of the antecedent conditions in a study.

A *dependent variable* is a variable suspected to be a consequent of the independent variable.

Quantitative and Qualitative Variables

Mill's distinction between events that occur in degrees or in their presence or absence is reflected today in the distinction scientists make between *quantitative* and *qualitative* variables.

A *variable* is *quantitative* if its possible values fall on a *numerical continuum;* the values represent the degree or amount of the dimension being measured.

A *variable* is *qualitative* if its possible values differ in *kind or quality* rather than in degree.

Height, weight, degree of extroversion, degree of depression, SAT scores, or the amount of a drug are all quantitative variables. Sex (male vs. female), political party (Democrat, Republican, or Independent), or type of treatment (drug vs. placebo) are qualitative variables.

This change in terms, from *events* to *variables*, is more than just a change in vocabulary. Mill chose the terminology of events because this was a natural way of expressing causal relationships, for example, event A causes event B. However, psychologists often wish to study other types of relationships, relationships of correlation, in addition to those of cause and effect. For example, a psychologist might test whether scores on a test reflect brain damage, or if certain childhood experiences increase the risk of adult disorders. Because the language of variables is general, it is convenient for expressing any type of relationship.

Stated in terms of variables, both Mill's method of difference and his method of concomitant variation require that observations on the dependent variable be made at different values (or levels) of the independent variable, while controlling for all other variables. The conclusion, given observed differences on the dependent variable, is that the variation of the independent variable causes the variation in the dependent variable. In the language of variables, both methods can be stated the same way, so in the discussion to follow, we will refer to both simply as Mill's experimental method.

LIMITATIONS OF MILL'S EXPERIMENTAL METHOD

Mill made a strong claim for his experimental method. He thought that, if properly applied, it could *prove* laws of causation. That is, Mill believed that the method could establish, for all occasions and for all times, that a law of causation is true. We now realize that experiments cannot offer such proof.

The problems lie in three aspects of the method:

1. The problem of controlling for all variables other than the independent variable—the question of the *internal validity* of the study;

2. The extent to which the conclusions of the study generalize to other circumstances—the question of the *external validity* of the study; and

3. The extent to which the independent and dependent variables are valid measures (or operational definitions) of theoretical concepts—the question of the *construct validity* of the study (Cook and Campbell, 1979).

Internal Validity

Today, if a study is well controlled, it is said to be internally valid.

A study is *internally valid* to the extent that important variables are controlled, so that the actual relationship between the independent variable and the dependent variable can be observed.

Mill's experimental method requires that all variables other than the independent and dependent variable be controlled. If this could be achieved, any change in the dependent variable would have to be caused by the change in the independent variable; there simply would be no other explanation.

However, the complete control called for by Mill's method is an unattainable ideal. In actual studies it is impossible to control for every single thing: Mesmer overlooked suggestion; von Frisch initially overlooked distance and thought that the bees' dances indicated the type of food they had found. All experimenters can hope to do is to control for variables known to be important. So, there is no way to *guarantee* that a study is internally valid.

It is not uncommon for pioneering studies on a topic to overlook variables that researchers routinely control in later stages of the inquiry. A good example of this is McGinnies's experiment on "perceptual defense" (McGinnies, 1949). Based on psychoanalytic theory, McGinnies hypothesized that threatening visual stimuli evoke defensive responses by the perceptual system to prevent the stimuli from being consciously recognized. He believed that these defenses prevent the anxiety that would accompany the recognition of threatening stimuli.

In his experiment, threat words, such as "whore" and "penis," and neutral words, like "stove," were presented to women college students for very brief exposure times using a tachistoscope. A tachistoscope is an apparatus that allows the researcher to present visual stimuli for a controlled period of time. The exposure times were gradually increased until each word could be identified correctly. McGinnies predicted that, because of perceptual defense, the threat words would require greater exposure times to be correctly identified. His prediction was confirmed.

This study appeared to be well controlled. Each subject was exposed to both threat and neutral words, to control for visual acuity. The lighting for both types of words was identical; the words were presented in the same size print; the threat and neutral words averaged the same number of letters. Nevertheless, the study immediately was criticized for not controlling for a critical variable. Any guesses?

Howes and Solomon (1950) pointed out that McGinnies did not control for word frequency, that is, for how often a word is encountered in reading and conversation. They presented evidence that common words, like McGinnies's neutral words, are more easily identified than infrequent words, like the threat words. McGinnies' interpretation of his results was put in doubt by this alternative explanation. Subsequent studies would have to control for word frequency.

External Validity

Even if Mill's ideal of complete control could be attained, the conclusion of his experimental method would still have to be seriously qualified:

> It is possible that a relationship between the independent and dependent variables exists only for the precise conditions present in the study.

Von Frisch used sugar water in his studies. The type of food was controlled, the same food being used at the different distances. Given just these observations, it could be that von Frisch discovered only the dance that bees do when returning from locating sugar water. Perhaps bees use a different method to indicate the distance of, say, clover, to other bees.

A study is *externally valid* to the extent that the relationship observed between the independent and dependent variables generalizes to circumstances other than those in the study. This would include generalizing to different types of subjects, different settings, and different types of measures.

Virtually all experiments today follow the pattern of control specified in Mill's experimental method. But the very act of controlling raises issues of generalization. For this reason, experiments have a serious problem with external validity. Do the results of studies done in laboratories generalize to other settings or other subjects? Does saccharine, shown to cause cancer in laboratory animals, also cause cancer in people? Do the results of psychotherapy evaluation studies, in which subjects are carefully selected and the therapy follows a standard protocol, generalize to patients being seen in private practice?

These are difficult questions to answer. It is clear that a single study can do little to establish the external validity of a finding; what is needed is a series of studies that vary in circumstances. Philosophers of science, like Hempel (1966), recommend that hypotheses be replicated under the widest possible range of circumstances for just this reason.

Construct Validity

The construct validity of an independent or dependent variable is the extent to which the variable is a valid measure of the theoretical construct (i.e., concept) it is supposed to measure (Anastasi, 1988).

If a variable measures something other than the construct intended by the experimenter, then the conclusions of the study may be wrong. For example, what Mesmer took as a valid definition of the construct "magnetic treatment" also could be understood in terms of the construct "suggestion"; these two constructs were confounded in his studies.

Mesmer's difficulty in understanding the true nature of his treatment raises an issue for all researchers—the possibility that an independent or dependent variable thought to measure a single construct actually is complex. In such cases, although researchers may get the results they predict, this may happen for entirely different reasons than they hypothesize.

The perceptual defense study illustrates this problem. Imagine that McGinnies had controlled for word frequency and still found the predicted relationship between the type of word, threat versus neutral (the independent variable), and exposure time (the dependent variable). Would this finding establish the reality of perceptual defense? Not necessarily. The same result could occur due to factors having nothing at all to do with perceptual defense, as Howes and Solomon (1950) suggested.

Howes and Soloman speculated that McGinnies's findings resulted from social factors rather than perceptual ones. It is possible that the subjects recognized the threat words as quickly as the neutral words but were reluctant to report them until they were certain that they were correct. Imagine how embarrassing it would be to announce "penis" and then find out the word that had been presented was actually "genius." To test this explanation, they suggested varying the social circumstances (e.g., having a female experimenter and male subjects).

The issues of internal validity, external validity, and construct validity make it clear that experiments can never *prove* a relationship between independent and dependent variables or guarantee the correct interpretation of one. In fact, the language used by modern researchers for stating their conclusions reflects the fact that the results of a study always are open to question and always require further confirmation. Read a modern study and you will see the conclusions couched in terms like "these results *support* the theory that . . . " or these results *suggest* that . . . ," or "the results confirm the hypothesis that . . . ." Scientists do not say that their results *prove* a theory true or false.

APPLYING THE METHODS

The two basic experimental designs used in psychology today are based on Mill's experimental method. Remember, this method requires that observations on the dependent variable be made at different levels of the independent variable, while controlling for other variables.

In a *within-subjects design,* each subject is measured on the dependent variable at *all* the different levels of the independent variable.

In a *between-subjects design,* each subject is measured on the dependent variable at only *one* level of the independent variable. Different subjects are measured at each level of the independent variable.

Franklin's studies, the studies by von Frisch, and McGinnies's perception experiment were all within-subjects designs. Franklin's group observed the same subject's responses to different treatments. Von Frisch observed the same bees returning from different distances. McGinnies's subjects were presented with both the threat words and the neutral words. By contrast, many studies evaluating psychotherapy and drug therapy use between-subjects designs. Each subject is given only one type of therapy, so there are different subjects in the different treatment groups.

In planning a study, you must choose whether you want to use a within-subjects design or a between-subjects design. In an influential analysis, Campbell and Stanley (1963) compared how these designs handle major threats to internal validity. We will follow their analysis, using a classic research problem, transfer of training, to illustrate the comparison. Since neither design proves to be ideal, the choice between them depends on the specifics of the hypothesis being tested.

Within-Subjects Design

Transfer of training refers to the transfer of skill acquired on one type of task, Skill A, to another task, Skill B. Students are taught Latin because it is assumed that this training will improve their understanding of English. Students study geometry to better their problem solving. Baseball players cross-train lifting weights to improve their hitting. The Head Start preschool experience is designed to provide disadvantaged children with cognitive skills that will be advantageous to them throughout their lives.

The first studies on transfer used a within-subjects design. The subjects were measured on Skill B to determine their level of performance, then trained on Skill A, and finally measured again on Skill B. Several subjects were observed, each receiving exactly the same instructions and procedures.

Campbell and Stanley (1963) identified five major threats to the validity of this type of study: the threats to internal validity of history, maturation, testing, instrumentation, and the threat to external validity (or construct validity; Cook and Campbell, 1979) of carryover effects.

History and maturation. In this design, if subjects' scores change from the pretest to the posttest, the change in scores is attributed to the training on Skill A. However, if events other than the training occur between the two measurements, the effects of these events may be confounded with the effects of the training.

The uncontrolled events can occur either in the environment, the threat of *history,* or within the subject, the threat of *maturation.*

> *History* refers to environmental events, other than those associated with the independent variable, taking place between the measurements in a study.

> *Maturation* refers to "processes within the [subjects] operating as a function of the passage of time per se (not specific to the particular events), including growing older, growing hungrier, growing more tired, and the like."

In the transfer of training study, if the training phase of the study takes a long time (say, a semester in school), history and maturation become serious threats. One, or several, of the other activities that subjects engage in over the semester could improve performance on Skill B (the threat of history). Also, at the end of the semester, because they are several months older, the subjects might perform many skills at a higher level than they did at the beginning of the semester, due to maturation.

Testing and instrumentation. In a within-subjects design, subjects are measured on the dependent variable at each level of the independent variable. These multiple measures give rise to two additional threats to internal validity: *testing* and *instrumentation.*

> *Testing* refers to "any effects of taking a test on the scores of a second testing."

> *Instrumentation* refers to "changes in the calibration of the measuring instrument or changes in the observers or scores used [that] may produce changes in the obtained measurements."

For example, if observers are being used to record behavior, the researcher must make sure that they do not change their methods as the study progresses. Observers may become blasé as they gain experience in the testing situation; or their ratings may change unintentionally as they become more familiar with the experimental design or the researcher's hypothesis. If measurements are done with instruments, they must be calibrated the same way during all phases of the research; if testing with different forms of a test, the researcher must make sure that they are equivalent.

In the transfer of training study, if the measures of skill were done with paper-and-pencil tests, instrumentation would not be a problem, but testing would be a serious threat. People usually do better the second time they take an ability test, even without any intervening training. This effect is a serious threat to the design since the anticipated effect of training on Skill A also is to increase the scores. Here the effect of testing is confounded with the effect of the independent variable.

Carryover effects. In a within-subjects design, each subject receives all the treatments being studied. If the first treatment a subject receives has a lasting effect, the subject's reaction to the second treatment may be affected. For example, in the perceptual defense study, if subjects are given a threat word first, this may increase their anxiety and influence their reaction to the next neutral word. Campbell and Stanley called this threat to external validity *multiple-treatment interference,* or, more simply, *order* or *carryover effects.*

> *Carryover effects* are "likely to occur whenever multiple treatments are applied to the same respondents, because the effects of prior treatments are not usually erasable."

In some cases, carryover effects would be so pronounced that the within-subjects design would not be a practical choice. In a study comparing different treatments for an illness, for example, if the first treatment cures the illness, there would be no point in giving the second treatment. A between-subjects design would have to be used in such cases, which occur frequently.

Between-Subjects Design

W. H. Winch (1908) conducted the first between-subjects design on transfer of training. His study is famous because E. G. Boring (1954), a historian of psychology, identified it as the first study in psychology to use a *control group design.*

> A *control group design* is a between-subjects design in which one group of subjects receives the treatment (the *experimental group*) and another group of subjects does not (the *control group*).

To study transfer using this design, the experimental group would be trained on Skill A; the control group would not. Once the experimental group finished its training, both groups would be measured on Skill B. If the experimental group scored higher on Skill B, this would be taken as evidence of transfer of training.

Since each subject is given only one treatment in this design, and is observed only once, the between-subjects design avoids the threats of maturation, history, testing, instrumentation, and carryover effects. However, because *different subjects* are observed in each experimental group, two new threats to internal validity are introduced: *selection* and *mortality*.

Selection and mortality. In Winch's study, the experimental group was a group of school children who received training at memorizing lines of poetry, such as Byron's

> She walks in beauty like the night
> of cloudless climes and starry skies. . . .

The control group did not get this training. The training was expected to facilitate memorization of passages from a history text, like

> At the beginning of the eighteenth century Britain was still chiefly an agricultural country.

The problem here is that any systematic differences between the children in the two groups, in ability, interests, motivation, etc., are confounded with the effects of the independent variable. This threat to internal validity is called *selection*:

> *Selection* refers to systematic differences in the types of subjects assigned to the experimental groups.

Winch tried to equate the groups on their ability to memorize, but who is to say if he was successful? Also, since he personally assigned the children to the groups, there is the possibility that he was biased and unwittingly assigned the best students to the training condition. In addition, one group of students may have matured faster than the other group, the threat of *selection-maturation*, or specific events may have happened to one group and not to the other during the course of the study, the threat of *selection-history*.

Winch's study lasted about three weeks. Because the subjects were children and under the control of their teacher, everyone finished the study. But in longer studies involving less control over the subjects or more demands placed on them, subjects may drop out. If differential dropout rates occur for the groups, and if subjects who drop out are different from those who don't, this would constitute another threat to internal validity, called *mortality* by Campbell and Stanley.

> *Mortality* refers to the differential loss of subjects from the experimental groups.

Mortality is a serious problem. Research evaluating the effects of psychotherapy, for example, can last several months, and when the treatment does not seem to be beneficial, subjects may drop out and seek therapy elsewhere. This is particularly likely to happen in the placebo group, which receives no active therapy.

Selection and mortality present difficult problems for the between-subjects design. If subjects in the experimental groups are different, the effects of these differences can be confounded with the effects of the independent variable. The within-subjects design avoids these problems by observing the same subjects in different conditions of the experiment. When subjects drop out of a within-subjects design, they can be dropped from all the conditions, so there will not be a differential dropout rate.

APPROACHES TO DEALING WITH UNCONTROLLED VARIABLES

Neither the within-subjects nor the between-subjects design offers the perfect control of variables that Mill's method requires. Mill offered no solutions to this problem; but since his day three distinct practical approaches have been developed for dealing with uncontrolled variables.

The Within-Subjects Design with Virtually Total Control

In his now classic research on conditioned reflexes, Ivan Pavlov (1927/1960), the Russian Nobel Prize-winning physiologist, introduced the strategy of handling the problem of uncontrolled variables by regulating virtually all aspects of the experimental situation. His research on the salivary reflex in dogs was carried out in a custom-built laboratory called the "tower of silence." The building was soundproofed to eliminate the influence of uncontrolled stimuli from outside. During the experiment, the animals were observed using a periscope, to avoid uncontrolled interactions between the dogs and the experimenters. Dogs were ideal subjects for this procedure because suggestion posed no threat and because the ease of controlling the animals' lives during and between experiments minimized any threats of history. The experiments on conditioned reflexes also were of short duration, minimizing maturation as a threat. The subjects had special surgery so that their salivary glands would discharge directly into a tube outside their mouths. The amount of saliva produced in response to a stimulus was accurately measured, eliminating the threats of instrumentation and testing. The experimental design was within-subjects, with only one animal observed at a time (a so-called $n = 1$ design). The results were replicated with other dogs.

The total control achieved by Pavlov is possible only in animal studies, and his approach is well suited for such research. B. F. Skinner (1938) adapted and extended Pavlov's approach to develop the experimental methods used in operant conditioning. Today Pavlov's and Skinner's single-subject designs are used frequently in experiments on animals and people. These designs, as well as the modern extensions of them, are discussed in Chapter 9, Single-Case Experimental Designs.

Statistical Control: Measure the Uncontrolled Variables and Remove Their Effects

In between-subjects designs, it is impossible to control perfectly for differences between subjects in the various groups; subjects may differ in age, education, attitudes, past experience, etc. (the threat of selection we discussed above). However, in some cases, the subjects can be measured at the beginning of the study on variables suspected to be threats to internal validity. Questionnaires can be developed to ask people about relevant past experiences, and standard measures can be used to assess their interests, abilities, and personality traits. Then when the study is over, statistical procedures can be used to remove the effects of these variables on the dependent variable. These variables then are said to be "statistically controlled."

Statistical control is a powerful technique in observational studies in which direct control, by holding variables constant, is impossible. Because understanding statistical control requires some knowledge of measurement and the mathematics of correlation, this technique will be discussed in Chapter 5, Correlation, following the presentation of these topics.

Randomized Experiments

In some between-subjects studies, researchers can control the assignment of subjects to conditions. In drug studies, for example, experimenters can decide which subjects to assign to the placebo and which to the active drug. When this is the case, the best approach for control purposes is to *randomly* assign the subjects to the groups.

> In *random assignment*, each subject is assigned to an experimental condition purely by chance, (e.g., by flipping a coin, or drawing the subject's name out of a hat, or by using computer-generated random numbers). This assignment gives subjects an equal chance of being assigned to any of the conditions of the study.

Random assignment avoids any systematic bias in assignment and permits a statistical estimate to be made of the magnitude of the effects of uncontrolled variables in the study. This estimate of the error due to uncontrolled variables is used in evaluating the results of the study.

The randomized experiment is considered the best available design for experiments because it offers the most powerful method developed so far for overcoming the threats of uncontrolled variables. Unfortunately, it is not always possible to randomly assign subjects to experimental conditions. The logic of randomization, the method of choice when it can be applied, is explained in Chapter 6, Randomized Experimental Designs.

The development of the two approaches to control that use statistics, statistical control, and randomization, occurred in a three-step sequence. First, procedures were developed to measure individual differences. Then, a novel method of analysis was invented to determine the degree of "correlation" between different measures. Finally, these new methods of measurement and correlation were applied to problems in experimental design.

In the next two chapters, we discuss how researchers measure individual differences and determine the correlation between variables.

KEY TERMS

Empiricism
Mill's methods
Utilitarianism
Laws of causation
The event analysis
Varying the circumstances
Methods of difference, concomitant
  variation, and agreement
Well-controlled vs. confounded study
Placebo
Double blind study
Variable
Independent vs. dependent variables
Quantitative vs. qualitative variables

Internal validity
External validity
Construct validity
Tachistoscope
Within-subjects design
Between-subjects design
Threats of history and maturation
Threats of testing and
  instrumentation
Threat of carryover effects
Control group design
Threats of selection and mortality
Statistical control
Random assignment

KEY PEOPLE

John Stuart Mill
James Mill and Jeremy Bentham
Karl von Frisch

Thomas D. Cook, Donald T.
  Campbell, and Julian C. Stanley
Ivan Pavlov
B. F. Skinner

REVIEW QUESTIONS

1. Describe John Mill's early childhood and explain how his education was an experiment testing the tenets of utilitarianism.

2. Describe Mill's two steps for establishing laws of causation.

3. Diagram and explain the logic of Mill's method of difference.

4. Analyze the cause of the visual illusion presented in the text using the method of difference.

5. Compare the method of difference and the method of concomitant variation.

6. Explain how von Frisch's study of bees illustrates the method of concomitant variation.

7. Compare the method of difference and the method of agreement. Why are the conclusions of studies that use the logic of the method of agreement often verified by experiments using the method of difference?

8. Explain how researchers used the method of agreement to find the cause of Legionnaires' disease.

9. Why do modern scientists use the language of variables rather than Mill's language of events?

10. Distinguish between independent and dependent variables.

11. What are the three major problems with Mill's experimental method that preclude researchers from reaching certain conclusions using it?

12. State two rival hypotheses to explain the results of McGinnies's experiment on perceptual defense.

13. Identify the major threats to the validity of a within-subjects design.

14. Identify the major threats to the validity of a between-subjects design.

15. Describe three approaches to deal with the threat to validity of uncontrolled variables.

4

Measurement

— ❖ —

Until the phenomena of any branch of Knowledge have been submitted to measurement and number it cannot assume the status and dignity of a science.

SIR FRANCIS GALTON

— ❖ —

*THE VARIETY OF MEASURES IN PSYCHOLOGICAL
   RESEARCH*
SCALES OF MEASUREMENT
STANDARD AND NORM-BASED SCALES
THE BEGINNINGS OF NORM-BASED MEASUREMENT
DESCRIBING INDIVIDUAL DIFFERENCES
      Percentiles
      The Normal Distribution
      Percentiles and the Normal Curve
      Why the Normal Distribution Is So Common
      Galton's Scaling Method
*NORMAL OR NON-NORMAL? THE LOGIC
   OF STATISTICAL TESTS*
KEY TERMS, KEY PEOPLE, REVIEW QUESTIONS

Many breakthroughs in science come directly from advances in measurement. Claims that sensory acuity is a sign of intelligence (Wissler, 1901), or that a mother's rejecting personality causes her child's autism (Schreibman & Koegel, 1975), or that prefrontal lobotomy effectively cures mental illness (Valenstein, 1986) are examples of theories that have been rejected after being evaluated using good measures. Improved measures of personality, intelligence, and cognitive abilities often lead to progress in understanding human behavior.

Even seemingly small modifications in measurement can result in major scientific advances. In his studies of children's intelligence, Jean Piaget (1952) switched from the standard measure, counting the number of correct answers on an intelligence test, to studying how children explain their answers, both right and wrong. With this change, Piaget started a line of research that revealed the logic of children's thinking. B. F. Skinner (1938) observed the rate of bar pressing of pigeons and rats instead of choosing other possible measures of learning. This choice was critical for his discovery of the effects of different schedules of reinforcement.

Given the importance of measurement, researchers must plan their measurement strategies with care. Independent and dependent variables must be operationally defined. Variables that the investigator is trying to control may have to be measured to ensure that they remain constant throughout an experiment. Even uncontrolled variables have to be measured if the experimenter plans on using statistical controls. Whether the results of a study are clear-cut or not will depend in large part on the type and quality of its measurements.

THE VARIETY OF MEASURES IN PSYCHOLOGICAL RESEARCH

Psychologists have at their disposal all the measurement techniques that have been developed in the physical and medical sciences. They can use computer-controlled displays to study perception, radio telemetry to track wild animals, deep-sea sonar to follow whales, and magnetic brain imaging to study brain dysfunction in children with attention deficit hyperactive disorder.

Psychologists also can choose from a vast assortment of psychological tests and observational schemes. *Tests in Print* IV (Murphy, Conoley, & Impara, 1994), a directory of the available commercial tests, lists over 3,000 tests for comparing peoples' aptitudes, abilities, interests, emotions, sensory acuities, personalities, disabilities, attitudes, and disorders. The questions used in surveys often are published along with results so that other researchers can use them. Ethograms profiling the behavioral repertoires of different animals also are available.

Psychological studies often use a combination of measures, some physical, some previously published psychological measures, some custom-made for the study. This blend of instruments is well illustrated in a study by Sheldon Cohen and his colleagues (Cohen, Tyrrell, & Smith, 1991) on the effects of psychological stress on susceptibility to the common cold. The researchers faced two measurement challenges in their study: (1) how to measure or manipulate stress, and (2) how to measure or manipulate exposure to the cold virus.

Ethically sound procedures for manipulating stress are severely limited and are not likely to result in the high levels of stress that would be needed to affect resistance to disease. Although it might be possible to show subjects a stressful movie or recount a sad story, for example, such brief events most likely would not have a lasting impact. An alternative would be to select participants who already have different levels of stress in their lives. Cohen et al. decided on this procedure.

To do this, they combined three previously published paper-and-pencil measures into their own custom-made stress index. The measures were: (1) a life event scale, on which participants reported the number of stressful life events that they had experienced in the previous year (events such as divorce or the death of a close friend; (2) a perceived stress scale, on which they reported the extent to which their lives felt overwhelming; and (3) a negative mood scale, measuring the degree to which they felt upset, shaky, irritated, sad, etc. Participants' scores on the combined measure indicated their levels of stress, from high to low. Since each component was known to be reliable, the composite also was expected to be reliable. The validity of the composite was unknown. (Procedures for assessing the reliability and validity of measures are discussed in Chapters 5, Correlation, and 12, Planning the Study.)

Cohen et al. decided to directly expose their high- and low-stressed subjects to disease by giving them nose drops containing an infectious dose of a respiratory virus and then quarantining them in hotel rooms. The subjects were told the nature of the study before volunteering; they knew that the virus was only a cold virus and would do no lasting harm; and they were paid for their participation. Exposing them to a measured dose of a virus, followed by a quarantine, ensured that high- and low-stressed subjects were exposed equally to the disease. The alternative to this procedure, measuring exposure, would have been very difficult.

Whether or not a subject was infected was determined by blood tests. Subjects were considered to be infected if the virus or antibodies to it could be isolated in their blood. A physician also rated the severity of the subjects' colds.

The researchers also measured a variety of other variables so that if stress and vulnerability to the cold virus were found to be related, alternative explanations of the results could be tested. For example, because smoking affects susceptibility to disease, the amount of the chemical cotinine in the blood was measured; this is an accurate index of how much a person smokes. The participants also took two standard personality scales to check whether the stress index was measuring personality differences rather than stress. How much the subjects exercised, their diets, and the quality of their sleep also were assessed by questionnaire.

All of the measures used in this study are subject to error, but to different degrees. The least error is expected for the measures that participants cannot influence, like the blood analysis. Such measures are called *nonreactive.*

Measures are *nonreactive* if subjects can have no control or influence over their outcomes; that is, if the act of measurement itself cannot result in a reaction from the subjects that could bias the results.

The questionnaires, interviews, and personality scales used in the study, by contrast, were *reactive.*

Measures are *reactive* if they are made with the subjects' awareness, and if this awareness could lead to a bias in their results.

Participants who want to create a favorable impression on investigators, for example, might present themselves on questionnaires and personality scales as less stressed than they actually are. On the other hand, some people may exaggerate their problems to gain an investigator's sympathy. Another problem with reactive measures is that the measurement itself may change the subject, thereby introducing other kinds of error into the study. Filling out the questionnaire on exercise and diet, for example, could suggest the benefits of exercise and a good diet to participants, leading them to change their normal routines.

Whenever possible, nonreactive measures should be used to supplement reactive measures. In the stress study, for example, the physiological measure of smoking, the amount of cotinine in the blood, served as a check on participants' self-reports of the number of cigarettes they smoked. The agreement between the results of these measures confirmed the validity of cotinine as an index of smoking and also helped to establish the self-report measure as valid for future research.

The only problem with using nonreactive measures is that they may be difficult to obtain. To collect blood samples, for instance, requires that a medical professional be on hand; such intrusive procedures may not be suitable for most psychological studies. Other nonreactive measures, such as archival records or covert observation, may violate subjects' rights to privacy. And nonreactive measures simply are not available for many variables. Cohen et al. most likely did not include a nonreactive measure of stress because such measures have not been developed. Webb, Campbell, Schwartz, Sechrest, and Grove's 1981 book, *Unobtrusive Measures: Nonreactive Research in the Social Sciences,* is a good source of ideas on ways to measure nonreactively.

When nonreactive measures are unavailable, multiple reactive measures should be considered.

Checking the agreement between multiple measures of the same variable gives investigators a way to evaluate error.

Agreement between the results of different measures establishes that the observations are not uniquely tied to a particular method. In psychotherapy evaluation research, for example, psychologists' ratings of their patients' improvement often are checked against the patients' own ratings. In the stress study, the severity of the participants' colds was rated both by a physician and by the subjects themselves. The close agreement between their ratings provided evidence for the validity of both measures.

Cohen et al. found that a higher percentage of high- than low-stressed subjects caught cold after being exposed to the virus. This result was replicated with five types of viruses and shown not to be due to differences in the personalities, diet, exercise, or smoking habits of the high- and low-stressed subjects. The study provides perhaps the best evidence available to date that psychological stress can lower a person's resistance to disease.

The results of this stress study were reported using numerical scales. The stress scale varied from 3, low stress, to 12, high stress; the severity of a subject's cold ranged from 0, no cold, to 4, severe cold; cotinine levels were recorded in parts per unit volume; scores on the personality scales were numbers in the range from 20 to 80; weight was measured in kilograms. Although these scales all involve numerical values, they are not interpreted or analyzed in the same way. To interpret scale scores, researchers must know both the *scale type* of the measure and whether the scale construction is based on *standards* or *norms*. We turn first to the distinction between scale types.

SCALES OF MEASUREMENT

The idea of different types of measurement scales was developed by S. S. Stevens (1946), a psychologist who studied sensation and developed many of the basic sensory scales used today. Stevens argued that there are four basic measurement scales: *ratio, interval, ordinal,* and *nominal,* distinguished from each other by four properties that determine how scores on the scale can be interpreted.

The first property is *equality.*

> A scale has the property of *equality* if two subjects who are assigned the same score are equal on what is being measured.

If Bob and Jane both are measured as 68 inches tall, then they actually are the same height. The scale of height has equality, the most basic property of a scale; without equality, you do not have a scale at all.

The second property is *rank order.*

> A scale has *rank order* if higher scale scores always indicate more of what is being measured.

The scale of height, for example, has rank order since higher numbers, 69 inches, 70 inches, etc., indicate taller people. The numbers assigned to players on a basketball team do not. Player number 23 does not have more of a trait than player number 8. Although qualitative measures, like sex, sometimes are coded numerically, for example, Female 2, Male 1, these "scale scores" also do not have the property of rank order.

The third property is *equal intervals.*

> A scale has *equal intervals* if equal-sized differences in scale scores always indicate equal-sized differences in the amount of what is being measured.

For height, the difference between 69 inches and 71 inches, a difference of 2 inches, is the same as the difference in height between 52 and 54 inches. A scale with equal intervals has a constant unit of measurement. The Richter earthquake scale is an example of a common scale that does not have equal intervals. A difference of 1 unit on this scale indicates an increase in the energy

TABLE 1 SCALES OF MEASUREMENT AND THEIR PROPERTIES

| | *Property* | | | |
| | *1* | *2* | *3* | *4* |
Scale	*Equality*	*Rank Order*	*Equal Intervals*	*Equal Ratios*
Ratio	Yes	Yes	Yes	Yes
Interval	Yes	Yes	Yes	No
Ordinal	Yes	Yes	No	No
Nominal	Yes	No	No	No

of the quake by a multiplication of 10, not the addition of a constant amount of energy. The difference in energy between a 6.0 and a 7.0 earthquake is much greater than the difference between earthquakes of 1.0 and 2.0 on the scale.

The fourth and last property is *equal ratios.*

A scale has *equal ratios* if ratios of scores are meaningful.

Height has this property, so two heights can be meaningfully compared by computing their ratio. If Paul is 7 feet tall and Tim is 3.5 feet tall, it is permissible to say that Paul is twice as tall as Tim. By contrast, ratios are not directly interpretable on the Richter scale. An earthquake of 6.0 is not twice as severe as a quake of 3.0; it is 1,000 times more severe.

We have numbered these properties from 1 to 4 to indicate their interrelationship. If a scale has property 4, it also must have all the properties with lower numbers, that is, properties 3, 2, and 1. Similarly, if a scale has property 3, it must have properties 2 and 1; and if a scale has property 2, it must have property 1. Because of this structure, Stevens pointed out that the four properties describe only four types of scales. These scales are shown in Table 1 along with their properties.

Ratio scales have all four properties. Many scales in the physical sciences, such as distance, weight, voltage, current, force, are ratio scales. These scales all have a natural zero point; that is, a score of zero means the absence of the property; zero weight, for example, means literally no weight. Few of today's psychological scales are ratio scales; and the ratio scales we are familiar with, scales of sensations, like the sone scale of noise, were all constructed by Stevens himself. A noise of 10 sones will sound twice as loud to the average person as a noise scaled 5 on this scale.

Interval scales have properties 3, 2, and 1. The best known interval scales are the Fahrenheit and Celsius temperature scales. Because the zero points on these scales do not correspond to the absence of heat, ratios cannot be computed to compare two temperatures; a 100-degree day is not twice as hot as a 50-degree day, for example. But the scale has a constant unit, so a 5-degree difference, from 10 to 15 degrees, is the same increase in temperature as a 5-degree difference from 95 to 100 degrees. The Kelvin temperature scale, by contrast, does have an absolute zero, --459.7 degrees Fahrenheit, the temperature at which all molecular motion stops. Ratios on this scale are meaningful; a 100-degree Fahrenheit day (310.9 °K) is 1.1 times as hot as a 50 degree day (283.1 °K).

TABLE 2 **BEAUFORT WIND SCALE**

| | Wind Speed | | |
Beaufort Scale	(Km/hr)	(mph)	Description
0	below 1	below 1	Calm
1	1–5	1–3	Light air
2	6–11	4–7	Light breeze
3	12–19	8–12	Gentle breeze
4	20–28	13–18	Moderate breeze
5	29–38	19–24	Fresh breeze
6	39–49	25–31	Strong breeze
7	50–61	32–38	Moderate gale
8	62–74	39–46	Fresh gale
9	75–88	47–54	Strong gale
10	89–102	55–63	Whole gale
11	103–117	64–75	Storm
12	above 117	above 75	Hurricane

From Microsoft Encarta, 1994.

Whether a scale has interval properties is verified by experimentation. If an object with a scale score of, say, 5 is "added to" an object with a scale score of 10, for the scale to have the interval property the combination must yield a score of 15. For example, if a 5-pound object is placed on top of a 10-pound object, the combination will weigh 15 pounds. For every interval scale, a process of combining, or adding, two objects to get a new third object must be found so that the new object's scale score is in agreement with arithmetical rules (see Cohen & Nagel, 1934).

Research to verify scale properties is straightforward with measures of weight, length, voltage, etc., but has not been possible for psychological scales, like self-confidence, degree of depression, or intelligence. Consider intelligence; say Bob has an IQ of 80, Jill's IQ is 60, and Mary's is 140. Is Mary's intelligence equal to the combination of Bob's and Jill's intelligence (80 + 60 = 140)? For this question to be meaningful, there has to be some concrete means to "add" IQ scores. For example, if Bob and Jill took the IQ test together could they get Mary's score? Probably not. Because no one has thought of a way of verifying the interval or ratio properties of such measures, such scales can only provide information about the rank ordering of people.

Ordinal or rank order scales have properties 2 and 1. A newspaper may rank order best-selling books from 1 to 10. This scale does not have a constant unit and the ratios of scores are not meaningful. The 5th best-selling book does not sell twice as much as the 10th best-seller, nor are the differences in sales the same between 1st and 2nd place as between 2nd and 3rd place. The Beaufort wind speed scale and the Mohs hardness scale are commonly used ordinal scales. The Beaufort scale, which is presented in Table 2, classifies wind speed into 13 categories from 0, calm, to 12, hurricane. You can see by looking at the

TABLE 3 MOHS HARDNESS SCALE

Mineral	Hardness	Common Tests
Talc	1	Scratched
Gypsum	2	by fingernail
Calcite	3	Scratched by copper coin
Fluorite	4	Scratched by a knife blade
Apatite	5	or window glass
Feldspar	6	Scratches a knife
Quartz	7	blade
Topaz	8	or
Corundum	9	window glass
Diamond	10	Scratches all common materials

From Microsoft Encarta, 1994.

wind speeds that this is not a ratio or interval scale. The difference between scale scores of 0 and 2, 3 mph, is not equal to the difference between scale scores of 10 and 12, 12 mph.

The Mohs hardness scale, presented in Table 3, is based on the operation of scratching one material against another. The harder of the two materials will scratch the other material, but not the other way around. Topaz will scratch quartz, but quartz is not hard enough to scratch topaz. A new material, like your fingernail, is measured by comparing it to these standard 10 materials. A fingernail will scratch gypsum but not calcite, so the scale score for a fingernail is 2.5. This scale does not have ratio or interval properties.

The *nominal scale* only has property 1, equality. If numbers are assigned with these scales (e.g., Democrats = 1; Republicans = 2), they are only for convenience in naming. Nominal scale scores cannot be compared numerically.

The type of scale used in measurement is critical because it limits the type of analysis that is possible on the scale scores. The mean and standard deviation, for example, are not meaningful when computed on scores from nominal and some ordinal scales. If you were to rank order 10 people on intelligence and compute the mean of the rankings, you would get a mean of 5.5. This number would reflect only the number of subjects studied and would say nothing about the average intelligence of the 10 people. Because nominal scales and many ordinal scales do not have normal distributions, statistics that assume this type of distribution are not recommended for use with them. Specific statistical procedures have been developed for analyzing data for these types of scales (see Liao, 1994).

STANDARD AND NORM-BASED SCALES

Physical measures are based on standards, objects with known properties that serve as the official definition of the unit for measuring the property. Prescientific standards were the foot, literally a person's foot, the hand width, and the distance from the elbow to the end of the middle finger, the cubit. Today's standards are considerably more precise. The meter is defined as the distance traveled by light in a vacuum in 1/299,792,458 of a second (Microsoft Encarta, 1994). The kilogram is defined by a cylinder of platinum-iridium alloy kept in France.

Psychological measures are not based on such standards. There is no person housed in Washington, D.C., who is the standard for "average neuroticism," although most people could nominate an acquaintance for this standard. Psychological measures are *norm-based*, meaning that the score for an individual is interpreted by comparing his/her score with the scores of a group of people who define the norms for the test. A person scores average on an intelligence test whose score is equal to the average of this group of people.

Norm-based measurement is unique to psychology and other social sciences. Although we know of no physical measure that is interpreted with norms, this type of measurement is common in psychology. In developing the Wechsler intelligence scales, for instance, the tests (there are three tests to span the age range from young children to adults) were given to a representative national sample of people of different ages. Their performances set the norms, that is, what is considered a high, average, or low score on the test.

The logic of norm-based tests was developed in the mid 1800s by Sir Francis Galton. Galton also developed the basic statistics for reporting norm-based scores—percentiles—and the statistic used in determining the reliability and validity of measures—the correlation coefficient. In the next section of this chapter, we discuss how Galton made these discoveries and explain the logic of norm-based tests. This logic is essential for understanding modern psychological measurement and analysis.

*T*HE BEGINNINGS OF NORM-BASED MEASUREMENT

Galton got involved in measuring individual differences because such measurement was essential to the success of his scientific program to improve the human race. Galton defined the nature extreme in the nature versus nurture debate—the question of whether differences between people in abilities, attitudes, and other characteristics are due to experience (nurture) or biological inheritance (nature, Galton's position). It was Galton who introduced the word heredity into English (from the French) to refer to the process of biological transmission of traits from parents to offspring.

Given his extreme biological position, it is not surprising that Galton saw educational programs as a waste of time and money. For Galton, social reform required intervention in the process of breeding itself. He coined the word *eugenics* (the science of improving the human race by judicious mating and other means that give more suitable people the advantage in having children) to name such reform. His eugenics program would encourage desirable people to have many children and discourage undesirable people from having any children at all. Then, by virtue of the laws of heredity, the human race would improve generation by generation.

To carry out his program, Galton needed to discover the laws of heredity. The then "state of the art" experimental methods of John Stuart Mill were not useful to Galton. Galton's problems in heredity could not be stated in terms of cause and effect. The characteristics of parents do not cause the characteristics of their offspring in any one-to-one manner. Galton needed methods for measuring traits and other methods for dealing with the co-relation or correlation between the traits of parents and offspring. He wanted to know, for example, if parents were intelligent, what that implied about the intelligence of their children. Galton had to invent these methods.

Galton's grandfather had amassed a fortune selling muskets to the British army during the war against Napoleon; the grandfather's factory turned them out at the rate of one per minute. When his father died, Galton inherited his share of the family fortune, which was enough so that he did not have to work again. He quit medical school and devoted his life to science (Galton, 1909). Galton's wealth was the capital that financed the beginning of statistics in the social sciences. (Students today might wish England hadn't needed so many muskets!)

Galton's wealth financed his scientific work on a wide range of topics, including geography and meteorology. After he read *Origin of the Species* in 1859, a book his cousin, Charles Darwin, has just published, his interests focused on eugenics. In Darwin's theory, the future of a species is determined by natural selection—the survival of the fittest. Galton thought it would be an error to trust the future of the human race to the capriciousness of natural selection. It would be a far better world, he argued, if the future were engineered through eugenics.

Galton's work on methods stemmed directly from problems he faced in his eugenics program:

- Galton wanted a way of describing the scores of a large group (population) of people on a trait like intelligence. This description would be the standard of comparison for any future changes on the trait brought about by eugenics.

- He needed a way of describing the degree of change on the trait, so he could find out if future generations were improving compared to the present one. His programs would be evaluated by these changes.

- He needed a quantitative measure of intelligence. This measure was needed to select the people to encourage to breed.

- He needed to identify which traits were biologically determined, because these were the traits that eugenics programs could influence. To do this, he had to find a measure of the degree to which offspring are similar to their parents on a trait.

Galton's eugenics program is history, but his methods are now basic in modern research.

In the early 1860s, Galton began studying the inheritance of intelligence. There were no established measures of intelligence at that time. (The Binet-Simon scale was not available until 1911.) Galton had to find one. He settled for eminence, "high reputation," as his measure. He decided to examine the family trees of eminent men—judges, statesmen, scientists, etc.—to see if eminence "ran in families." The answer was yes. Galton found for judges that:

> More than *one in every nine* of them have been either father, son or brother to another judge. . . . There cannot, then, remain a doubt but that the peculiar type of ability that is necessary to a judge is often transmitted by descent. (Galton, 1864/1892, p. 62)

Galton found similar results for other categories of eminent men. We now know that this result, that eminence runs in families, does not necessarily mean that it is biologically inherited. Families share a common culture as well as common genes. Galton ignored the latter possibility and concluded that intelligence is highly heritable.

DESCRIBING INDIVIDUAL DIFFERENCES

Galton was happy with the results of his study of eminence, but he was not satisfied with using ratings of "eminent" or "not eminent" to measure intelligence. He wanted to study heredity with *quantitative* measures. His dream was to obtain "exact measurements relating to every measurable faculty of body or mind, for two generations at least" (Galton, 1909, p. 244).

To this end, Galton set up a unique laboratory in London at the International Health Exhibition. For threepence, visitors to his laboratory could take a series of tests and measures, and compare how they did with the results from other visitors. Galton's measurements included hearing and visual acuity; color sense; reaction time; pulling, squeezing, and hitting strength; as well as height, weight, and arm span.

On first reading, it seems that this list of measures did not include the one trait of most interest to Galton—intelligence. Not so. For Galton had included measures of sensory acuity and reaction time, the measures thought by scientists of his day to be the best indicators of intelligence. Scientists believed that intelligent people were quick to react and, like the fairy-tale princess who could feel a pea through a stack of mattresses, highly sensitive to stimuli. Retarded people were expected to be slow and insensitive.

Percentiles

Galton wanted to let visitors to his exhibit compare themselves to other visitors. To do this, he developed a novel statistical method called *centiles* or *percentiles.*

Percentiles are calculated from a group of scores. First, all the scores are rank ordered from high to low; then they are divided into 100 groups, with an equal number of scores in each group. If 500 people were tested, each of the 100 groups would contain 5 scores. The values dividing these groups are called percentiles and are numbered from 0 to 100.

ANTHROPOMETRIC
LABORATORY

For the measurement in various ways of Human Form and Faculty.

Entered from the Science Collection of the S. Kennington Museum.

This laboratory is established by Mr. Francis Galton for the following purposes:—

1. For the use of those who desire to be accurately measured in many ways, either to obtain timely warning of remediable faults in development, or to learn their powers.

2. For keeping a methodical register of the principal measurements of each person, of which he may at any future time obtain a copy under reasonable restrictions. His initials and date of birth will be entered in the register, but not his name. The names are indexed in a separate book.

3. For supplying information on the methods, practice, and uses of human measurement.

4. For anthropometric experiment and research, and for obtaining data for statistical discussion.

Charges for making the principal measurements:
THREEPENCE each, to those who are already on the Register. FOURPENCE each, to those who are not:— one page of the Register will thenceforward be assigned to them, and a few extra measurements will be made, chiefly for future identification.

The Superintendent is charged with the control of the laboratory and with determining in each case, which, if any, of the extra measurements may be made, and under what conditions.

H. & W. Brown, Printers, 20 Fulham Road, S.W.

Poster advertising Galton's Anthropometric Laboratory.

A *percentile* is one of the values that divide a set of scores into 100 groups of equal frequency. One percent of the scores fall below the value of the 1st percentile, 2% fall below the 2nd percentile, 80% fall below the 80th percentile, and so on.

The 50th percentile, called the *median*, divides the scores into two equal-sized groups; 50% are below the median, and 50% above.

For the heights of males, Galton found that the 50th percentile was at 67.9 inches, the 70th percentile at 69.2, and the 90th percentile at 71.3. A visitor who was 69 inches tall would know that about 70% of the visitors were shorter and 30% were taller than he was.

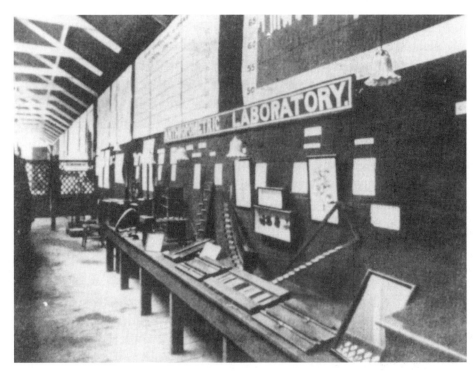

Galton's laboratory at the International Health Exhibition.

Table 4 shows the results for some of Galton's measures, collected in 1884. Besides the simplicity of the percentile system, what is striking is the marked difference in the size of people just over 100 years ago. Back then the 95th percentile for men's weights was 172 pounds; today the 50th percentile man weighs 170 pounds!

No one could have devised a simpler method for conveying a person's relative standing on a measure, and no one has since. Educators today still use Galton's percentiles to report the results of standard tests, such as the SATs; physicians use percentiles to evaluate the height and weight of children; and psychologists use these statistics to describe a person's standing on all kinds of measures of personality and ability.

The Normal Distribution

When the exhibition closed, Galton moved his laboratory to the South Kensington Museum, where he collected data for six more years. He used the data for a variety of projects, including replicating a remarkable discovery that had been made some 30 years earlier by M. A. Quetelet, a Belgian astronomer.

TABLE 4 PERCENTILES

					Values surpassed by percents, below										
					95%	90%	80%	70%	60%	50%	40%	30%	20%	10%	5%
					Values unreached by percents, below										
Character measured	Age	Unit of measurement	Sex	No. of Persons	5%	10%	20%	30%	40%	50%	60%	70%	80%	90%	95%
Height standing	23–	Inches	M.	811	63·2	64·5	65·8	66·5	67·3	67·9	68·5	69·2	70·0	71·3	72·4
without shoes	51	"	F.	770	58·9	59·9	61·3	62·1	62·7	63·3	63·9	64·6	65·3	66·4	67·3
Height sitting from seat	23–	Inches	M.	1013	33·6	34·2	34·9	35·3	35·4	36·0	36·3	36·7	37·1	37·7	38·2
of chair	51	"	F.	775	31·8	32·3	32·9	33·3	33·6	33·9	34·2	34·6	34·9	35·6	36·0
Span of Arms	23–	Inches	M.	811	65·0	66·1	67·2	68·2	69·0	69·9	70·6	71·4	72·3	73·6	74·8
	51	"	F.	770	58·6	59·5	60·7	61·7	62·4	63·0	63·7	64·5	65·4	66·7	68·0
Weight in ordinary	23–	Pounds	M.	520	121	125	131	135	139	143	147	150	156	165	172
indoor clothes	26	"	F.	276	102	105	110	114	118	122	129	132	136	142	149
Vital or Breathing	23–	Cubic	M.	212	161	177	187	199	211	219	226	236	248	277	290
Capacity	26	Inches	F.	277	92	102	115	124	131	138	144	151	164	177	186
Strength of Pull as	23–	Pounds	M.	519	56	60	64	68	71	74	77	80	82	89	96
archer with bow	26	"	F.	276	30	32	34	36	38	40	42	44	47	51	54
Strength of Squeeze	23–	Pounds	M.	519	67	71	76	79	82	85	88	91	95	100	104
with strongest hand	26	"	F.	276	36	39	43	47	49	52	55	58	62	67	72
Swiftness of Blow	23–	Feet per	M.	516	13·2	14·1	15·2	16·2	17·3	18·1	19·1	20·0	20·9	22·3	23·6
	26	second	F.	271	9·2	10·1	11·3	12·1	12·8	13·4	14·0	14·5	15·1	16·3	16·9
Keenness of Sight by	23–	Inches	M.	398	13	17	20	22	23	25	26	28	30	32	34
distance of reading	26	"	F.	433	10	12	16	19	22	24	26	27	29	31	32
diamond type															

Values surpassed and values unreached, by various percentages of the persons measured at the Anthropometric Laboratory at the late International Health Exhibition.

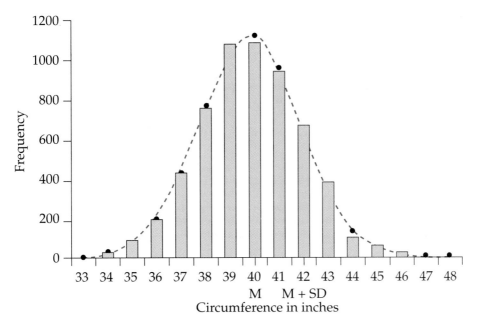

FIGURE 1

Histogram of the circumferences of the chests of Scottish soldiers (based on Quetelet, 1849).

Quetelet discovered that differences between people in height and other physical measures have a simple mathematical form—a form that allows accurate description of the physical characteristics of thousands of people using only two numbers (Quetelet, 1849). In one demonstration Quetelet arranged the chest circumferences of 5,738 army recruits in a special pattern which we now call a *histogram*.

A *histogram* is a graph showing the frequency of occurrence of different values of a measure. The graph is made up of a series of rectangles; the width of each rectangle indicates an interval of values on the measure and the height of the rectangles is in proportion to the frequency of cases that have values in that interval of scores.

Quetelet took the continuum of chest measures from 33 to 48 inches and divided it into a series of consecutive categories each with a width of 1 inch. He then placed each of his 5,738 measurements into its appropriate category.

The resulting histogram (shown in Figure 1) had a "bell-curve" shape that was familiar to Quetelet. Astronomers had been using this curve to describe the distribution of errors they made, for example, in locating stars in the heavens. It was called the *normal distribution* or *Gaussian distribution* (after the mathematician Carl Gauss).

A *normal distribution* is a theoretical frequency distribution that is specified by a mathematical equation. The distribution has the shape of the cross-section of a bell; the high point of the curve is at the median, and the curve is symmetric around the median.

The form of the ideal normal distribution, shown by the dotted line in Figure 1, is described mathematically by a formula that depends upon only two values, the *mean* and *standard deviation* of the measure.

The *mean* is the average value of a measure. It is computed by adding all the scores and dividing by the number of scores.

For a normal distribution, the mean is equal to the median; this is not true for every distribution.

The *standard deviation* is an index of the width of a frequency distribution. The smaller the standard deviation, the closer the scores cluster around the mean score. The greater the standard deviation, the greater the differences between the scores and the mean. The standard deviation is computed by calculating the average squared distance of the scores from the mean and taking the square root of this value.

The mean's location on the histogram in Figure 1 is shown with the letter M; here it is the average chest size of recruits. The standard deviation is the distance, in units of the trait being measured (for chest size the unit is inches), from the mean to the place on the curve marked by M + SD. The height of the normal curve at M + SD is about 60% of its height at M, its maximum height.

Percentiles and the Normal Curve

Galton could have used Quetelet's normal distribution method to describe the distribution of peoples' scores on his measures; there is a mathematical relationship between the normal curve and percentiles, the measure that Galton preferred. Percentiles can be calculated from the mean and standard deviation of normally distributed traits. Figure 2 shows that the mean is at the 50th percentile; M + SD is at the 84th percentile; M – SD is at the 16th percentile.

Once the values of M and SD are calculated for a measure, the values at various percentiles can be read from Figure 2. Using Galton's data for the height of males, M = 67.9 inches and SD = 2.5 inches; so the 16th percentile is M – SD = 67.9 – 2.5 = 65.4 inches; the 50th percentile is 67.9 inches; and the 84th percentile is M + SD = 67.9 + 2.5 = 70.4 inches. Figure 2 also shows the percent of cases falling within intervals expressed using M and SD.

Galton published the results of his measurements at the exhibition using percentiles rather than means and standard deviations. He did this because he thought percentiles would be easier for people to understand and use to determine their standings on the measures. Yet in scientific journals today, it is the mean and standard deviation, not percentiles, that are used routinely to describe distributions. The reason is that these statistics afford a more economical description than percentiles; only two numbers, M and SD, are needed to generate all the percentiles (for normal distributions).

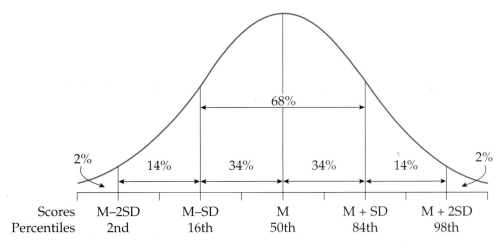

| 2% | 14% | 34% | 34% | 14% | 2% |

FIGURE 2
Percentiles and the normal curve, with percents under curve rounded to whole numbers.

Why the Normal Distribution Is So Common

Galton's explanation for why human characteristics are normally distributed was different from Quetelet's. Quetelet thought that "errors of creation" had a normal distribution because this distribution was characteristic of all errors. Galton based his explanation on a mathematical theorem discovered by Carl Gauss. Gauss's *central limit theorem* was concerned with the distribution of a variable that is formed by adding together a series of other variables. Gauss showed that such aggregate variables would tend more toward a normal distribution as the number of variables added together became larger. This would occur *regardless* of the distribution of the variables being added together. The theorem predicted that, in practice, any aggregate of variables would have approximately a normal distribution.

Height and weight, the measures studied by Quetelet and Galton, were such aggregates. Height is the sum of the heights of a series of body parts, the height of the foot bone plus the ankle bone, etc., up to the head bone. Weight is the sum of the weights of all separate body parts. Today many psychological measures are purposely constructed so that the score on the scale is an aggregate of other scores. Scale scores then will tend to have a normal distribution. This method of scale construction is discussed in the next section.

The discovery that many human characteristics are normally distributed was exciting to Galton because it showed that individual differences follow exact mathematical laws. Quetelet's beautiful results were possible because of quantitative measures. Galton was impressed with Quetelet's work. He thought that progress in studying heredity also would come only with refinements in measurement that would allow quantification of complex human traits, like intelligence.

This view is not unique to Galton. It is shared by many scientists. Peter Medawar, for example, who has written extensively on the scientific method, concludes:

> The art of research is that of making a problem soluble by finding out ways of getting at it. . . . Very often a solution turns on devising some means of quantifying phenomena or states that have hitherto been assessed in terms of "rather more," "rather less," or "a lot of," or workhorse of scientific literature—"marked." (Medawar, 1979, p. 18)

Galton's Scaling Method

Height and weight are easily quantified, but Galton was not particularly interested in these variables; they were simply convenient to try out his methods. Galton wanted to study intelligence. Like height and weight, intelligence could be considered an aggregate—an aggregate of different skills, such as sensory acuity, quick thinking, ability in arithmetic, problem solving, etc. He expected that a quantitative measure of intelligence would show the normal distribution; but no measures were available to test this hypothesis.

To construct a quantitative interval scale of intelligence, Galton devised a clever method of scaling that would produce an interval scale from an ordinal (rank order) scale. The ordinal measure would come from teachers' judgments of their pupils. One hundred pupils, say, would be assigned a score from 1 to 100 to indicate their rank order; the student with the highest intelligence would get a score of 100.

These ordinal scores then would be transformed to an interval scale of intelligence using the properties of the normal curve. First, the student with average intelligence, the one who scored 50 on the ordinal scale (the 50th percentile in the group of 100 students), would be given an arbitrary intelligence score of, say, 100. Next, the student who scored 84 on the ordinal scale (the 84th percentile) would be given an intelligence score one standard deviation above the mean, since the 84th percentile is exactly one standard deviation above the mean on the normal curve. Setting the standard deviation to 15, this student would be assigned a score of 100 + 15 = 115. The value of 15 is arbitrary. Any positive number could be chosen for the standard deviation. The rest of the scores are not arbitrary; the remaining scores on the ordinal scale would be converted to intelligence scores by translating their percentile scores to the corresponding score on a normal distribution with a mean of 100 and a standard deviation of 15. For example, an ordinal score of 98 (the 98th percentile) is two standard deviations above the mean, and would be assigned a score of 100 + 15 + 15 = 130. An ordinal score of 16 would get an intelligence scale score of 100 − 15 = 85.

This new scale, Galton argued, would be an interval scale of intelligence. In support of this conclusion, he showed that this method would work for physical characteristics, like height and weight. If you rank order 100 people on height and then go through the scaling procedure, you will end up with an interval scale of height. So Galton expected the method to work for intelligence as well. In discussing Galton's scaling method, Stigler (1986) points out that his argument is based only on an analogy to height. It is not necessarily true that if the method works for height it also will work for intelligence. Direct evidence is needed that the intelligence scale has equal intervals. As we mentioned earlier, such evidence has not been found.

Since Galton's method requires the judges to be familiar with the intelligence of all the students (to rank order them), such a method would be impractical for measuring intelligence in clinical work. Clinicians need measures that can be administered to one person, or to larger samples for research. But a practical variant of Galton's procedure is used in modern measurement: A questionnaire is devised that is made up of a series of, say, 50 to 100 items, and presented to subjects one at a time. The items for an ability test could be problems to solve; for a personality test, questions about feelings, beliefs, and behaviors. Each item is scored either 1 or 0, depending on the subject's answer. A "correct" answer gets the higher score. The subject's score on the scale is the sum of the item scores. Since this is an aggregate score, it would be expected, by the central limit theorem, to tend to have a normal distribution and, following Galton's logic, to be an interval scale.

The Wechsler Adult Intelligence Scale (WAIS), today's most popular clinical scale, consists of a series of items from different content areas related to intelligence: vocabulary, general information, arithmetic problems, similarities, etc. The subject's scores on the individual items are added together to give a total score for the test. Since these scores are aggregates, they are normally distributed. Similarly, the Minnesota Multiphasic Personality Scale, MMPI, the most popular measure of personality, consists of over 500 true/false items. The scores on particular sets of items are added to form aggregates measuring personality traits that have normal distributions.

NORMAL OR NON-NORMAL?—THE LOGIC OF STATISTICAL TESTS

Quetelet's and Galton's demonstrations that human characteristics have normal distributions, together with the work of astronomers and other scientists showing that this distribution describes errors of measurement, resulted in the normal distribution acquiring almost a cult status. In the 1890s, scientists revered the normal distribution as a "universal law of nature," a distribution with limitless applications.

Usually when extravagant claims are made in science, there are skeptics ready to challenge them. In this case, the skeptic was Karl Pearson, Galton's friend, colleague, and fellow eugenicist. Pearson had a clear interest in showing that the normal distribution did not have limitless applications. In fact, he had developed an elaborate system of equations for describing different *nonnormal distributions.*

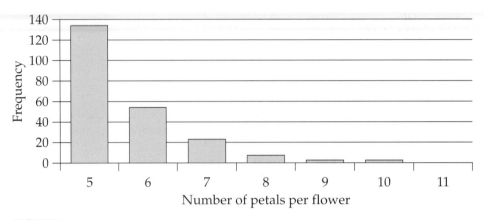

FIGURE 3
Skewed distribution of buttercup petals. (From Pearson, 1900.)

Pearson knew that many distributions of natural events are not normally distributed. One whimsical example he cited (Pearson, 1900) was the distribution of buttercup petals, which is a *skewed* distribution, not a normal distribution.

> In a *skewed distribution*, the mean and median are not equal, as they are in the normal distribution. A distribution is *positively skewed* if the mean is greater than the median and *negatively skewed* if the mean is less than the median.

Figure 3 shows the positively skewed distribution for 222 buttercups.

Pearson suspected that the data cited by other scientists to demonstrate normal distributions really were not a good fit to the normal curve either! Professor Merriman, for example, illustrated the normal distribution of errors using data from one thousand rifle shots at a target by soldiers of the U.S. Army. For this demonstration, different areas of the target were marked with the numbers from 1 to 11. Table 5 shows the number of shots that hit each of these different areas, called the *observed frequencies*, and the number of shots that were expected to hit these areas if the distribution of errors was normal, the *expected frequencies*.

If you compare the observed and expected frequencies, they look fairly close. As expected, the highest number of shots, 212, hit area 6, and areas 1 and 11 were hit the least number of times, also as expected. The observed and expected frequencies for the other areas also appear to be in close agreement. But visually comparing the frequencies is not an objective procedure. Different people certainly would disagree, as Pearson and Merriman did, on whether the observed frequencies were a good fit with the expected frequencies.

What was needed, then, was an objective test to resolve such differences of opinion. Pearson developed such a test, the first widely used *statistical test*.

> A *statistical test* is a mathematical procedure to compare observed results with theoretically expected results in order to reach a conclusion as to whether or not the observations fit the theory.

TABLE 5 DISTRIBUTION OF SHOOTING ERRORS (FROM PEARSON, 1900)

Area	Observed Frequency	Expected Frequency for Normal Distribution
1	1	1
2	4	6
3	10	27
4	89	67
5	190	162
6	212	242
7	204	240
8	193	157
9	79	70
10	16	26
11	2	2

The test Pearson developed for this case is now called the Pearson chi-square, χ^2, Xtest. (The Greek letter chi is pronounced kï.)

The first step in the test is to state exactly the theory or hypothesis to be tested. For Pearson, the hypothesis was that the shooting errors had a normal distribution. The second step was to calculate a test statistic, a numerical value, to measure the similarity between the observed frequencies and the expected frequencies. This statistic is called χ^2. It is calculated by subtracting each corresponding observed and expected frequency squaring these differences, dividing by the expected frequency, and then adding up the values.

The formula for χ^2 is:

$$\chi^2 = \Sigma \, (O - E)^2 / E$$

where O is an observed frequency, E is the corresponding expected frequency, and the summation is over the set of observed frequencies. The smaller the value of χ^2, the less the discrepancy between the two sets of frequencies, and the better the fit between the observations and the normal curve. When $\chi^2 = 0$, the corresponding frequencies are equal. Using Professor Merriman's data, Pearson calculated $\chi^2 = 45.8$.

Next, Pearson determined what values of χ^2 to expect if the distribution of shooting errors was normally distributed. Note that even if the errors are really normally distributed, we would not expect χ^2 to be exactly zero. Pearson showed that in this case χ^2 is expected to be a small positive number and to vary, sometimes being larger, sometimes smaller, over replications of the study. Pearson figured out the exact probability distribution of χ^2, assuming the distribution of errors was really normal (see Figure 4).

This distribution shows that values of χ^2 from, say, 3 to 15 are most likely to occur, while large values of χ^2, indicating a poor fit, and values of χ^2 close to zero, indicating an extremely good fit, are unlikely to occur.

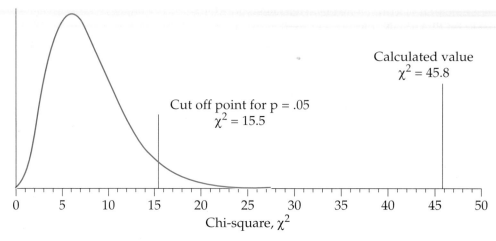

FIGURE 4
The distribution of chi-square if the shooting errors have a normal distribution.

The third step was to compare the calculated value of χ^2 with the probability distribution of χ^2. The calculated value was 45.8. The probability distribution shows that this is a very unlikely value. Pearson determined that the probability, p, of getting this value or an even larger value ($\chi^2 \geq 45.8$) was only .00000155.

Pearson based his decision about whether the distribution of shooting errors was normal or not normal on the probability, p. We do the same thing today in all statistical tests. We call p the *significance probability*.

The *significance probability, p,* is the probability, if the hypothesis being tested is true, of getting the observed value of the test statistic or an even larger value. (The larger the value of the test statistic the poorer the fit of the data to the hypothesis being tested.)

In this case, the hypothesis being tested is that the distribution is normal. If p is too small, say, .05 or less, the fit is not good; that is, the observed data would be quite unlikely to occur if the distribution were normal. If, however, p is relatively large, greater than .05, then the fit is satisfactory, and the conclusion would be that the observed frequencies have an underlying normal distribution. The cutoff point of .05 is called the *alpha level* of the statistical test.

The *alpha level* is the critical value of p used in the statistical test. If p is equal to or smaller than the value of α ($p \leq \alpha$), the hypothesis being tested is rejected; if p is greater than α ($p > \alpha$), the hypothesis is not rejected. The alpha level is set by the experimenter before conducting the test. The value $\alpha = .05$ is commonly used.

Pearson furnished a table that allows researchers to determine the p value for any calculated value of χ^2 for several different values of α. This chi-square table is published in modern statistics texts.

For Professor Merriman's data, p was very small, well below .05. In Pearson's words:

> If shots are distributed on a target according to the normal law, then such a distribution as that cited by Mr. Merriman could only be expected to occur, on an average, some 15 or 16 times in 10,000,000 trials. (Pearson, 1900, p. 355)

Although the data appeared to confirm the hypothesis that they were normally distributed, Pearson's test indicated that, in fact, the distribution was not normal. Pearson had made his point, and the hypothesis that the errors had a normal distribution was rejected. The normal distribution was not a universal law of error.

You might expect that Pearson's demonstration would have resulted in a decline in the popularity of the normal curve, but this did not happen. In fact, the normal curve still is the major probability distribution taught today. The routine use of the mean and standard deviation to describe scores is based on the normal distribution being a good approximation to the actual distribution of the scores.

So Pearson's conclusion that the normal curve should have a narrow application in science was not convincing. Ironically, his χ^2 test, the method he used to reach this conclusion, became immensely popular. It has become a standard method for analyzing non-normal data, that is, data from ordinal or nominal scales. The χ^2 test is used, for example, in modern medical studies to see if a particular high incidence of a disease at a particular place is more than the frequency expected by chance. In studies of birth order, the test is used to study whether firstborns are more likely to be eminent than people with other birth orders. These are just two of the many possible applications of the χ^2 test.

The use of statistical tests in data analysis is now virtually universal, and these tests have become standard for comparing observations with theoretical expectations. The most popular tests assume that the observed scores being analyzed are normally distributed.

In 1984, the Association for the Advancement of Science published an issue of their journal *Science 84* celebrating the top 20 discoveries of the 20th century that have made a "significant impact on the way we think about ourselves and our world" (Hammond, 1984). The award winners included antibiotics, nuclear fission, Einstein's theory of relativity, the computer, television, birth control pills, and Pearson's chi-square test! In presenting the award for Pearson's discovery, Ian Hacking (1984) wrote:

> The chi-square test was a tiny event in itself, but it was the signal for a sweeping transformation in the ways we interpret our numerical world. . . . For better or worse, statistical inference has provided an entirely new style of reasoning. The quiet statisticians have changed our world—not by discovering new facts or technical developments but by changing the ways we reason, experiment, and form our opinions about it. (Hacking, 1984, p. 70)

KEY TERMS

Reactive and non-reactive measures
Multiple measures
Scale properties
  equality, rank order, equal intervals,
  equal ratios
Scale types
  ratio, interval, ordinal, and nominal
Standard vs. norm-based measures
Eugenics
Percentiles
Median

Histogram
Normal distribution
Mean, standard deviation
Aggregate measures
Central limit theorem
Skewed distributions, positive and
  negative
Statistical test
Pearson's χ^2 test
Significance probability, p
Alpha level, α

KEY PEOPLE

Sheldon Cohen et al.
Francis Galton
Charles Darwin
S. S. Stevens

M. A. Quetelet
Carl Gauss
Karl Pearson

REVIEW QUESTIONS

1. Cohen, Tyrrell, and Smith (1991) used multiple measures of their subjects' smoking and the severity of their colds. Explain why they used multiple measures.

2. Classify the following measures as reactive or nonreactive. Explain your answers.
     cotinine in the blood as a measure of smoking
     self-report of stress
     presence of antibodies in the blood
     Wechsler IQ test
     subjects' weight

3. Describe the relationship between scale properties and scale types in Stevens' classification of scales.

4. Identify the scale type and scale properties of the following:
     weight in grams
     temperature in degrees Fahrenheit
     temperature in degrees Kelvin
     Richter scale
     Mohs hardness scale
     Beaufort wind scale

5. Classify the following scales according to whether they involve standard or norm-based measurement:
   weight in grams
   Mohs hardness scale
   Wechsler Adult Intelligence Scale
   MMPI Depression scale

6. Explain how Galton's goal of developing a eugenics program led him to become interested in statistical methods.

7. Describe Galton's system of percentiles and explain why this system is important in norm-based measurement.

8. What is the advantage of describing sets of scores with the mean and standard deviation rather than percentiles? When would percentiles be preferred?

9. What percentiles correspond to the following scores on a normal curve?
   two standard deviations below the mean
   one standard deviation below the mean
   at the mean
   one standard deviation above the mean
   two standard deviations above the mean

10. Compare Quetelet's and Galton's explanations for why human characteristics, like height, are normally distributed.

11. Describe how you would construct an interval scale of creativity using Galton's scaling method. Could you be sure that it was an interval scale? Why or why not?

12. Describe the logic of Pearson's chi-square test in your own words.

13. Explain why Pearson's statistical test was selected by the Association for the Advancement of Science as one of the top 20 discoveries of the 20th century.

5

Correlation

❖

It will be shown how the closeness of co-relation in any particular case admits of being expressed by a simple number.

SIR FRANCIS GALTON

❖

THE DISCOVERY OF REGRESSION
    The Concept of Regression
    The Regression Coefficient
THE SCATTERPLOT: THE GRAPH OF CORRELATION
THE CORRELATION COEFFICIENT
    The Independence of Variables
    z Scores
    r, an Index of Correlation
    Calculating r
    r and the Reliability and Validity of Measures
CORRELATION AND PREDICTION: THE METHOD
  OF LEAST SQUARES
    Nonlinear Relationships
    Statistical Control
CORRELATION'S BAD REPUTATION
    Causal Relationships
        Common cause
        Direct causation
        Partial causation
    Noncausal Relationships
        Correlation by chance
        Correlation by custom
        Common correlates
KEY TERMS, KEY PEOPLE, REVIEW QUESTIONS

Today norm-based measurement is the dominant method in psychology for assessing individual differences. In fact, all of our most popular scales (e.g., the Wechsler intelligence tests, the Minnesota Multiphasic Personality Inventory, and the Strong Interest Inventory) use this type of measurement. But the success of this approach depended on additional methodological advances that enabled researchers to evaluate the scales and use them in empirical studies.

First, methods were needed for evaluating how well the scales measured what they were designed to measure—whether the Wechsler Intelligence Scale for Children (WISC) is a good measure of intelligence, for example. Second, investigators needed a method for studying individual differences. Variation between people in personality, social class, education, sex, political beliefs, and culture cannot be studied experimentally, because it is impossible to manipulate such characteristics. These needs were met with the development of a statistical method called "correlational analysis."

This highly mathematical technique was not devised, as you might expect, by a mathematician concerned with the abstract problem of describing the relationship between variables. The initial work on this method was done by Sir Francis Galton, the inventor of norm-based measurement. Galton, who was studying inheritance by breeding peas, was looking for a method to assess how similar parents and offspring are on different traits. The story of his research and of his subsequent invention of the correlation coefficient reveals the close association between correlation and norm-based measurement. Perhaps more than any other single event, the introduction of correlational analysis brought quantitative methods to the social sciences. With correlation, psychology for the first time had a powerful, objective method for observational research.

THE DISCOVERY OF REGRESSION

In his initial studies of heredity, Galton compared different generations of people on distributions of physical traits. The comparisons showed that the distributions were surprisingly constant across generations. There was little change in either the means or standard deviations of the scores. Further, fossil records of plants revealed constant distributions of characteristics over thousands of years.

This consistency was puzzling to Galton. He thought that if the physical traits he was observing were highly determined by heredity, they would *not* be constant over generations. If heredity is highly influential, he thought, there would be an increasing standard deviation in traits from generation to generation.

Let's look at Galton's reasoning using height in people as an example. Galton thought that height is determined mostly by heredity; so the children of tall parents should end up as tall adults, and the children of short parents should be short adults. But Galton knew that height is not completely determined by heredity; all children in the same family are not the same height even though they have the same parents.

Most likely, Galton supposed, about half the children in a family grow taller than their parents, and half end up shorter. But if this is true, there should be ever *increasing standard deviations* of the trait in the population. To understand why, consider, as Galton did, two tall people who have children; say, half their children are taller than they are as adults. The tall children marry other tall people and have children, half of whom grow taller than themselves. If this is repeated, generation after generation, we would end up with some very tall people, say, people 30 feet tall, having even taller children! The same process would occur for short parents; half of their children would end up shorter than them. As adults, the short people would have some shorter kids, and so on—until we would have some people, say, 1 foot tall, having even shorter kids! The increasing numbers of very short and very tall people would dramatically increase the variability of height in the population.

But people have been on earth for thousands of generations and there are no gigantic or teeny-tiny people. Perhaps, thought Galton, children are not equally likely to be taller or shorter than their parents. He wrote to his cousin Charles Darwin that he "was very desirous of ascertaining the facts of the case." In response, Darwin suggested that he investigate the question using sweet peas.

Galton then designed an experiment to determine the exact relationship between the sizes of parent peas and their offspring. Peas had the advantage over other plants of being self-fertilizing, so each offspring had only one parent.

Galton decided to study quantitative characteristics of peas (of course)—diameter and weight. (At about the same time as Galton's experiments, Gregor Mendel studied qualitative traits of peas, such as tall versus dwarf plants, by interbreeding plants and arrived at an entirely different theory of heredity from Galton's.) Galton selected seeds of seven different, evenly spaced sizes: three below average, one average, and three above average. (He was using Mill's method of concomitant variation here, but he would reach an entirely different type of conclusion than the method would reach.) He picked 10 seeds of each size, for a total of 70 seeds, to form a set. Nine sets were sent to friends in the country with explicit instructions on how to plant them. At harvest time, the plants were sent back to Galton.

The Concept of Regression

After measuring the sizes of the offspring, Galton classified them into the seven groups defined by the size of their parents. Table 1 shows the *average size* of the offspring with the sizes of their parents for all seven parent sizes. (The results are simplified here to clarify the relationship between parent and offspring.)

Put yourself in Galton's shoes and see if you can see a relationship between the parent sizes and the *average* offspring sizes. Can you state the relationship with a simple principle? Hint: Forget about the absolute size of the peas and think in terms of size measured as a *deviation* from the mean; the average pea had a diameter of 18. Table 1 shows these deviations in parentheses. Can you state the relationship now?

TABLE 1 PARENTS VERSUS AVERAGE OFFSPRING, SIZE IN HUNDREDS OF AN INCH (DEVIATION FROM THE MEAN OF 18 IN PARENTHESES)

	Parent Size		Offspring Average Size	
Biggest	21	(+3)	19	(+1)
	20	(+2)	18⅔	(+⅔)
	19	(+1)	18⅓	(+⅓)
Average	18	(0)	18	(0)
	17	(−1)	17⅔	(−⅓)
	16	(−2)	17⅓	(−⅔)
Smallest	15	(−3)	17	(−1)

Galton described the relationship as one of *"regression to mediocrity"* or *"regression to the mean."* The average offspring was closer to the average-sized pea than its parent was. Big parents had smaller offspring; tiny parents had bigger offspring. Only average-sized parents had offspring who were the same size, on the average, as their parents.

The Regression Coefficient

Galton found that a single number, a fraction, described the regression to the mean. For each of the seven groups of peas, the average offspring deviation from the mean was ⅓ the deviation of its parent. Table 1 shows that if you divide the parent deviation from the mean by 3, in each case you get the average offspring deviation. Galton called this number the *regression coefficient,* and gave it the symbol *r*, for regression.

This simple result could only be discovered using norm-based measurements on the peas. The regression coefficient relates the *deviation* of the parent from the *mean* to the *deviation* of the offspring from the *mean.*

This result was astounding. Could it really be true that a single number is sufficient to describe the relationship between relatives? Galton wrote:

> This curious result was based on so many plantings . . . that I could entertain no doubt of the truth of my conclusions. (Galton, 1886, p. 246)

But people were another story. There were no good data available that could be used to test regression to the mean for people.

Galton immediately began to collect family records of height for two generations. After five years, he had collected about 300 cases of parents' and their children's heights as adults, enough, he judged, for a fair test of regression.

The results confirmed his understanding that the distribution of height changes little from generation to generation. The mean and standard deviation for fathers and sons were virtually identical; the same result was found for mothers and daughters. Now for the critical point. Was there regression to the mean?

THE SCATTERPLOT: THE GRAPH OF CORRELATION

The test for regression followed the same design as the pea study, with one exception: People have two parents, not one; and the offspring are of two types—men and women, each with a different distribution of height; men are taller, on the average, than women. To solve this problem, Galton multiplied the heights of all the women in the study by 1.08, a factor chosen to equalize the average heights of men and women. Then he averaged the parents' heights to obtain a single number called the mid-parent value.

Before describing what Galton found, let's look at the range of logical possibilities for the regression. We can better appreciate his specific result if we first see the full range of possibilities.

Let's start with the degree of regression Galton found for peas, $r = \frac{1}{3}$ or .33. For this value of r, the children's deviation from the mean would be $\frac{1}{3}$ of their parents' deviation from the mean. Figure 1 shows this regression for height. The graph shows the heights expected for the *average* child, if $r = .33$. The straight line in the graph is called the *regression line*. Using this line, you can determine the *average* height of the children for any height mid-parent (assuming here that $r = .33$). For example, mid-parents who are 71 inches tall can expect children who average 69 inches. This case is shown on the graph.

The regression line shows only the results for the *average* child. It doesn't show the variability in height among the children in the same family (or among children with the same sized parents). This variability can be seen if we plot the individual parent/child cases on the graph with the regression line, as in Figure 2. Sixty cases are plotted there, less than Galton used, but enough to clearly show the results. Each diamond in the graph, ◊, is one case and is located by the height of the mid-parent (on the horizontal axis) and the height of their child (on the vertical axis). This type of graph, which is known by a variety of different

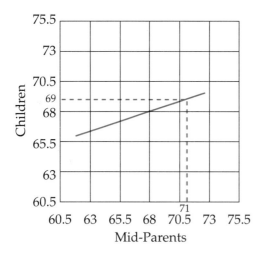

FIGURE 1
$r = .33$

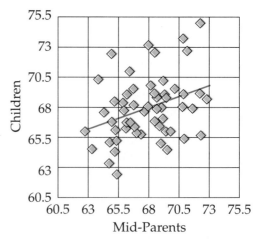

FIGURE 2
$r = .33$

names—scattergram, dot diagram, X-Y chart, or *scatterplot*—is still the best technique we have for displaying the relationship between two measures.

A *scatterplot* is a graph showing, for a group of subjects, the values for each subject on two measures. Each subject is plotted as a point; the point is located by the values of the subject on the two measures. The measures are plotted on the horizontal and vertical axes of the graph.

The scatterplot for $r = .33$ shows considerable variability, or *scatter*, around the regression line. Pick a mid-parent height and look at the wide range of heights of the children. With $r = .33$, there is only weak similarity in the heights of parents and children.

Figure 3 shows the regression line and individual cases for $r = .66$. There is more similarity between parent and child here than for $r = .33$. The plot shows that very tall parents do not have very short children, and vice versa; very short parents do not have very tall kids. There also is less scatter around the regression line than for $r = .33$. Children in the same family would not vary widely in height if $r = .66$.

The next plot (Figure 4) shows how parent and child heights would be related if $r = .90$. The children would be very similar in height to their parents here; the child deviation from the mean is %0 of the parents' deviation, so there is only a small regression to the mean. There also is little scatter around the regression line.

The maximum value for r is 1 (Figure 5). (If r were greater than 1, the children would be farther from the mean than their parents; consequently, the standard deviation of height also would *increase* from generation to generation. But since the standard deviation is equal for the parents and children, r cannot be greater than 1.) With $r = 1$, every case falls on the regression line, so

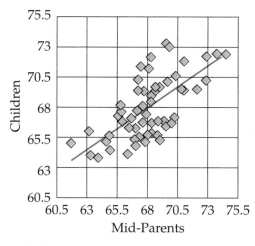

FIGURE 3
$r = .66$

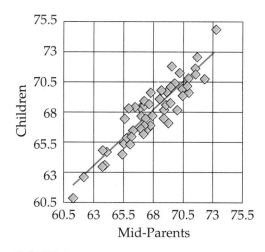

FIGURE 4
$r = .90$

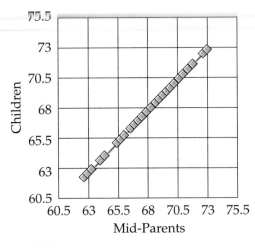

FIGURE 5
r = 1

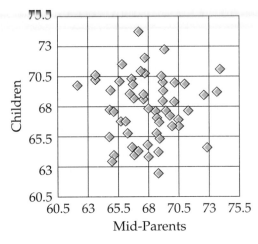

FIGURE 6
r = 0

all children are identical in height to their mid-parent. Galton was positive he would *not* find $r = 1$, since he knew that all sons (or daughters) of the same parents are not the same height.

There is one more possibility to examine, which Galton also thought would not happen, $r = 0$ (Figure 6). The regression line is horizontal at the mean in this case; with $r = 0$, the heights of the children are not related to the heights of the parents. Tall parents are just as likely to have short, average, or tall children; the same expectations hold for the children of tall parents as for those of short parents. There is simply no similarity in height between parent and child. Galton was fairly sure he would not find $r = 0$, because casual observation indicated some degree of similarity between parent and child.

Now, the actual result. Galton found the regression coefficient was $r = .66$. On the average, children have ⅔ of their mid-parent deviation. The plot, Figure 3, shows a marked similarity between parent and child. This result was better than Galton could have hoped for. First, his paradox was explained. Regression to the mean of $r = .66$ allows the parent and child to be quite similar in height and still have constancy in the mean and standard deviation across generations. Second, the usefulness of the regression coefficient was confirmed for people. The index was clearly a measure of similarity between relatives; $r = 1$ indicated perfect similarity; $r = 0$ indicated no similarity; values between 0 and 1 could be interpreted as degrees of similarity. The higher the value of r, the less the regression to the mean and the greater the similarity between relatives. Since Galton considered the effects of the environment negligible, for him r was an index of biological inheritance.

These results suggested a lifetime of research. Galton and his followers could find the degree of inheritance for all major human faculties and characteristics, for all possible pairings of relatives—child versus parent, grandpar-

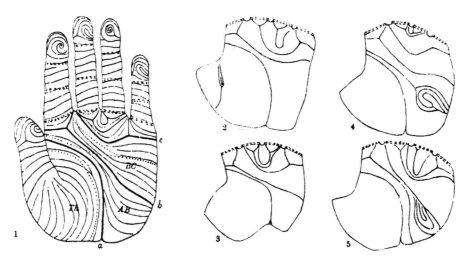

Galton's fingerprinting system, showing ridges and the creases of the palm. (The Granger Collection, New York.)

ent versus grandchild, uncle versus nephews, etc. The research would be time-consuming (and pretty dull), but the results would form the empirical foundation for eugenics.

Galton did not realize the full importance of his regression analysis yet. He thought its use was limited to studies of inheritance—studies examining the relationship between relatives on the same trait. It was only several years later, while he was working on a project unrelated to inheritance, that the real significance of his method suddenly struck him. It was a moment of joy for Galton.

THE CORRELATION COEFFICIENT

The Independence of Variables

Galton became interested in the problem of personal identity when he was invited to give a lecture on the system of criminal identification developed by Alphonse Bertillon. "Bertillonage" was the only systematic method of establishing personal identity at the time. The method involved careful measurement of different characteristics of the body, such as height, foot length, and head size. Criminologists believed that this set of measurements was sufficient to accurately establish a person's unique identity and guard against false impersonation. (Fingerprinting, the modern system for establishing identity, was developed by Galton as an alternative to Bertillon's system.)

Fingerprints were a sidelight of Galton's main work on heredity, but a sidelight that gave the occasion for Galton's most fruitful insight—the invention of correlation analysis. This insight occurred while Galton was considering a criticism of Bertillonage.

According to Galton, the claimed high accuracy of Bertillonage was based on the presumed "independence of the variables measured."

> Two variables are said to be *independent* of each other if the variation in scores on one variable is in no way related to the variation in scores on the other variable.

Galton thought that the accuracy of the method was not as high as claimed because the variables used by Bertillon were *not independent* of each other. He thought, for example, that tall people would most likely have big feet and that short people would have small feet. If this were true, the two measures would not be independent, and including foot size in the system would add little information over knowing a person's height. But how could Galton demonstrate this lack of independence?

z Scores

The problem of comparing variables was related to the heredity problem that Galton had been working on already. Galton had demonstrated that the regression coefficient, *r*, is basically a measure of similarity; *r* could index the degree of similarity between the heights of fathers and sons, for example. But could *r* be computed between different measures taken on the same person? Does it make sense to ask what is the similarity between, say, head length and height? One measure varies around a mean of 67 inches, while the other varies around a mean of 7.5 inches. How can you say a person's height is identical, or slightly different, or very different from his head size?

This was the question Galton was thinking about while visiting the grounds of Naworth Castle when, in his words:

> A temporary shower drove me to seek refuge in a reddish recess in the rock by the side of the pathway. There the idea flashed across me, and I forgot everything else for a moment in my great delight. (Galton, 1909, p. 300)

He had figured out how to compare different measures and determine an index of correlation.

The solution was based on an extension of Galton's norm-based measurement scheme of describing a person's score as a *deviation* from the mean. For example, let's say that Big Joe is 72 inches tall and the average man's height is 67 inches. Then Joe is 5 inches above the mean. If the standard deviation of height is 2.5 inches, then Joe is 5/2.5, or 2, standard deviations above the mean. Next consider Big Joe's head. Let's say it is 8.1 inches long, and the mean head length is 7.5 inches, and the standard deviation of this measure is 0.3 inches. Joe's head length is .6 inches above average; this is 2 standard deviations above average, since the standard deviation is 0.3 (.6/.3 = 2). Now we can compare Joe's height with his head size: Both are 2 standard deviations above average, so Joe's height is identical with his head size! In this special sense, Joe is as tall as his head is long!

This comparison of a person's scores on two different measures is made by transforming the scores to a new scale, a scale where the unit of measure is based on the standard deviation of the measure. Today these new scores are called *z scores:*

A *z score* is equal to the difference between a score and the mean divided by the standard deviation. A z score expresses how far a score is from the mean in units of the standard deviation.

The formula for computing a z score from an original or *raw* score is

$$z = \frac{X - M}{SD}$$

where, X is the original score, M is the mean of the X scores, and SD is the standard deviation of the X scores.

A z score of zero occurs when the X score is equal to the mean; positive z scores occur when X scores are above the mean, and negative z scores when the X scores are below the mean. If a person, like Big Joe, has the same z score on two different measures, then he falls at the same percentile on both measures. Two standard deviations above the mean is at the 98th percentile; so Joe is taller than all but 2% of people, and his head also is longer than all but 2% of other heads.

r, an Index of Correlation

With the z score, Galton could determine the similarity of head size and height. Transforming the original scores to z scores puts both measures on the same scale so that the scores can be directly compared. The value of r can then be computed on these scores just as if it were a problem in heredity. (The computation of r will be discussed in the next section.) If r turned out to be equal to zero, the variables would be independent. Positive values of r would indicate similarity between the z scores on the two measures, that is, a lack of independence. Galton found for head size versus height $r = +.35$, indicating lack of independence. This finding confirmed his criticism of Bertillonage.

Galton called r an index of co-relation or *correlation* (the second spelling caught on). In his own words:

Two variable organs are said to be co-related when the variation of the one is accompanied on the average by more or less variation of the other, and in the same direction. Thus the length of the arm is said to be co-related with that of the leg, because a person with a long arm has usually a long leg, and conversely. If the co-relation be close then a person with a very long arm would usually have a very long leg; if it be moderately close then the length of his leg would only be long, not very long; and if there were no co-relation at all then the length of his leg would on the average be mediocre. . . .Between these two extremes are an endless number of intermediate cases, and it will be shown how the closeness of co-relation in any particular case admits of being expressed by a simple number. (Galton, in Pearson, 1930, p. 50)

This passage, the first public presentation of correlation, was read at a meeting of the British Royal Society on December 20, 1888. This was the start of a revolution in research methods.

Calculating r

Galton computed *r* by a graphical method. Today the easiest, most accurate computation is by computer. The computer is programmed to follow the computational formula developed by Karl Pearson, the inventor of the χ^2 test we discussed in the last chapter. Pearson developed and extended the mathematical basis of correlation and derived the modern formula for *r*. Because of this work, *r* is now known as the *Pearson correlation coefficient*. In a strange twist of history, Galton's name is no longer linked with correlation, and many scientists now must think it was developed by Pearson!

r and the Reliability and Validity of Measures

The correlation coefficient provides an important tool for evaluating the reliability and validity of norm-based scales. A good example of the application of this statistic is found in the manual for the latest revision of the Wechsler Intelligence Scale for Children (WISC-III, Wechsler, 1991).

The reliability of the WISC was reported for children in age groups from 6 to 16 years old. For each age group, 200 children were tested. Reliability was studied using the split-half method: The test, composed of numerous items with differing content, was split in half to form, in effect, two IQ tests with similar content. Each subject was scored on both halves of the test and these scores were correlated. A high correlation would indicate that scores on the two halves of the scale are consistent with each other. If the correlation is close to zero, the implication would be that the test is inconsistent and does not even correlate with itself. The split-half correlation was high for the WISC. For example, for 11-year-olds, the correlation was .90. This high value places the test among the most reliable psychological tests available.

The validity of the WISC was studied by correlating WISC scores with other established measures of intelligence and determining the correlations of WISC scores with other variables that should correlate with intelligence for theoretical reasons. If the WISC is valid, the correlation of the WISC and other intelligence tests should be high, close to the reliability of the WISC. The correlation between WISC scores and school grades was expected to be positive but lower than the correlation with other intelligence tests because grades depend on more than intelligence.

The WISC manual reports that the WISC correlates with the Stanford-Binet Intelligence test, *r* = .83, and with mathematics and English grades in school, *r* = .41 and *r* = .40, respectively. These correlations support the validity of the WISC. We will discuss the reliability and validity of measures further in Chapter 12, Planning the Study.

CORRELATION AND PREDICTION: THE METHOD OF LEAST SQUARES

As we have discussed, Galton saw the correlation coefficient as an index of similarity—a measure of the degree of co-relation between different variables. His interpretation still is in common use today, for example, whenever we compute the correlation between two measures to determine the degree of similarity between them. But there also is a different interpretation of correlation today. This interpretation was discovered by George Yule (1897). Yule, a mathematician working in Pearson's laboratory saw that Galton's and Pearson's work on correlation was a specific case of a general method of analysis that astronomers and physicists had been using for almost a century—the *method of least squares.*

Scientists had used this method to develop mathematical models *to predict* events such as the movement of the moon and planets and the occurrence of high and low tides. The method involved calculating equations to minimize the error in predicting one variable, the dependent variable, from a set of independent variables. Astronomers would take a set of observations of the position of the moon at different times during the year and with the method of least squares calculate an equation to predict the moon's position in the future. The method calculated the equation so it would be the best possible fit to the observations. The method got the name *least squares* because it guaranteed that the fit had the least squared error. The error is the difference between the value predicted by the equation and the observed value.

Yule thought that Galton's problem of describing the relationship between parents and offspring also could be considered as a problem in prediction: How well can you predict offspring characteristics from parent characteristics?

When Yule worked out the least squares solution to this problem, the result was astonishing. The equation for prediction calculated by the method of least squares was the exact equation for Galton's regression line. Yule's calculations also showed that the correlation coefficient, r, was a measure of the accuracy of the predictions: $r = 1$. was characteristic of perfect prediction (zero error) and $r = 0$ was the worst possible prediction (maximum error).

The equation from the method of least squares for predicting height (based on Galton's data) was

$$Y = 26.8 + .6(X),$$

where Y was the predicted height of the offspring and X was the height of the parent. This is the equation for a straight line, a *linear relationship* between the variables Y and X.

Two variables, Y and X, are said to have a *linear relationship* if they are related by an equation of the type $Y = a + bX$.

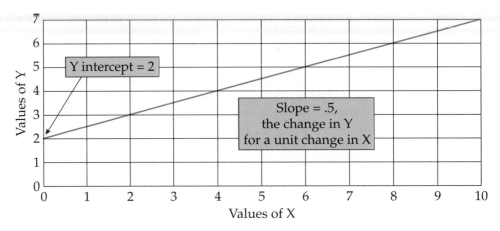

FIGURE 7
Graph of the linear relationship $Y = 2 + .5X$.

The constant b is the slope of the line and the constant a is the Y intercept of the line. The slope of the line is equal to the change in Y for a change in X; the Y intercept is the value of Y for $X = 0$, the point where the line crosses the Y axis. Figure 7 shows the slope and Y intercept for the equation $Y = 2 + 0.5X$.

Yule's work demonstrated that what Galton was doing when he calculated a correlation coefficient was predicting one variable from another variable assuming a linear relationship. If you examine the scatterplots shown earlier in this chapter, you will see that the higher the value of r, the closer the data points fall to the regression line.

> The Pearson correlation coefficient, r, is a measure of how well one variable, Y, can be predicted from another variable, X, using the linear relationship $Y = a + bX$. A value of $r = 1$ indicates perfect, error-free prediction. A value of $r = 0$ indicates prediction at a chance level.

Yule's insight linked Galton and Pearson's work to an established area of mathematics and led to the development of two methods of enormous importance in the social sciences: (1) methods for studying *nonlinear* relationships, and (2) a new method of *statistical control*.

Nonlinear Relationships

The method of least squares is not limited to linear relationships. With a simple change of the model, nonlinear relationships can be studied. Let's consider the relationship between anxiety and test performance in school. Optimal performance is expected at a middle level of anxiety—anxiety that is neither too high to hinder performance nor too low to motivate the student to do well. This curvilinear relationship is shown in Figure 8. The curve follows the equation $Y = a + bX + cX^2$, where a, b, and c are constants calculated to minimize er-

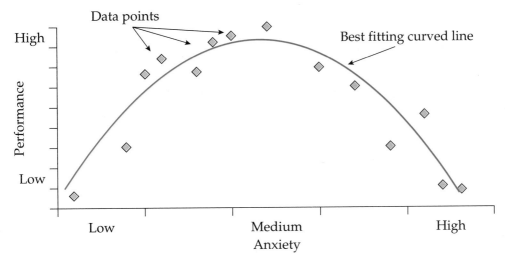

FIGURE 8
Curvilinear relationship between anxiety and performance

rors in prediction. This equation differs from the equation for the straight line by the addition of the term cX^2.

With the method of least squares, experimenters can determine the extent to which observed scores match what is expected for a curvilinear relationship. The degree of fit of this model is measured by a generalization of the correlation coefficient that is called the *multiple correlation coefficient*.

This development was important for psychology because nonlinear relationships are common in psychological research. Growth curves, which show how physical and psychological characteristics change over time, are typically nonlinear. Psychophysical relationships, which show how sensory acuity changes as a function of the magnitude of a physical stimulus, also are nonlinear.

Statistical Control

In Mill's methods, variables are controlled by holding them constant over different conditions in an experiment. But such control is not always possible. In studies of diseases, like cancer, or disorders, like depression or schizophrenia, experiments to find the causes are impossible. Such research must be correlational. The method of least squares provides a powerful tool for analysis in such cases.

Let's take breast cancer as an example. A recent theory holds that exposure to sunshine *reduces* the risk of a woman developing breast cancer (Cowley, 1992). According to the theory, the vitamin D produced by sunshine helps the body absorb calcium which, in turn, controls the growth of cancerous cells. But how can this suspected relationship be studied? One way would be to compare rates of breast cancer in groups of women who get different amounts of sunshine, say, women in Seattle versus women in Florida. But how can we control other variables that we already know are linked with cancer? For example, we know that the risk of cancer increases directly with age, so age must be accounted for in studies of cancer.

Age can be "controlled" in such studies by using the method of least squares in a two-stage process. In the first stage, age is measured, then used in a mathematical model to predict the incidence of cancer:

Model 1: $Y = a + b$ (Age)

where Y is the incidence of cancer, the dependent variable,
and Age is the independent variable.

We can fit this model to the data to determine how well cancer is predicted by age. In the second stage, we fit the model:

Model 2: $Y = a + b$(Age) $+ c$(Sunshine)

and calculate how much better Model 2 fits the data compared to Model 1. If Model 2 fits the results significantly better, this constitutes evidence that the amount of sunshine is related to the risk of cancer.

Note that the logic here is a variation of the logic of Mill's method of difference. Models 1 and 2 differ in only one independent variable, Sunshine. So if Model 2 fits the data better than Model 1, it must be due to this variable. The variable Age is *statistically controlled* since it is present in both equations.

The sunshine–breast cancer hypothesis was supported by correlational research that used statistical controls for age and other variables linked to cancer. The hypothesis currently is undergoing a more rigorous experimental test by the National Institute of Health. Sixty thousand women are receiving either vitamin D and calcium supplements or a placebo in a 9-year experiment. Because this type of research does not expose subjects to harmful agents, there are no ethical problems to prevent its use with people.

Yule's contribution to research methods was enormous. Least squares is now the most popular method of analysis in psychology. It is used, for example, in studies evaluating how well SAT scores can predict college grades, in studies predicting what kinds of patients will benefit most from psychotherapy, in studies predicting what types of prisoners will violate parole, and in studies of the link between stress and susceptibility to colds. Its applications are limitless.

CORRELATION'S BAD REPUTATION

We have seen that the correlation coefficient can be interpreted as a measure of similarity between two variables and as a measure of the degree of accuracy in predicting one variable from another assuming a linear relationship. However, sometimes scientists wish to go beyond these interpretations to infer cause-and-effect relationships between the variables being correlated. Scientists can run into problems here.

To understand how, let's try to state the logic of correlation in the language of Mill's methods of induction. As you remember from Chapter 2, Mill's methods have an *if. . . then . . .* format. *If* specific observations are made, *then* you can reach a specific conclusion. Let's try this for correlation:

> *If* you observe each of n subjects on two variables, V_1 and V_2, and compute the correlation coefficient, r, and find that r is not zero, *then* you can conclude that V_1 and V_2 are related by . . .

How should we finish the conclusion? If V_1 and V_2 are correlated, what exactly does this mean? It is possible that V_1 is the cause or part of the cause of V_2; or vice versa, V_2 might be the cause of V_1; or V_1 and V_2 both might be caused by a third variable, V_3; or V_1 and V_2 might not be linked by any fact of causation. There is no single conclusion that follows logically from the fact that two variables are correlated. We cannot write a simple ending for our method of induction. This ambiguity in what correlation implies about the relationship between variables is the reason for correlation's bad reputation.

To better understand correlation, we need to be familiar with the variety of relationships between variables that can lead to correlation. Let's start our discussion by looking at how Galton used the relation of causality to interpret his own results on heredity and Bertillonage.

Causal Relationships

Common cause. Galton's first correlations were computed comparing different relatives on the same variable, height for parents, V_1, and height for their children, V_2; and comparing two variables, the sizes of different body parts for the same people, for example, length of the right arm, V_1, and length of the left arm, V_2. In both cases, Galton interpreted the correlations as being due to a common cause; V_1 and V_2 correlate because both are caused, in part, by another factor that they share. Parents and children share the same genetic material, which determines height. The lengths of both of a person's arms result from the same biological process of growth. This process is shared by both arms.

Common cause is a popular explanation for why variables correlate. IQ test scores correlate with school grades, it is claimed, because both are influenced by the individual's intellectual skills. Two measures of extraversion correlate because both measure the trait of extraversion. However, variables may correlate for other reasons. Instead of sharing a common cause, one variable may directly cause, or at least be involved in the cause, of the second variable.

Direct causation. Suppose we visit a New Year's Eve party. Just after midnight, we interview the revellers to find out how many drinks they have had, V_1, and administer a blood test for alcohol, V_2. No doubt the correlation between V_1 and V_2 will be high, maybe $r = +.90$. People who have had many drinks will have a high concentration of alcohol in their blood; teetotalers will have no alcohol in their blood. Does this correlation indicate a common cause? In other words, is there a third factor that causes people to drink and also causes alcohol to form in the blood? No, not at all—the relationship is simpler; the alcohol you drink goes into your bloodstream. This direct causation is the explanation for the high correlation.

Partial causation. Correlations also are found when the causation is not as direct as in the alcohol example. "Partial causation" or "indirect causes" frequently occur in studies of risk factors for disease and psychopathology. Several studies have shown, for example, that separation from a parent before age 11 increases a child's risk of developing depression as an adult. The separation may result from the death of a parent, divorce, or a temporary circumstance.

Separation is called a "risk factor" here because separation before age 11 (yes or no), V_1, is correlated with adult depression (yes or no), V_2. Approximately 40% of depressed adults report separation from a parent as a child (Roy, 1981); many children separated from a parent do not develop depression, though, and many depressed adults were not separated from their parents as youngsters.

Although separation and depression are related, the correlation in this case does not reflect a common cause or direct causation; separation does not cause depression in itself. The relationship is understood instead as one of partial causation: For some children, separation initiates a chain of events that eventually leads to depression. But why this occurs for some children and not others is a mystery; circumstances other than the separation must be involved.

Noncausal Relationships

Common cause, direct, and indirect causation involve cause-and-effect relationships between variables; but other noncausal relationships can result in substantial correlations as well.

Correlation by chance. Correlations can occur between variables simply by chance. Let's say a scientist measures the visual acuity and height of 20 people and calculates r as +.60. For this group, the taller people have better eyesight than the shorter people. This correlation could result from bias in the selection of participants for the study; by chance, the group may include a disproportionate number of tall, eagle-eyed, and short, nearsighted people. With a larger, more representative sample of subjects, the correlation might be zero.

This interpretation of a correlation as due to chance can never be entirely discredited, since there is always some possibility, even if very small, of getting a biased sample of subjects. Replicating the result with another group of subjects helps to discredit this explanation. In addition, there is a statistical test that allows the experimenter to investigate the credibility of the chance interpretation. This test calculates the probabilities of getting correlations by chance and uses these results to help decide if the observed correlation is due to chance or reflects a systematic relationship between the variables.

Correlation by custom. Go out on a busy street corner and note for each of the men and women who walk by, V_1: M or F, the number of earrings worn, V_2: 0, 1, 2 earrings, or more. Make perhaps 200 observations. You can anticipate a substantial correlation between V_1 and V_2. Men will usually be wearing 0 or 1 earring, women 0 or 2 earrings. Few woman wear 1 earring and few men wear 2 earrings. Is this a causal relationship? Hardly.

This is a correlation due to fashion or custom. Since our culture makes sharp distinctions between men and women, there are many correlations between gender and other variables, such as interests, skills, and values; these correlations reflect the different experiences of men and women in our culture. We can call these examples correlations due to *custom*. Often they are easy to spot as noncausal because the variables form no logical causal chain or have no common cause. How, for example, can gender cause the number of earrings worn? But sometimes it is difficult to identify whether the relationship is causal or noncausal, especially in cases that involve a *common correlate*, as in the next example.

Common correlates. The psychiatrist Alfred Adler maintained that a person's personality was determined, in part, by birth order. According to his theory, firstborn children develop different personalities than later borns, because they have different relationships with their siblings and parents. Adler thought that firstborns were more ambitious, more responsible, more organized, and less peer oriented than people of other birth orders. One prediction, based on these ideas, is that there will be a correlation between birth order, V_1, and the occupational prestige of a person's job, V_2, with firstborns having the higher prestige positions.

This prediction has been supported. If you were to survey, say, physicians and car salesmen in your town, you would probably find a higher percent of firstborn physicians than firstborn salesmen. Adlerians would interpret this correlation as one of partial causality; in their view, experiences associated with different birth orders set up a chain of events terminating in the individual's employment. But there is another plausible interpretation of the correlation, one that has nothing to do with birth order or personality.

The alternative explanation concerns money, the money it takes to become a physician or lawyer. It is known that families with more money have fewer children than families with less money; families with money, therefore, have a higher proportion of firstborn children than poorer families. (If you have just 2 children, 50% are firstborn; if you have ten children, only 10% are firstborn.) It takes money to go to college, and then on to medical or law school. Put these two facts together and you would expect to find more children of well-to-do parents in medical and law school, and lots of them should be firstborn! Since it takes less money to become a car salesman, there should be fewer firstborns in the showroom.

This alternative hypothesis explains the correlation between V_1 and V_2 by evoking money as a *common correlate*. If we statistically control money, the correlation between V_1 and V_2 should be reduced to zero.

Which explanation is right? We don't know. We would have to do further research to find out. And that is precisely the problem with correlational findings. After the fact, you usually can create several plausible, and distinctly different, explanations for any correlation you find. Does the correlation reflect *common cause, partial cause, chance, custom,* or a *common correlate?* The answer will come only with more studies. This ambiguity in interpretation is behind the derogatory phrase "just a correlational study."

But don't let these problems prejudice you against correlational studies. As we will see in the next chapters, all types of studies have their problems and all require additional research to provide further evidence in support of their conclusions. Although the history of correlational research is short, its successes have been great. Determining the severe consequences of smoking (over 1,000 deaths per day in the United States alone), discovering the role of fluoride in fighting cavities, and demonstrating that rapid eye movements are an index of dreaming, are all classic results of correlational research.

KEY TERMS

Regression to the mean
Regression coefficient, r
Regression line
Scatterplot
Scatter
Bertillonage
Independence of variables
z scores
Pearson correlation coefficient
Method of least squares

Linear versus curvilinear relationship
Statistical control
Multiple correlation coefficient
Common cause
Direct causation
Partial causation
Correlation by chance
Correlation by custom
Common correlates

KEY PEOPLE

Francis Galton
Alphonse Bertillon
Karl Pearson

David Wechsler
George Yule
Alfred Adler

REVIEW QUESTIONS

1. Why was the constancy of the distribution of physical traits of plants and animals across generations puzzling to Galton?

2. Describe Galton's pea study and summarize its results.

3. Galton was excited about discovering regression to the mean, but he was troubled about its implications for his program of eugenics. Why would Galton find regression troublesome?

4. What were the differences between Galton's study of peas and his study of people's heights? Did Galton find regression to the mean for people?

5. Sketch a scatterplot showing the relationship between parents' and children's heights (as adults) that Galton discovered. Draw the regression line on your plot.

6. Why did Galton think that the accuracy of Bertillonage may have been inflated?

7. What would the value of the correlation coefficient be for two independent variables?

8. Describe how Galton used z scores to demonstrate that height and head size are not independent.

9. Explain why Galton's correlation analysis can be considered as a special case of the method of least squares.

10. Describe the difference between a linear and a curvilinear relationship. Give an example of each.

11. Describe how age was statistically controlled in the study on sunshine and the risk of breast cancer.

12. Explain how statistical control follows the logic of Mill's method of difference.

13. Describe five different relationships that can exist between variables that are correlated. Give an example of each.

6

Randomized Experimental Designs

---------- ❖ ----------

It is the method of reasoning, and not the subject matter, that is distinctive of mathematical thought. A mathematician, if he is of any *use*, is of use as an expert in the process of reasoning, by which we pass from a theory to its logical consequences, or from an observation to the inferences which must be drawn from it.

SIR RONALD FISHER

---------- ❖ ----------

A MEASURE OF ERROR
THE RANDOMIZED BLOCKS DESIGN
     Replication
     Random Assignment
     Determining the Measure of Error
     The Null Hypothesis
     The Significance Probability, p
     Interpreting p
     The t Test
COMPLETELY RANDOMIZED DESIGN AND THE LATIN
   SQUARE DESIGN
FISHER'S DESIGNS IN PSYCHOLOGY
     Completely Randomized Design: Evaluating Cognitive
       Therapy
     Randomized Blocks Design: Stimuli Necessary
      for Perceptual Development
     Latin Square: High Sugar Diet for Children

POWER ANALYSIS: DECIDING ON THE NUMBER
OF SUBJECTS
> *Type I and Type II Errors*
> *The Treatment Effect Size*
> *How to Estimate the Effect Size in Your Own Research*
> *Other Strategies to Increase Power*
>> *Increasing power by increasing MD*
>> *Increasing power by reducing the standard*
>> *deviation*
>> *Increasing power by increasing the alpha level*
>> *or using one-tailed tests*
STATISTICAL CONCLUSION VALIDITY
> *Low Statistical Power*
> *Violation of Assumptions*
> *Error Rate Problem*
> *Instability*
FINAL COMMENT
KEY TERMS, KEY PEOPLE, REVIEW QUESTIONS

At the beginning of the 20th century, Mill's methods defined the concept of control in experimental design. But, as we discussed in Chapter 3, there are problems in applying Mill's methods in experimental work in the social sciences because in these fields it is impossible to achieve the perfect control the methods require. In psychology, there always will be uncontrolled variables introduced by the many differences among people—in attitudes, personality, abilities, and prior experiences.

Given such uncontrollable variables, how can experimenters reach valid conclusions from the results of experiments? We discussed one solution to this problem, involving correlational analysis, in the last chapter; if the uncontrolled variables can be measured, their effects can be corrected for by statistical methods. In this chapter, we consider a second solution to the problem of uncontrolled variables, one developed by Sir Ronald A. Fisher, a British scientist, who was a follower of Galton's ideas in eugenics and a colleague of Pearson and Yule.

Fisher's innovative experimental designs incorporated the controls of Mill's methods and introduced the new technique of randomly assigning subjects to treatments. Today his methods are the standard of excellence for experimental research.

Fisher was a child prodigy in mathematics. He graduated from Cambridge University in England in 1913, with concentrations in mathematics and the new field of genetics. When World War I interrupted his scientific career, Fisher was excluded from military service because his eyesight was poor. So he did "war work" instead, and took the teaching position of another man who went to war. On Armistice Day, he quit teaching, which was not to his liking, and started looking for another job.

Fisher was considering two very different careers—subsistence farming, an occupation that would let him live an "ideal eugenic life" and raise a large family, and research in the new field of biometry, the application of mathematics to biology and genetics. While deliberating on these radically different alternatives, he heard of an available position for a statistician at the experimental agriculture research station at Rothamsted. Although this was just a temporary position, analyzing data already collected at the station, the unusual combination of mathematics and farming must have attracted him, because he decided to set aside his dream of subsistence farming and take the position. Fisher's choice was fortunate for science.

The director of the research station soon realized Fisher's immense talent and the temporary job was made long-term: "It took me a very short time to realize that he was more than a man of great ability, he was in fact a genius who must be retained" (Box, 1978, p. 97). Within a few years, Fisher would develop a remarkable theory of experimentation, complete with experimental designs and a method of data analysis, which he called the analysis of variance.

Fisher's experimental designs were presented in a 1926 paper entitled "The Arrangement of Field Experiments." In this paper Fisher developed the logic and the advantages of his new methods. We will introduce his methods by closely following the examples from agriculture that he used in that paper; these examples illustrate the logic of the methods especially clearly. Once the basic designs are discussed, we will go on to consider how they are applied in psychology.

A MEASURE OF ERROR

Imagine, as Fisher did, a large field divided into two equal plots. Wheat is planted in both plots and the plots are treated exactly the same except that one is fertilized and the other is not. For convenience, let's refer to the fertilized plot as A1 and the other plot as A2. The experimenter wants to discover the effect of the fertilizer on wheat yields.

The design of this experiment follows the logic of the method of difference: Only one antecedent is different for the two plots, A1 versus A2 (the independent variable), while other variables are controlled. According to Mill's method, if a difference is found in the wheat yields of the two plots (the dependent variable), it would be due to the fertilizer.

Let's say, as Fisher did, that plot A1 produces the greater yield. To make the outcome numerical, say that A1 yields 100 bushels and A2 yields 82 bushels. Mill's method would lead to the conclusion that the 18-bushel advantage of A1 over A2 is due to the fertilizer. However, in practice, we couldn't be confident in drawing this conclusion—because Mill's method could not be applied perfectly. It is not possible to control for every difference between the plots. Plot A1 might have better soil than A2, or better drainage, or less insect or bird damage. As Fisher put it, "What reason is there to think that, even if no [fertilizer] had been applied, the [plot] which actually received it would not still have given the higher yield?" (Fisher, 1926, p. 504).

**TABLE 1 FARMER'S RECORDS COMPARING
WHEAT YIELDS (IN BUSHELS) OF PLOTS A1 AND A2**

Year	Plot A1	Plot A2	A1 − A2
1906	88	80	+8
1907	89	87	+2
1908	84	90	−6
1909	95	100	−5
1910	94	92	+2
1911	85	80	+5
1912	80	79	+1
1913	87	83	+4
1914	79	85	−6
1915	87	90	−3
1916	93	92	+1
1917	98	87	+11
1918	98	90	+8
1920	95	97	−2
1921	94	89	+5
1922	86	80	+6
1923	82	77	+5
1924	82	85	−3
1925	91	87	+4

Here, then, is a perfect illustration of the major problem with the method of difference. The advantage of A1 could be due to the fertilizer, or due just to uncontrolled events. How can the researcher decide between these possibilities? Fisher considered two types of evidence that might help. First, what if the farmer stated that he chose the plots fairly and had no reason to believe that one plot had better soil than the other? Or second, what if the farmer had kept records over several years of the wheat yields of these two plots? Fisher dismissed the farmer's opinion as evidence, since it could not be substantiated, but he felt the records would provide valuable information.

Let's say the farmer had records for the past 19 years of the wheat yields for both plots *without fertilizer on either plot*. Table 1 shows these yields; the difference in the yields of the plots also is shown there and plotted as a histogram in Figure 1.

The results for the first 19 years show the differences in the yields of plots A1 and A2 when the plots were treated *uniformly;* these differences would be due to uncontrolled variables. The differences vary from +11 bushels (the greatest advantage for A1) to −6 bushels (the greatest advantage for A2). Now compare these differences with the result of the experiment, which is marked on the histogram. Not once in the 19 years did A1 have an advantage as large or larger than the 18-bushel advantage that occurred when A1 was fertilized.

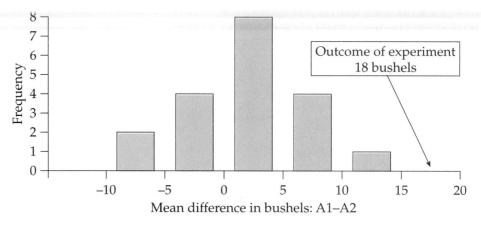

FIGURE 1
Histogram of farmer's records for 19 years prior to the experiment.

On the basis of this finding, Fisher concluded: "Either there is something in the treatment, or a coincidence has occurred such as does not occur more than once in twenty trials" (Fisher, 1926, p. 504).

What kind of coincidence? The coincidence would be that the year selected for the experiment just happened to be the year of the maximum advantage observed for plot A1, the actual effect of the fertilizer being nil. If the fertilizer is ineffective, the probability of this coincidence is ¹⁄₂₀, or 5%. Since Fisher judged this probability small enough to argue against the hypothesis that the fertilizer was ineffective, he concluded that the fertilizer was effective.

With this design, Fisher offered a solution to the problem of the method of difference. By collecting additional information on the results that would occur due just to uncontrolled variables, the researcher would be able to make a reasoned decision about the effectiveness of the treatment. Using this design, however, it would take many years to complete even a simple experiment. But Fisher didn't intend this method as a practical model for research. In presenting this design, he wanted only to show the kinds of information needed to interpret the outcome of the experiment. He argued that:

> what is required to interpret the outcome of an experiment is a *valid measure of error*, a measure of which outcome will occur due to uncontrolled variables.

This is the heart of Fisher's approach—finding a valid measure of error. Mill had argued for perfect control in the experiment, so that errors could be reduced to zero. Because Mill's solution is impossible to achieve in practice, Fisher proposed to *measure the extent of the error* instead, and to use this measure in interpreting the outcome of the study. From Fisher's viewpoint, if you can't eliminate all error, the best alternative is to measure it, so that you can take account of the error in drawing your conclusions.

A2	A1	A2	A1
A1	A2	A2	A1
A2	A1	A1	A2
A2	A1	A2	A1
A1	A2	A1	A2

FIGURE 2
Randomized block design with two treatments, A1 and A2, and 10 blocks.

Fisher went on to show how to derive this measure of error from experiments that could be done in a single growing season. We will discuss his designs with one independent variable in this chapter and devote Chapter 8, Factorial Designs and Interactions, to the more complex designs with more than one independent variable.

THE RANDOMIZED BLOCKS DESIGN

Fisher's *randomized blocks design,* now a standard in psychological research, was used first in agriculture. The researcher would divide the field chosen for the experiment into a number of smaller areas, called *blocks.* Let's pick 10 as a number to work with. Each of the 10 blocks would be further divided into two plots. Then, within each block one plot would be *randomly selected,* say, by a coin toss, to receive treatment A1, the fertilizer, and the other would receive no fertilizer, treatment A2. Figure 2 shows a randomly selected arrangement of the treatments in the field. Notice that treatments A1 and A2 appear in each of the 10 blocks, but their positions within the block vary randomly.

Replication

At the end of the growing season, the crops on each of the 20 plots would be harvested and their yields measured and recorded. As in the previous design, half of the total area of the field would be treated with fertilizer and half would not. But now, instead of comparing the yields in the two halves of the field, we can compare yields within each of the 10 blocks. In effect, the original experiment is *replicated* 10 times using smaller plots, and the method of difference is applied 10 times, once in each block. This replication, an innovation of Fisher's, is necessary to measure the error in the experiment.

> *Replication,* a major feature of all of Fisher's designs, was not present in any of Mill's methods.

Random Assignment

The *random assignment* of treatments to plots (or randomization) is the second major feature of this design.

With random assignment, each plot has an equal probability of receiving each treatment.

randomization is done for two reasons. First,

randomization avoids any bias that may occur if a nonrandom or systematic assignment is used.

If, for example, representatives from the fertilizer company made the assignment, they might select the better looking soil to receive the fertilizer, thereby creating a bias in the study. Even a neutral observer might bias the assignment unconsciously. Also, a systematic assignment, such as alternating the treatments in successive plots (for example, A1 A2 A1 A2), could bias the study if uncontrolled soil conditions in the field also had this pattern of variation.

The second reason for using random assignment is that

random assignment is necessary to determine a valid measure of error for the experiment, a measure of which outcomes to expect due to uncontrolled variables.

Without this measure of error, there is no good way to interpret the results of the study.

Random assignment, like replication, was not used in Mill's methods.

Fisher felt that randomization was so critical for experimentation that he and a colleague published tables of random numbers to make it easy for researchers to randomly assign treatments (Fisher & Yates, 1953).

Determining the Measure of Error

Now let's look closely at the outcome of the experiment to see why randomization and replication are necessary to calculate a measure of error. Figure 3 shows the wheat yields in bushels for each of the 20 plots in the field.

The average yield for the plots getting A1 is 26.0 bushels; the average yield for A2 is 23.7 bushels. These means were calculated by adding the yields for each type of plot and dividing by the total number of plots getting that treatment, 10 in this case. Since the distribution of yields across different plots is expected to have a normal distribution, the mean is the appropriate summary statistic.

The results show that the mean difference between the fertilized and unfertilized plots is $26.0 - 23.7 = 2.3$ bushels per plot, the advantage going to the fertilized plots. The question is whether this difference is due to the fertilizer or uncontrolled variables, such as soil fertility or bird damage? To answer this question, we need a measure of error. Fisher's solution to this problem was ingenious.

Assume, for now, that the fertilizer is completely ineffective. If this is true, what we have done in the study is simply to label plots of the field randomly

A2 18	A1 20	A2 13	A1 12
A1 32	A2 27	A2 19	A1 23
A2 29	A1 27	A1 11	A2 5
A2 22	A1 25	A2 35	A1 34
A1 36	A2 33	A1 40	A2 36

FIGURE 3
Yields in bushels for the
20 plots: Mean
A1 – mean A2 = 2.3 bushels.

A1 18	A2 20	A2 13	A1 12
A1 32	A2 27	A1 19	A2 23
A2 29	A1 27	A2 11	A1 5
A2 22	A1 25	A2 35	A1 34
A2 36	A1 33	A2 40	A1 36

FIGURE 4
Relabeling the plots: Mean
A1 – mean A2 = –1.5 bushels.

A2 18	A1 20	A2 13	A1 12
A1 32	A2 27	A1 19	A2 23
A1 29	A2 27	A1 11	A2 5
A2 22	A1 25	A2 35	A1 34
A1 36	A2 33	A2 40	A1 36

FIGURE 5
Relabeling the plots: Mean
A1 – mean A2 = +1.1 bushels.

as A1 or A2 and compare the means of plots that have been given these arbitrary labels. If the fertilizer is ineffective, plots A1 and A2 actually were treated uniformly, and the observed mean difference of 2.3 bushels would be a result of uncontrolled variables.

With a different assignment of labels, the outcome of the study would have been different. Figure 4 shows a different labeling done following the same scheme of randomization used in the actual experiment.

With this labeling, and assuming the fertilizer does not work, the mean difference between the plots would have been –1.5 bushels. Figure 5 shows yet another labeling that could have happened. With this labeling, the mean difference would be +1.1 bushels.

If we continued relabeling the plots and computing the resulting mean difference, we would end up with a set of values for the mean difference, values that would be expected if the fertilizer did not work. These values show us the mean differences to expect due just to uncontrolled variables.

This set of values is exactly the measure of error we are looking for!

Fisher thought that 500 values would be sufficient to accurately measure the error of the study. We did the relabeling 500 times and recorded the resulting mean differences. They are collected and presented in the histogram in Figure 6.

The Null Hypothesis

The histogram shows the mean differences between plots A1 and A2 that would be expected if the fertilizer is ineffective. Fisher called the hypothesis that the fertilizer is ineffective the *null hypothesis.*

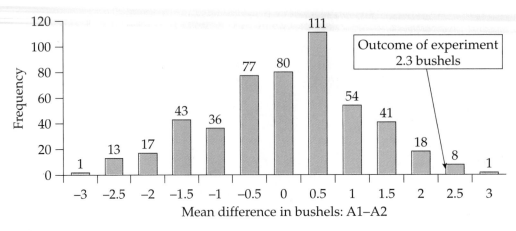

FIGURE 6
Mean differences in yields expected due to uncontrolled variables, A1 – A2: Results of 500 random assignments.

The *null hypothesis* in an experiment states that the independent variable has no effect on the dependent variable.

The histogram shows that the mean differences, given that the null hypothesis is true, range from a low of –3 bushels to a maximum of +3 bushels.

The Significance Probability, p

Now we can compare the outcome of the study with this measure of error. The actual outcome, a mean difference of 2.3 bushels, is marked on the histogram. In the 500 relabelings, only 9 assignments gave a mean difference of 2.3 or more. If the fertilizer is ineffective, the probability of getting a mean difference of 2.3 or more is $p = 9/500 = .018$.

The statistic p is the *significance probability* for the test of the null hypothesis.

The *significance probability, p,* is the probability, if the null hypothesis is true, of getting the observed mean difference or an even larger value.

Interpreting p

Fisher contended that the conclusion drawn from a study should depend upon the value of p. He suggested that the cutoff point of $p = .05$ be used in reaching a conclusion according to the following rule:

If p is less than or equal to .05, $p \leq .05$, then reject the null hypothesis, since the results are inconsistent with this hypothesis.

If p is greater than .05, $p > .05$, then do not reject the null hypothesis, since in this case the results are consistent with this hypothesis.

If you remember from Chapter 4, the cutoff point for p is called the alpha (α) level of the test. In our example, $p = .018$, which is *less than* the $\alpha = .05$ (5%) cutoff point, so the null hypothesis is *rejected.* The conclusion is that there is good evidence that the fertilizer works.

When the null hypothesis is rejected, the result, the observed mean difference, is said to be *statistically significant* at the 5% *alpha level* or the 5% *level of significance.*

> The *level of significance* is the alpha level, the cutoff point for p in reaching a conclusion about the null hypothesis; 5% is the accepted standard today.

It is important to realize that this evidence, a statistically significant mean difference, is *not proof* that the fertilizer worked, just *good evidence* that it worked.

> A statistically significant result is one that is unlikely to occur due just to the uncontrolled variables in a study.

But it may have occurred. In fact, if the fertilizer is ineffective, the conclusion of the statistical test will be wrong 5% of the time. Because of the possibility of this error in interpretation, it is necessary to replicate experimental results in many different studies before they become accepted as fact. According to Fisher:

> A scientific fact should be regarded as experimentally established only if a properly designed experiment *rarely fails* to give this [5%] level of significance. (Fisher, 1926, p. 504)

The randomized blocks design is a practical design for agriculture that takes only a single growing season to yield results. The statistical procedure of doing 500 relabelings, called a *randomization test* or a *Monte Carlo test*, is practical today because we have computers. In the 1920s, it took hours of boring work by hand.

The t Test

Fisher recommended using an approximation to the randomization test to avoid these laborious computations. In 1908, William Gosset, a colleague of Pearson's, publishing under the name "Student," developed a statistical test, called the *t test* (Student, 1908).

> The *t test* is used to test for differences between the means of two groups in a study in which the subjects are randomly sampled from a large (actually infinite) population.

Even though in the randomized blocks design the subjects (plots of land) are not randomly selected from a large population, Fisher showed that Student's *t* test was a good approximation to the randomization test.

A1	A2	A2	A2
A2	A1	A2	A1
A2	A1	A2	A1
A1	A1	A1	A2
A2	A1	A1	A2

FIGURE 7
Completely randomized design with two treatments, A1 and A2, and with 20 plots.

Student's *t* test is quick and easy to compute. A value of the statistic, called *t*, is computed from the results of the study, and this value can be looked up in a table to see if the mean difference is significant. The computations and use of the table are presented in statistics texts. Today, even though modern computers make calculating Fisher's preferred test, the randomization test, easy, the *t* test is still the more popular procedure. In most cases, the choice between these two tests is, as they say, "academic," since their results agree closely; in the example computed above, the randomization test gives $p = .018$; the *t* test gives $p = .013$.

If you go to any shopping mall today, you will be able to find inexpensive pocket calculators that have the *t* test built in; the user only has to enter the data from a study and the computer does the entire computation. Student would have been shocked to learn how popular his test would become. Its popularity is due to the fact that it can be used with Fisher's designs.

COMPLETELY RANDOMIZED DESIGN AND THE LATIN SQUARE DESIGN

In the *completely randomized design*, instead of using the blocking of the randomized blocks design, the treatments are randomly assigned to plots throughout the whole field. The field is divided into a number of plots and the treatments are randomly assigned to them. When two treatments, A1 and A2, are being compared, half the plots are randomly assigned to A1 and the other half go to A2. Figure 7 shows a completely randomized design with 20 plots.

Because the pattern of randomization is different in this design than in the randomized blocks design, the computations of the statistical test also are different. Fisher developed a modification of Student's *t* test, called the *t* test for independent groups, as an approximation to the randomization test for this case.

As we will see, the completely randomized design is popular in psychology, but it is used infrequently in agriculture because of the possibility of an apparent imbalance in the assignment of treatments to plots. If most of the A1 treatments were assigned by chance to the north section of a field and most of the A2 treatments ended up in the south section, there would be an apparent bias in the study. No experimenter would want to conduct an agricultural study with this assignment. The randomized blocks design avoids this type of apparent bias by restricting the random assignments to within blocks, guaranteeing that both treatments are applied evenly all over the field.

BETTGELERT FOREST LAYOUT

Elevation:

1730–1800′	B	A	E	D	C
1530–1730′	C	E	B	A	D
1460–1590′	A	C	D	E	B
1340–1460′	D	B	A	C	E
1250–1340′	E	D	C	B	A

A. Sitka spruce
B. Japanese larch
C. Sitka spruce/Japanese larch 50/50
D. Sitka spruce/Pinus contorta 50/50
E. Norway spruce/European larch 50/50

Two rows of Beech planted on each side of the series.

FIGURE 8
Photo taken at Bettgelert Forest 16 years after the trees were planted, with the layout of the planting.

Fisher's *Latin square design* also uses very restricted randomization to avoid apparent bias in assignments. In the Latin square design, the field first is divided into rows and columns, the number of rows and columns corresponding to the number of treatments being compared. With 2 treatments, there would be 2 rows and 2 columns; with 5 treatments, there would be 5 rows and 5 columns. Treatments are assigned to this grid so that one and only one treatment falls in any given row or column.

Figure 8 illustrates how the Forestry Commission in Wales used a 5 x 5 Latin square to study the effects of altitude on the growth of different varieties of pine trees at Bettgelert Forest in 1929. The researchers laid out the Latin square on a steep hill so that each row was at a different elevation. Soil fertility at each altitude was controlled by randomly assigning different varieties and combinations of trees to different positions in the row. The photograph, taken 16 years after planting, clearly shows the differential effects of altitude on the trees.

Fisher published tables giving all possible arrangements of treatments for Latin squares of sizes 2, 3, 4, 5, and 6. The experimenter would lay out the field in the appropriate number of rows and columns and then pick at random an arrangement of treatments from Fisher's table. This randomization ensures that there will be no systematic bias and provides the basis for the measure of error in the study. Again, since the pattern of randomization is different from the previous designs, the calculations of the statistical test also are different.

The computations of the Latin square are found in advanced statistics texts and in handbooks of experimental design (see Kirk, 1982).

The Latin square is a popular design in agriculture because it does a good job of controlling for gradients of soil fertility in a field. Imagine that the soil in the field is best at the north end and becomes progressively worse going from north to south. In the Latin square design each treatment appears in each row and column, so each treatment would be equally applied to the good and poor soil, thus controlling for soil quality. Gradients of soil fertility are common, so the Latin square design is well suited for agricultural research.

Fisher's randomized designs were revolutionary. When Fisher proposed them, other scientists were recommending systematic designs for agricultural experiments. They were skeptical at first about Fisher's randomization method. Student, for example, thought that some systematic designs would result in a smaller error than randomized designs and therefore would be more sensitive. As late as the 1940s, agriculture texts posed the question of which design, systematic or random, was better (Leonard & Clark, 1939).

Today, systematic designs are not even classified as "true" experiments (see Chapter 10, Field Research). When either type of design is possible, randomized designs are preferred. Randomized designs replaced systematic designs for the reasons Fisher presented in his 1926 paper:

> Random assignment avoids any systematic bias in assigning treatments and is essential for calculating a valid measure of error.

FISHER'S DESIGNS IN PSYCHOLOGY

Fisher developed his designs for agricultural research. In psychology we are not interested in treating plots of land, and our subjects do not come laid out in a field so that they can be easily blocked, and we do not face problems of bird damage or differences in soil fertility. But there are enough parallels between agricultural studies and psychological experiments to make Fisher's designs the methods of choice for experiments in psychology. Table 2 outlines these similarities.

The subjects in psychological research are people or animals. The independent variable is the type of treatment they receive. The treatments, in psychology, vary widely, from schedules of reinforcement, to differently shaped visual stimuli, to different types of psychotherapy. The dependent variable is a measure of the subjects' behavior in the study, behavior that is thought to be influenced by the independent variable. The dependent variable might be the rate of bar pressing in an animal learning experiment, the perceived intensity of a stimulus in a perception study, or the severity of depression in research evaluating psychotherapy.

In the completely randomized design, subjects are randomly assigned to treatments with the sole restriction being that equal numbers of subjects be assigned to each treatment. (Equal numbers are not necessary but do lead to the most sensitive design; see the discussion of power later in this chapter.)

TABLE 2 COMPARISON OF AGRICULTURAL AND PSYCHOLOGICAL EXPERIMENTS

Term	Agriculture	Psychology
Subjects	Plots in field.	People (or animals) who meet the criteria for inclusion.
Independent variable	Different treatments applied to the soil.	Different treatments given to the subjects.
Dependent variable	Measure of yield of crops, e.g., wheat yield in bushels.	Measure of subjects' behavior, e.g., severity of depression.
Random assignment	Random assignment of plots to treatments.	Random assignment of subjects to treatments.
Completely randomized design	Plots in field are randomly assigned to treatments with the only restriction being that equal numbers of plots are assigned to each treatment.	Subjects are randomly assigned to treatments with the only restriction being that equal numbers of subjects are assigned to each treatment.
Randomized blocks design	The field is divided into blocks, blocks are subdivided into plots, and then plots within a block are randomly assigned to treatments. Random assignment is restricted to within blocks.	Subjects are divided into blocks. A block is a group of subjects who are similar to each other on specified criteria. Subjects within each block are randomly assigned to treatments. Random assignment is restricted to within blocks.
Latin square design	Randomization is restricted to preset patterns of applying treatments to the plots. The patterns have each treatment in the study in each "row" and "column" of the field.	Randomization is restricted to preset patterns of assigning subjects to treatments. The design is used in psychology to test for effects within subjects.
Conditions held constant	Application of seed, preparation of soil, duration of study, method of harvest, amount of watering and weeding, etc.	Initial description of study to subjects, duration of study, instructions, methods of measuring dependent variables, etc.
Uncontrolled events	Bird damage, weather, insect damage, etc.	Equipment failure, experimenter mistakes in the protocol, fire alarm during study, missed appointments, etc.
Uncontrolled differences among subjects	Differences in soil fertility, water drainage, etc.	Differences in personality, abilities, interests, past history, etc.

One way to assign subjects randomly to treatments is to write their names on pieces of paper, put the pieces in a hat, shake well, pick out half the subjects for one treatment, and assign the remaining subjects to the other treatment.

Another method of randomly assigning subjects to treatments is by computer. We have included computer programs for random assignment in Chapter 12, Planning the Study.

The randomized blocks design uses more restricted random assignment to groups than the completely randomized design. In agriculture, adjacent plots of land form a block and the randomization takes place within blocks. Because adjacent plots should be more similar in soil fertility than nonadjacent plots, blocking helps to control for differences in fertility. The best parallel to adjacent plots in psychology would be identical twins. Each pair of twins would be one block; the study would have several blocks. Within each block, one twin would be randomly assigned to one treatment and the other would get the second treatment. Since twins are similar in many ways, the study would achieve good control over differences among the subjects.

Twin studies are rare because so few twins are available. But, as the following experiment illustrates, when twin studies can be done they often are models of control. One recent well designed experiment in medicine, for example, may change the way parents feed their children (Johnston et al., 1992). This 3-year study examined the effects of calcium supplements on the bone density of 70 pairs of identical twins, ages 6 to 14. One twin in each pair was randomly chosen to receive 1,000 mg of calcium daily; the other received a placebo that only looked and tasted like the calcium supplement. The results showed that the supplements increased the children's bone density.

If twins are not available, the next best alternative is for researchers to form the blocks themselves.

> Subjects can be *paired*, or *matched*, based on their similarity on variables that the experimenter wishes to control.

Matching might be done on sex, age, education, ability, or degree of illness, for example. Random assignments then would be made by selecting subjects for each of the treatments from within these matched blocks of subjects.

In agricultural research using the Latin square design, the treatments are assigned to different plots of a field so that each treatment falls only once in each "row" and "column" of the field. In psychology, there is no single parallel to the rows and columns of a field.

> A common application of the Latin square in psychology is in experiments where each subject receives all of the treatments at different times.

Let's say a psychologist wants to study the effects of caffeine on cognitive functioning, as measured by performance on simple arithmetic problems. The researcher decides to use a within-subjects design. Each subject receives each of four doses of caffeine: no caffeine, dose 0; low caffeine, dose 1; medium caffeine, dose 2; and high caffeine, dose 3. To minimize carryover effects, a one-day interval is planned between the doses.

Figure 9 shows a Latin square design for this study. The columns of the square correspond to the orders, 1st, 2nd, 3rd, or 4th, of administering the doses. The rows correspond to groups of subjects. All the subjects in a group receive the doses of caffeine in the same order. The subjects are randomly assigned to the groups. The entries in the square show the specific doses. The subjects in Group 1, for example, are tested first on dose 2, then dose 0, followed by dose 3, and finally, on the fourth day, dose 1. This particular arrangement of doses was picked at random from a table of possible 4 x 4 Latin squares (Fisher & Yates, 1953).

		Order		
	1st	2nd	3rd	4th
Group 1	dose 2	dose 0	dose 3	dose 1
Group 2	dose 0	dose 1	dose 2	dose 3
Group 3	dose 1	dose 3	dose 0	dose 2
Group 4	dose 3	dose 2	dose 1	dose 0

FIGURE 9
Latin square design showing the order of giving
4 different does of caffeine to 4 groups of subjects.

The Latin square balances the order of administering the caffeine. Each dose is given to one group of subjects in each possible order; that is, dose 0 is presented first to one group; dose 1 is presented first to another group, etc. This helps to control for carryover effects and to balance out any effects of practice on test taking.

In the next section, we present three psychology experiments to illustrate the completely randomized design, the randomized blocks design, and the Latin square. The Rush, Beck, Kovacs, and Hollon experiment (1977) was the first to find that a psychotherapy was better than a standard drug therapy for a major psychiatric disorder. The study by Held and Hein (1963) established a basic fact about the development of visual perception. The findings of the study by Wolraich et al. (1994) contradict conventional wisdom about the effects of sugar on children's behavior.

Completely Randomized Design: Evaluating Cognitive Therapy

In the mid 1970s, cognitive psychotherapy was a promising treatment for depression. Clinical experience treating patients was positive; however, the effectiveness of the therapy had not been tested in a controlled experiment using random assignment of patients to treatments. In 1977, Rush et al. published the first such test.

The subjects were depressed patients referred to the University of Pennsylvania Hospital for treatment. To participate in the study, patients had to meet rigorous inclusion criteria, including moderate to severe levels of depression, a diagnosis of depressive syndrome based on published criteria, no history of schizophrenia or alcoholism, and no contraindications for antidepressant medication. Over 110 applicants were screened to find the 41 patients included in the study.

The patients signed a consent form agreeing to receive either cognitive therapy or drug therapy with imipramine, a tricyclic antidepressant (a standard drug therapy for depression). Then they were randomly assigned to one of the therapies. The severity of each patient's depression was monitored throughout the 12-week treatment using three measures: the Beck Depression Inventory, the Hamilton Rating Scale for Depression, and the Raskin Depression Scale.

At the end of the treatment, the mean depression scores on all three measures of patients in the cognitive therapy group were significantly lower than those in the drug therapy ($p < .05$). This study, published in 1977, in volume 1 of a new journal, *Cognitive Therapy and Research,* inspired many other studies of cognitive therapy.

Randomized Blocks Design: Stimuli Necessary for Perceptual Development

By the early 1960s, there was evidence that normal vision in cats depends upon their experiencing varied visual stimulation as kittens. Kittens deprived of normal stimulation, either by being physically restrained or by having their eyes covered with hoods that let in only diffuse light, later showed visual deficiencies when compared to litter mates raised normally. Based on these results, Richard Held and Alan Hein (1963) considered two alternative hypotheses about the kind of stimulation needed for normal visual development. According to one hypothesis, stimulation received while the animal is passive would be sufficient to produce normal vision. According to the second hypothesis, young animals must be free to *create changes* in their visual stimulation through their *own movements* for normal vision to occur.

To decide between these hypotheses, Held and Hein tested 8 pairs of kittens, each pair from a different litter. All 16 kittens were raised in darkness until they were strong enough to be in the study (at 8 to 12 weeks). Then they were exposed to carefully controlled visual stimulation for three hours a day. One kitten in each pair was randomly assigned to the "Active" condition and the other to the "Passive" condition. The active member (A) of the pair was allowed to walk inside an illuminated circular pen that was 4 feet in diameter with 1-inch-wide black-and-white vertical stripes on its wall. The passive member (P) was placed on the other side of the pen from A, in a physical apparatus with rods, gears, and pulleys that operated so that when A moved, P moved an equivalent distance.

The apparatus permitted P to make only slight head and eye movements on its own. By this means the visual stimulation of both kittens was kept nearly equal; but A's stimulation was self-produced, whereas P's was not. Each pair thus provided a test between the two hypotheses.

This study involved two types of matching. First, the kittens in each pair were litter mates; so they were expected to be more similar to each other than unrelated kittens. Second, the kittens in each pair were "yoked" together; that is, they were placed in an apparatus that operated so that the movements of the active kitten controlled the visual stimulation of the passive one.

> Designs in which one subject's behavior controls the outcome of another are called *yoked control designs;* these designs are used to control for variables that are directly affected by the behavior of the subjects themselves.

Held and Hein used this design to control the variety of visual stimulation presented to both kittens, while simultaneously allowing one kitten to be active and one to be passive.

The daily experimental sessions continued until one member of the pair could pass the "paw placement test." In this test, the kitten was carried forward and downward toward the edge of a table; it passed if it showed visually mediated anticipation of contact by extending its paws as it approached the table. As soon as one of the kittens passed, both kittens were given additional visual tests.

Held and Hein's apparatus for controlling visual stimulation of active and passive kittens.

The results confirmed the researchers' expectations: In each pair, the active kitten passed the paw placement test first ($p < .05$) and also performed better on the other two measures of visual development. The authors concluded that the results "provide convincing evidence for a developmental process, in at least one higher mammal, which requires for its operation stimulus variation concurrent with and systematically dependent upon self-produced movement" (Held & Hein, 1963, p. 876). These results provided an impetus to the development of "feedback" toys for human infants, toys that would give babies varied stimulation dependent on their own movement.

Latin Square: High Sugar Diet for Children

Many parents and schoolteachers are convinced that children are overly sensitive to sugar—that sugar creates a "sugar high" that leads to hyperactivity and poor conduct. This idea was tested by Mark Wolraich and his colleagues (1994) in an elaborate study that controlled the total diets of 48 families for a 9-week period.

Two groups of children were recruited by advertisements and by contacting preschool programs: 25 children, 3 to 5 years old, and 23 children, 6 to 10 years old, all of whom were identified by their parents as being sugar sensitive. At the beginning of the study, the researchers removed all food from the subjects' homes and replaced it with food prepared for the study.

	Order		
	1st	*2nd*	*3rd*
Group 1	diet 1	diet 3	diet 2
Group 2	diet 2	diet 1	diet 3
Group 3	diet 3	diet 2	diet 1

FIGURE 10
Latin square design showing the order of three diets.

Each subject and the subject's family followed three different diets, each for a 3-week period: Diet 1 was high in sugar, with no artificial sweeteners; diet 2 was low in sugar, with aspartame (the ingredient in NutraSweet) as a sweetener; diet 3 also was low in sugar, but with saccharin as the sweetener. The order of presenting the diets was balanced, using a 3 x 3 Latin square (see Figure 10).

Clearly, suggestion is a major threat to the internal validity of this study; if the families knew which diet they were on, their child's behavior might be influenced by their strong expectations that sugar causes behavior problems. To guard against this, the subjects, family members, and experimenters testing the children were not told which diet the subjects were on at any time. Also, although the actual diet changed only every three weeks, the appearance of the diet was changed on a weekly basis. Only one parent correctly guessed the order of the diets.

The children were tested weekly on a battery of tests assessing their academic skills, motor skills, and general activity levels. Their parents, teachers, and the experimenters also rated them on behaviors such as conduct, hyperactivity, and aggression.

The data were analyzed by averaging the scores on these measures during the periods of the three diets. The results showed virtually no differences in the children's behavior associated with diet. The experimenters concluded that "neither sucrose nor aspartame produces discernible cognitive or behavioral effects in normal preschool or in school-age children believed to be sensitive to sugar" (Wolraich et al., 1994, p. 306). We are left with the mystery of why so many parents are convinced that sugar is a factor in the misbehavior of their children.

POWER ANALYSIS: DECIDING ON THE NUMBER OF SUBJECTS

Type I and Type II Errors

On the basis of their results, Rush et al. concluded that cognitive therapy was more effective than drug therapy for the patients in their study. But this conclusion could be wrong. Rush et al. did their statistical test at the 5% level of significance. This means that there is a probability of 5% that they could conclude that one treatment is more effective than the other when, in fact, the treatments do not differ in effectiveness (that is, when the null hypothesis is true). This error is called a *Type I error*.

A *Type I error* occurs when the null hypothesis is rejected when it is true.

Using the 5% level of significance, 5 out of 100 experiments will reach an incorrect conclusion that there is an effect of the experimental treatment when there actually is no difference in the treatments.

As a test of this possibility, Rush's study was replicated by Irene Elkin and her colleagues (1989), who found no significant difference between cognitive therapy and drug therapy. But this finding also may be in error. Elkin's group may have committed the error of *not rejecting* the null hypothesis when it is false, a *Type II error.*

A *Type II error* occurs when the null hypothesis is not rejected when it is false.

Experimenters can never know whether they have made a Type I or Type II error since they can never know the *actual* or *true* effects of the treatments. Experimenters know only the observed results, which always are subject to error. As we have discussed, the probability of making a Type I error is controlled by the statistical test. Doing the test at the 5% level of significance means that the probability of a Type I error is exactly 5%. The Type II error is controlled by the design of the study. A well-designed study with good measures and enough subjects will have a low probability of making a Type II error. This means that the probability will be high of detecting a difference between the treatments if such a difference exists. The probability of drawing this correct conclusion is called the *power* of the statistical test.

The *power* of a statistical test is the probability of correctly rejecting the null hypothesis. The power is equal to one minus the probability of a Type II error.

The concept of power was introduced by Jersey Neyman and Egon Pearson; both men were colleagues of Fisher in the late 1920s. Egon Pearson was the son of Karl Pearson, Galton's colleague.

A power of .50 or 50% (we will express power as a percent to avoid the decimal) means that the probability is 50-50 (the same as getting heads on the flip of a coin) that the experiment will detect a true difference between the treatments. A power of 90% means that the probability is 90% that an actual effect will be detected. Other things being equal, the experimenter wants the power to be as high as possible.

Setting the number of subjects in the study is the primary method the experimenter has of controlling the power of an experiment: The more subjects, the greater the power. The power can be set as close to 100% as the experimenter wants by including enough subjects. But large-sized experiments can be expensive to conduct and time-consuming to administer. In addition, it may be difficult or impossible to find enough subjects for a large study. So experimenters must strike a balance between these practical concerns and power in deciding on the number of subjects.

Successful studies with a completely randomized design are possible with a wide range of numbers of subjects—from just a few subjects in a group, to as many as 11,000 subjects per group, for example, in an experiment on the relationship between taking aspirin and heart attacks (Steering Committee of the Physicians Health Study Research Group, 1988).

Deciding on the number of subjects is critical for experimenters. Too few subjects and the study can be a complete washout with no significant findings. When this happens an effective treatment may be overlooked. Too many subjects wastes time and money that could be better spent investigating other aspects of the problem. To make a reasonable decision on the number of subjects, experimenters must understand the relationship between the design of an experiment and power.

The Treatment Effect Size

The power of a statistical test depends not just on the number of subjects, but also on the size of the treatment effect. If the effect is strong (e.g., if everyone getting the treatment changes dramatically and no one in the control group changes), an experiment with only a few subjects will lead to the correct conclusion that the treatment is effective. If the treatment effect is slight, however, many more subjects will be needed to ensure a good likelihood of reaching the correct conclusion.

The fact that power depends on the actual size of the treatment effect presents a problem in designing studies. The experimenter planning the study does not know the size of the treatment effect, since, of course, the study is designed to find this out. So the experimenter must estimate the effect size and plan the study accordingly. Let's look at an example and see how this is done.

Consider an experiment to study the effectiveness of a training program for increasing scores on the SAT verbal exam. The subjects, high school seniors, are randomly assigned to two groups. The treatment group receives the training; the control group gets no training. After the training is completed, the subjects in both groups take the SAT exam. In the data analysis, the experimenters plan to compare the mean SAT scores for the two groups using the t test at the 5% level of significance. They know that in a national sample the mean SAT verbal score is set to 500, with a standard deviation of 100. Now, how many subjects should they observe in each group? 10? 20? 50? 100?

Let's consider three possibilities for the size of the training effect.

1. A small sized effect: Let's say SAT scores in the treatment group average only 20 points higher than scores in the control group. Since the standard deviation of the SAT is 100 points, this would be an increase of only $20/100 = 0.20$ of a standard deviation. An average student, at the 50th percentile without training, would be at the 58th percentile with training. (The 58th percentile is 0.20 standard deviations above the mean on a normal curve.)

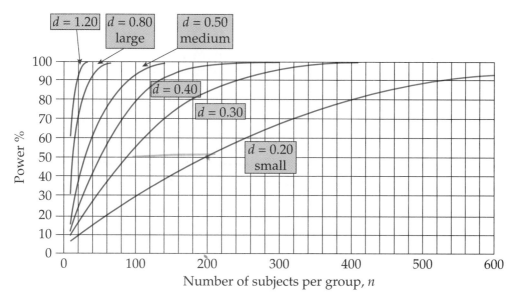

FIGURE 11
Power versus number of subjects per group for different treatment effect sizes, d = MD/SD.

Dividing the mean difference by the standard deviation, as we just did to get $20/100 = 0.20$, gives a good measure of the size of a treatment effect. This statistic is commonly used in the analysis of power and is called the *standardized mean difference (or Cohen's measure of effect size), d.*

2. A medium-sized effect: Scores are raised by 50 points; $d = 50/100 = 0.50$. The average student before training would be at the 69th percentile after training.

3. A large-sized effect: Scores are raised by 80 points; $d = 80/100 = 0.80$. The average student before training would be at the 79th percentile after training.

Let's first consider the small effect ($d = 0.20$). The graph in Figure 11 shows the relationship between power (in %) and the number of subjects per group, n, for different sized treatment effects.

Find the curve for $d = 0.20$. Next, find the point on the curve where it intersects the 50% power value and read that the corresponding number of subjects is about 190. This means that 190 subjects per group, a total of 380 subjects for the study, are needed to have a 50% chance of detecting this small effect. It probably would not be worthwhile to do the study with a power this low, since half the time you would not expect significant results.

Jacob Cohen (1988), who has been advocating power analysis to psychologists planning research, suggests doing studies with a power of at least 80%. With a small effect size of $d = 0.20$, this would take about 400 subjects per group. Unless you have access to lots of subjects, doing a study to detect a small effect might be a waste of effort.

With a medium-sized effect ($d = 0.50$), many fewer subjects would be needed. The graph shows that for a power of 80%, it would take about 65 subjects per group, and for a power of 90%, about 85 subjects per group. For a strong effect, $d = 0.80$, 25 subjects per group would yield a power of 80%; 35 subjects would give about 90% power.

So what is the bottom line on how many subjects to use? With a medium-sized effect, plan on around 65–85 subjects per group to have a high-powered study. If the size of the effect is large, the study could use as few as 25 subjects per group and still have high power. On the other hand, if you expect a small treatment effect, plan on a large number of subjects (800+). If this is not feasible, consider going back to the drawing board and improving the treatment, or try one of the strategies discussed below to increase power.

How to Estimate the Effect Size in Your Own Research

Estimating the effect size is straightforward if you are doing research on a problem that has been studied before. For example, there is extensive literature on the effectiveness of different treatments for depression, from psychotherapies to electro-convulsive therapies. If you were interested in doing research on depression, you could get a good idea of what effect sizes to expect in your own research by studying the available literature. Virtually all studies publish means and standard deviations on the outcome measures for each treatment group, so calculating the effect size ($d = MD/SD$) is simple.

If you can find no previous research on your problem, then the power analysis is difficult because you have no basis for estimating the effect size. In such cases, one approach would be to do a *pilot study:*

> A *pilot study* is a small-scale rehearsal of the actual study to test procedures and practice interacting with the subjects.

The results from a pilot study will give you a rough idea of the standard deviation of your measure and the differences to expect between groups. Without a pilot study, your best bet would be to make an educated guess about the effect size, or simply plan for a medium-sized effect and include 40 to 50 subjects per group. This would give you high power for a strong effect, good power for a medium effect, and poor power for a weak effect.

Other Strategies to Increase Power

If the power analysis suggests observing more subjects than is practical, you can consider alternative methods to create a high-powered study with fewer subjects. These methods involve increasing the size of the treatment effect or changing the alpha level of the statistical test that you plan to use. We will consider effect size first.

Effect size, as you recall, is defined as the mean difference between the treatments, divided by the standard deviation of the scores: $d = MD/SD$. Effect size can be increased either by increasing MD or by decreasing SD.

Increasing power by increasing MD. Let's reconsider the study on the effect of training on the SAT. Imagine the training program is a 2-hour seminar covering strategies for answering multiple-choice questions and working examples of the types of questions that can be expected on the test. Compare this to a training program involving 1 hour a day for a full year, in which the content of the test is studied extensively. This yearlong program should be more effective than the 2-hour session. Consequently, the effect size for the yearlong program should be larger and the power to detect the more effective program greater.

The lesson here is that by selecting a treatment with a high likelihood of being effective and comparing it to a treatment expected to be ineffective, for example, a control group, you can expect a larger effect, which will require fewer subjects to achieve adequate power.

> To increase power, plan your study to compare treatments with markedly different effects.

Increasing power by reducing the standard deviation. The SAT training example, discussed above, used an unselected group of high school seniors expected to have a SD of 100 on the SAT verbal exam. By systematically selecting subjects, it is possible to reduce this SD and thereby increase the effect size and the power. Since SAT scores are correlated with grades, subjects could be selected who have average grades; say, a C average. For this select group, the variability of SAT scores should be lower than 100, since there would be fewer high scores and fewer low scores. Doing the study with these students would increase power through reducing SD.

> The more homogeneous the subjects in a study, the smaller will be the SD and the greater the power to detect a difference between treatments.

There is a disadvantage to improving power by systematically selecting subjects, though. By restricting the subjects, you reduce your ability to generalize the results. In the new version of the SAT study, for example, you would find out nothing about how the training would affect students with averages above or below C.

> The standard deviation also can be reduced by using a more reliable measure for the dependent variable, if one is available, and by tightening the controls in the study.

If you are using a "home-made" measure or rating scale, you might look instead for a published measure with established validity and reliability. Controls could be improved in any number of ways depending on the specifics of the study. It might be possible to increase control by reducing distracting or extraneous events during the experiment or by using uniform procedures, for example, conducting the study in a quiet room, free of interruptions, and tape recording the instructions so that they are the same for all participants.

Increasing power by increasing the alpha level or using one-tailed tests. It is traditional to set alpha equal to .05, guaranteeing a 5% probability of a Type I error. If alpha is set at a higher value, say, .10, the power of the test will be increased. At first glance, this seems appealing; however, it usually is not a good idea because this change also increases the probability of making a Type I error to 10%.

Researchers customarily test the null hypothesis against the alternative hypothesis that the experimental conditions have different effects (direction unspecified); the researcher rejects the null hypothesis if the mean of one condition, say, A1, is sufficiently *greater than* the mean of the other condition, A2, or if the mean of A1 is sufficiently *lower than* the mean of A2. Here the statistical test is called *two-tailed* because the researcher rejects the null hypothesis if either of these outcomes occurs. The power chart in Figure 10 is based on a two-tailed test with alpha equal to .05.

However, a researcher might decide instead to test the more specific hypothesis that one of the conditions, say, A1, has a greater mean than the other, A2. Here the null hypothesis would be rejected only for one outcome, when the mean of A1 is sufficiently *greater than* the mean of A2, a *one-tailed test.* One-tailed tests, which are more powerful than two-tailed tests, are appropriate, for example, when comparing new treatments with placebo treatments or when testing a prediction deduced from a theory.

A program for computing power for one- and two-tailed tests at different alpha levels can be downloaded from our Website (see the preface).

STATISTICAL CONCLUSION VALIDITY

Virtually every modern experiment that employs random assignment of subjects to conditions also uses statistical tests. Even though the results of statistical tests give the most accurate conclusions possible, these results may be in error. Cook and Campbell (1979) discuss the accuracy of conclusions based on statistical tests as *statistical conclusion validity:*

> *Statistical conclusion validity* refers to the validity of the conclusion of a statistical test.

As you know, statistical tests are subject to two types of error, Types I and II. Cook and Campbell's analysis focuses on the circumstances leading to these errors. Here, we will consider four major threats to valid inference they discuss: low statistical power, violated assumptions of statistical tests, the error rate problem, and experimental instability.

Low Statistical Power

If the power of a statistical test is low, there is a high risk of overlooking the effect of an independent variable. After studying experimental designs in psychology, Cohen (1988) concluded that too many research studies are done with low power. In the previous section, we discussed the steps that researchers can take to increase the power of their studies.

Violation of Assumptions

In order to calculate the p value associated with a statistical test, assumptions must be made about the nature of the observations. The t test, for example, assumes that the observations are samples from a large set of scores and that the observations in this large set have a normal probability distribution. If this assumption is incorrect, the p value may be inaccurate and the conclusion based on p invalid. The impact of the violation of assumptions is a technical problem that is studied in statistics. To avoid such problems, researchers should be familiar with the assumptions of the tests they use and be confident that any violations of these assumptions, if present, will not affect their conclusions.

Error Rate Problem

As we have discussed, the Type I error rate of statistical tests is controlled by the experimenter. It is customarily set at 5%, meaning that in 5 out of 100 experiments when the null hypothesis is true, the experimenter will incorrectly reject this hypothesis. This is the case if the experimenter conducts only *one* test; when multiple tests are done, the error rate increases. If an experimenter conducts, say, 100 tests, the probability of making *at least one* Type I error can be as high as .99. If you do enough tests, you are virtually certain to make a Type I error, that is, falsely claiming statistical significance.

The increased error rates associated with multiple tests can make the results of research difficult to interpret. For example, a large-scale study done in Sweden reported a statistically significant risk of disease associated with living close to power lines (Feychting & Ahlbom, 1993). However, this conclusion now is in doubt because the researchers conducted hundreds of statistical tests but published only selected results. Although the error rate problem with multiple tests has been recognized for over 30 years (see Ryan, 1959), there still is no satisfactory solution.

Instability

Instability is the threat that circumstances in the experimental situation, other than those associated with the independent variable, may affect subjects' scores on the dependent variable. Such circumstances would include unreliable measures, unwanted variation in treatments, unexpected events during the experiment (e.g., equipment malfunction), and differences among the subjects in characteristics that influence their behavior in the study. All these factors can increase the variability of subjects' scores on the dependent variable, consequently reducing the power of the study and its statistical conclusion validity. The threat of instability can be reduced by using reliable measures and uniform treatments, and by selecting more homogeneous subjects.

FINAL COMMENT

With this discussion of power and statistical conclusion validity, we complete our presentation of the basic technical aspects of psychological research. We have seen how Mill's methods are applied and how statistical controls and randomization are used in overcoming the problems of uncontrolled variables. We also presented the basic designs used in experimental and correlational research. These technical issues, however, do not give a complete picture of the concerns involved in conducting research. We have yet to discuss the ethics of research, the moral rights and wrongs that must be considered in studying animals and people.

The ethical codes that we use in psychological research developed in a different manner from advances in technical methods. Methodological advances typically have come from single scientists trying to solve problems in their own research. Correlation was invented by Galton to study heredity; Fisher developed randomization to improve agricultural research. As we discuss in the next chapter, ethical codes and procedures came from committees reacting to the abuse of subjects by researchers. These committees worked to define the basic rights of subjects in research and to develop effective procedures to help researchers safeguard them.

KEY TERMS

Measure of error	t test
Randomized blocks design	Completely randomized design
Replication in the randomized blocks design	Latin square design
	Yoked control designs
Random versus systematic assignment	Type I and Type II errors
	Power
Null hypothesis	Standardized mean difference, d
Significance probability	Pilot study
Alpha level	One- and two-tailed tests
Statistical significance	Statistical conclusion validity
Level of significance	Error rate problem
Randomization test	Instability

Ronald A. Fisher
William Gosset, pen name "Student"
Mark Wolraich et al.
Richard Held and Alan Hein

A. J. Rush et al.
Irene Elkin et al.
Jersey Neyman and Egon Pearson
Jacob Cohen

*R*EVIEW QUESTIONS

1. Why did Fisher think that past records of wheat growth on plots A1 and A2 would help him to interpret the results of his experiment on the effect of fertilizer?

2. How did Fisher use these past records to determine a measure of error?

3. Describe how treatments are randomly assigned to plots in the randomized blocks design.

4. What are two advantages of random assignment over systematic assignment?

5. State the rule for reaching a conclusion about the null hypothesis based on the value of p.

6. Explain why rejecting the null hypothesis does not mean that the results of a study prove that the null hypothesis is false.

7. Describe how treatments are assigned to plots in a Latin square design.

8. Describe how participants can be grouped into blocks in a psychological experiment using a randomized blocks design.

9. Describe a common application of the Latin square design in psychology.

10. Explain how the yoked control design used by Held and Hein controlled for the visual stimulation the kittens received.

11. How is the probability of a Type I error controlled?

12. What factors in research affect the probability of a Type II error?

13. Use the power chart to determine the power of an experiment with $d = 0.50$ and 50 subjects in each group.

14. Present four strategies for increasing the power of an experiment.

15. Identify four major threats to drawing valid conclusions with a statistical test.

7

Ethics of Research

— ❖ —

Experimentation was originally sanctioned by natural science.
There it is performed on inanimate objects, and raises no moral
problems. But as soon as animate, feeling beings become the
subjects of experiment, . . . this innocence of the search for
knowledge is lost and questions of conscience arise.

HANS JONAS

———— ❖ ————

THE NUREMBERG CODE
     Informed Consent
     Risk/Benefit Analysis
THE NEED FOR LEGISLATIVE CHANGE
THE BELMONT REPORT
     Respect
     Beneficence
     Justice
CODE OF FEDERAL REGULATIONS FOR THE
  PROTECTION OF HUMAN SUBJECTS
AMERICAN PSYCHOLOGICAL ASSOCIATION (APA) CODE
  OF CONDUCT FOR RESEARCH
ETHICS IN ANIMAL RESEARCH
     Animal Welfare Act of 1985
     APA Code of Conduct: Care and Use of Animals
      in Research
FINAL COMMENTS
KEY TERMS, KEY PEOPLE, REVIEW QUESTIONS

Syphilis had become a public health problem in the United States during the first decades of the 20th century. People who contracted this highly contagious and much dreaded disease faced dismal life prospects. The lucky ones experienced symptoms only temporarily, shortly after contracting the disease. The unlucky ones could look forward to prolonged illness, blindness, arthritis, dementia, and premature death. After the spirochete that causes the disease was discovered in 1905, fear of the syphilis germ grew along with general support for treatment programs that prevented its worst symptoms and rendered it noninfectious. It was with great hope of bringing syphilis under control that the physician-scientists of the United States Public Health Service began six pilot treatment programs in the South in the 1930s (DiIanni, 1993).

Macon County, Alabama, was selected as a treatment site for this program. Most of its poverty-stricken residents were black sharecroppers, among the poorest of the poor, who welcomed the medical treatment that the government offered them. Unfortunately, the funds available for the treatment program soon ran out; those involved in the planning had underestimated the expense of the lengthy course of injections that was then the only therapy available for treating the disease. The program came to an abrupt halt, despite the fact that many people had received less than the full series of injections needed for a cure and some had not been treated at all.

It was at this point that the scientists of the Public Health Service made a decision that would be momentous for the people of Macon County and for the future of research ethics. Although there were no funds to continue treating the patients, they thought that something of value still might be garnered from the project. So in the fall of 1932, they began a six-month research project designed to study "the effects of untreated syphilis in the Negro male." They reasoned that the men would not be treated in the six-month period anyway, so they wouldn't be harmed by the research and the results of this project might discredit the popular and dangerous myth that syphilis is not a fatal disease in African Americans.

The researchers enlisted the aid of the Tuskegee Institute, a local college, founded by Booker T. Washington in 1881 to educate freed slaves and their descendants, that had the staff and facilities needed to do the required medical testing and the respect of Macon County's residents. The officials at Tuskegee agreed to do the testing in the hope of improving the future treatment prospects of the region's residents.

Four hundred men in the late stages of the disease were recruited for the study. The men were told only that they had "bad blood," a euphemism that they might have understood to mean anything from anemia to syphilis, and offered "special free treatment" for it. In fact, they received no treatment, only X-rays, blood tests, physical exams, and extremely painful and dangerous spinal taps, which were used only to study the effects of the disease.

In this first phase of the research, the investigators were able to demonstrate that syphilis had the same physical consequences for the residents of Macon County as it had for other groups. Encouraged by these results, they decided to continue the research beyond the initial six-month period. The study had changed from a short-term to a long-term study of the progression of untreated syphilis. At this point, two hundred more men were recruited to serve as controls.

UNTREATED SYPHILIS IN THE
MALE NEGRO

A COMPARATIVE STUDY OF TREATED AND
UNTREATED CASES

R. A. VONDERLEHR, M.D.
TALIAFERRO CLARK, M.D.
O. C. WENGER, M.D.
AND
J. R. HELLER Jr., M.D.
Assistant Surgeon General, Medical Director (Retired), Surgeon,
and Assistant Surgeon, Respectively, United States
Public Health Service
WASHINGTON, D. C.

A determination of the effectiveness of treatment in preventing the transmission of syphilis is one of the basic problems in the control of this disease. Second in importance to it is the effect which treatment has in preventing late and crippling manifestations. The administration of adequate treatment in early syphilis is recognized as the most important factor in the prevention both of communicable relapse and of the early complications so detrimental to the health of the individual patient. As the result of surveys of a few years ago in southern rural areas it was learned that a considerable portion of the infected Negro population remained untreated during the entire course of syphilis. Such individuals seemed to offer an unusual opportunity to study the untreated syphilitic patient from the beginning of the disease to the death of the infected person. An opportunity was also offered to compare this process, uninfluenced by modern treatment, with the results attained when treatment has been applied.

First published report of the Tuskegee syphilis study: *Journal of the American Medical Association* (1936).

For the next 40 years, the research participants suffered through annual tests masquerading as treatment, including the painful spinal taps. To keep up the appearance of treatment, three kinds of pills, all placebos, were given to the men. In exchange for their continued participation and for permitting autopsies to be performed on them when they died, each man was paid $35 to $50 "life insurance," just enough to give him a decent burial.

The researchers never told the men that they had syphilis, and none received treatment. In fact, the investigators enlisted the aid of other government agencies to prevent them from being diagnosed and treated elsewhere. Early on it became clear that the disease was devastating the subjects. By 1936, 75% of the test group suffered from complications of the disease; 50% were experiencing cardiovascular problems; and a third had neurological damage. By 1972, 128 of the participants had died of syphilis or syphilis-related complications, 40 of their wives had contracted the disease, and 19 children had been infected at birth (Associated Press, 1997).

Despite its horrific nature, the study was never a secret. Its results were published periodically in leading journals and even reported to Congress. The research continued long after the discovery of penicillin, the wonder drug that cures syphilis even in its late stages. It even went on through large-scale government efforts to eradicate the disease. Finally, in 1972, 40 years after it began, Pete Buxton, an epidemiologist who worked for the Centers for Disease Control, passed information about the study on to the press. When the public learned about the research, a government investigation began and the study was halted. In the end, the survivors of this experiment were paid less than $38,000 each in compensation in an out-of-court settlement. On May 16, 1997, President Clinton apologized to the 8 elderly survivors of this shameful government-sponsored research.

In the 1930s, when the Tuskegee syphilis study began, there were no laws or formal codes of conduct to protect research subjects. At that time, physician-researchers, who are bound by the Hippocratic oath to bring no harm to their patients, were trusted to take care of the people who participated in their research. Studies like Tuskegee demonstrated that in some cases that trust was misplaced.

When the abuses of human subjects in this and other medical studies became the focus of public attention in the 1970s, the result was widespread debate about the proper treatment of participants in research and legislative action to prevent future abuses. As a consequence, scientists who conduct research on people today have federal regulations to guide their work. These regulations now have the authority of law, and mechanisms are in place to ensure compliance.

In this chapter, we discuss the current ethical guidelines for human and animal research of the American Psychological Association (APA). Our presentation here focuses on ethical guidelines related to the design and conduct of research. Ethical issues involved in the analysis and communication of research results will be taken up in Chapter 13, Communicating Research. As we shall see, developments in medicine have played a critical role in shaping the ethical standards of research psychologists. But because the risks to research subjects differ in medicine and psychology, there also are important differences in their ethical requirements.

The men in the Tuskegee syphilis study had been subjected to incalculable abuse. They had been tricked into participating in research disguised as treatment, denied information about its nature and risks, lied to about the benefits they would receive from it, subjected to excruciating pain and the continuing ravages of a deadly and infectious disease—all in the name of science. Ironically, while this was going on, the United States government had been involved in developing the Nuremberg Code, the first internationally accepted code of ethics for medical research. The Nuremberg Code specifically prohibited each of the violations of human subjects committed by the scientists involved in the Tuskegee syphilis study.

*T*HE NUREMBERG CODE

In 1945 a military tribunal of American judges met at Nuremberg, Germany, to decide the fate of 23 Nazi doctors on trial for their involvement in atrocious medical experiments on concentration camp inmates during World War II. The tribunal learned of experiments in which people were exposed to extremely high altitudes to study their endurance; experiments in which parts of people's bodies were deliberately frozen; experiments in which healthy people were infected with malaria, epidemic jaundice, and spotted fever to test treatments and vaccines, or merely to keep a virus alive for future experimentation; and experiments in which people were poisoned so that researchers could study the effects at autopsy (Katz, 1972). In these experiments, the torture and death of the research participants were part of the research plan.

The 23 defendants were found guilty of war crimes and crimes against humanity. Despite their arguments to the contrary, the court judged the defendants to have violated certain fundamental principles that they believed define what is legal, moral, and ethical conduct of medical researchers toward human participants in research. The judges argued that only "certain types of medical experiments on human beings, when kept within reasonably well-defined bounds, conform to the ethics of the medical profession generally." These "bounds" were spelled out in 10 principles for medical research, now known as the Nuremberg Code.

The Nuremberg Code, which is presented in its entirety in Box 1, provided the first widely accepted ethical guidelines for medical experimentation on humans. The code has since served as the prototype for many other ethical codes for research, including those of the U.S. federal government and the APA.

BOX 1　THE NUREMBERG CODE

The great weight of the evidence before us is to the effect that certain types of medical experiments on human beings, when kept within reasonably well-defined bounds, conform to the ethics of the medical profession generally. The protagonists of the practice of human experimentation justify their views on the basis that such experiments yield results for the good of society that are unprocurable by other methods or means of study. All agree, however, that certain basic principles must be observed in order to satisfy moral, ethical, and legal concepts:

1. The voluntary consent of the human subject is absolutely essential.

   This means that the person involved should have legal capacity to give consent; should be so situated as to be able to exercise free power of choice, without the intervention of any element of force, fraud, deceit, duress, over-reaching, or other ulterior form of constraint or coercion; and should have sufficient knowledge and comprehension of the elements of the subject matter involved as to enable him to make an understanding and enlightened decision. This latter element requires that before the acceptance of an affirmative decision by the experimental subject there should be made known to him the nature, duration, and purpose of the experiment; the method and means by which it is to be conducted; all inconveniences and hazards reasonably to be expected; and the effects upon his health or person which may possibly come from his participation in the experiment.

The duty and responsibility for ascertaining the quality of the consent rests upon each individual who initiates, directs, or engages in the experiment. It is a personal duty and responsibility which may not be delegated to another with impunity.

2. The experiment should be such as to yield fruitful results for the good of society, unprocurable by other methods or means of study, and not random and unnecessary in nature.

3. The experiment should be so designed and based on the results of animal experimentation and a knowledge of the natural history of the disease or other problem under study that the anticipated results will justify the performance of the experiment.

4. The experiment should be so conducted as to avoid all unnecessary physical and mental suffering and injury.

5. No experiment should be conducted where there is an *a priori* reason to believe that death or disabling injury will occur; except, perhaps, in those experiments where the experimental physicians also serve as subjects.

6. The degree of risk to be taken should never exceed that determined by the humanitarian importance of the problem to be solved by the experiment.

7. Proper preparations should be made and adequate facilities provided to protect the experimental subject against even remote possibilities of injury, disability, or death.

8. The experiment should be conducted only by scientifically qualified persons. The highest degree of skill and care should be required through all stages of the experiment of those who conduct or engage in the experiment.

9. During the course of the experiment the human subject should be at liberty to bring the experiment to an end if he has reached the physical or mental state where continuation of the experiment seems to him to be impossible.

10. During the course of the experiment the scientist in charge must be prepared to terminate the experiment at any stage, if he has probable cause to believe, in the exercise of the good faith, superior skill, and careful judgment required of him that a continuation of the experiment is likely to result in injury, disability, or death to the experimental subject.

Informed Consent

The concentration camp inmates had no choice about whether to participate in the medical experiments. They were at the mercy of their captors. It was to prevent such coercion in future research that the judges at Nuremberg formulated their first principle, *the principle of informed consent.* It reads: The voluntary consent of the human subject is absolutely essential.

This principle requires that before the decision to participate in research is made, potential subjects must be fully informed about the "nature, duration, and purpose of the experiment; the method and means by which it is to be conducted; all inconveniences and hazards reasonably to be expected"; and any effects upon health or person that could result from their involvement. Subjects must be free to withdraw from the study at any time.

In conducting their research at Tuskegee, the Public Health Service doctors clearly violated this fundamental principle. The participants in that research thought that they were being treated for "bad blood." They did not know that they were in a research study at all, nor were they told of the risks associated with their participation. For their part, the investigators of the Tuskegee study claimed that their research was not comparable to the experiments conducted by the Nazis and therefore that the Nuremberg Code was not relevant to it.

Most medical researchers since the Nuremberg trials have agreed on the validity of informed consent as a guiding principle for research (Katz, 1972). When controversy has arisen in medicine, it usually has been over questions of how the principle should be interpreted and applied, not over the principle itself. One problem is that the procedures used to solicit participation may affect the sense of freedom experienced by potential subjects. Variations in who discusses the research with them, who asks for their participation, in what ways, and under what circumstances can all be important. Another problem in applying the principle is that many life circumstances can threaten people's perceived freedom of choice. Subjects recruited in business may see little choice in whether to be a part of research, since they may believe that their job security depends upon participating. Dying patients may be willing to undergo extreme risks; they may see the research as providing their only hope for recovery. Prisoners may believe that their cooperation in risky experimental procedures will affect the length or conditions of their imprisonment. Clients of human service agencies may believe that the services they receive depend upon their involvement in the research. Prisoners or other inmates may be unduly swayed by monetary inducements, since even small sums of money can materially change institutional life for them.

A separate question is how best to protect subjects who are incapable of clearly understanding the nature of an experiment or of making decisions for themselves; that is, how should informed consent be obtained in the case of children, mental patients, severely retarded people, and psychotherapy patients whose intense involvement with their therapists might jeopardize a reasoned consideration of whether they should take part in research conducted by them? More generally, how can we ensure that failures of communication and of understanding are avoided?

Finally, there are differences of opinion about how the principle of informed consent should be applied outside the context of medical experimentation. How should it be applied in psychology, where physical risks are rare? Many psychological studies could not be conducted if the principle of informed consent was strictly followed; complete informed consent would require the experimenter to reveal in full the intent of the research, perhaps even its hypotheses. The effects of such full disclosure would prevent unambiguous interpretation of the results and seriously compromise the value of research. The question of how to apply the principle of informed consent in behavioral research was not resolved at Nuremberg.

Risk/Benefit Analysis

A second basic ethical requirement of the Nuremberg Code is that, before conducting research, there should be a careful assessment of whether the *risks* of the research are justified by its *potential fruitfulness* for society. All unnecessary risks should be scrupulously avoided and precautions should be taken to protect participants from even the remote possibility of injury or disability. Research should be undertaken only when the risks of physical and mental damage and suffering "do not exceed that determined by the humanitarian importance of the problem to be solved by the experiment."

To decide for or against research using this principle, the importance of the research must be assessed. Gauging this can be difficult because there are no agreed-upon standards for what qualifies as important research. Differences of opinion are common. Some scientists look at immediate or potential applications in assessing the value of research. Others regard a contribution to knowledge as sufficient justification for research, even when no potential applications of its findings seem likely.

Assessing the nature and extent of the risks in research also can be difficult. Katz (1972) distinguished *three types of risk* that can arise in research with human participants: *interference with bodily integrity, interference with psychological integrity,* and *interference with self-determination and privacy.* In the Nazi experiments and in the Tuskegee study, interference with bodily integrity was certain. Pain and death were expected. Neither the psychological distress nor the right of participants to determine their own destinies entered into the deliberations of the researchers.

Although risks of physical injury are a major concern in medical research, other sorts of risk are more likely in psychology. Psychological research involves physical dangers only occasionally, for example, in drug or stress research, or in sleep or food deprivation experiments. Threats of death or physical disability are rare in psychological research. Threats to psychological well-being and privacy are more common.

To illustrate the controversy that can arise over the extent and nature of research risks in psychology, let's look at an experiment conducted by Stanley Milgram (1963). Milgram, who was concerned with the claim of the Nazi researchers that they had only been following orders, decided to test whether people in this country would blindly obey an authority. Milgram asked his subjects, who had been recruited through an advertisement, to shock another "subject" (actually an accomplice of the experimenter who received no shocks) whenever the subject made a mistake on a learning task. Facing the participants was a shock generator with 30 switches, each apparently increasing the shock by 15 volts and delivering shocks ranging in intensity from 15 to 450 volts. Each time the "learner" made an error, the "teacher," the actual subject, was told to increase the shock level one notch. Milgram gave the teachers a real 45-volt shock so that they could experience how painful it was.

Milgram was surprised to find that 87% of the participants continued to shock the learner after he kicked loudly on the wall of the room where he was strapped into the electric chair and stopped answering any of the teacher's questions. Two-thirds delivered 450 volts, the highest level of shock. Although subjects continued to obey the experimenter, they did so with great tension. One "mature and initially poised businessman" was "reduced to a twitching, stuttering wreck, who was rapidly approaching a point of nervous collapse" (Milgram, 1963, p. 377).

The public disclosure of Milgram's experiment led to debate over the ethics of exposing people to deceptive and stressful procedures in research. Milgram's critics claimed that the psychological distress experienced by his subjects, both during and after their participation, could not be justified by the importance of the problem and that his subjects also had to live, after the experiment, with the painful knowledge of what they had been willing to do in the name of science. They also argued that by conducting this experiment Milgram had exploited his subjects' trust (Baumrind, 1964).

Milgram (1964) countered these claims with reports from participants collected in postexperimental interviews. Many said that they were glad to have been involved and that they knew themselves better because of it. In response, Milgram's critics argued that experimenters should not be in the business of providing such disturbing insights to participants and that the statements of Milgram's subjects most likely reflected only their need to believe that something of value came from this painful experience.

In addition to threats to psychological well-being, psychologists also must be sensitive to potential threats to the anonymity and reputation of research participants. Special care must be taken to avoid such risks when observing people's behavior in private places or in institutional settings; in deciding whether to give researchers access to confidential records of inmates or clients; and in reaching conclusions about whether or not to collect data about people from third parties who might learn confidential information (e.g., about their mental or legal status) during the questioning (Kelman, 1977).

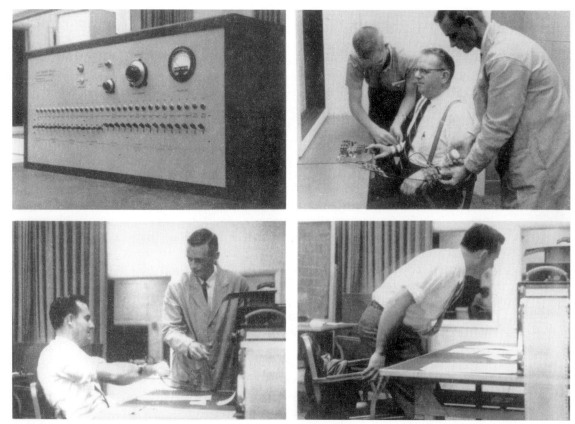

The photo at the top left shows the shock generator used by the "teacher" in Milgram's experiment; in the top right photo, electrodes are attached to the "learner;" the pictures at the bottom show a "teacher" getting a sample electric shock (left) and refusing to continue (right).

THE NEED FOR LEGISLATIVE CHANGE

Although the guidelines set forth at Nuremberg were widely accepted, in the decades following World War II several more medical experiments that violated the Nuremberg Code's most fundamental principles came to light. These experiments were conducted in the United States, the country responsible for the Nuremberg Code, by well-respected scientists, with financial support from the federal government. The moral outrage that resulted from the public disclosure of these studies led to legislative action that has shaped current research practice in medicine and psychology.

In 1966, Henry Beecher, an American physician, reported on 22 experiments that he believed violated both the principle of informed consent and the Nuremberg Code's injunction against risking the health and well-being of research participants. In one study, retarded children were injected with the hepatitis virus so that a controlled test of the effectiveness of a vaccine could be conducted. In another, elderly hospital patients were injected with live cancer cells to study their immune reactions. They were told that they would be receiving "some cells" but no mention was made of cancer. Beecher claimed that the 22 studies in his report were a small fraction from a list he had compiled reviewing one prestigious medical journal in a single year.

Several ethically controversial research studies in the behavioral sciences, in addition to Milgram's, also came to light in the decades following World War II. The violation of the right to privacy was at issue in the Wichita jury study of 1954. This study was conducted by law professors who were interested in studying federal jury deliberations by secretly recording them. Although the prior consent of the judge and the opposing lawyers was sought, the consent of the jurors was not (Diener & Crandall, 1978).

In 1970, four years after Beecher's report, Laud Humphreys published observations he collected secretly while he acted as "watchqueen" in a public rest room where homosexual encounters regularly took place. Humphreys copied down the men's license plate numbers, found out where they lived, and a year later collected more information from them by carrying out a phony health survey.

The ethics of a simulated prison experiment conducted by Philip Zimbardo and his students (Haney, Banks, & Zimbardo, 1973) also aroused concern. The experiment, which was to have gone on for two weeks, had to be called off after only a few days because Zimbardo found the students who were role-playing guards becoming frighteningly sadistic toward the students who had been assigned, purely by chance, to the role of prisoners.

Prompted by such revelations, in 1973 Congress established the National Commission for the Protection of Human Subjects in Biomedical and Behavioral Research. The mandate of the commission, the majority of whose members were from outside the health professions, was to "provide a public review of the ethical and legal problems of human subjects research" (Veatch, 1989, p. 15). Two documents resulted from their work: *the Belmont Report*, a statement on the basic values that they believed ought to underlie research on human subjects, and *new federal regulations* to provide the means for ensuring that these values are upheld in research. We will consider each of these in turn.

THE BELMONT REPORT

The Belmont Report, which is reprinted in Appendix A, was the result of nearly four years of monthly meetings by members of the National Commission as well as four days of deliberations that took place at the Smithsonian Institution's Belmont Conference Center in 1976. Over these years, the commissioners worked to identify the basic values behind "the many particular ethical prescriptions and evaluations of human actions" (National Commission, 1979, p. 3–4) in previous codes of ethical conduct for research. Among the documents they studied were the Nuremberg Code, the federal regulations then in effect for research on human subjects, and the APA's 1972 code of conduct for research.

When their analyses were complete, the commissioners articulated *three fundamental values*, which they believed are essential for researchers to uphold in studies with human participants. They are: (1) *respect*, (2) *beneficence*, and (3) *justice*.

Respect

The first principle of the Belmont Report requires investigators to respect the autonomy of human participants in research. This value preserves the right of subjects to make their own decisions about the activities in which they will be involved, and if they are incapable of such autonomous decision making, to be protected from harm. This principle requires researchers to give potential subjects sufficient information about the study initially to allow them to make an informed and free choice about whether to participate, and once the study begins to decide whether to continue. Those with diminished capacities of self-determination, who cannot capably make decisions for themselves, must be protected from harm.

Respect is the value underlying the Nuremberg Code's principle of informed consent and, in the case of persons judged incapable of self-determination, its requirement to protect research participants from unnecessary physical and mental suffering and from "even the remote possibility of injury, disability, or death."

Beneficence

The second principle of the Belmont Report, the principle of beneficence, is the requirement that researchers treat participants in such a way as to secure their well-being. Beneficence requires researchers, first, to follow the injunction of the Nuremberg Code and the Hippocratic oath to "do no harm" and, second, to "maximize possible benefits and minimize possible harms" to participants in research (National Commission, 1979, p. 4).

The principle of beneficence goes beyond the Nuremberg Code's requirement that researchers weigh the humanitarian importance of research against its risks to assert that research should aim at benefiting the participants themselves, not just humanity. Based on this principle, placebo control groups now are controversial in medical research. Although many researchers continue to assign control subjects to an inactive placebo group or to a waiting list in treatment studies, some medical researchers believe that such control subjects instead should receive the best alternative to the treatment being tested; should the new treatment prove more effective than the alternative, they believe, it should be made available to all participants in the study (Rothman & Michels, 1994).

Justice

The third principle of the Belmont Report is the requirement that researchers treat subjects justly by distributing the benefits and harms associated with research equitably. "An injustice occurs," according to the commissioners, "when some benefit to which a person is entitled is denied without good reason or when some burden is imposed unduly" (National Commission, 1979, p. 5). When people are subjected to the risks of research but reap none of its benefits, as they were in the Nazi experiments and in the Tuskegee syphilis study, and as poor ward patients were in countless medical experiments in the 19th and early 20th centuries, they are being treated unjustly.

The powerful rarely serve in psychological experiments. Members of minority groups, the poor, those with special health care needs, and others perceived as vulnerable do. Injustice occurs whenever such subjects are "systematically selected simply because of their easy availability, their compromised position, or their manipulability, rather than for reasons directly related to the problem being studied" (National Commission, 1979, p. 5).

The *principle of justice* adds to the Nuremberg Code the requirement of fairness in the distribution of benefits and burdens of research through the avoidance of biased selection and unfair treatment of participants.

CODE OF FEDERAL REGULATIONS FOR THE PROTECTION OF HUMAN SUBJECTS

The federal regulations formulated by the National Commission in conjunction with the National Research Act were designed to implement the principles of the Belmont Report through specific behavioral guidelines and procedures for research. The intent of the regulations was to remove the ambiguities of previous codes by mandating specific procedures for researchers and to shift some of the burden of ethical decision making from the individual researcher, who has a personal stake in it, to committees representing the views of the broader community. The new regulations also provided a mechanism for preventing and correcting questionable ethical practices in research.

The regulations require that *Institutional Review Boards (IRBs)*, committees that review proposed research to ensure that it complies with federal regulations, be established. Such IRBs must include at least one member not affiliated with the institution to represent community views. Box 2 gives the criteria that IRBs are to use in evaluating research.

The first task of the IRB is to ensure that risks to human subjects are minimized and reasonable in relation to the benefits they derive from their participation. If the research involves more than minimal risk, IRBs also ensure that the regulations for acquiring informed consent are followed and documented appropriately, and that procedures for recruiting participants are equitable. Procedures for applying for IRB approval of research, including the documentation of informed consent, are discussed more fully in Chapter 12, Planning the Study.

Although the federal regulations incorporate the principles of the Nuremberg Code, they differ from that code in allowing research on human subjects to be done without informed consent when three conditions are met: (l) the research involves no more than *minimal risk* to subjects; (2) subjects' rights or welfare will not be interfered with; and (3) the research could not be carried out without such a waiver.

BOX 2 EXCERPTS FROM HEALTH AND HUMAN SERVICES POLICY FOR PROTECTION OF HUMAN RESEARCH SUBJECTS, CODE OF FEDERAL REGULATIONS, REVISED AS OF OCTOBER 1, 1994

Criteria for IRB approval of research

(a) In order to approve research covered by this policy the IRB shall determine that all of the following requirements are satisfied:

1. Risks to subjects are minimized: (i) By using procedures which are consistent with sound research design and which do not unnecessarily expose subjects to risk, and (ii) whenever appropriate, by using procedures already being performed on the subjects for diagnostic or treatment purposes.

2. Risks to subjects are reasonable in relation to anticipated benefits, if any, to subjects, and the importance of the knowledge that may reasonably be expected to result. In evaluating risks and benefits, the IRB should consider only those risks and benefits that may result from the research. . . . The IRB should not consider possible long-range effects of applying knowledge gained in the research . . . as among those research risks that fall within the purview of its responsibility.

3. Selection of subjects is equitable. In making this assessment the IRB should take into account the purposes of the research and the setting in which the research will be conducted and should be particularly cognizant of the special problems of research involving vulnerable populations, such as children, prisoners, pregnant women, mentally disabled persons, or economically or educationally disadvantaged persons.

4. Informed consent will be sought from each prospective subject or the subject's legally authorized representative, in accordance with, and to the extent required by [the law].

5. Informed consent will be appropriately documented, in accordance with, and to the extent required by [the law].

6. When appropriate, the research plan makes adequate provision for monitoring the data collected to ensure the safety of subjects.

7. When appropriate, there are adequate provisions to protect the privacy of subjects and to maintain the confidentiality of data.

(b) When some or all of the subjects are likely to be vulnerable to coercion or undue influence, such as children, prisoners, pregnant women, mentally disabled persons, or economically or educationally disadvantaged persons, additional safeguards have been included in the study to protect the rights and welfare of these subjects.

A study involves *minimal risk* when "the probability and magnitude of harm or discomfort anticipated in the research are not greater in and of themselves than those ordinarily encountered in daily life or during the performance of routine physical or psychological examinations or tests." (Office for Protection from Research Risks, 1994, p. 119)

This relaxing of the informed consent requirement enables psychologists to do certain kinds of low-risk research that would not be possible if informed consent procedures were mandatory. One common type of research in social psychology, for example, involves the naturalistic observation of people's behavior in public places. The APA notes that in such research "the experience of the participants is not affected by the research, and there are no direct positive or negative effects on them" (APA, 1982, p. 37). Because the behavior being observed is public, and the subjects are anonymous and their involvement minimal, no threats to their privacy or self-determination are involved either.

AMERICAN PSYCHOLOGICAL ASSOCIATION (APA) CODE OF CONDUCT FOR RESEARCH

The APA's code of ethics for research, first published in 1973, has since been revised, most recently in 1992. As you can see from studying Box 3, where the current version is reprinted, the code owes much to the Nuremberg Code and the Belmont Report. In addition, it requires psychologists to comply with federal and state regulations governing behavioral research. What is unique about this code is that it was based not only on past codes and government guidelines but also on input from APA members about specific research practices that were of ethical concern to them and extensive discussion by psychologists.

BOX 3 AMERICAN PSYCHOLOGICAL ASSOCIATION CODE OF CONDUCT FOR RESEARCH (STANDARDS FOR PLANNING AND CONDUCTING RESEARCH ON HUMAN SUBJECTS), 1992

6.06 Planning Research

(a) Psychologists design, conduct, and report research in accordance with recognized standards of scientific competence and ethical research.

(b) Psychologists plan their research so as to minimize the possibility that results will be misleading.

(c) In planning research, psychologists consider its ethical acceptability under the Ethics Code. If an ethical issue is unclear, psychologists seek to resolve the issue through consultation with institutional review boards, animal care and use committees, peer consultations, or other proper mechanisms.

(d) Psychologists take reasonable steps to implement appropriate protections for the rights and welfare of human participants, other persons affected by the research, and the welfare of animal subjects.

6.07 Responsibility

(a) Psychologists conduct research competently and with due concern for the dignity and welfare of the participants.

(b) Psychologists are responsible for the ethical conduct of research conducted by them or by others under their supervision or control.

(c) Researchers and assistants are permitted to perform only those tasks for which they are appropriately trained and prepared.

(d) As part of the process of development and implementation of research projects, psychologists consult those with expertise concerning any special population under investigation or most likely to be affected.

6.08 Compliance With Law and Standards

Psychologists plan and conduct research in a manner consistent with federal and state law and regulations, as well as professional standards governing the conduct of research, and particularly those standards governing research with human participants and animal subjects.

6.09 Institutional Approval

Psychologists obtain from host institutions or organizations appropriate approval prior to conducting research, and they provide accurate information about their research proposals. They conduct the research in accordance with the approved research protocol.

6.10 Research Responsibilities

Prior to conducting research (except research involving only anonymous surveys, naturalistic observations, or similar research), psychologists enter into an agreement with participants that clarifies the nature of the research and the responsibilities of each party.

6.11 Informed Consent to Research

(a) Psychologists use language that is reasonably understandable to research participants in obtaining their appropriate informed consent (except as provided in Standard 6.12, Dispensing With Informed Consent). Such informed consent is appropriately documented.

(b) Using language that is reasonably understandable to participants, psychologists inform participants of the nature of the research; they inform participants that they are free to participate or to decline to participate or to withdraw from the research; they explain the foreseeable consequences of declining or withdrawing; they inform participants of significant factors that may be expected to influence their willingness to

BOX 3 CONTINUED

participate (such as risks, discomfort, adverse effects, or limitations on confidentiality, except as provided in Standard 6.15, Deception in Research); and they explain other aspects about which the prospective participants inquire.

(c) When psychologists conduct research with individuals such as students or subordinates, psychologists take special care to protect the prospective participants from adverse consequences of declining or withdrawing from participation.

(d) When research participation is a course requirement or opportunity for extra credit, the prospective participant is given the choice of equitable alternative activities.

(e) For persons who are legally incapable of giving informed consent, psychologists nevertheless (1) provide an appropriate explanation, (2) obtain the participant's assent, and (3) obtain appropriate permission from a legally authorized person, if such substitute consent is permitted by law.

6.12 Dispensing with Informed Consent

Before determining that planned research (such as research involving only anonymous questionnaires, naturalistic observations, or certain kinds of archival research) does not require the informed consent of research participants, psychologists consider applicable regulations and institutional review board requirements, and they consult with colleagues as appropriate.

6.13 Informed Consent in Research Filming or Recording

Psychologists obtain informed consent from research participants prior to filming or recording them in any form, unless the research involves simply naturalistic observations in public places and it is not anticipated that the recording will be used in a manner that could cause personal identification or harm.

6.14 Offering Inducements for Research Participants

(a) In offering professional services as an inducement to obtain research participants, psychologists make clear the nature of the services, as well as the risks, obligations, and limitations. . . .

(b) Psychologists do not offer excessive or inappropriate financial or other inducements to obtain research participants, particularly when it might tend to coerce participation.

6.15 Deception in Research

(a) Psychologists do not conduct a study involving deception unless they have determined that the use of deceptive techniques is justified by the study's prospective scientific, educational, or applied value and that equally effective alternative procedures that do not use deception are not feasible.

(b) Psychologists never deceive research participants about significant aspects that would affect their willingness to participate, such as physical risks, discomfort, or unpleasant emotional experiences.

(c) Any other deception that is an integral feature of the design and conduct of an experiment must be explained to participants as early as is feasible, preferably at the conclusion of their participation, but no later than at the conclusion of the research. (See also Standard 6.18, Providing Participants With Information About the Study.)

6.16 Sharing and Utilizing Data

Psychologists inform research participants of their anticipated sharing or further use of personally identifiable research data and of the possibility of unanticipated future uses.

6.17 Minimizing Invasiveness

In conducting research, psychologists interfere with the participants or milieu from which data are collected only in a manner that is warranted by an appropriate research design and that is consistent with psychologists' roles as scientific investigators.

6.18 Providing Participants With Information About the Study

(a) Psychologists provide a prompt opportunity for participants to obtain appropriate information about the nature, results, and conclusions of the research, and psychologists attempt to correct any misconceptions that participants may have.

(b) If scientific or humane values justify delaying or withholding this information, psychologists take reasonable measures to reduce the risk of harm.

6.19 Honoring Commitments

Psychologists take reasonable measures to honor all commitments they have made to research participants.

The APA's ethical standards for research agree with the Nuremberg Code in stating that it is the obligation of the researcher to obtain subjects' informed and voluntary consent to participate in research when there are risks to their physical or psychological integrity. Participants must be informed of "all features of the research that reasonably might influence their willingness to participate" and any other aspects of the research about which they inquire. The decision to participate must be made without coercion, informed consent must be fully documented, and subjects must be informed that they are free to terminate their involvement in the research at any time.

For those legally incapable of giving informed consent, whether because of age or disability, psychologists are required to explain the study as fully as possible, obtain potential subjects' agreement to participate, and seek the informed consent of their legal representatives (see the discussion of consent forms in Chapter 12, Planning the Study).

Research participants also must be informed about any anticipated sharing or further use of data gathered from them in which they might be identified, as well as any possibility of unanticipated future uses of data collected from them (e.g., by depositing it in an archive). The APA guidelines are based on the idea that people have a right to privacy which must be protected by psychologists who conduct research. Participants must decide for themselves whether personally identifiable data can be shared with others.

As we have said, the federal regulations allow researchers to waive the requirement of informed consent under certain circumstances. The APA guidelines permit some research to be conducted without informed consent and even allow researchers to misinform subjects when methodological considerations require it and when the risks to participants are negligible. *Deception* is not discussed in the federal guidelines, although it is not ruled out.

Deception was common in behavioral research some decades ago; but current APA standards require that deception be used only as a last resort, and only when the problem is important and no alternative procedures (e.g., simulation or role-playing techniques) are available. They also specify that "psychologists never deceive research participants about significant aspects" of the research "that would affect their willingness to participate, such as physical risks, discomfort, or unpleasant emotional experiences."

The opinions of responsible professionals vary on the question of whether and to what extent deception should be permissible in psychological research. Some researchers believe that deception is harmful and never ethically justified, since it violates the principle of informed consent and destroys the nature of the researcher-participant relationship by violating the participant's trust. Other psychologists believe that deception in experiments, which usually is very mild, is harmless, since its effects are transitory, and in specific cases, they argue, the importance of the research justifies the minimal loss of human dignity that might be entailed. Keith-Spiegal and Koocher (1985) summarize the kinds of suggestions that researchers have developed to help make deception more acceptable to subjects. One of these is giving participants the option of removing their data from the study if they wish to do so.

Although the APA guidelines allow deception under certain circumstances, they also state that gaps in participants' understanding of the study should be removed when data collection is complete. Explanations then should be given for why there was no informed consent and/or why the deception was used (see Chapter 12, Planning the Study). Although such *debriefing* is intended to restore the nature of the researcher-participant relationship to its preresearch status, it is difficult for researchers to know whether this has been successful. Participants who have been lied to during the experiment may not believe researchers when they tell the truth at the end of an experiment, and in the future such subjects may suspect deception in research even when none is present.

ETHICS IN ANIMAL RESEARCH

So far, we have discussed the ethics of research involving human participants, but this is only one part of research ethics in psychology. Animals are used in about 7 to 8% of psychology's experiments; of these animal studies, most involve rodents and birds (90%) and about 5% use primates (APA, 1994). The genes, environment, and experience of animal subjects can be controlled and experimental conditions manipulated to a greater extent than is possible with human participants.

The benefits of psychological research with animals are less well known than the medical ones, but they are many and important. Research with animals has led to important insights that have greatly improved people's lives. To give just a few examples, principles of learning and behavior acquired from animal studies have resulted in new educational methods, life-enhancing treatments for disorders like enuresis, and lifesaving treatments for disorders like anorexia (Miller, 1985). Studies done on primate communication have inspired improved strategies for communicating with retarded children (APA, 1994). In behavioral medicine, animal research has yielded important advances in rehabilitating victims of stroke, brain injury, and neurological damage (Miller, 1985).

Despite the benefits to people and animals themselves of animal studies, the ethics of such research has been a continuing concern of scientists and members of the general public for the past two hundred years. And feelings on this issue have often run high.

In the first decades of the 19th century, the pioneering physiological researchers Françoise Magendie and Claude Bernard aroused moral outrage by conducting surgical procedures on live unanaesthetized animals. These men ran private research laboratories and conducted public demonstrations of surgery for their livelihood. Although Magendie and Bernard justified such practices by saying that animals lack consciousness and feel no pain, other scientists who witnessed these demonstrations disagreed, calling them unnecessary and cruel (Orlans, 1993).

The antivivisectionists who were active in Magendie's day wanted to eliminate or reduce surgery done on animals for scientific research or for purposes of demonstration. Their main method was to read scientific publications and expose studies that they judged to be cruel, trivial, and repetitive. Psychologists did not escape their attention. Early in the 20th century, John Watson, the father of behaviorism, was severely criticized in the popular press for surgically depriving rats of their sense modalities to learn how their ability to run mazes would be affected (Dewsbury, 1990).

Public concern over animal experimentation continued throughout the century. The beginning of what has been called the animal rights movement can be traced to 1975 when Peter Singer published his popular and controversial book *Animal Liberation.* In it, Singer argued that the exploitation of animals in research reflects an attitude of speciesism, analogous to racism or sexism, which he defined as "a prejudice or attitude of bias toward the interests of members of one's own species and against those of members of other species"

(Singer, 1975, p. 7). Singer's book led to widespread political action to end cruelties in animal farming and the use of animals in testing chemicals and beauty products in industry. It also led to organized protests against animal research in medicine and psychology.

After the publication of Singer's book, many animal rights organizations, varying in size and strategies, sprang up in the United States and other countries. These include *People for the Ethical Treatment of Animals (PETA); the Animal Liberation Front (ALF); Ethics and Animals,* an association of philosophers; the *Animal Legal Defense Fund,* an association of attorneys; and *Psychologists for the Ethical Treatment of Animals.*

The late 1970s and 1980s ushered in demonstrations and sit-ins and other peaceful methods of protesting animal research, as well as a variety of more violent and militant strategies. Radical animal rights groups began infiltrating research labs, destroying data and equipment, bombing and setting fire to buildings, and removing research subjects. Acting in part as a response to publicity raised by the animal rights activists, in the mid-1980s Congress passed the amendments to the Animal Welfare Act, to which we now turn.

Animal Welfare Act of 1985

In 1985, experimental procedures came under the Animal Welfare Act and thereafter were regulated by the Office for Protection from Research Risks (OPRR) at the National Institutes of Health (NIH), the same office that oversees human subjects research. As of 1985, research proposals that involve subjecting animals to pain must be reviewed by an *Institutional Animal Care and Use Committee (IACUC),* pronounced "I, a cook." IACUCs must include a scientist, a veterinarian, and at least one member who is not affiliated with the institution to represent community views on the care and treatment of animal subjects. The job of the IACUC, as described by Holden, is "to judge whether the experimental design is sufficient to yield important new knowledge, whether the animal model selected is appropriate (or whether nonanimal alternatives exist), the adequacy of procedures for pain control and euthanasia, environmental conditions, and qualifications for personnel" (Holden, 1987, p. 880).

The 1985 amendments to the Animal Welfare Act also required for the first time that the environment of primates promote their psychological well-being. Jane Goodall, author of *The Chimpanzees of Gombe* (1986), had lobbied for such legislation, arguing that because of the similarity of primates to humans, chimpanzees "should be provided with a rich and stimulating environment" and the company of caretakers "selected for their understanding of animal behavior and their compassion and respect for, and dedication to, their charges" (Goodall, 1987, p. 577). Psychologists have been active in research investigating the types of living conditions best suited for that purpose (see Novak & Petto, 1991).

As a result of these changes in the federal regulations, proposals for research involving animals now are evaluated to determine whether they are likely to yield important new knowledge. The research problem should be important; there should be a reasonable prospect that the study will generate the knowledge being sought; and needless repetition of procedures must be avoided. To accomplish this, researchers must select the most appropriate animal for the research, as well as the best experimental procedures and instruments, based on a firm grounding in the literature of animal research.

APA Code of Conduct: Care and Use of Animals in Research

The APA regulations on the ethical treatment of animals in research, reprinted in Box 4, require psychologists to comply with federal, state, and local regulations, to treat animal subjects humanely, and to make every effort

---

BOX 4 APA STANDARD 6.20: CARE AND USE OF ANIMALS IN RESEARCH, 1992

(a) Psychologists who conduct research involving animals treat them humanely.

(b) Psychologists acquire, care for, use, and dispose of animals in compliance with current federal, state, and local laws and regulations, and with professional standards.

(c) Psychologists trained in research methods and experienced in the care of laboratory animals supervise all procedures involving animals and are responsible for ensuring appropriate consideration of their comfort, health, and humane treatment.

(d) Psychologists ensure that all individuals using animals under their supervision have received instruction in research methods and in the care, maintenance, and handling of the species being used, to the extent appropriate to their role.

(e) Responsibilities and activities of individuals assisting in a research project are consistent with their respective competencies.

(f) Psychologists make reasonable efforts to minimize the discomfort, infection, illness, and pain of animal subjects.

(g) A procedure subjecting animals to pain, stress, or privation is used only when an alternative procedure is unavailable and the goal is justified by its prospective scientific, educational, or applied value.

(h) Surgical procedures are performed under appropriate anesthesia; techniques to avoid infection and minimize pain are followed during and after surgery.

(i) When it is appropriate that the animal's life be terminated, it is done rapidly, with an effort to minimize pain, and in accordance with accepted procedures.

"to minimize the discomfort, infection, illness, and pain of animal subjects." As of 1992, the regulations specify that psychologists can subject animals to pain, stress, or privation only when there are no alternative procedures and when the research is of sufficient "scientific, educational, or applied value" to justify such procedures. According to the APA's statistics, few behavioral studies involve pain, stress, or privation to animal subjects (APA, 1994).

When pain is involved, the APA code requires that every effort be made to reduce the animals' suffering. One way to do this is to choose procedures for research that are the least painful and least invasive. Specialists in animal behavior should be consulted to ensure that the best animal species is selected for the research. Species differ in their appropriateness as models for studying particular phenomena. They also vary in the amount of discomfort that a particular procedure will produce in them; the age of the animal also can make a difference. Observations of animals in the wild might replace laboratory experiments. Whenever possible, positive incentives should be used in place of deprivation.

A second strategy is to reduce the number of animals involved in research to a minimum and, when appropriate, to search for alternatives to animal subjects. Power analyses can be used to determine the minimum number of animals needed for meaningful statistical testing (see Chapter 6), and research designs can be selected that require the fewest subjects. In the future, the availability of animal clones may increase the precision of experiments and reduce the number of animals needed in research. Occasionally it has been possible for nonanimal models to substitute for animals. Some experiments on predation, for example, have used lifelike models in place of animal prey. Finally, when appropriate, post hoc (after the fact) analyses of data gathered on people who have experienced the conditions of interest might be considered.

The debates on the ethics of animal research in the past two centuries have been characterized by extremes of opinion and passion on both sides. At one extreme are animal rights advocates who argue that all animal research should be abolished, disregarding the benefits of such research to people and animals. At the other are those researchers who believe that the interests of humans should take precedence over any concerns about animal welfare. Most researchers today would take a position somewhere in the middle and almost all would acknowledge the moral obligation of researchers to treat animal subjects with compassion.

The changes in the law and in the thinking of scientists and nonscientists alike about the ethics of animal research that have taken place in the past decades have been nothing short of revolutionary. One can only imagine how a scientist in Magendie's day would react to the following statement made by the editors of *Animal Behaviour*, one of today's most prestigious journals of animal behavior:

> To stop, to think and to weigh up the value of the research against all of the costs for the animals involved before anything is done to them at all should be part and parcel of any scientific inquiry. (Dawkins & Gosling, 1992, p. 1)

*F*INAL COMMENTS

Although guidelines and committees are an indispensable aid to ethical decision making, it is not necessary to rely exclusively on such external standards in making judgments about the ethics of research. There is a simple strategy that anyone, including you, can use as a check in considering the ethics of specific research techniques. It is to put yourself in the place of the people who will be participating in the research and then decide whether you would be willing to be treated in precisely the same way as you plan to treat them. If you conclude that you would, you can rest assured that the research most likely is ethically sound.

Of course, you recognize this simple and powerful principle as the *golden rule,* a guide to moral conduct that your parents and teachers taught you as a child. Indeed, the golden rule is a principle of right conduct in all the major religions of our time (Seldes, 1972, pp. 432–4).

In Buddhism:
Hurt not others in ways that you yourself would find hurtful. (Udana-Varga: 5, 18).

In Christianity:
All things whatsoever ye would that men should do to you, do ye even so to them: for this is the Law and the Prophets. (Matthew: 7,12)

In Confucianism:
Tsze-kung asked, saying: "Is there one word which may serve as a rule of practice for all one's life?" The Master said, "Is not Reciprocity such a word? What you do not want done to yourself, do not do to others." (Confucius: *Analects*)

In Islam:
No one of you is a believer until he desires for his brother that which he desires for himself. (Sunnah)

In Judaism:
What is hateful to you, do not to your fellow-men. That is the entire Law; all the rest is commentary. (Talmud: Shabbat, 31 a)

This principle also appears as the central prescription in a classic treatise in philosophy. Immanuel Kant, the 18th-century philosopher, called it the *categorical imperative* and claimed it to be the only moral rule needed to live the good life. The categorical imperative reads:

Act as if the principle on which your action is based were to become by your will a universal law of nature. (Kant, 1785; cited in *Microsoft Encarta,* 1994)

Finally, this principle also is central in the thinking of people who have suffered abuse at the hands of researchers. Eva Mozes Kor, a survivor of the Nazi medical experiments on twins, for example, offered the following guideline for scientists to use in designing and conducting studies with human participants (Kor, 1992, p. 8):

Treat the subjects of your experiments in the manner that you would want to be treated if you were in their place.

Charles Pollard, a survivor of the Tuskegee syphilis study, described his feelings after learning of the deadly deception that had been practiced on him for over 40 years in similar terms. He remembers muttering some curse words to himself and thinking:

I wouldn't have did them like that.

KEY TERMS

Tuskegee syphilis study
Trial of Nazi doctors at Nuremberg
Nuremberg Code
Principle of informed consent
Milgram's obedience study
Wichita jury study
Zimbardo's prison experiment
Belmont Report
Principles of respect, beneficence, and justice

Institutional Review Board (IRB)
Code of federal regulations for the protection of human subjects
APA Code of Conduct for Research
Speciesism
Institutional Animal Care and Use Committee (IACUC)
APA Code: Care and use of animals in research

KEY PEOPLE

Stanley Milgram
Henry Beecher
Laud Humphreys
Philip Zimbardo

Françoise Magendie and Claude Bernard
Peter Singer

REVIEW QUESTIONS

1. Describe the purpose, procedures, and duration of the Tuskegee syphilis study.

2. Why were charges brought against the Nazi doctors on trial at Nuremberg?

3. What are the two most fundamental principles of the Nuremberg Code?

4. What problems are encountered by medical and psychological researchers in applying the principle of informed consent?

5. According to the Nuremberg Code, under what conditions should research involving risks to subjects be undertaken?

6. According to Katz, what three types of risk can arise in research with human participants?

7. Describe the purpose, procedures, and results of Milgram's obedience experiment.

8. What were the ethical problems Milgram's critics saw in his experiment? What was Milgram's reply to his critics?

9. What types of violations of research ethics did Beecher find in the medical literature?

10. What were the ethical problems in Humphreys's study of gay men?

11. According to the Belmont Report, what three fundamental values must be upheld in research with human participants?

12. Describe how research should be done to be in accord with the following principles:
    a) respect,
    b) beneficence,
    c) justice.

13. In what way does the principle of beneficence go beyond the Nuremberg Code?

14. What is the purpose of the Institutional Review Board?

15. Under what conditions do the federal regulations permit research on human subjects without informed consent?

16. What is the definition of "minimal risk" in the federal regulations for human research?

17. According to APA guidelines, how should a participant's right to privacy affect procedures in research?

18. What is the APA position on deception in psychological research?

19. What proportion of psychological research involves animals?

20. What are some benefits to people that have resulted from psychological research on animals?

21. What is the job of the IACUC?

22. What are the concerns addressed in the APA Code of Conduct for Animal Research?

23. What strategies can be used to reduce the number of animals in research?

24. Explain Kant's categorical imperative.

8

Factorial Designs and Interactions

❖

In expositions of the scientific use of experimentation it is frequent to find an excessive stress laid on the importance of varying the essential conditions *only one at a time . . . .* this simple formula is not very helpful.

R. A. FISHER

❖

THE FACTORIAL DESIGN
    Assigning Subjects to Treatments
    Comparisons between Conditions
    The Interaction between Factors A and B
    Main Effect of Factor A
    Main Effect of Factor B
    The Analysis of Variance
VARIATIONS IN FACTORIAL DESIGNS
    Between-Subjects Factors
    Within-Subjects Factors
    Subject Factors
    The Number of Factors
ADVANTAGES OF THE FACTORIAL DESIGN
    Efficiency
    Comprehensiveness
    External Validity
THE GENERAL LINEAR MODEL
KEY TERMS, KEY PEOPLE, REVIEW QUESTIONS

If you pick up a can of Diet Coke and read the label, you will notice a mysterious tongue-twister:

Phenylketonurics: Contains Phenylalanine.

This message is a warning to phenylketonurics, people suffering from phenylketonuria (PKU), a genetic disorder that prevents the normal metabolism of the amino acid phenylalanine. When this acid, an ingredient in aspartame (the sweetener in Diet Coke), is not metabolized properly, it builds to toxic levels, causing brain damage. Today all newborns are tested for PKU. If the test is positive, the baby immediately is put on a special diet low in phenylalanine. Without this diet, PKU babies (one in about every 15,000 births) would end up brain damaged and institutionalized with the diagnosis of inherited mental retardation.

The discovery of the dietary "cure" for PKU was a fortunate result of scientific advances in how scientists think about development. Most researchers today no longer try to measure the degree of inheritance of traits, as Galton did; geneticists now assume that both heredity and environment *interact* in setting the course of development, as the following quote from Richard Lewontin illustrates:

> To predict what an organism will be like at some future moment, it is not sufficient to know what it is like now, nor is it enough to describe the environment through which the organism is about to pass. We must know both. (Lewontin, 1982, p. 17)

PKU is a perfect example. Most people thrive on a diet containing phenylalanine; only the rare people with PKU suffer brain damage because of it.

To develop a cure for PKU, scientists had to be aware of the possibility of *interactions* in human development.

> An *interaction* occurs when the effect of one variable, *A*, on another variable, *X*, depends on a third variable, *B*.

Table 1 illustrates the interaction between diet, variable *A*, and genetic type, variable *B*, in determining brain functioning, variable *X*.

In everyday language, if the effect of one treatment *depends on* something else, this is an interaction. If you were to ask, for example, "What are the effects on health of drinking alcohol?", a good answer would be that it depends on your age, your sex, and how much you drink. For a woman older than 50, light drinking reduces the risk of death; but if the woman is between 30 and 50, light drinking increases it (Fuchs et al., 1995). Age and drinking *interact* in determining risks to health, in other words. (Heavy drinking at any age increases the risk of death!)

Given the complexity of organisms, it is not surprising that scientists are discovering that interactions are the norm rather than the exception. Few treatments affect every person or animal in the same way. In fact, it is difficult to

TABLE 1 INTERACTION OF DIET AND GENETIC TYPE IN DETERMINING WHO SUFFERS BRAIN DAMAGE FROM PKU

| | | Diet, Variable A | |
		With phenylalanine	Without phenylalanine
Genetic Type	PKU	Brain Damage	Normal
Variable B	No PKU	Normal	Normal

think of treatments that do not interact with other conditions. Should you take aspirin for headaches? It depends on your age. Children can get Reye's syndrome, an often fatal disorder, from taking aspirin; but aspirin is fine for adults and may even reduce the risk of heart disease. How about penicillin for a strep throat? Again, it depends. Some people have a severe allergic reaction to penicillin. If you become clinically depressed, should you take Prozac? Once more, it depends. If the depression is bipolar, you might be better off on lithium.

Because experience has shown that interactions occur so frequently, researchers now deliberately hunt for them. Numerous studies have been done to find out whether two common treatments for psychological disorders, drug therapy and psychotherapy, combine additively or interact in affecting patients' behaviors. If the drugs alone result in a certain amount of improvement, A, and psychotherapy also results in a fixed improvement, B, when the patient receives both, what will the outcome be? Will the effects add so that the patient improves by $A + B$, or will the treatments interact to produce a super treatment (a greater improvement than $A + B$), or no effects at all (if the effects cancel each other out)? The answer is critical to finding the best possible therapy.

Psychologists also investigate whether particular treatments interact with patient types. Such research can yield important information on the generality of treatments and the causes of disorders. For example, Stewart, Quitkin, Terman, and Terman (1990) investigated whether two types of depression share the same underlying cause by examining the interaction between treatment and type of depression.

Stewart and his colleagues knew that seasonal affective disorder (SAD), a winter depression, could be treated successfully by exposing patients to bright artificial light during the winter months (the light makes up for the reduced natural sunlight at that time). But they wondered whether light therapy also would help atypical depression, a mood disorder that shares symptoms in common with SAD. They reasoned that if light treatment works as well for atypical depression as it does for SAD, the two disorders actually might be variants of the same underlying problem. When they did the study, they found that SAD responded well to light treatment but atypical depression did not. Their finding, an interaction between treatment and type of depression, supported the standard classification of SAD and atypical depression as separate disorders calling for different treatments.

Experiments such as this one, which test for interactions, must include at least two independent variables and one dependent variable. Until the 1920s, when R. A. Fisher introduced the factorial design, there were no experimental designs for testing interactions. The available research designs before Fisher were modeled exclusively on Mill's method of difference, which states that experimental conditions should be varied only one at a time. This requirement prevented researchers from studying interactions. Fisher's factorial design, to which we now turn, is one of the most commonly used research designs in psychology today.

Fisher (1926) introduced the factorial design by discussing an experiment testing the effects of fertilizers on the yield of winter oats. We will use a psychological example, the effect of drugs on memory, instead of his example from agriculture. Our discussion will follow the logic of this design presented by Joan Fisher Box (1978), Fisher's daughter and his biographer.

THE FACTORIAL DESIGN

Let's begin by imagining that an experimenter is interested in testing the effects of two drugs, A and B, on memory. Some common social drugs that affect memory are alcohol, caffeine, and nicotine (Kerr, Sherwood, & Hindmarch, 1991). In the experiment, participants would learn a list of nonsense syllables, then, after a period of time, receive the drug treatment, then try to recall the previously learned materials.

The two independent variables would be (1) the presence versus absence of Drug A (e.g., caffeine) and (2) the presence versus absence of Drug B (e.g., nicotine). The dependent variable would be a measure of the amount of material recalled. Since there are two independent variables and each variable has two different values or *levels* (presence vs. absence), there are 2 × 2, or four, different treatments in the study (see Table 2).

> In a factorial design, the total number of treatments is equal to the product of the number of levels of each of the independent variables.

A list of the treatments in this experiment can be generated by multiplication. If we call the levels of independent variable A, $a1$ and $a2$, and the levels of independent variable B, $b1$ and $b2$, then the product of $(a1 + a2)$ times $(b1 + b2)$ gives the full set of treatments:

$$(a1 + a2)(b1 + b2) = a1b1 + a1b2 + a2b1 + a2b2$$

where $a1b1$ stands for treatment $a1$ and $b1$ given together.

The factorial design gets its name from this process of multiplying to yield the experimental treatments. If you recall from algebra, an equation like

TABLE 2 THE FOUR TREATMENT CONDITIONS IN THE 2 × 2 FACTORIAL DESIGN STUDYING THE INTERACTION OF DRUGS A AND B

	Drug A	
Drug B	Absent	Present
Absent	Placebo	Only Drug A
Present	Only Drug B	Drugs A & B

$X^2 + 3X + 2$ can be factored into the product of two terms involving X. These terms, $(X + 1)$ and $(X + 2)$ in this case, are the factors of the equation. Similarly, the terms $(a1 + a2)$ and $(b1 + b2)$ are the factors of the experimental design, since they can be multiplied together to give the full set of possible treatments. The terms *factor* and *independent variable* are used interchangeably.

> A *factorial design* is an experimental design with two or more independent variables, in which the complete set of treatments or conditions is generated by multiplying together the levels of the independent variables.

Factorial designs are described by giving the number of levels on each factor. The memory study is called a 2×2 ("two by two") factorial design, because each of the factors has two levels. If one factor had 4 levels and the other factor 3 levels, it would be called a 4×3 ("four by three") factorial design.

If the full set of treatments is not used, the experiment does not have a factorial design. If the memory study had only three conditions, for example, Drug A, Drug B, and Placebo, it would not be a factorial design, even though each level of each independent variable would be present.

Assigning Subjects to Treatments

There are two general procedures for assigning the subjects to the four different treatments of our 2×2 memory study. In a within-subjects design, each subject would receive all four treatments. In a between-subjects design, each subject receives only one treatment, so different subjects would be used in each condition.

Which of these two designs to use would depend upon the specifics of the study. Within-subjects designs have the advantage of controlling for individual differences among the subjects, because subjects' characteristics are constant across the treatments. In addition, this design requires a fraction of the subjects needed for a between-subjects design. In the memory study, if we wanted to have, say, five observations in each treatment group, the between-subjects design would require $5 \times 4 = 20$ subjects, but the within-subjects design would require only 5 subjects.

The problems of the within-subjects design result from the repeated measurement of the same subjects. When each subject participates in all the treatments, fatigue and practice effects can result. If the treatments are given in different orders, interaction effects are possible (e.g., drug A may have a particular effect on memory when preceded by drug B but not when preceded by a placebo). Procedures for controlling for these problems are discussed later in the chapter. The between-subjects design avoids the problems of repeated measures by having each subject receive only one treatment.

We will explain the logic of the factorial design using the 2×2 memory study with a between-subjects design. Let's assume that 20 people are randomly assigned to the four drug treatment conditions, with 5 people in each of the four conditions: Placebo (P), Drug A (A), Drug B (B), and Drugs A and B (AB). The last treatment, giving participants both drugs simultaneously, would not be included in an experiment varying the treatments one at a time. In fact, at first glance this treatment seems to make it impossible to untangle the effects of the two drugs. How is it possible to figure out the influence of each drug when both are given to the same subjects? Fisher had an ingenious answer to this question that, oddly enough, is based on the logic of varying one thing at a time!

Comparisons between Conditions

The first step in analyzing the results of a factorial experiment is to calculate the mean (average) values of the dependent variable for the different experimental conditions. Table 3 shows the individual subject scores and the means for each treatment in the memory study. The scores are the results of the memory test given to the subjects after taking the drugs—the higher the score the better the recall.

The Interaction between Factors A and B

In Table 3 there are two comparisons between the means of the conditions that provide information about the effects of Drug A. Each of these comparisons is based on the logic of the method of difference; as required by the method, only one condition is varied for each comparison.

1. $M_A - M_p$
   The mean of condition A, M_A, can be compared to the mean of condition P, M_p; the difference between these means gives the advantage of Drug A over the placebo. Getting the means from Table 3, $M_A - M_p = 15 - 10 = 5$. The observed effect of Drug A here is to increase recall by 5 points.

2. $M_{AB} - M_B$
   The mean of condition AB, M_{AB}, also can be compared to the mean of condition B, M_B. The difference between these means gives the advantage of giving Drug A to subjects who also are receiving Drug B. The result is $M_{AB} - M_B = 33 - 20 = 13$. The effect of A *in the presence of B* is to increase recall by 13 points.

TABLE 3 SCORES ON RECALL AND MEAN RECALL SCORES FOR EACH TREATMENT CONDITION IN THE 2 × 2 FACTORIAL DESIGN

		Drug A	
		Absent	Present
Drug B	Absent	P S 1: 10 S 2: 7 S 3: 9 S 4: 9 S 5: 15 $M_p = 10$	A S 6: 10 S 7: 14 S 8: 16 S 9: 15 S 10: 20 $M_A = 15$
	Present	B S 11: 18 S 12: 16 S 13: 19 S 14: 23 S 15: 24 $M_B = 20$	AB S 16: 30 S 17: 37 S 18: 34 S 19: 30 S 20: 34 $M_{AB} = 33$

Both comparisons show an increase in recall when the participants take Drug A, but the advantage of A is greater when B is present, 13 points, than when B is absent, 5 points. This result is evidence of an interaction between A and B. If A had the same effect in the presence or absence of B, there would be no evidence of an interaction.

> To evaluate the possibility of an interaction between Factors A and B, comparisons must be made of the effects of A at different levels of B.

In our example, the effect of A differs by $13 - 5 = 8$ points depending on whether B is present or absent. This difference provides a numerical measure of the strength of the interaction; the greater this number, the more evidence of an interaction.

The null hypothesis, that the interaction value is equal to zero, is tested by computing the significance probability, p, which is the probability if the null hypothesis is true of getting the observed value, or one even greater. As in every statistical test, if p is less than or equal to the alpha level chosen for the test (usually alpha = .05), the null hypothesis is rejected. In the example, the statistical test results in $p < .05$, so there is a significant interaction.

This statistical test for the interaction, devised by Fisher, now is called the F (for Fisher) test to recognize his work. The computations for the F test are explained in statistics texts and handbooks of experimental design (see Winer, 1991, or Kirk, 1982).

Main Effect of Factor A

In some experiments, the researcher may be interested in the average effect of an independent variable. In our example, Drug A increases recall by 5 points when B is absent and 13 points when B is present; so in this case, the average or *main effect* of A is $(13 + 5)/2 = 9$ points.

> The *main effect* of Factor A is determined by computing the effect of A at each level of B and averaging these values.

The main effect of a factor, like the effect of an interaction, can be tested for significance by an F test. The null hypothesis in this case is that the main effect is equal to zero. In the example, the computations of the F test show that $p < .05$, so the null hypothesis is rejected and we conclude that there is a significant main effect of the factor.

When the interaction is not significant, the main effect gives complete information about the effect of the factor. When the interaction is significant, the effect of A is not uniform, but depends on B. In this case, the main effect may not be of interest.

Main Effect of Factor B

In the 2×2 factorial design, the analysis that is done for Factor A is repeated for Factor B. Again, two comparisons are needed to judge the effect of Factor B:

1. $M_B - M_P$
   The mean of condition B, M_B, first is compared to the mean of condition P, M_P. The difference gives the advantage of Drug B over the placebo. Getting the means from Table 3, $M_B - M_P = 20 - 10 = 10$ points.

2. $M_{AB} - M_A$
   The mean of condition AB, M_{AB}, then is compared to the mean of condition A, M_A. The difference gives the advantage of Drug B for *subjects who also receive Drug A*. The result is $M_{AB} - M_A = 33 - 15 = 18$ points.

The main effect of B is calculated by averaging the results of these two comparisons: $(18 + 10)/2 = 14$. Averaged over levels of A, the main effect of B is 14 points. The F test of this main effect is significant at $p < .05$.

We also can use the observed effects of B at the different levels of A to determine if there is an interaction between B and A. The effect of B when A is absent is 10 points; when A is present, it is 18 points. So the effect of B differs by $18 - 10 = 8$ points, depending on the level of A. Notice that this is the same value, 8, that we got when we calculated the interaction of A and B before. This is no coincidence.

> The evidence for an interaction between Factors B and A is always the same as the evidence for an interaction between A and B. Consequently, there is only one F test for the interaction.

TABLE 4 ANALYSIS OF VARIANCE SUMMARY TABLE FOR RECALL SCORES

Source	df	F
Drug A	1	38.12*
Drug B	1	92.24*
A × B	1	7.53*
Error	16	(10.63)

The value in parentheses is the mean squared error.
* $p < .05$.

The context of the experiment usually will favor one or the other way of stating the interaction—either that the effects of A depend on B, or that the effects of B depend on A.

The Analysis of Variance

The complete analysis of the two factor design, called the *analysis of variance*, includes three F tests—one test for each main effect and one test for the interaction. These tests are presented in an analysis of variance summary table. A standard format for such tables is shown in Table 4. The first column, labeled Source, lists the names of the main effects, the interaction, and the error term. The error term is used in computing the F tests. Its value (shown in parentheses) is a measure of the extent to which differences among the scores on the dependent variable are due to uncontrolled variables.

The second column shows the *degrees of freedom, df,* associated with the main effects, the interaction, and the error. These numbers are based on the size of the study. For each main effect, *df* is equal to one less than the number of levels of that factor. In our example, each factor has two levels; so, $df = 2 - 1 = 1$. The *df* of the interaction is the product of the *df*s of the two main effects, $1 \times 1 = 1$. The *df* for error depends upon the number of subjects and the number of treatments. In the example, *df* is equal to the total number of subjects (20) minus the number of treatments (4); df error $= 20 - 4 = 16$.

The third column shows the value of the test statistic, F, for each statistical test. The larger the value of F, the smaller the value of the significance probability, *p*. Fisher published tables of the critical values of F for different values of alpha. The table, available in most statistics texts, shows that each F test in our example is statistically significant at $p < .05$.

VARIATIONS IN FACTORIAL DESIGNS

In Chapter 5, we discussed how Fisher's agricultural experiments with one independent variable translated into experiments in psychology. We considered three designs: (1) between-subjects designs in which subjects are assigned to the conditions completely at random (the completely randomized design), (2) the between-subjects design in which subjects are blocked before being randomly assigned to conditions (the randomized blocks designs), and (3) the within-subjects designs in which each subject is observed in each condition of the study (the repeated measures Latin square design). Each independent variable in a factorial design can be based on any one of these three designs. Subjects in a factorial design can be

- Assigned completely at random to the levels of a factor,
- Be matched into groups (blocks) and then randomly assigned to levels of the factor (randomized blocks), or
- Observed at each level of the factor (repeated measures).

There is one additional way that subjects can be assigned to the levels of a factor, one that we did not discuss in Chapter 6; namely,

subjects can be *systematically* placed in, not randomly assigned to, particular levels of a factor. Systematic assignment is based on characteristics of the subjects, like gender, age, or personality type. An independent variable based on systematic assignment is called a *subject factor.*

Two between-subjects factors—completely randomized (no matching) and randomized blocks (matching)—were discussed in Chapter 6. Applying these methods in factorial designs raises no new issues. The other two methods—repeated measures and subject factors—do have special problems that we will discuss after we look at some examples of factorial experiments with between-subjects factors.

Between-Subjects Factors

Factors with complete randomization are routine in psychological research. In studies using this method, subjects first are selected who are similar on variables that the researcher suspects might influence the outcome of the treatments (e.g., age, severity of a disorder); the subjects then are randomly assigned to the treatment groups. Often repeated measurements are made on the dependent variable before and after the treatment.

This design has much to recommend it. There are no major threats to its internal validity and it is easy to use. The randomization can be preplanned and subjects can be assigned to the conditions when they volunteer for the study. Randomization also allows the investigator to calculate a measure of error due to uncontrolled variables.

Elkin et al. (1989) used this design in a National Institute of Mental Health sponsored large-scale experiment comparing drug therapy and psychotherapy for depression. The patients in the study were randomly assigned to either (1) drug therapy, (2) cognitive psychotherapy, (3) interpersonal psychotherapy, or (4) a placebo drug treatment. Their depressive symptoms were assessed before, during, and at the end of therapy, as well as at 6-, 12-, and 18-month intervals following termination. In this evaluation study, patients were randomly assigned to the levels of the first factor, the type of treatment, and the degree of their depression was measured at each level of the second factor, the time of measurement. The first factor is a between-subjects factor because different patients are observed at each of its levels; the second is a within-subjects factor because the same subjects are observed at every level. A design having both between and within factors, like this one, is called a *mixed design*.

Randomization also can be used for both factors of an experimental design. This was done by Sigall and Ostrove (1975) who investigated the role of a convicted felon's appearance on the sentence she was given in a criminal trial. The subjects, who played the role of jurists in the study, read a description of a crime committed by a woman whose photograph was attached to the description. In fact, the photographs and the felony described to the subjects varied. The photo was either of an attractive or an unattractive woman (Factor A) and the crime either was a swindle or a burglary (Factor B). The participants were randomly assigned to one of the four possible conditions (2×2) and were asked to decide how many years in prison would be a suitable punishment for the crime. The results revealed an interaction between the type of crime and the attractiveness of the felon. The attractive burglar was given a shorter sentence than the other three combinations.

Between-subjects factors with complete randomization were ideal for this problem, since the alternative, using within-subjects factors, would require subjects to sentence all four cases. If this design were used, most likely the nature of the manipulation, varying attractiveness and the type of crime, would become apparent to the subjects, possibly affecting the outcome of the study.

Randomization with prior matching is a good alternative to complete randomization. Subjects can be matched on important variables and then randomly assigned to levels of a factor. Matching is an excellent method for reducing error due to uncontrolled individual differences between subjects. Azrin and Peterson (1990) used matching in this way to evaluate a behavioral treatment for Tourette syndrome, a disorder characterized by involuntary motor tics and embarrassing verbal outbursts.

The experimenters wanted to evaluate the effects on patients of receiving a behavioral treatment for their disorder. However, only 10 subjects with Tourette syndrome were available for the study, and they had very different ages, varying degrees of severity of their symptoms, and they differed on whether they took medication for the problem. Random assignment to the two planned experimental groups (treatment vs. no treatment) would have been unwise with such a small, diverse subject pool, because the groups might have ended up being quite different on some combination of these variables. As an alternative, the authors used a randomized blocks design.

Five pairs of subjects were formed, with both members of a pair matched so that they were almost the same age and had symptoms of about the same severity. Both were matched on whether they were on or off medication. Then one member of each pair was randomly assigned to the habit reversal treatment and the other to a waiting list to be treated at the end of the study. Type of treatment is a between-subjects factor because different subjects are assigned to the levels of the factor. The frequency of the subjects' tics was observed before and after the treatment (or waiting period), a within-subjects factor based on repeated measures. The results showed an astounding 92% reduction of tics for the behavioral treatment, far better than the 50% reduction rate with medication alone. These results raise hope of a major breakthrough in the treatment of this devastating disorder.

This study used matching to control for differences among the patients on age, severity of symptoms, and medication. The investigators could have used a different strategy based on the factorial design if they had had more subjects. Using this new design, the variables that Azrin and Peterson controlled through matching could have been introduced as separate factors. Such a factorial design would permit statistical tests of the main effects and interactions of these variables. The Drug × Treatment Interaction, for example, would test whether the behavioral treatment worked better or worse when the patient was on medication. Unfortunately, introducing new factors requires large numbers of subjects, so this design is not useful for studying rare conditions, like Tourette syndrome.

Within-Subjects Factors

Both of the therapy evaluation experiments we have discussed had repeated measures on one factor. There are no special problems with within-subjects factors when they are used in this way, to record changes in subjects over time. Problems do arise, however, when within-subjects factors are used to evaluate different treatments. In such cases, the order of presenting the treatments becomes an issue. An experiment by Hall and Kataria (1992), which evaluated different treatments for attention deficit hyperactive disorder (ADHD), a condition characterized by impulsive, overactive, and inattentive behavior, illustrates one solution to this problem.

The children in the study were randomly assigned to either a behavioral, cognitive, or control (inactive) treatment. Repeated measures were taken on each child under medication (Ritalin) and with no medication. Hall and Kataria found a significant interaction between the medication and the psychological treatment for the children's performance on a delayed response task. Medication combined with cognitive treatment resulted in the best performance.

The delayed response task was given to the children twice, when they were taking Ritalin and when they were not. When the same task is repeated, as it was in this study, there is always the danger of order effects; that is, repeating the task may affect the results, either through practice, fatigue, or boredom. So, in this case, it would not be desirable to give every child the drug first, followed by the no drug condition.

For this reason, the experimenters decided to *counterbalance order* by giving half the children the Ritalin first, and giving it to the rest of the children second. With this procedure, any order effects are balanced, since equal numbers of subjects receive the treatments in each possible order. The Latin square design discussed in Chapter 6 is based on this logic.

Counterbalancing effectively controls for changes that take place in subjects during an experiment, like fatigue or boredom, but does not guard against interactions among the treatments. If, for example, treatment B is very effective when it follows A but ineffective otherwise, the results for treatment B will depend on how many times B follows A. If B never follows A, the researcher would erroneously conclude that B is an ineffective treatment. For this reason, counterbalancing should not be used when investigators suspect the possibility of interactions involving order.

The logic of the factorial design offers an excellent alternative to counterbalancing for dealing with order effects. Order can be introduced as a separate factor in the design. Using this strategy, each possible order of the treatments would be a level of the factor to which subjects would be randomly assigned. This procedure would allow the experimenter to test for order effects as well as interactions between order effects and the other factors in the design.

Although this may be the best way to control for order effects, it is not problem free. With several treatments, the number of levels of the order factor becomes excessively large, requiring large numbers of subjects. With five treatments, for example, there are 120 possible orders; assigning subjects to each of these orders would require many subjects. With only two or three treatments, having two and six possible orders respectively, this technique would be worth considering.

The simplest procedure for dealing with order effects is randomization, a popular method when an experiment involves many treatments or tasks. Using randomization, subjects are assigned to the treatments in an order selected at random. With four treatments, for example, there are 24 possible orders. Each subject would be assigned, by chance, to one of these. This method of assigning subjects to orders deals with order effects in the same way that randomly assigning subjects to groups handles uncontrolled individual differences. It avoids any systematic bias. Of course, the possibility remains that the orders that are selected will favor some treatments.

Regardless of which strategy is used to deal with order effects, the experimenter's job is to set the procedures of the study to minimize them. This might be done by introducing a break between treatments (e.g., giving the treatments on different days) or by designing the treatments with a view to minimizing fatigue, boredom, and practice effects. In the Ritalin study, for example, a 24-hour period during which the subjects were off the drug preceded the no-drug condition.

Subject Factors

Subject factors, as you remember, are factors in a study that are based on characteristics of the subjects. The levels of a subject factor are classifications of the subjects on such variables as personality, age, or gender. Because different subjects are assigned to the levels of subject factors, they are between-subject factors.

Such factors are included in psychological research for many reasons. They might be:

- The primary focus of the study. In personality research, for example, people are classified into types, such as the Type A or Type B personality, and compared to see whether their behaviors differ. The competitive, achievement-oriented Type A person has a greater risk of coronary heart disease than the more relaxed, mellow Type B person, for example (Jenkins, Zyzanski, & Rosenman, 1979).

- A substitute for factors that cannot be manipulated for practical or ethical reasons. It would be unethical, for instance, to subject people to high levels of stress to observe changes in their immune systems. However, people can be measured on stress and then studied, as Cohen et al. did (Cohen et al., 1991; see Chapter 4). These researchers gave a viral challenge, nose drops loaded with common cold virus, to subjects who were either high or low on measured stress. They found that a higher percentage of the high stressed subjects caught the cold.

- Used for assessing external validity. If a main effect or interaction between factors can be shown to hold for subjects differing on characteristics like age or gender, its generality is assured. This is commonly done in survey research in which sample sizes are large enough to study several factors at once.

- Used as a first step before beginning a more elaborate study. Subject factors can be used to establish differences between participants, which then can be examined more fully in a more extensive study. For example, research has shown that there is a sex difference in alcohol metabolism. When alcohol consumption is proportional to body weight, less alcohol is found in men's bloodstreams than in women's. This finding, which confirms the folklore that men "hold their liquor" better than women, was a necessary preliminary to later research testing hypotheses about the basis for this difference. We now know that men have an enzyme in their stomachs that breaks down alcohol before it reaches the bloodstream; because women have less of this enzyme, more alcohol reaches their bloodstream (Frezza et al., 1990). Men apparently hold their liquor in their stomachs!

Subjects, of course, cannot be assigned randomly to the levels of a subject factor, and sometimes the differences between levels of such a factor are not unitary. Consider "gender," for example. Subjects are not randomly assigned to a gender and there is not a single difference between men and women. Consequently, if the main effect of a subject variable is significant or if the interaction between a subject variable and another variable is significant, the result often is difficult to interpret. Finding a significant subject factor is the same as finding a significant correlation between variables, so the same problems arise in interpreting such effects as in interpreting correlations (see the discussion of these problems in Chapter 5). The following study illustrates the use of a subject factor in a factorial design.

CALVIN AND HOBBES by Bill Watterson

Many adults are convinced that eating sugar negatively affects both the behavior and cognitive abilities of children (see the *Calvin and Hobbes* cartoon) but not of adults. But this was not what was found in an elaborate, well-controlled study that varied the amount of sugar in children's diets over nine weeks. In Chapter 6, we presented Wolraich et al.'s (1994) study which used a Latin square design to examine the effects on children of diets high in sugar, aspartame, and saccharin. They found no effects, adverse or beneficial, of the high sugar diet. After reviewing that study, we were left with the mystery of why sugar has such a bad reputation if, in fact, its effects are not negative.

This mystery may have been solved by Jones et al. (1995) in an experiment that used a different method of giving the sugar to the children as well as a different experimental design. Jones and his colleagues studied the short-term effects of having children ingest a large amount of sugar at one time, what they called a "standardized large glucose load." Their method was comparable to real-life situations where children eat a large amount of sugar (e.g., at parties, and for Calvin, at breakfast). Unlike Wolraich et al.'s study, participation was not restricted to children. They loaded adults with glucose as well.

The Jones study also had two independent variables rather than one. Each of the variables had two levels: (1) Sugar Treatment, pre- and post-, and (2) Age, children and adults. The sugar treatment factor involved repeated measures—the participants were observed before and after the glucose load and age was the subject factor. This mixed design had one between-subject factor, Age, and one within-subject factor, Sugar Treatment.

The hypothesis of the study was that age and treatment *interact* in determining subjects' reactions to sugar. Specifically, the authors expected that the reaction to sugar, measured by self-reported symptoms, would be greater for

TABLE 5 MEAN SYMPTOM LEVELS BEFORE AND AFTER SUGAR LOADING FOR CHILDREN AND ADULTS (FROM JONES ET AL., 1995)

| | Sugar Treatment | |
Age	Pre-sugar	Post-sugar
Children	12.8	22.0
$n = 25$		
Adults	10.0	13.0
$n = 23$		

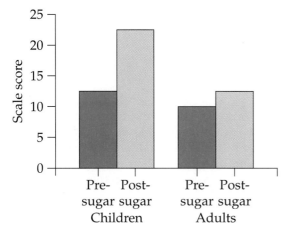

FIGURE 1
Bar chart showing mean symptom scale scores.

FIGURE 2
Line chart showing mean symptom scale scores.

children than adults. Each symptom (shaky, heart pounding, headaches, feeling weak, anxious, difficulty concentrating, slowed thinking, and feeling sweaty) was rated on a scale from 1 to 7, 1 being "the symptom is not present at all," and 7, "the symptom is present in the extreme."

The symptom levels for both children and adults are shown in Table 5. Before the sugar load (administered on a per body weight basis to control for the size differences between children and adults), the symptoms were comparable for both groups. After ingesting the sugar (for the child, an amount equivalent to drinking a 24 ounce bottle of Coke), the symptoms of the children increased more than did those of the adults.

Figures 1 and 2 show these results using two popular types of charts. In Figure 1, a *bar chart*, each experimental condition is shown as a bar, with the height equal to the mean value of the reported symptoms. Figure 2 is a *line chart*; each line on this chart connects the pre- and post-treatment means on the symptom scale for one group of subjects. Although investigators choose one of these three methods—the table, bar chart, or line chart—to present their findings in publications, the evidence for interactions can be seen most clearly in the line chart. If its two lines are not parallel, there is some evidence for an interaction.

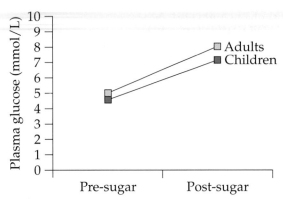

FIGURE 3
Mean glucose levels pre- and post-sugar ingestion for children and adults.

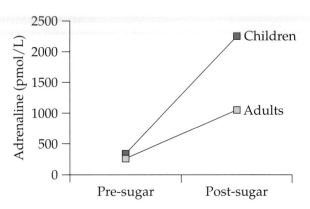

FIGURE 4
Mean adrenaline levels pre- and post-sugar ingestion for children and adults.

Although Jones et al.'s study demonstrated that children and adults react differently to sugar, it still isn't clear why. Children and adults differ in more ways than one, so there also are many possible explanations for this finding. Such problems in interpretation are common for subject factors.

A general strategy, used frequently by researchers to help them later interpret results involving subject factors, is to formulate one or more hypotheses that would account for the expected effects and then to collect additional observations to evaluate them. Plans to collect the additional observations are included in the original design of the study.

Jones et al. anticipated that children and adults would react differently to sugar and speculated that this was because children's adrenal glands are more responsive to blood sugar level than adults'. To test this hypothesis, the participants' blood, which was drawn before and after the sugar load, was analyzed to determine how much glucose, that is, metabolized sugar, and adrenaline it contained. The results of these analyses showed virtually identical levels of glucose in the children and adults following the sugar load (see Figure 3), but different levels of adrenaline, the children's levels increasing much more than the adults (see Figure 4). This result confirmed the experimenters' expectations.

The Number of Factors

The Jones et al. study tested men and women as well as boys and girls. If a different reaction to sugar had been expected for males and females, the design could have introduced sex as a subject factor, a third factor in the design. This additional factor would allow the investigators to test whether sugar loading affects males and females similarly.

Every additional factor that is included in a design increases the number of statistical tests that are calculated. In a three-factor design, there are tests for three main effects, A, B, and C; tests for three "two-way interactions," $A \times B$, $A \times C$, and $B \times C$; and a test for the "three way interaction," $A \times B \times C$.

"Two-way" interactions are the same as the interactions we already have discussed. The $A \times B$ interaction is tested by examining the effects of Factor A at the different levels of Factor B. The other two-way interactions are defined similarly; the $B \times C$ interaction, for example, is sensitive to whether the effects of Factor B on the dependent variable differ across levels of Factor C.

The three-way interaction, $A \times B \times C$, is a complex idea; it involves four variables, the three independent variables and the dependent variable. A three-way interaction results when a two-way interaction, say $A \times B$, is different for different levels of C.

> The $A \times B$ interactions at different levels of C are compared to test for the possibility of a $A \times B \times C$ interaction.

The $A \times B \times C$ interaction could be described as the $B \times C$ interaction varying across levels of A; or the $A \times C$ interaction varying across levels of B. These are equivalent descriptions. There is only one three-way interaction in a three-factor design.

There is no upper limit to the number of factors in a factorial design, except perhaps human understanding. Trying to interpret a "four-way" interaction, for example, is a serious challenge. If the ideas being tested require such complexity, however, the factorial design is unequaled.

ADVANTAGES OF THE FACTORIAL DESIGN

In his book *The Design of Experiments,* Fisher (1935) presented three major advantages of the factorial design over traditional experiments that vary one variable at a time. Over 60 years of experience with the factorial design have borne out Fisher's original assessment.

Efficiency

In a factorial design with a given number of subjects, it is possible to test the effects of two (or more) factors with the same precision as a traditional study of equivalent size that tests only one variable. To understand this, imagine that 40 subjects are available for a study. In a traditional experiment, 20 subjects would be assigned to Treatment $a1$ and 20 to Treatment $a2$. In like manner, in the 2×2 factorial, 20 subjects would get Treatment $a1$ and 20 would get Treatment $a2$; but 20 of the subjects also would get Treatment $b1$ and 20 would get Treatment $b2$. For each factor, it is possible to compare 20 subjects against 20 other subjects. Since this is the same number of subjects we compared in the traditional study, the factorial design is more efficient, yielding more information from the same number of subjects.

Comprehensiveness

The factorial design also permits tests of interactions. Such tests are not possible in one variable at a time studies. In addition, the precision we saw for main effects also applies to testing interactions.

External Validity

In a traditional study, the effects of a single variable are evaluated holding other conditions constant. But this design severely limits the possibility of generalizing from the study, because there is no evidence that the results will replicate across other conditions. In a factorial design, by contrast, the effects of each factor are evaluated at the same time as the other factors are varied, so an assessment of external validity is built into the design. When the interaction is not significant, there is direct evidence that the effects generalize across these conditions. When the interaction is significant, information is gained about the limits of the generalization. In Fisher's words:

> As the factorial arrangement well illustrates, we may, by deliberately varying . . . some of the conditions of the experiment, achieve a wider inductive basis for our conclusions, without in any degree impairing their precision. (Fisher, 1935, p. 100)

THE GENERAL LINEAR MODEL

So far, we have discussed two statistical approaches to the basic problem of uncontrolled variables in research, statistical control and randomization. In Chapter 5, we saw how statistical controls are used in correlational research when random assignment of subjects to conditions is impossible. As you remember, if you can measure subjects on an uncontrolled variable, it is possible to remove the influence of this uncontrolled variable on the dependent variable by using the mathematics of multiple correlation.

In experimental designs, the random assignment of subjects to experimental conditions avoids systematic bias and allows the experimenter to calculate a measure of the error due to uncontrolled variables (see Chapter 6). This measure of error is used in statistical tests.

We usually are taught that these two methods, statistical control and randomization, should be applied in different types of studies. Researchers use randomization whenever possible; otherwise they are forced to rely on statistical controls. And the methods are taught as different mathematical procedures. In statistical control, the experimenter fits different mathematical models to the data and evaluates their fit. Randomization is followed by statistical tests, such as the analysis of variance, which test differences between the means of experimental groups.

Within the last 25 years, however, a new approach to data analysis that unifies these two traditional approaches has become increasingly popular. The *general linear model (GLM)* is a generalization of multiple correlation that can be used to analyze the results of experiments and correlational research.

GLM not only simplifies the logic of data analysis, since one general method can analyze data from almost any research project, but GLM provides the experimenter with techniques that are not available in the traditional data analysis. The unification provided by GLM permits the best feature of correlational data analysis, statistical controls, to be used in experimental studies, and allows one of the best features of experimental work, the testing of interactions, to be used in correlational research.

GLM is taught today in advanced methods books after the traditional data analysis procedures are presented (e.g., see Winer, 1991, or Kirk, 1982). But the efficiency and scope of GLM is so great that we would not be surprised if, within the next 25 years, it becomes the dominant method of analysis taught even in introductory texts.

*K*EY TERMS

Phenylketonuria
Interaction
Levels
Factor
Factorial design
Between-subjects designs vs. within-
  subjects designs
F test
Main effect
Analysis of Variance
Analysis of Variance summary table

Degrees of freedom, df
Between-subjects factor
Within-subjects factor
Counterbalancing
Order effects
Mixed design
Subject factor
Bar chart
Line chart
General linear model

*K*EY PEOPLE

R. A. Fisher
Joan Fisher Box

T. W. Jones et al.

*R*EVIEW QUESTIONS

1. Explain what researchers mean by an interaction between variables.

2. Give three examples of interactions from everyday life.

3. Why were Stewart et al. testing for an interaction between type of patient and type of treatment?

4. How can the full set of treatments in a factorial design be generated from the individual factors?

5. Describe a 4 × 3 factorial design.

6. How many subjects would be required in a 3×3 between-subjects factorial design to have 10 subjects in each condition of the experiment? How many subjects would be needed if it were a within-subjects design?

7. In a 2×2 factorial design, describe how a numerical measure of the strength of the interaction is calculated.

8. How many F tests are there in the analysis of a 2×2 factorial design? What effects do they test?

9. What are the degrees of freedom for the main effects and interaction in a 2×2 factorial design?

10. Present the four ways of assigning subjects to the levels of an independent variable in a factorial design.

11. Give two examples of factorial designs with random assignment of subjects to at least one factor of the design.

12. How was matching used in the study of the behavioral treatment of Tourette syndrome?

13. What are the problems of using repeated measures in a factorial design?

14. Describe three techniques for dealing with order effects in a within-subjects design.

15. Describe four reasons for including subject factors in a factorial design.

16. Describe the factorial design used in the Jones et al. study. Why is this design called a mixed design? What other studies described in this chapter are mixed designs?

17. What strategy did Jones et al. use to help them interpret the interaction between sugar treatment and age in their experiment?

18. List all the statistical tests possible in a $2 \times 2 \times 2$ factorial design.

19. According to Fisher, what are the three advantages of the factorial design?

20. The general linear model allows a major feature of correlational analysis to be used in experimental research and a major feature of factorial designs to be used in correlational research. What are these two features?

9

Single-Case Experimental Designs

❖

When you have the responsibility of making absolutely sure that a given organism will engage in a given sort of behavior at a given time, you quickly grow impatient with theories of learning. Principles, hypotheses, theorems, satisfactory proof at the .05 level of significance . . . nothing could be more irrelevant. No one goes to the circus to see the average dog jump through a hoop significantly oftener than untrained dogs.

B. F. SKINNER

❖

THE 0 X 0 SINGLE-CASE DESIGN
LIMITATIONS OF RANDOMIZED CONTROL GROUP
    DESIGNS
        Getting Enough Subjects
        Misleading Summary Statistics
        Relevance
SKINNER'S BASIC EXPERIMENTAL DESIGN
REPLICATION IN MODERN SINGLE-CASE DESIGNS
        Sequential Replication Designs
            1) ABAB Designs
            2) Alternating Treatment Designs (ATDs)
        Illustration of the ATD Design: Temporal Discrimination
            in Goldfish
        Simultaneous Replication Designs
        Illustration of the Multiple Baseline Design: Behavioral
            Treatment of Depressive Behaviors

PRINCIPLES OF DESIGN AND ANALYSIS
  Choice of Design
  The Size of the Study
  Handling Threats to Internal and External Validity
  Data Analysis
KEY TERMS, KEY PEOPLE, REVIEW QUESTIONS

In the early 1990s, a young girl who was enrolled in a special education class in a New England school stunned her teachers by revealing that she was being sexually abused by every member of her family (Palfreman, 1993). Serious doubts arose concerning the truth of her story, however, because the girl did not report the abuse directly. She was autistic and could not speak normally. Instead, she had typed her message with the help of another person using a new technique called facilitated communication. Although her family denied the allegations, the authorities initiated a court case to see whether the child should be removed from her home.

Facilitated communication had just recently been introduced as a breakthrough in treating autism. Autistic children exhibit severe social withdrawal, gravely impaired communication, and restricted and ritualized behavior. Most autistic children score in the subnormal range on measures of intellectual development. However, the advocates of this new form of communication claimed to have discovered that autism is a disorder that traps normal, even gifted minds inside poorly functioning bodies, which are physically unable to produce speech or make signs. With the help of facilitated communication, they believed, many autistic children would be shown to have normal intellectual abilities.

Facilitated communication is done with a trained adult, called the facilitator, and a computer. With the help of the facilitator, the child types out messages with one finger on the keyboard. The facilitator steadies the child's hand and helps keep the child focused by placing his or her hand on the child's arm. This gesture also is thought to provide the child with much-needed emotional support.

The new technique produced astounding results. Autistic children who could hardly communicate before began expressing their thoughts and feelings with amazing clarity, using advanced vocabulary, and with good grammar and punctuation. Autistic children took advanced mathematics and English courses with their facilitators. Some typed out messages of relief at having been set free from the prison of their autism. The method, which was hailed as a miracle that would enable autistic children to lead productive lives, was introduced into many school systems.

But not everyone accepted these findings. The method was not based on solid research and there was an unresolved question about the nature and extent of the facilitator's influence over what was being communicated by the child. In fact, this issue became the focus of the court case. Was the claim that the child was being sexually abused coming from her or from her facilitator? Could the facilitator be controlling what the child typed by guiding her hand rather than just steadying it?

The court agreed to a scientific experiment to answer this question. The experiment was designed and carried out by Howard Shane, an expert on the communication of handicapped people. Because the court needed to resolve the question of whether the facilitated communications revealed the thoughts of the child or her facilitator, by necessity, the experiment had to involve only one subject, the autistic child. In addition, it was vital that the experiment be internally valid. Any error in its conclusion would lead to tragedy, either needlessly separating a child from loving parents, or reuniting her with abusive ones.

Shane used an ingenious experimental method to test the validity of facilitated communication. The experiment consisted of a series of trials on each of which the child was shown a picture of an everyday object, for example, a key or shoes, and asked to type the name of the object with the aid of her facilitator. The facilitator was shown the same picture as the child on half the trials; on the other trials, the facilitator saw a different picture than the child. Neither the child nor the facilitator could see the picture shown to the other person. The two types of trials were presented in random order and a record was kept of what was typed.

The logic of the experiment is clear. If the facilitator is merely helping the child to express her own thoughts, the words typed should not be influenced by what the facilitator sees. However, if the facilitator is controlling the content of the typing, then, if they see different pictures, the child should type the name of the object that the facilitator sees.

The results were definitive. On every trial in which the child and facilitator saw different pictures, the child named the object seen by the facilitator. Statistical tests were not needed. The probability that this pattern of typing occurred due to uncontrolled variables was negligible. The conclusion was inescapable. The child was not communicating her own thoughts. Accordingly, the charges were dropped and the family reunited.

Other researchers subsequently did their own tests of facilitated communication with similar results to Shane's. As a result, many experts no longer consider facilitated communication a breakthrough for understanding autism (Delmolino & Romanczyk, 1995, and Jacobson, Mulick, & Schwartz, 1995) and some programs using facilitated communication have been discontinued. Children previously placed in advanced classes with facilitators have been removed from them and put back into classes appropriate to their abilities. Shane's simple experiment, which tested only one subject, saved a young girl and her family. It also led to a clearer understanding of a once promising method for reaching autistic children.

Shane's experiment is a dramatic example of the need in psychology for *single-case* or *n = 1 designs*. These designs were developed so that psychologists could study the conditions affecting behavior experimentally with single subjects. The research designs we have focused on previously in this book (e.g., Galton's correlational studies and Fisher's factorial designs) require many subjects, to permit random assignment of subjects to conditions and/or to compute the necessary correlations. Of course, these methods cannot be applied to single cases. So researchers using single-case designs have had to devise different techniques for dealing with uncontrolled variables. In this chapter, we discuss the logic and variety of these experimental designs.

THE O X O SINGLE-CASE DESIGN

Previous chapters of this book have pointed to two advances in methods that have had a dramatic impact on how psychologists conduct research. They are Fisher's invention of randomized experimental designs (see Chapters 6 and 8) and the development of statistical controls (see Chapters 5 and 8). So popular are these methods that, if you were to pick up a major psychology research journal and browse through the articles in it, you would discover that randomized groups, statistical controls, or both, would be used in the great majority of them.

If you were to look through a major journal in the physical sciences, however, you would not find these methods to be anywhere near as popular as they are in psychology. In fact, undergraduate curricula in physics and chemistry usually don't even consider these methods. The reason is that courses in the statistical aspects of experimental design are unnecessary in these fields. In physics and chemistry, the basic experiments simply follow Mill's experimental method exactly; everything is controlled except for one condition that is varied.

Consider a simple experiment in chemistry. Suppose a chemist wants to test the hypothesis that if a drop of Chemical A is added to a beaker of Chemical B there will be a reaction that releases heat. The experiment would be straightforward: first measure the temperature of the chemicals to make sure that both are at room temperature, then add the drop of Chemical A to B, and finally measure the temperature of the mixture again. A sudden increase in temperature would confirm the hypothesis.

The results of this experiment would be convincing because: the time of the mixing is determined by the experimenter; external conditions are well controlled; the treatment takes only a moment to complete; the expected result occurs immediately after the chemicals are mixed; and the result is dramatic—there is an unmistakable rise in temperature. The procedure could be replicated over and over with the same result.

This type of study can be diagrammed as:

O X O

where O stands for an observation and X stands for a treatment (Campbell & Stanley, 1963). The "subjects" in this experiment are objects or chemicals. The experiment involves repeated measures; the same "subject," in this case Chemical B, is measured twice, once before the treatment (a pretest) and again after the treatment, adding Chemical A (a posttest). This would be called a single-case design in psychology, since one "subject" rather than a group of subjects is observed.

The pioneers of psychological research patterned their experiments after this popular design in the physical sciences. Franklin's evaluation of Mesmer's magnetic cure (see Chapter 1) used the O X O single-case design. A patient was observed, given a fake magnetic treatment, and tested once again. Hermann Ebbinghaus (1895/1913) did his experiments on memory using a repeated measures design with himself as the only subject. He studied how variations in lists of nonsense syllables that he memorized affected his subsequent recall of them. Ivan Pavlov (1928), in his classical conditioning experiments, first observed that a dog did not salivate at the sound of a bell, then he exposed the dog to many pairings of the bell with food, and finally he retested the dog to see whether it now salivated to the sound. John Watson, the behaviorist (1928/1972), used this design to demonstrate how a phobia could be created in a young child.

The O X O single-case design lost favor in psychology once it became apparent that it was inadequate for studying many problems of interest to psychologists. This design has problems, for example, when the treatment, X, is not one that produces immediate and dramatic effects, a common occurrence in psychological research. In evaluating an educational program, like Head Start, for example, the treatment, early education for children, would take months or years to administer, the effects would not be apparent immediately, and the effects would not be dramatic for every child—some would benefit, others would not. Also, when a long time intervenes between the Os in the design, the threats of history (external events that affect the posttest measure) and maturation (changes in the subject over the course of the study) are problematic.

Psychologists have adopted the control group design with random assignment of subjects to conditions to control for these threats. This two-group design can be diagrammed as follows:

Experimental group: R O X O

Control group: R O   O

where R indicates that subjects are randomly assigned to the groups, X, the treatment, is given only to the experimental group, and the control group receives no treatment. As we have discussed in previous chapters, this randomized design is considered by many psychologists to be the ideal method for psychological research.

However, some experimental psychologists do not use this control group design at all in their research. Instead, they argue that for the research problems of interest to them the single-case O X O design and similar designs are preferable to the randomized control group design. The views of these psychologists are a legacy of the pioneering advances in single-case methodology that B. F. Skinner made starting in the 1930s.

Skinner used the O X O single-case design, with important modifications, in his experiments on animal learning. His treatments involved giving a subject, usually a pigeon or rat, a reinforcer, food, for performing a particular type of response. The reinforcement produced immediate and dramatic effects, comparable to those found in experiments in physics and chemistry.

Skinner's success with the method inspired others to adopt his operant conditioning procedures and his experimental methods. During the 1950s and 1960s, researchers showed the effectiveness of behavioral techniques for treating phobias, autism, obsessive compulsive disorders, enuresis, addictions, anorexia and obesity, using a modified single-case O X O design. In 1960, Murray Sidman published *Tactics of Scientific Research*, which became the bible of single-case research design. Nothing succeeds like success, and the single-case design was reestablished as a viable method in psychology.

Psychologists who advocate the use of single-case experimental designs in psychology do not see them as a replacement for the randomized groups design. Instead, they consider the single-case experiment to be a superior method for certain applications and the only possible one for others. Before discussing modern developments in single-case designs, we will look at some of the problems with randomized control group designs that have led to the renewal of interest among psychologists in single-case designs.

LIMITATIONS OF RANDOMIZED CONTROL GROUP DESIGNS

Getting Enough Subjects

Randomized control group designs require many subjects in each group. We learned in Chapter 6, for example, that an experiment must have about 60 subjects in each of two groups for the recommended power of 80% to detect a moderate-sized effect. It is sometimes difficult to gather such large samples. For example, to collect enough subjects for a study of depression with three treatment groups and one control group, researchers had to recruit participants from several different hospitals and clinics in three separate cities (Elkin et al., 1989). And depression is often called the "common cold" of psychological disorders. If the research focuses on rare conditions, like dissociative disorders or pica (compulsive eating of nonnutritive substances), finding enough subjects for a randomized design may be impossible.

Single-case research designs are naturally suited to the study of rare phenomena. In addition, they have proven popular among clinical psychologists who are interested in assessing the effectiveness of treatments for particular clients rather than in conducting large-scale studies involving many people.

Misleading Summary Statistics

Between-subjects designs typically use the mean and standard deviation as summary statistics to describe the experimental results. Individual scores of subjects usually are not reported. In fact, the *Publication Manual of the American*

TABLE 1 CHANGE SCORES ON THE
HAMILTON DEPRESSION SCALE FOR
INDIVIDUAL SUBJECTS DIAGNOSED WITH
SAD: PRE- MINUS POSTTHERAPY DEPRESSION
SCORES[1] (FROM ROSENTHAL ET AL., 1985)

Bright Light		Dim Light	
S1	−1	S8	−5
S2	7	S9	−3
S3	8	S10	3.5
S4	13	S11	4.5
S5	14	S12	5
S6	14.5	S13	6
S7	18.5	S14	9
		S15	9.5
		S16	25
Mean = 10.6		Mean = 6.1	

[1]Patients classified as atypical depression were not
included in this table.

Psychological Association recommends against reporting individual scores in research using group designs (1994, p. 15). Unfortunately, summary statistics
may not accurately reflect what happens to some subjects in a study, giving a
misleading picture of the effects of the experimental treatments.

To illustrate, let's look at an experiment on the effects of light therapy for
patients suffering from seasonal affective disorder (SAD), a winter depression
thought to be caused by reduced light during the winter months. Rosenthal et
al. (1985) tested the effectiveness of daily exposure to bright, full-spectrum artificial light in reducing the symptoms of patients with this disorder. The subjects, all diagnosed with SAD, were randomly assigned either to bright light
therapy or to a placebo treatment, dim light. Ratings were made on the severity of their symptoms before and after a week of treatment.

Table 1 shows the change scores for individual subjects on the measure of
depression from pretherapy to posttherapy. Positive numbers indicate an improvement in symptoms over the one-week experimental period. The mean
change scores show that, overall, bright light resulted in a greater reduction in
depression ($M = 10.6$) than dim light ($M = 6.1$). However, inspection of the results for individual subjects reveals considerable variation in the effectiveness
of the treatment.

The change scores of subjects 2 through 6, who received the bright light,
were close to the mean of 10.6 (7 to 14.5). For these subjects, the mean accurately reflects the effect of the treatment. But the results for S1 and S7 were
exceptions; S1 got slightly worse during the therapy and S7 improved a remarkable 18.5 points. The mean change of 6.1 for the placebo group accurately reflects only the effect of the treatment for S10 through S15, not for

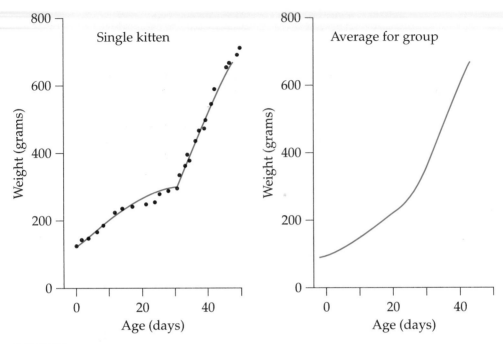

FIGURE 1
Growth curves for a single kitten and the average for a group of kittens. (From Bateson &
Young, 1981.)

the other three subjects; S8 and S9 got worse under the dim light, but S16
improved by 25 points, the largest improvement in the entire study. S14 and
S15, who also received dim light, improved to an extent close to the mean
improvement of the subjects who got the bright light. If only the summary
statistics had been presented, these exceptions would not have been noted
and an incomplete understanding of the effect of the therapy would have
resulted.

In addition to burying the results for exceptional subjects, summary statistics can mask patterns that occur in all subjects. The data from Bateson and
Young's research on the growth of cats (1981, cited by Martin & Bateson, 1993)
is a good example. Figure 1 plots weight as a function of age for one kitten in
their study and for the combined data of several kittens. As you can see, the
kitten whose weight is plotted in the individual record shows abrupt growth
at about 30 days. This same rapid weight gain occurs in all kittens, but at different times. Because of the different timing of this increase, the growth curve
for a group of kittens fails to reflect the abrupt change in weight that takes
place in all kittens. Combining the data leads to the misleading conclusion that
growth in kittens is smooth and uniform.

Single-case research avoids the problems of summary statistics by not
using them. The results for each subject are reported separately, so it is always
clear how the results apply to individual subjects.

Relevance

The randomized control group design is not suitable for certain research problems, such as testing the validity of facilitated communication for a particular child. Single-case designs are appropriate when the research focuses on the study of unusual problems (e.g., a rare disease), or unusual skills (e.g., photographic memory), or in certain invasive medical procedures (such as mapping the brain by stimulating various locations prior to surgery). Single-case designs also are widely applied in diagnostic work when the researcher is interested in determining the cause of a particular patient's disorder. An allergist, for example, might conduct a series of O X O experiments to determine the substances to which a patient is allergic.

SKINNER'S BASIC EXPERIMENTAL DESIGN

The necessity of single-case research was impressed upon B. F. Skinner early in his career. In the 1940s, Skinner was involved in a project that required him, like the circus trainer in the quote at the start of this chapter, to be "responsible for making absolutely sure that a given organism will engage in a given sort of behavior at a given time." The project was not for a circus act, though. Skinner had obtained grants from General Mills and the U.S. Department of Defense to finance the training of pigeons for military combat in World War II! The quote at the beginning of this chapter was inspired by this project. Skinner's plan was to have individual pigeons placed in the nose cone of missiles to guide them by pecking at a display showing the target. Whether the animals were accurate in performing this task was a life-or-death matter.

The standard control group research design was as useless to Skinner as it would be to the circus animal trainer. Skinner wasn't interested in demonstrating that pigeons trained according to a particular theory of learning would peck more accurately than untrained pigeons at an alpha level of .05. He had to find a method that would guarantee that each pigeon would perform accurately and consistently—and not under controlled conditions in the lab, but through all sorts of distractions, including heavy antiaircraft fire.

Skinner developed the basis for such a method while he was a graduate student in psychology at Harvard University. Skinner had entered graduate school without having taken a single psychology course. He had been an English major as an undergraduate, and apparently a good one. After reading some of his short stories, the famous poet Robert Frost suggested that he try writing as a career. Skinner spent a disappointing year after graduation trying before giving up this plan and entering Harvard. Except for some study of physiology, Skinner's background in psychology before graduate school was limited to reading Pavlov's work on conditioned reflexes and Watson's writings on behaviorism. Because he was untrained in the standard research methods of the field, Skinner developed his own, fashioned after the single-case methods of these pioneers.

Pigeons in Skinner's lab learning to cooperate. The pigeons are reinforced if they simultaneously peck matching buttons.

In his 1956 essay entitled "A Case History in Scientific Method," Skinner described the steps and lucky breaks that led to his invention of the method of operant conditioning. As a graduate student, Skinner wanted to develop a method for studying the effects of environmental manipulations empirically, by trial and error, without having to advance fancy principles or hypotheses. He decided to first establish the behavior of interest, then expose the subject to a particular treatment, then look again at the behavior. Instead of randomly assigning subjects to groups to deal with uncontrolled variables, Skinner adopted Pavlov's strategy of controlling for sources of variability before measurement by carefully controlling the animal's environment. (Recall Pavlov's "tower of silence" from Chapter 3.) With such control, Skinner reasoned, the effects of changing aspects of the environment should be immediately apparent. Statistical analyses of the data would be unnecessary.

Skinner built an ingenious apparatus for his experiments and developed a unique method for recording the animal's behavior. As you are probably aware, this apparatus is the "Skinner box," a special cage equipped with a bar or lever that the animal presses to get a pellet of food. The experimenter can program the box's food magazine according to a preset "schedule of reinforcement." The animal might be given a pellet for each bar press, for example, or for every 50 presses, or once every 5 minutes.

Skinner used a kymograph, an instrument that records the rate of response as a line on a strip of paper, to visually display the rate of bar pressing of individual subjects in the Skinner box. In kymograph recordings, called *cumulative records,* each response of the animal moves the stylus up, so that the slope of the line is proportional to the rate of the animal's responding—the steeper the slope, the greater the frequency of bar pressing.

The format for Skinner's experiments, which tested the effects of different treatments (e.g., schedules of reinforcement) on bar pressing, is as follows: Prior to the experiment, a food-deprived animal is conditioned to associate the

B. F. Skinner with a rat in a Skinner box. The kymograph is shown at the bottom right.

click of the food magazine with food. Then the animal is placed in the apparatus and the experiment begins. A *baseline phase*, during which bar pressing is not reinforced, comes first. Its purpose is to determine the animal's response rate prior to the treatment. Next, during the *treatment phase*, which follows the baseline, bar pressing is reinforced, either continuously or intermittently. In the third phase, *extinction*, reinforcement is discontinued, baseline conditions are reestablished, and bar pressing no longer operates the food magazine. Finally, in the last phase, the reinforcement is reintroduced.

This study can be diagrammed as:

$$\text{O} \qquad \text{X O} \qquad \bar{\text{X}}\text{O} \qquad \text{X O}$$

| Baseline | Treatment | Extinction | Treatment |

2nd Baseline

where O stands for continuous observation of the subject's behavior for a period of time; X is the start of the treatment; and $\bar{\text{X}}$ (read "not X") represents the start of extinction, when the treatment is withdrawn and baseline conditions are reinstated. An alternative system of notation that is used in the literature on single-case experiments labels the baseline phases "A" and the experimental phases "B" (see Barlow & Hersen, 1984). The design is known as an *ABAB design*, or a *reversal* or *withdrawal design*.

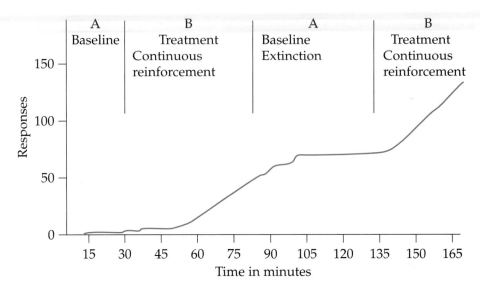

FIGURE 2
Cumulative record for an ABAB design

Figure 2 shows a cumulative record for an ABAB design. During the initial baseline the food-deprived subject presses the bar only a few times, as reflected in the flat cumulative record. In the first treatment phase, the slope of the cumulative record accelerates rapidly, indicating a steady high rate of bar pressing for this subject. The slope of the graph decelerates during extinction as the rate of bar pressing decreases. Finally, when the treatment is reintroduced, a high rate of bar pressing is quickly reestablished.

The results for this ABAB study demonstrate that the behavior of this subject is under the control of the experimenter. The rate of bar pressing is changed by giving or withholding reinforcement. Because everything other than the reinforcement is held constant throughout the experiment, there are no competing hypotheses to explain the pattern of the animal's behavior. Summary statistics and statistical tests are not needed, since the pattern of results is clear from visually inspecting the cumulative record.

Skinner's single-case design modified the O X O design used in chemistry in two ways. First, instead of a single pretest and posttest observation, Skinner used *continuous observations* of the subject before and during the treatment. Continuous observations are not needed in chemistry because variations in external conditions, which are the only concern of the experimenter, can be controlled very well. But when the subjects are living creatures, changes in behavior occur spontaneously, without any apparent external causes. Continuous observations in the baseline phase enable the researcher to record the variability of the subject's behavior that is due just to uncontrolled external and internal events.

In addition, Skinner built replication into his design; once applied, the treatment is removed, then reintroduced later. In Skinner's research, the effect of the treatment extinguishes when reinforcement is discontinued, so it is possible for the experimenter to replicate the original experiment.

Skinner's modifications greatly improved the internal validity of the O X O design for research in psychology. The continuous observations in the baseline phase provide a check for the threats of history and maturation, since the effects of uncontrolled external events or changes in the subject would show up in the baseline record. The replication guards against any external event coincident with the treatment being confounded with the treatment. It is implausible that such coincidental events would occur repeatedly in the same experiment at the precise times that the experimenter introduces the treatments.

In addition to replicating the experiment for each subject, Skinner also replicated between subjects. To show that the treatment could be generalized to other subjects, as a rule Skinner would replicate the ABAB study for three more subjects. If the results were consistent for all four subjects, Skinner believed there was sufficient evidence to establish the generality of the effects of the treatment for the type of animal studied.

REPLICATION IN MODERN SINGLE-CASE DESIGNS

Skinner's ABAB design illustrates the distinctive features of many modern single-case experiments:

- The behavior of one subject is continuously observed for a period of time across different experimental conditions that are introduced by the experimenter.
- The subject's behavior during the treatment phase is contrasted with the same behavior during a baseline or no-treatment phase.
- The experiment is replicated within a single subject, for example, the AB sequence is repeated in the ABAB design.
- A graph showing all the observations made on each subject during each phase of the study is presented.
- The results can be analyzed with or without a statistical analysis.
- The experiment is replicated for additional subjects.

Earlier we noted that the internal validity of the single-case design is strengthened by replicating the treatment for a given subject. As the following discussion of modern variants of the single-case design illustrates, it is possible to replicate either sequentially or simultaneously:

1. In *sequential replication designs*, different experimental conditions are presented one at a time in sequence. The ABAB design is an example.

2. In *simultaneous replication designs*, several variations of the experiment are conducted at the same time on a single subject.

Sequential Replication Designs

1. ABAB Designs. Several variations of the ABAB design have been developed since Skinner did his original experiments. Modern experimenters sometimes elect to use partial replication rather than the complete replication that was Skinner's trademark. This can be done by dropping the first baseline, to give the *BAB design*, or by not reintroducing the treatment in the *ABA design*. Or two or more experimental conditions can be studied in sequence. For example, the *ABABCBC design* might be used to assess the effect of an experimental drug: *A* would be the baseline (no drug); *B*, the placebo drug (included to control for suggestion); and *C*, the active drug. This design actually combines two experiments in sequence: the ABAB design, to test the placebo effect, and the BCBC design, to test the active drug against the placebo. Other designs of this general type can be created by using different numbers of treatments in varying orders (Barlow & Hersen, 1984).

In one variation of the sequential replication design, a single treatment is applied in varying degrees during the course of the experiment. A popular application of this *changing criterion design* is in evaluating the treatment for addictions, like smoking or drinking caffeine. In this application, the experimenter establishes a contract with the patient governing, say, the number of cups of coffee the patient can consume on any given day. The goal, or behavioral criterion, changes during the study. If the patient normally drinks 15 cups/day, the criterion for the first period might be 12 cups/day, then 10 cups/day for the second period, and so on, until the final goal is reached. The experiment would be diagrammed as

$$O\ X_{12}\ O\ X_{10}\ O\ X_8\ O\ X_6\ O\ X_4\ O\ X_2\ O\ X_0$$

where X_8 indicates a criterion of 8 cups of coffee per day.

During the study, if the patient meets the criterion, by drinking the specified number of cups of coffee or less, a reward is given; otherwise there is a penalty. The treatment's effectiveness is demonstrated if the patient's behavior changes to match the criterion.

2. Alternating Treatment Designs (ATDs). The *alternating treatments design (ATD)*, also called the *multi-element design*, differs by degree from the ABAB design. In both designs, the subject is exposed to a series of conditions, one after the other. Skinner's ABAB design had two experimental conditions, each presented twice in a fixed order, with many observations in each condition. In the ATD, more changes are made in the conditions and fewer observations are taken in each phase of the experiment. Shane's experiment on facilitated communication, in which he showed the child and the facilitator the same or different pictures, is an example of an ATD. In place of the fixed order of the ABBA design, the conditions in the ATD may be presented in a randomized order. For example, an ATD might have three conditions, each presented 30 times, in random order, with one observation in each condition.

Using the O X system of notation, an ATD alternating randomly between three treatments (X,Y, and Z) could be diagrammed as:

O Y O X O Z   O Z O X O Y   O Z O Y O X, . . . ,O Y O Z O X
   Block 1   Block 2   Block 3   Block *n*

The randomization here is within blocks; all three treatments are presented in a random order, then all three are presented again in a random order, and so on. Such *block randomization* guarantees that no one treatment is presented too many times in a row or left out for an extended period of time.

The ATD has two major advantages over the ABAB design. First, it usually involves many more replications of the basic AB experiment, providing an opportunity to demonstrate over and over that the subject's behavior can be controlled by the experimenter's choice of experimental conditions. Second, the order of the treatments can be randomized. This is an advantage because randomization helps to control for order effects among the treatments.

The following example illustrates one of the many applications of the ATD and demonstrates how the design can be modified to investigate different problems. In it, the ATD was used to demonstrate that goldfish can be taught to make a difficult temporal discrimination using operant conditioning techniques.

Illustration of the ATD Design: Temporal Discrimination in Goldfish

In fixed-interval schedules of reinforcement, particular behaviors are reinforced after a specific time interval, for example, every 10 minutes, every hour, or even every 12 hours. Mammals can coordinate their behavior accurately to long intervals of time and can be taught to start bar pressing close to the start of the reinforcement period, even when there are no external cues for the animals to use to time the interval. These findings suggest the presence in mammals of a "biological clock," a cyclical physiological process that the animals use as a stimulus for marking the passage of time.

Gee, Stephenson, and Wright (1994) studied whether goldfish are able to learn the kind of long-interval temporal discrimination that mammals can. Demonstrating that fish can make such discriminations would be of practical, as well as theoretical, interest. In a technique used in commercial fishing, called "recall ranching," fish are raised in open waters but conditioned using sound to stay in a particular location for feeding. Then, when they are large enough, the fish are harvested. If fish can learn long-interval temporal discriminations, such temporal conditioning might be substituted for auditory conditioning, saving the cost of expensive sound-generating equipment.

The subjects in the Gee et al. experiment, 8 goldfish (*Carassius auratus*), were individually housed in controlled aquariums and exposed to an artificial light cycle of 12 hours of bright light (8 a.m. to 8 p.m.) and 12 hours of dim light (8 p.m. to 8 a.m.). Each tank was equipped with a fish-activated lever that could be programmed to release food when pressed.

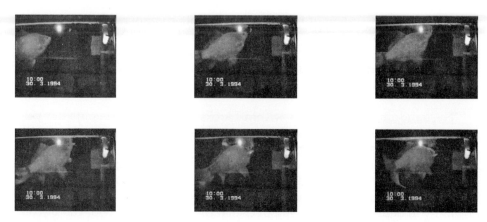

One of the goldfish from the Gee et al. experiment approaching and pressing the lever to release food.

The experimental plan was eventually to feed the fish, by means of the lever, for only 1 hour a day starting at 2 p.m. There was no cue to this feeding time except the temporal one. If the fish could learn the temporal discrimination, it was expected that they would start pushing the lever in the minutes preceding 2 p.m. in anticipation of feeding. The study was conducted in five phases (see Figure 3):

Baseline: During the first phase, a fish was put on continuous reinforced feeding (CRF); food was released every time the fish pressed the lever. The baseline continued for 14 days, to observe the fish's natural feeding rhythms.

Shaping: During the second phase, continuous reinforcement was discontinued by gradually restricting the time intervals during which lever pressing was reinforced. On the first day, starting at 2 p.m., the feeding interval lasted 12 hours; it was reduced to 10 hours on the second day. Then, on each succeeding day, it was reduced by 2 more hours, so long as the fish had eaten on the previous day, until the final feeding time was down to 1 hour, still beginning at 2 p.m..

Restricted Feeding: The-1-hour-per-day feeding interval, beginning at 2 p.m., was continued for 4 weeks.

Extinction: During the 6-day extinction period, lever pressing no longer resulted in reinforcement. The fish was not fed for 6 days.

Baseline: Following extinction, the baseline condition of continuous reinforcement (CRF) was reestablished.

The observations in the study alternated between two time periods, from 1:30 p.m. to 2 p.m., a 30-minute period prior to the 1-hour-per-day restricted feeding time; and from 1:30 a.m. to 2 a.m., a 30-minute period selected as a control condition. The feeding and control conditions are the two treatments in this alternating treatment design. The total number of lever presses made by the fish was recorded during each of these periods, throughout the course of

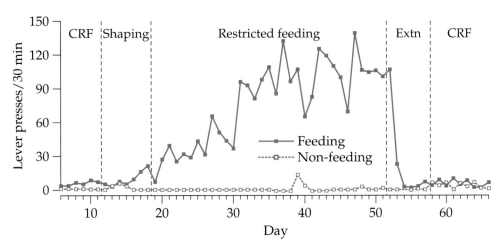

FIGURE 3
Goldfish lever presses during the 30-minute period before feeding and during a 30-minute control period before no feeding. (From Gee et al., 1994.)

the study. Order effects were not an issue because the control condition involved only passive observation of the subject.

The results of the experiment for one fish are shown in Figure 3. Notice that, in contrast to Skinner's cumulative record, this graph charts the number of lever presses made by the fish in two separate 30-minute time intervals over the 60 days of the experiment. The blue squares show the rate of lever pressing in the 30 minutes prior to the 1-hour feeding period; the open squares show the rate of lever pressing for the 30-minute no-feeding control period.

The baseline responding for this fish was low for both time periods. During shaping and the restricted feeding phases, the lever pressing prior to the 2 p.m. feeding time increased, with no change in the rate of response in the control condition. Lever pressing dropped back to the baseline level during extinction, remaining low in the terminal baseline phase. The results provide clear evidence that this fish acquired the temporal discrimination and the results replicated with other fish. One fish died during the experiment, but the six remaining fish behaved similarly to this one.

Simultaneous Replication Designs

ABAB and alternating-treatment sequential replication designs require the experimenter to withdraw a treatment or switch between treatments. Although this does not present an ethical dilemma in many cases, in some it does. If the subject's disorder is serious or long-standing, it may be inadvisable to withdraw an effective treatment or switch to a new one, to make the experiment internally valid.

Another problem with sequential replication designs is that they are practical only when there are minimal carryover effects of the treatment (see Chapter 6 for a discussion of carryover effects). Carryover effects often are not a problem. In Shane's experiment on facilitated communication, for example, the "treatments" only involved presenting pictures to the subject and her facilitator. Because neither the child nor the facilitator was given feedback on the outcome of each trial, the result for one trial couldn't have affected the result for the next trial. But the possibility of carryover effects rules out the use of this design for some problems. When students are taught new skills, like mathematics, writing, or a foreign language, for example, the learning endures beyond the end of the teaching period, making an ABAB design or ATD inappropriate for such cases.

Simultaneous replication designs avoid both the ethical problem of switching between treatments and the problem of carryover effects. In this type of design, two or more O X O subexperiments are carried out at the same time on the same subject. A study with three subexperiments would be diagrammed as:

Subexperiment 1: O X O O O O O O O O

Subexperiment 2: O O O O Y O O O O O

Subexperiment 3: O O O O O O O Z O O

where X, Y, and Z denote the beginnings of different treatments.

The subexperiments all are designed to test the same type of treatment, but they differ either (1) in the behaviors being treated or (2) in the settings in which the treatment is applied. A child might be given a behavioral treatment to reduce three different inappropriate classroom behaviors, like talking to other students, walking around the room, and not attending to work, for example, or the child might be treated for the same problem behavior, say, walking around the room, in three different classrooms.

This type of design is called a *multiple baseline design* because the design has two or more distinct baselines, one for each subexperiment. The study begins by making observations on all the baselines. After recording the behaviors for a period of time, a treatment then is started for one subexperiment. Then, after a second interval of time, another treatment is begun, and so on, until all the treatments have been introduced. A treatment, once started, continues throughout the study.

Each subexperiment is a replication, a separate test of the effectiveness of the treatment. The treatments begin at different times to guard against confounding by an external event. If the behavior in each separate experiment responds to the treatment, the evidence of its effectiveness is clear. The continuous observation of multiple behaviors or of the same behaviors in different contexts also provides a check on maturation.

The following experiment used the multiple baseline design in one of the first experiments to show the successful application of behavioral techniques to reduce depressive behavior in a child.

Illustration of the Multiple Baseline Design: Behavioral Treatment of Depressive Behaviors

A 10-year-old boy, Dale, who was diagnosed as having a major depressive disorder, had been admitted to a children's psychiatric intensive care unit because of the seriousness of his symptoms. In addition to other symptoms of depression, Dale was uncommunicative in interpersonal situations. Frame, Matson, Sonis, Fialkov, & Kazdin (1982) used a multiple baseline design to test the effectiveness of a behavioral approach to reducing his depressive behaviors.

The behaviors that were selected for reduction were classified into four types:

1. Inappropriate body position (e.g., turning away from the interviewer, covering his face with his hands, bending backward or forward inappropriately).

2. Lack of eye contact (e.g., not looking the interviewer in the eye while talking).

3. Poor speech quality (e.g., speaking too softly or in a garbled fashion, answering questions with one or two words, waiting more than 3 seconds before answering).

4. Bland affect (e.g., lack of emotional tone in voice, lack of hand gestures while speaking).

The frequency of each of these target behaviors was assessed at the beginning of the experiment by having Dale role-play situations that were likely to come up in his home or in the hospital, for example, helping another child to get food in the cafeteria. Each day Dale was asked to role-play 12 different situations. During these role-plays, each of the four target behaviors was rated as present or absent. Dale was assigned 0 to 12 points for each behavior daily, depending on his performance in the role-plays. The higher the score, the more evidence there was of depressed behavior and the less the evidence of the treatment's effectiveness.

A behavioral skills training program, involving instruction, role-playing, modeling, and performance feedback, was developed to reduce these four target behaviors. The design of the experiment is shown in Figure 4. The study lasted for 28 days, with a one-day follow-up 12 weeks after the end of the study. Baselines were recorded for each behavior for the first 8 days. Then, on day 9, the treatment sessions for body position and eye contact were started; on day 14, the treatment for speech quality began; and, finally, on day 20, the experimenters began treating bland affect. Once started, a treatment continued until the 28th day of the study.

Figure 4 shows the frequency of the target behaviors in each phase of the experiment. The results reveal a marked reduction in each of the target behaviors after the treatment for it began and no improvement before that. Bland affect, for example, did not improve when the treatments for eye contact and

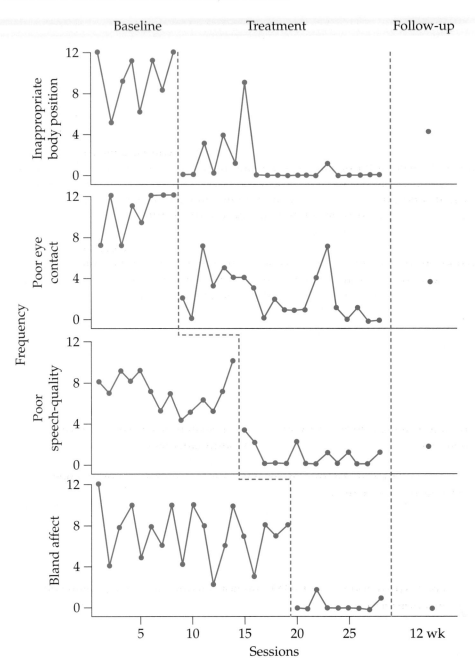

FIGURE 4
Behavioral record for depressed boy during a multiple baseline study. (From Frame et al., 1982.)

speech quality were started but did reduce after its direct treatment began. Finally, the treatment effects lasted well beyond the end of the experiment, as indicated by the observations made at the 12-week follow-up.

PRINCIPLES OF DESIGN AND ANALYSIS

In single-case research, the experimenter has to make choices like those made by researchers using between-subjects designs: The single-case researcher must (1) select a particular experimental design; (2) decide on the size of the study, that is, the number of observations per subject, the number of experimental conditions; (3) determine how to maximize internal and external validity; and (4) make decisions on how to analyze the results.

Statistical procedures have been developed for dealing with some of these design and analysis issues in between-subjects designs: Designs can be compared on their relative power to detect treatment effects; the number of subjects needed to ensure a desired level of power can be calculated; and data analysis can be done using descriptive and inferential statistics. But statistical procedures for single-case studies have not been developed to the same extent as they have for between-subjects designs. So in single-case studies, design and analysis decisions must be based on established practice and rules of thumb rather than on formal principles.

Choice of Design

The main design decision in single-case research is whether to replicate sequentially (ABAB designs and ATDs) or simultaneously (multiple baseline designs). The experimenter's choice will depend on the specific treatments being studied. ABAB or alternating treatment designs are practical only when carry-over effects are minimal. Ethical concerns also may rule out withdrawal or alternating treatment designs or even the baseline phase of designs. Patients should be given the best known treatment or experimental treatments that promise even better results. Patients with serious problems cannot be switched to placebos, or inferior treatments, or observed for any length of time without treatment (as in the baseline).

When ABAB designs and ATDs are not possible, multiple baseline designs may be appropriate. But these designs are more complicated to conduct than ABAB studies because they involve multiple measures. They also have a potential limitation: If in a design with, say, three baselines, O1, O2, and O3, behaviors O2 and O3 should change after the treatment for O1, then the different experiments would not yield independent evidence of the effectiveness of the treatment. Such a study would have questionable internal validity because the threat of history could not be ruled out. Only experience with the specific behaviors and treatments to be studied will help researchers to decide when this might be a problem.

The Size of the Study

Of course, the number of subjects in a single-case design is not an issue, but the number of observations per phase, the length of the phases, and the number of phases are. Although no formal procedures for making these decisions have been established, the following guidelines have been suggested.

The baseline should have a sufficient number of observations to give a good measure of error. The number of observations needed will depend on the stability of the behavior being observed. If the behavior varies only slightly across several observations, relatively few observations will suffice. When there is considerable variability in the behavior, more observations will be needed. Instead of proceeding in such cases, the experimenter may want to consider canceling the study, trying to figure out the source of the variability, and continuing once the behavior is stabilized. If the baseline shows a pattern or systematic trend, like a steady increase or decrease, or if it has a cyclical form, the experimenter should try to identify the reasons for this pattern before using the baseline to evaluate the treatment.

After the experimenter has established a length for the baseline, the other phases of the study should be matched for duration and for the number of observations collected. Matching the phases for length improves the study by providing a common time interval for the influence of any uncontrolled variables that may affect behavior in the different phases, for example, fatigue, maturation, or daily or weekly cycles. An exception to this guideline would be experiments assessing the effectiveness of treatments for problem behaviors; in such research, the length of time that successful treatments are withdrawn should be minimized for ethical reasons.

The number of phases in a study will depend on the number of treatments being evaluated and the number of replications desired for each subject. A general rule, based on Mill's method of difference (see Chapter 3), would be to vary only one aspect of the treatment from phase to phase of the experiment. According to Mill, only one antecedent should be varied, while all others are held constant. Consistent with this guideline, the more treatments are being evaluated, the more phases will be needed.

There are no guidelines for deciding on the number of replications in sequential replication designs. Withdrawal studies can involve as few as one replication, as in the standard ABAB study. ATDs, like the design in the goldfish study, use numerous replications of the AB pattern.

For multiple baseline designs, single-case methodologists recommend four separate baselines. If the behavior responds selectively and consistently to four separate treatments, they consider the evidence good that the treatment worked for that subject.

Handling Threats to Internal and External Validity

Single-case designs are vulnerable to the threats to internal validity of history, maturation, instrumentation, and testing (see Chapter 3). Campbell and Stanley (1963) consider the major threat to the O X O design, the building block of all the single-case designs, to be history. As you recall, the threat of history is that external events that occur coincidentally with the application of the treatment are the real causes of changes in the subject's behavior.

In laboratory research, the threat of history can be controlled by isolation. Pavlov, as we noted before, did his research in a "tower of silence" that was isolated from interference by thick sod walls and a moat! In field research, where isolating subjects is not possible, the effects of history can be assessed by replication, using either an ABAB type design or a multiple baseline design. When the effect of the treatment is demonstrated many times with the same subject, the likelihood that a correlated external event produced the effects is negligible. Replication makes the single-case design a powerful procedure.

There is one threat that cannot be controlled by replication, however. This threat is associated with the fact that human participants in such experiments are aware that they are being tested. In single-case research, the same person is observed in all conditions of the experiment and may know when different phases begin. As a result, the confounding effects of suggestion are especially likely in such studies (see Chapter 12, Planning the Study).

External validity is a more serious problem than internal validity for single-case research. It is this limitation that leads advocates of single-case research to emphasize the importance of replicating findings. As we have seen, replications often are included in the original studies. (The goldfish study, for example, replicated its results with six additional subjects.) But the problem of generalizing results is not restricted to single-case studies. Even when a study is done with, say, 60 subjects, we still do not know if its results would generalize to subjects other than those tested in the research.

For this reason, establishing the generality of findings necessarily proceeds in a hit-or-miss fashion in experimental research. When one investigator publishes a study, others attempt to replicate and extend it. If studies conducted with very different subjects yield a consistent finding, the result is considered to be general. *Meta-analysis* is a recently developed formal method for making sense of the results collected in multiple studies on a particular problem (see Rosenthal, 1984).

Data Analysis

Comparisons between different phases of a single-case experiment often are done by "visual" analysis. The experimenter inspects the graph of the results; if the data show unequivocal results, like most of the experiments discussed in this chapter, the conclusion is straightforward. However, borderline results, that is, results from which different researchers might draw different conclusions, are inevitable.

Researchers disagree on how to proceed when faced with such results. Some experts believe that in such cases the study should be rethought and redone with better controls or a revised treatment. Others think that appropriate statistical analyses are needed to reach an objective conclusion and that such statistics should be used as routinely in single-case experiments as they are in between-subjects research.

If the history of the development of statistics for between-subjects designs is any guide, in the future we can expect to see new statistical methods and more frequent applications of existing statistical methods for single-case designs. But not all researchers would welcome these methods. Some researchers think that an overemphasis on statistics actually would slow the progress of psychology as a science by shifting the focus away from observed behavior and onto mathematical models. Most likely, in the years to come, we will see advances in both statistical and nonstatistical approaches.

KEY TERMS

Facilitated communication	Sequential replication design
Single-case (n = 1) experiments	Simultaneous replication design
O X O design	ABABCBC design
Control group design, with random assignment of subjects	Changing criterion design
	Behavioral criterion
Skinner box	ATD
Kymograph	Block randomization
Cumulative record	Multiple baseline design
Baseline vs. treatment phase	Meta-analysis
ABAB design	

KEY PEOPLE

Howard Shane	John Watson
Donald T. Campbell and Julian C. Stanley	B. F. Skinner
	Murray Sidman
Hermann Ebbinghaus	Philip Gee et al.
Ivan Pavlov	C. Frame et al.

REVIEW QUESTIONS

1. What characteristics of the simple chemistry experiment described in the text make its results so convincing?

2. Explain the notation system used by Campbell and Stanley to diagram experiments.

3. Describe the single-case experiments of Ebbinghaus and Pavlov.

4. What problems can be studied with the control group design that cannot be studied with the single-case O X O design?

5. Diagram a two group control group design with random assignment of subjects to groups.

6. What are the three major limitations of control group designs?

7. How can summary statistics mask patterns that occur in all subjects? Give an example.

8. In which of Skinner's projects was proof at the .05 level of significance irrelevant?

9. What was Skinner's background before studying psychology in graduate school?

10. Describe the three basic phases of a typical experiment Skinner would conduct?

11. What two basic modifications of the O X O design did Skinner introduce? What purposes did these modifications serve?

12. What are the distinctive features of a modern single-case experiment?

13. Describe the two types of replication in modern single-case experiments.

14. Describe how the ABABCBC design might be used to evaluate a new drug.

15. What are the two major advantages of the ATD design over the ABAB design?

16. Describe the ATD design that was used to demonstrate temporal discrimination in goldfish.

17. What problems of an ABAB or ATD design are avoided by using a multiple baseline design?

18. Describe the multiple baseline design that Frame et al. used to evaluate a behavioral treatment for depressive behaviors.

19. What is the main decision researchers must make in designing a single-case experiment?

20. What factors should researchers consider in deciding on the length of the baseline?

21. What is the major threat to the internal validity of a single-case experiment and how is it controlled in practice?

10

Field Research

---- ❖ ----

The person who must have certitude, who cannot embrace
conclusions tentatively, should not be engaged in social
scientific research.

NORVAL GLENN

---- ❖ ----

THE DESIGN OF FIELD EXPERIMENTS
   (QUASI-EXPERIMENTS)
      Pretest-Posttest One-Group Design: O X O
      Replicating the O X O Design with Different Measures
        and Subgroups
      Replicating the O X O Design with Repeated Measures,
        Time-Series Designs
      Nonequivalent Control Groups
NATURALISTIC OBSERVATION
      Deciding on Behavioral Units
      Reducing Observer Bias
          Controlling observer knowledge
          Separating fact from interpretation
          Sampling methods
      Observer Reliability
      Reducing Subject Reactivity
          Acclimation and concealment
          Unobtrusive measures
          Archival data
SURVEY RESEARCH
      Probability Sampling
      Measuring Error
      Modes of Administering the Survey
      The Wording of Questions
FINAL COMMENTS
KEY TERMS, KEY PEOPLE, REVIEW QUESTIONS

Laboratory experiments show that watching television has an immediate impact on behavior. In one experiment, for example, children who watched a film showing aggressive behavior engaged in more aggressive acts than children who had just seen a neutral control film (Bandura, Ross, & Ross, 1963). In another, children's preferences for sex-neutral toys were affected by seeing a film that presented the toys as appropriate only for a specific sex (Cobb, Stevens-Long, & Goldstein, 1982). But restrictions on the conditions to which people can be exposed and on the types of measures that can be made limit the usefulness of laboratory experiments for discovering how television affects people's lives.

We now know, for example, that television has changed how children spend their time. Before the 1950s, children grew up without television; today, they spend about the same amount of time watching television as they spend in school. On the average, children watch television 3 to 4 hours a day, 7 days a week (Eron, Gentry, & Schlegal, 1994). One major consequence of such extensive television viewing is the displacement of other activities. If people watch television for many hours each week, they can't do other things, like spending this time in community activities or sports. This type of displacement cannot be studied in laboratory experiments.

It also may be difficult to manipulate many variables of interest to psychologists, like children's television watching over extended periods of time, in the laboratory. In fact, it may be unethical to deliberately expose children to the kinds of intense and frequent violence found on network television shows.

Clearly, assessing the full impact of television on people's lives requires field research, that is, research done outside the laboratory in the subjects' day-to-day natural environment. Such research conducted over the last 40 years points to the conclusion that television viewing does affect children's behavior and that often the effects are negative (Eron et al., 1994).

Other sorts of projects also require field research. Social programs, like Hawaii Healthy Start, in which home visitors provide overburdened parents with help in raising their children, must be evaluated in the environment outside the laboratory. Studying the behavior of animals in their natural habitats is necessary because animals behave differently in the wild than they do in captivity. Consumer products also often are best evaluated in the field. For example, *Consumer Reports* magazine (1996) tested motor oils using a fleet of New York City taxicabs. The researchers chose this setting because cabs travel many miles, in a short time, under very demanding conditions. *Consumer Reports* (1995) also evaluated psychotherapies by asking readers to report their experiences with different therapies. Surveys such as this are not hampered by the artificial restrictions that are usual in experimental evaluations of psychotherapy (Seligman, 1995).

Finally, some behaviors develop only in natural settings. For example, aggression most often is directed toward family members, friends, and acquaintances. Because such relationships are difficult or impossible to replicate in the laboratory, studies conducted there have had to focus on aggression against strangers and inanimate objects, different targets than are standard in everyday life.

Although field studies avoid the limitations of laboratory research, this advantage often is purchased with a loss of control. The two hallmarks of laboratory experiments, controlling external conditions by holding them constant and randomly assigning subjects to groups, frequently are impossible in the field, so field researchers have invented other strategies for reducing error. This chapter focuses on how this is done (1) in experimental designs, when random assignment is not possible; (2) in naturalistic observation; and (3) in survey research.

THE DESIGN OF FIELD EXPERIMENTS (QUASI-EXPERIMENTS)

When scientists can control who gets what treatment, as well as when and how behaviors are observed, field experiments are equivalent to laboratory experiments. The real design challenges of field experiments occur when such controls are impossible. Then the task becomes one of developing the best possible research plan, the design that will eliminate the greatest number of potential alternative explanations of the results.

Campbell and Stanley (1963) introduced the distinction between *true* and *quasi-experiments* to distinguish between studies with full experimental control and those falling short of this ideal.

> *True experiments* have random assignment of subjects to conditions and no major threats to internal validity (see Chapter 3).

Fisher's randomized experiments (see Chapter 6) and factorial designs (see Chapter 8) are examples of true experiments.

> *Quasi-experiments* are experiments with threats to internal validity inherent in their designs.

Most of the quasi-experiments that Campbell and Stanley discuss lack random assignment of subjects to conditions and those which have it suffer from the threats of history and/or maturation.

We will use two studies to illustrate how researchers reduce error in quasi-experiments. The first is a study of the effects of introducing television into a community; the second is an evaluation of a program to reduce highway traffic deaths. The highway study, a classic in the literature on field research, was analyzed by Campbell and Ross (1968). For both cases, we present an experimental design that would have been barely adequate for answering the questions of interest to the researchers, followed by the improved design that the researchers actually used.

Pretest-Posttest One-Group Design: O X O

In 1973, the residents of a rural town in Canada, population 658, watched television at home for the first time. Unlike its neighbors, "Notel," as the town was dubbed by the researchers, was in a valley and required a special transmitter to get adequate reception. Many families bought sets in anticipation of the promised transmitter. A group of psychologists, led by Tannis Williams (1986), saw the abrupt introduction of television into this community as a marvelous opportunity to assess the impact of television on people's lives. Because they knew that television would be coming a year ahead of time, they had ample opportunity to plan their study. The research assessed the effects of television on a variety of behaviors, including reading, vocabulary, creativity, gender-role attitudes, aggression, and leisure activities. We will discuss only the study designed to evaluate television's impact on children's aggression (Joy, Kimball, & Zabrack, 1986).

The study's basic design was a *pretest-posttest one-group design.* Using Campbell and Stanley's notation, which we introduced in Chapter 9, this study would be diagrammed as:

$$O \; X \; O,$$

where X stands for the introduction of television, the treatment, and O is an observation of aggressive behavior.

Here we see how the O X O design, which we introduced in the last chapter as a basic $n = 1$ design, can be used in research on groups of subjects. The two observations can be made on different groups of people, in a *cross-sectional design*, or on the same people, in a *longitudinal design*. The Notel researchers used a longitudinal design. They wanted to observe the children's aggressive behavior on the school playground before (the pretest) and two years after the introduction of television (the posttest). They believed that the two year interval would be adequate for the effects of television to become apparent.

The design of the Connecticut study to reduce highway deaths also was O X O. The study compared the incidence of accidental deaths before and after an intense program of ticketing speeders and imposing stiff penalties on those who were convicted. This crackdown on speeders followed a year in which a record number of people, 324, died in automobile accidents. The year of the crackdown, fewer people, 284, died in accidents. Because the study focused on the incidence of accidental deaths, the design had to be cross-sectional.

There are serious threats to the internal validity of both of these O X O studies, as described so far. If the children in Notel were found to be more aggressive after two years of television, for example, this might simply reflect the fact that older children (they now are two years older) behave more aggressively than younger ones (the threat of maturation). Or there might have been a change in the financial status of town residents during the two years of the study. The children's aggression might have increased because of their own or their parents' frustrations over their economic circumstances (the threat of history). A reduction in accidental deaths following the Connecticut crackdown might have been due to improved safety standards for new cars, increased seat belt use, or less driving occasioned by a gas shortage (all threats of history). If effects were found in these studies, they also might have resulted from normal year-to-year fluctuations in the measures; Cook and Campbell (1979) call this type of fluctuation *the threat of instability.*

Because the scientists who conducted these studies understood the threats inherent in the O X O design, they planned their research so that they could evaluate them by means of two general methods:

- *Replicating* the design using different measures and subgroups of subjects, and making repeated observations before and after the treatment.
- Using *nonequivalent control groups,* that is, different groups of subjects selected to enable the researchers to evaluate rival hypotheses.

Replicating the O X O Design with Different Measures and Subgroups

The Notel researchers wanted to find out whether the effects of television on aggression were general, as expected, or limited to one gender or the other, to a certain age group (1st- and 2nd-graders vs. 4th- and 5th-graders), to a particular type of aggression (physical vs. verbal), or to a particular measure of aggression (direct observation of playground behavior vs. peer and teacher ratings). The researchers replicated the O X O design separately for each of these variations in subjects and measures to assess the generality of television's effects.

They found that television was associated with increased aggression on each measure, for both genders, and for all age groups. The consistency of these results argued against explaining them as normal year-to-year fluctuations because such fluctuations would be unlikely to affect different subgroups and measures uniformly.

To evaluate the rival hypothesis of maturation (that older children might be more aggressive), the experimenters repeated the study using cross-sectional data. They compared first graders' aggression before television to the aggression of first graders two years later, after television was introduced. Because the comparison groups were the same age, maturation could not explain observed differences in their levels of aggression. As expected, the researchers found that the children who had watched television were more aggressive.

The researchers used nonequivalent control groups to test for one additional major threat in the Notel study, history, the possibility that event(s) other than the introduction of television might have produced the increase in aggression. We will discuss their strategy for evaluating the effects of history later in the chapter.

Replicating the O X O Design with Repeated Measures, Time-Series Designs

The researchers studying the Connecticut crackdown did not replicate their O X O design with subgroups of drivers or multiple measures. Instead, they decided to replicate the pre- and posttreatment observations using a different design. This *interrupted time-series design* is diagrammed as:

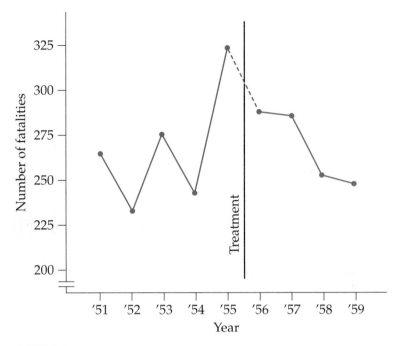

FIGURE 1
Driving fatalities in Connecticut, 1951–1959. (From Campbell & Ross, 1968.)

O O O O O O O X O O O O O O

The addition of several pretreatment observations in this design allowed the researchers to measure the natural variability in traffic fatalities and to detect systematic trends (upward or downward changes) in them. These repeated observations provided a benchmark for evaluating changes in trend following the treatment. In their absence, it is difficult to judge whether a change immediately following the treatment results from it or from normal fluctuation. You will recall that this strategy also is used in $n = 1$ research; in such designs, the repeated pretreatment Os establish the baseline for evaluating the effects of the treatment on the subject (see Chapter 9).

In the Connecticut study, each O refers to an observation of automobile fatalities in a given year. The data for the 5 years prior to and the 4 years after the crackdown are shown in Figure 1.

Figure 1 illustrates an upward trend in fatalities prior to the crackdown and a downward trend after, showing a reduction in deaths each year after the new policy. Before the crackdown, there were two increases, a smaller increase from 1952 to 1953, and a larger increase from 1954 to 1955. The large increase just prior to the treatment is a good example of the kind of problem encountered in field research. This alarming increase was what led Connecticut officials to initiate the program; it also made evaluation of the program's effect difficult.

Any year following one with such a large increase in fatalities would be likely to show a reduction in fatalities, even when no treatment is introduced. This is because the increase probably would be caused by a coincidence of factors that would be unlikely to repeat two years in a row. The drop in deaths after the crackdown could have resulted from a *statistical regression* to the mean rather than from the program itself.

As you recall, Francis Galton discovered statistical regression in his research on heredity (see Chapter 5). He found that the heights of children of very tall (or short) parents are closer to the population average for height than their parents. But such *regression to the mean* is not limited to height; regression is a general phenomenon that can occur in any series of repeated observations. If any extreme value (high or low) in the series is selected as the starting point in a study, the odds are that the next value in the series will be closer to the series' mean.

Statistical regression is a threat to the internal validity of a study whenever the researcher schedules a treatment following high (or low) scores on the dependent variable (as in the Connecticut study), or selects subjects for the study on the basis of their extreme scores. The extreme scores are likely to "regress," that is, change toward the mean in subsequent observations, a change that could be attributed erroneously to the treatment (Cook & Campbell, 1979). The results for the first year of the crackdown were inconclusive because it was impossible to know whether the reduction in fatalities resulted from regression or the program. The steady reduction in fatalities observed over the next several years, however, supported the researchers' claim that the program was effective.

The interrupted time-series design, which the Connecticut researchers used, is equivalent to the "AB" design, which we discussed in the chapter on n = 1 designs (see Chapter 9); the design has a series of observations before the introduction of the treatment and a series of observations after the treatment. Two other n = 1 designs also are used with groups of subjects in field research: the *alternating treatment design (ATD)* and the *multiple baseline design.*

The ATD and the ABAB design are called *interrupted time-series designs with multiple replications* in the field research literature. Cook and Campbell (1979) diagrammed such designs as follows:

$$O X O \quad O \overline{X} O \quad O X O \quad O \overline{X} O \quad O X O \quad O \overline{X} O \quad O X O,$$

$$\overline{X} = \text{absence of Tx}$$

where X is the absence of the $\overline{X}$ treatment, and the schedule of treatments, that is, the order of applying X or $\overline{X}$, can alternate or be randomized. X and $\overline{X}$ also can be different treatments, rather than one treatment and its absence.

Neither the Notel nor the Connecticut studies could use the interrupted time series design with multiple replications, but it was ideal for a medical study comparing two treatments for gunshot or stab wounds to the torso (Bickell et al., 1994). The standard emergency treatment for such wounds is to start an intravenous infusion (IV) of fluids immediately. However, Bickell and his coworkers were concerned that it might be harmful to administer an IV before the bleeding could be controlled by surgery. They designed their field experiment to resolve this issue.

Their study, done at the Ben Taub General Hospital in Houston, Texas, compared immediate IV to IV delayed until the patient was in the operating room. Patients who sought treatment on even numbered days of the week received immediate IVs; those who came to the hospital on odd days got delayed IVs. (The normal ethical requirement that patients give informed consent was waived by three different institutional review boards.) The results of the study showed better survival rates with delayed IV (203 of 289 patients, 70%, lived) than with immediate IV (193 of 309 patients, 62%, lived), $p < .05$.

We discussed the $n = 1$ multiple baseline design in Chapter 9. In one application of this design, several different behaviors are observed for one subject (these are the multiple baselines) and treatments are started for each behavior on a staggered time schedule. The *interrupted time series with switching replications* design, the equivalent group design, also uses the strategy of staggering the start of treatments (Cook and Campbell, 1979). The design is diagrammed as:

Group 1 O O O X O O O O O O O

Group 2: O O O O O O O X O O O

In this design, the same behavior is observed for both groups, with Group 1 receiving the treatment, X, first, and Group 2 receiving it later. Group 2 serves as a control for Group 1 because any historical events that affect Group 1 when it receives the treatment are unlikely to affect Group 2 subjects at precisely the moment that they receive the treatment. Similarly, Group 1 serves as a control for Group 2; when the treatment is introduced for Group 2, the scores in Group 1 are not expected to change. Although we have diagrammed this design with two groups, it actually could be used with any number of groups, each group serving as an independent replication for testing the effect of the treatment.

Nonequivalent Control Groups

The *randomized control groups design*, which is used so effectively in laboratory experiments, controls well for threats of history and maturation (see Chapters 6 and 8). Although this design can be used in some field studies (e.g., different motor oils were randomly assigned to particular taxis in the *Consumer Reports* study), often randomization is not possible. Because this was the case in the Connecticut crackdown and Notel investigations, the researchers in these studies had to find existing groups that would control as well as possible for history and maturation. The design they chose, the *nonequivalent control group design,* is diagrammed as:

Control Group: O   O

Experimental Group: O X O

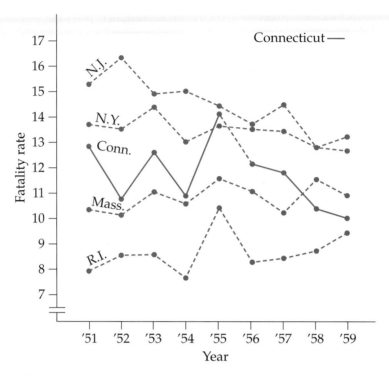

FIGURE 2
Driving fatalities per 100,000 persons in Connecticut and neighboring states. (From Campbell & Ross, 1968.)

The comparable time series design that includes such a control group is called an *interrupted time series with a nonequivalent no-treatment control group time series.* Its diagram is simpler than its name:

Control Group: O O O O O O O O O O O O O

Experimental Group: O O O O O O X O O O O O O

The control groups in both designs are called nonequivalent because the subjects are not randomly assigned to the groups and, as a result, there may be systematic differences between them. Although such nonequivalence is a problem, a nonrandomized control group usually is preferable to no control group at all.

In the Connecticut study, the best control groups available were drivers in adjacent states. The drivers and driving conditions in these states were similar to Connecticut's, but the adjacent states did not have Connecticut's crackdown on speeders. Figure 2 compares the fatalities in Connecticut and in these control states. Notice that this graph compares fatalities per 100,000 people rather than directly comparing the absolute numbers of fatalities. Expressing the fatalities as a rate controls for differences in the populations of the states. (Although the researchers could have adjusted the rates for differences in the ages and genders of drivers, they did not do so.)

If the pattern of fatalities in the control states was the same as Connecticut's (an upward trend before 1955 and a downward trend afterwards), there would be no evidence of an effect of the crackdown. But this proved not to be the case. Both New Jersey and New York showed continual downward trends before and after the Connecticut crackdown began, and Massachusetts and Rhode Island had upward trends throughout the same time period. Only Connecticut had a change in fatalities coincident with the start of the crackdown, providing good evidence for the program's effectiveness in preventing fatal accidents.

The Notel researchers had more difficulty in finding suitable control groups than the Connecticut researchers did. The ideal control for Notel would have been a twin city that had no television, like Notel, and did not get it when Notel did. But Notel's no-television status was unique in the early 1970s; there was no twin. So the researchers used other small cities adjacent to Notel as controls; these cities had television for several years before Notel got it—"Unitel" had one channel, "Multitel" had several.

The researchers observed residents of these cities and of Notel at the same times to control for history and maturation. Any general effects of history or maturation would be expected to affect the levels of aggression in Unitel and Multitel in the same ways as Notel. Because neither physical nor verbal aggression changed significantly in these control cities during the two years in which they increased in Notel, the researchers rejected history and maturation as explanations of the increased aggression in Notel (see Figure 3).

As the Notel and the Connecticut studies illustrate, nonequivalent control groups play a major role in improving the internal validity of field studies when it is not possible to randomly assign subjects to conditions. Without the evidence from the control groups, both studies would have been inconclusive. Using the control groups, the researchers were able to rule out plausible alternative explanations for the results. In general, the combination of using appropriate nonequivalent control groups and, if possible, taking multiple observations before and after the start of the experimental treatment greatly improves field studies.

*N*ATURALISTIC OBSERVATION

We used the term "observation" in the diagrams above to refer to any measures that are taken on subjects in a study. Actually, the direct observation of subjects' behaviors is rare in psychological research; ratings, tests, interviews, and questionnaires are much more common. Bakeman and Gottman (1986), experts on the naturalistic observation of social interaction, reported that only about 8% of psychological studies are observational. They implored psychologists to begin observing in their research.

Bakeman and Gottman admitted that they were looking for colleagues ("we are lonely"), but they also claimed that observation made for good research. They reported that observational studies had permitted them to find consistent results in areas previously recalcitrant to quantitative analysis, including: "how

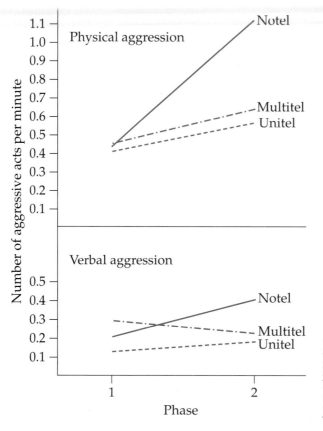

FIGURE 3
Levels of aggression in
Notel, Unitel, and Multitel
before (phase 1) and after
(phase 2) television. (From
Joy et al., 1986.)

babies learn to interact with their parents and organize their behavior; how
young children make friends or are rejected by their peers; how marriages suc-
ceed or fail by how spouses interact; how families weather stress or create
pathology" (Bakeman & Gottman, 1986, p. 201). They hoped that reporting their
successes would encourage others to use observation in their own research.

We already have discussed one study that used observational techniques.
The Notel researchers observed children's aggressive behaviors in a natural
situation, the school playground (Joy et al., 1986). They did so because they believed that behavioral observations were the best way to determine children's
levels of aggression in day-to-day life. The researchers also collected peer and
teacher ratings of aggression but concluded that such measures afford less certainty about what children actually do than seeing and recording their activities firsthand.

Direct observations enjoy a validity that can only be hoped for with less
direct measures of behavior. To illustrate, Anderson and Lorch (1983, as cited
in Joy et al., 1986) compared parents' ratings of the time their children
watched television with records made by a videocamera mounted in the viewing room. The two measures correlated only .21, a low value. Joy et al. suggested that the poor validity of these parents' ratings may help explain why

correlational studies that use them find low or nonsignificant relationships between extent of television watching and other behaviors.

One reason that observations are used less frequently than other methods in research may be that developing a scheme for observing behavior is more difficult than constructing a rating scale or questionnaire. The researcher has to devise a coding system for recording behaviors and observers must be trained to achieve adequate levels of accuracy, a time-consuming process. Goodall (1986) reported that college students were able to make reliable ratings of chimpanzee behavior only after a month of training in the field, and this following extensive instruction on the chimpanzee's ethogram in the classroom.

> An *ethogram* is an elaborate, sometimes pictorial, system for classifying the behavior of a species.

Part of the chimpanzee ethogram describing facial expressions is shown in Box 1. Although the term "ethogram" originated in the field of ethology, that is, the scientific study of animal behavior, researchers are beginning to publish ethograms for limited aspects of human behavior. Joan Bottorff and Janice Morse (1994), for example, developed an ethogram for nurse-patient interactions. Whenever an ethogram or more restricted category system is unavailable for a given group of subjects, which often is the case, researchers must develop their own category systems for recording behavior.

Deciding on Behavioral Units

If you remember from Chapter 3, John Stuart Mill identified two basic steps in research. The first is the event analysis, in which nature, as perceived, is broken down into discrete events, and the second is designing the research, in which events are manipulated or observed to determine cause and effect. Naturalistic observation is concerned with Mill's first step, the event analysis. Because Mill concentrated on his second step, the logic of research design, he presented little information on how to do the event analysis. Today there are many good examples of how to do what Mill called "the event analysis."

The first step in the event analysis is classifying the observed behaviors into discrete categories, so that the behaviors of interest can be differentiated from other behaviors. The major differences between classification schemes can be characterized according to two dimensions: the type of description, *functional versus empirical* (Lehner, 1979), and the *size (or molarity)* of the behavioral unit (Brandt, 1981).

> *Empirical descriptions* classify behaviors in physical terms, for example, muscle movements or bodily movements, such as walking or eating.

Such descriptions are designed to be objective, avoiding interpretations of behavior. In animal research, they prevent anthropomorphism, the attribution of human characteristics to animals (e.g., describing an animal as "envious" or "disappointed").

BOX 1 CHIMPANZEE FACIAL EXPRESSIONS (FROM GOODALL, 1986)

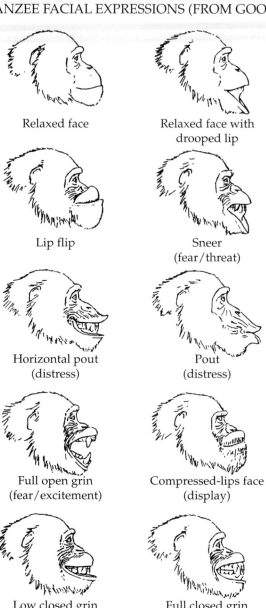

Relaxed face

Relaxed face with
drooped lip

Lip flip

Sneer
(fear/threat)

Horizontal pout
(distress)

Pout
(distress)

Full open grin
(fear/excitement)

Compressed-lips face
(display)

Low closed grin
(fear/excitement)

Full closed grin
(fear/excitement)

Full play face

BOX 2 ONE CHIMP'S MORNING (FROM GOODALL, 1986)

Report from the Field
Target: Adult male Jomeo, 14 October 1982
Field Assistants: Esiom Mpongo and Gabo Paulo

0617   Jomeo, Satan, Beethoven, and Freud in nests at KK10.
0634   Climb down. Beethoven presents, pant-grunts to Satan; Satan, hair out, stamps on Beethoven, who screams and falls 3 meters to the ground. Jomeo and Freud pant-grunt. Jomeo climbs a tree and sits.
0640   Satan feeds on *mitati* leaves. Beethoven watches, then feeds on the same.
0655   Jomeo feeds on *mitati* leaves too. They continue feeding and slowly head southeast.
0703   They stop feeding and travel. Freud does not feed.
0708   Freud pant-hoots, all pant-hoot, and Jomeo stamps. These pant-hoots are in response to calls from KK9 and KK8.
0710   The group arrives at KK9 and climbs, feeds on *kirukia* fruit. Goblin, who was feeding at KK9 before the arrival of the group, displays. Beethoven pant-grunts. Jomeo and Satan, no response. Goblin displays around, swaying, hitting saplings.
0715   Goblin climbs, feeds with the others, and food-grunts. Freud vanishes.
0725   They stop feeding, climb down. Goblin pant-hoots; the others are silent.
0726   All climb, feed on fruits at KK9 with pant-hoots.
0738   They stop feeding, climb down. Goblin displays, silently, not toward anyone. They travel southeast.

Functional descriptions classify behaviors in terms of their purposes or goals, for example, scavenging for food or making a sexual display.

When such goals are obvious (e.g., chimpanzees fishing for termites), functional descriptions replace complicated and tedious empirical accounts (e.g., picks up a stick, walks to the termite mound, inserts the stick into the mound, etc.). Both empirical and functional descriptions are popular and they often are combined in a single descriptive scheme.

In addition, functional and empirical descriptions can use different-sized behavioral units; that is, they can be at either the fine-grained "molecular level" or at the large-scale "molar level."

A description of an animal's movement in terms of the contractions and extensions of individual muscles of its legs is called *molecular;* a description focused on larger behavioral units, like walking or trotting, is *molar.*

Box 2 shows an excerpt from a field record of one chimpanzee's morning (Goodall, 1986). The target chimp is named Jomeo, and his companion chimps are Satan, Beethoven, and Freud. The record gives an empirical description with a relatively large behavioral unit, referring to patterns of behavior, like traveling, feeding, stomping, and "pant-hooting" (a particular cry).

BOX 3 UNITS OF PHYSICAL AGGRESSION (FROM JOY ET AL., 1986)

1. Hits, slaps, punches, or strikes with body part above waist.

2. Hits, slaps, punches, or strikes with a held object.

3. Kicks, steps on, sits on, lies on, or trips with body part below waist.

4. Bites or spits.

5. Pushes, holds, pulls, grabs, drags, or chokes.

6. Snatches property of another (without damage to that property).

7. Damages the property of another.

8. Tries to create a reaction; that is, teases, annoys, or interferes in the activity of another (except where chasing is involved and 11 or 12 is scored).

9. Threatens with some part of the body.

10. Threatens with a held object.

11. Chases another.

12. Chases with a held object.

13. Growls, grimaces, or makes sounds of dislike or anger toward another.

14. Throws or kicks an object at another, except as required (e.g., ball in game).

The observational categories used in the Notel aggression study are listed in Box 3. As you can see there, these are functional categories (e.g., spitting to show aggression) and, like Goodall's, focus on relatively large behavioral units.

The choice of the behavioral unit depends on the purpose of the study. In his research on human facial expressions associated with emotions, for example, Eibl-Eibesfeldt wanted to explore similarities in the expressions of people in different cultures (Eibl-Eibesfeldt, 1967, as cited in Lorenz, 1981). To do this, he recorded their facial expressions on film, which he then played back in slow motion and analyzed for similarities in facial muscle movements. This "microscopic" analysis revealed striking regularities in how culturally diverse groups express emotions like grief and enjoyment.

Reducing Observer Bias

An observer is not a mechanical device that simply records facts. Konrad Lorenz, one of the founders of ethology, expressed this idea when he wrote, "[The observer] is himself a subject, so like the object he is observing that he cannot be truly objective" (Lorenz, 1935; in Lehner, 1979, p. 92). The subjectivity of observers means that their perceptions and interpretations of events are influenced by their knowledge, interests, and needs. Researchers must take pains to minimize biases that they bring to their observations.

A good example of the subjectivity of observers came to light in Rubin, Provenzano, & Luria's (1974) study of how parents perceive their newborns. When asked to estimate the height and weight of their babies, parents systematically rated boys as taller and heavier than girls, even though there were no measurable differences between them. Apparently, the parents' beliefs that boys are bigger than girls biased their estimates in the direction of their expectations.

Controlling observer knowledge. Biases can be reduced in some studies by controlling what the observer knows about the experimental situation.

> Withholding potentially biasing information from an observer is called *blinding* the observer.

This strategy works because observers can't be biased by what they don't know. The parents' size judgments of their newborns could not have been biased by gender if they hadn't known their baby's sex when they made their ratings.

Separating fact from interpretation. However, in many studies, potentially biasing knowledge cannot be hidden; in others, there is no information to withhold, for example, in observations of animals in the wild. In these cases, observers must be trained to separate fact from interpretation and expectation. Goodall's observers, for example, were taught to record behaviors first and then to list possible interpretations of them with a special notation. This procedure reduced bias by constantly reminding the observers to distinguish between fact and interpretation.

Sampling methods. Bias also can be reduced by removing observers' choices about which subjects or behaviors to observe; the less choice, the less the opportunity for personal bias. For example, the observer could be given a set protocol of what to observe. The protocol might specify when the observer should start and stop recording, and which behaviors and subjects to observe during the sampling time interval.

Both Goodall and the Notel researchers used *continuous sampling* focused on one subject at a time. Goodall recorded the behaviors of single chimps from dawn to dusk (Goodall, 1986). In the Notel study, each child on the playground was observed for 1-minute intervals, during which all the aggressive acts of the child were recorded. Once the 1-minute observation was complete for one child, the next was selected, at random, and observed for 1 minute. This protocol continued until each child was observed for 21 minutes spread over two days. The choice of who to observe and for how long was controlled by the researchers, minimizing observer bias.

There are many different behavior-sampling schemes for controlling observer bias. Recording intervals can vary from almost instantaneous to very long periods. Recording can start and stop according to a preset time signal or be contingent on subjects' behaviors. Observations can focus on a single subject or include all the subjects who are visible to the observer. The various sampling schemes that are common in ethology and psychology were analyzed by Jeanne Altmann (1974), who discusses the pros and cons of each method. We recommend her article to anyone planning an observational study.

Observer Reliability

Error also can creep into a study when the rating system is ambiguous, when the raters fail to understand it, and when observers do not pay attention or are bored or tired. These sources of error can be detected by checking the reliability, or consistency, of the observations. In fact, a reliability assessment should be built into every observational study.

To establish reliability, the researcher must demonstrate that an observer's ratings are consistent with those of other raters or of an expert observer.

> The *interobserver* (or *interrater*) *reliability* of observations can be assessed by having different observers rate the same behavior sequence, and then checking the ratings for interobserver consistency.

If the ratings do not agree, this should be a warning to the researcher to retrain the observers or rewrite the rating system. It is wise to establish interobserver reliability before the study begins.

It also is good practice to check on *intraobserver reliability:*

> *Intraobserver reliability* is established by having an observer rate the same behavior sequence at different times throughout the study. Such checks reveal whether observers' ratings are stable (i.e., reliable) or whether they change as the study progresses.

Unreliability can result from fatigue or boredom or because a shift has occurred in the observer's use of the rating system. A lack of intraobserver reliability suggests the necessity of retraining the observer. Additional procedures for assessing reliability are discussed in Chapter 12, Planning the Study.

Reducing Subject Reactivity

In Chapter 1, we presented what may be the first documented example of subject reactivity in psychological research. Benjamin Franklin's commission demonstrated that patients' reactions to Mesmer's magnetic treatment depended upon their *knowing* that they were being treated. Franklin's group eliminated subject reactivity by "magnetizing" subjects without their awareness, a strategy that would be considered unethical by modern standards. Today's researchers use several strategies for handling the problem of reactivity, including: acclimation, concealment, and the use of unobtrusive measures and archival data.

Acclimation and concealment.
Acclimation refers to the tendency of subjects to become accustomed to the presence of an observer with the passage of time.

Konrad Lorenz described acclimation as a methodological ideal for naturalistic research:

> In the observation of highly organized creatures, the methodological ideal is achieved when it has become possible to accustom free-ranging wild animals to the observer to such an extent that their behavior is not influenced by his presence and he can, in fact, conduct experiments with them in a natural environmental setting. (Lorenz, 1981, p. 52)

Acclimation occurs both with human and animal subjects. Jane Goodall (1986) was able to learn many new things about how chimpanzees behave in the wild because her subjects gradually grew accustomed to her presence. To promote acclimation, Goodall dressed in similar dull-colored clothes every day and kept at least five meters between her and the chimps. The Notel observers tried to acclimate the children to their presence by coming to the playground for several days prior to rating the children's aggression; while the children were getting used to their presence, the observers took care not to interfere with their play. Although acclimation works well with some animals and with young children, it is less successful with other animals, with older more self-conscious children, and with adults.

Concealment is a good strategy for preventing reactance in animal studies, but there are ethical problems with secretly observing people's private behaviors. One study involving secret observation, in which an observer hid in a men's rest room stall and used a periscope to observe how long the men took to begin urinating, has become a classic example of what not to do in ethical research, for example (Middlemist, Knowles, & Matter, 1976; Koocher, 1977; Middlemist, Knowles, & Matter, 1977).

Concealment also has been used to promote acclimation in studies in which the subjects know they are being observed. Pepler and Craig (1995), for example, described a technology that worked well for audiovisual recording of children's playground behavior. They mounted telephoto cameras in windows overlooking a school playground and put a live microphone and receiver on the particular child they were monitoring. The other children were given dummy microphones and receivers, so they would not know who was being recorded during a play session.

Unobtrusive measures. In cases in which acclimation or concealment would not work, an alternative strategy to reduce subject reactivity would be to use unobtrusive measures of behavior. We are all familiar with the kinds of physical evidence used by forensic experts to reconstruct a crime (e.g., footprints, fingerprints, patterns of blood spatter, DNA from blood samples, and fiber traces). These are called *unobtrusive measures*.

A chimpanzee fishing for termites.

Unobtrusive measures give indirect, circumstantial evidence that certain behaviors have occurred.

Such measures have zero subject reactivity.

Suzuki, Kuroda, and Nishihara (1995) used unobtrusive measures in their study of tool use among chimpanzees in the northern Congo. They were able to get direct eyewitness records of chimps using tools to "fish" for termites on only three occasions, and then only for a moment. As soon as they were aware that they were being observed, the chimps fled into the jungle dropping their tools as they ran (an example of extreme reactivity!).

The researchers retrieved two types of tools: long rigid "perforating" sticks, which they thought the chimps used to poke holes in hard termite mounds, and flexible "fishing pole" sticks with a frayed end, with which they fished for termites. When a chimp sticks the fishing pole into the termite mound, the termite soldiers bite the frayed end and are pulled out by the fish-erchimp. When the researchers later analyzed fecal samples collected in the area, they found that the chimps were eating soldier termites and that other animals were not, providing indirect evidence of the chimps' tool use. Fecal samples often prove to be a good source of information on the diets and location of animals in the wild.

Unobtrusive measures are less frequent in research on people because more direct ways of observing them usually are available. Nevertheless, unobtrusive measures can prove invaluable in research on people, as they were in one probe into alleged tampering with a standard academic test by school officials in a prestigious elementary school in Connecticut (Avenoso, 1996). No direct eyewitness reports of tampering (changing students' answers to increase scores) were available, but an analysis of the answer sheets for the Iowa Test of Basic Skills produced damaging evidence.

The publisher of the test compared the number of erasures on the answer sheets of the suspected school with the sheets from other schools in the same district. They found that the suspect school had 26.4 erasures per student, compared to only 7 erasures per student at the comparison schools; and 89% of the erasures for the suspect school resulted in correct answers, compared to only 65% for the comparison schools. In addition, the analysis revealed several different patterns of pencil strokes on many of the answer sheets from the suspect school, suggesting that more than one person had answered questions on the same form. At the time of the newspaper report, the investigation was ongoing.

Archival data. The availability of *archival data* allows researchers to conduct studies that otherwise would be impossible. Recall, for example, that the researchers in the Connecticut highway study did not make observations of their own, but relied instead on data collected by state agencies. Because we are acclimated to record taking by government and other agencies, subject reactivity is likely to be reduced with such data. Box 4 discusses several archives that can be used in psychological research.

At first thought, the extensive databases and wide availability of archival data seem to be a researcher's dream. The data from elaborate scientific samples of people interviewed by professionals are readily available for your own analyses. In fact, for many projects this truly is a dream come true; but for others, archival data may just result in insomnia.

First of all, the data archived may not answer the precise questions that the researcher is posing. After all, it would be incredible to find that the precise data you need to test your original ideas has already been collected by a state agency! Archival data will not help if original questions or procedures are needed to test a hypothesis.

Second, archival data may be flawed. Webb and his colleagues (Webb, Campbell, Schwartz, & Sechrest, 1966) identified two major problems with archival records, selective deposit and selective survival.

Selective deposit refers to systematic bias in how archival records originally were recorded and in how data were selected for the archive.

Selective survival is the bias introduced when certain types of records in an archive are lost or destroyed.

A study comparing crime rates in Seattle and Vancouver (Sloan et al., 1988), for example, ran into the common problem of selective deposit. These

---

BOX 4 SOURCES OF ARCHIVAL DATA

The federal government is a major source of information on the population of the United States (the census is taken every 10 years), labor and farm information, import-export data, and information on education and safety. State and local governments, private and commercial enterprises, and the United Nations all publish archives.

In addition to such records, there also are large-scale research projects devoted to data collection and storage. Peter Marsden has edited a series of user guides to major social science databases for Sage Publications. The first guide in the series describes the General Social Survey (GSS), a project that began in 1972 (Davis & Smith, 1992). This survey, which is conducted every year, samples English-speaking adults living in households in the United States. Its questions and data, covering such topics as employment, sex, family life, education, religion, politics, crime, health and television viewing, are available to the public. This survey is associated with similar surveys in other countries, permitting cross-cultural research on many topics.

The Henry A. Murray Research Center at Radcliffe College is another major social science data archive. The Murray Center is a repository for data collected by many researchers on a variety of topics. The studies focus primarily on human development, social change, and the life experiences of American women. The center hosts visiting scholars and offers small grants to cover some research expenses incurred while using the archives.

The Aesthetics Research Archive at Boston University is a collection of videotaped interviews with creative artists, including the playwright Arthur Miller and the novelist Saul Bellow, on the creative process. This archive, which was established by Sigmund Koch, the psychologist who edited the six-volume *Psychology: A Study of a Science* (1959–1963), is a major source of data on creativity.

The Internet is rapidly becoming the primary archive for social science databases. "Publishing" archival data on the Internet is easy, and once published the data are available worldwide. Descriptions of the Murray Center archives are available on the Internet, for example, as are statistics collected by the federal government (www. fedstats.gov). If you search the Web for social science archives, you should be able to find many more sites. Commercial organizations also post data on the Internet. The Gallup survey research firm posts the results of recent polls and offers surveys that can be completed at its site (www.gallup.com).

---

cities are almost twins, but Vancouver has much stricter gun control laws than Seattle. During the years chosen for the study, the Washington State legislature passed the Domestic Violence Prevention Act, which mandated changes in the reporting of arrests in cases of domestic violence. The result was a marked increase in the number of recorded assaults in Seattle. During this same period, Vancouver had no such change in record keeping. In this case, the researchers avoided bias by not using data collected after the law was passed.

Changes in record keeping are a common occurrence in government archives. New legislation and new technology often mean new record-keeping systems, and computerization can lead to changes in the records themselves. These problems also can arise in databases for research. The GSS archive, which we described in Box 4, has undergone two changes in its sampling scheme since it began in 1972. Other potential problems in this database, caused by measurement changes, were identified by Smith (1988), who recommends that users check his article to see if their analyses are affected (Davis & Smith, 1992). The Murray Center holds seminars on how to deal with problems in archival data, like incomplete or noncomparable data.

Selective survival is no longer a problem in modern social science databases and government records because records now are preserved on computers. But selective survival can be a serious problem when older records and personal documents are used in research. Controversial or unflattering letters in a private collection may be destroyed and embarrassing political records may disappear, for example.

Webb et al. (1966) recommended the use of multiple measures to overcome potential biases in archival data. If different measures of the same behaviors all point to the same conclusion, confidence in its validity increases.

SURVEY RESEARCH

A critical component of every scientific study is selecting subjects. In this section of the chapter, we discuss how strategies used to select subjects affect the researcher's ability to generalize the results to people not observed in the study, an aspect of external validity.

The two basic procedures for selecting subjects in research are probability and nonprobability sampling.

> In *probability sampling,* each subject selected for the study is a member of a larger group of potential subjects, called the *population,* and each member of the population has a probability of being selected that is known and set by the researcher.

An example of probability sampling would be selecting, say, 25 students from a class of 100 by writing the names of all 100 students on separate slips of paper, placing the papers in a bowl, and drawing (as in a lottery) the 25 sample members. Here the population is the group of 100, and the probability of selecting any one person is $25/100 = 1/4$.

> In *nonprobability sampling,* the population is not specified and the probability of selecting a particular subject is unknown.

An example of nonprobability sampling would be selecting the next 25 people who enter a school cafeteria. The population, the group of potential subjects, is unspecified in this case. A potential subject would be anyone who might enter the cafeteria, and the probability of this event happening is not controlled by the researcher.

Both probability and nonprobability sampling are popular, with virtually all laboratory experiments using nonprobability sampling and all well-done surveys using probability sampling. Probability sampling has both a major advantage and a major disadvantage compared to nonprobability sampling. On the positive side, probability sampling permits findings from the sample to be generalized to the population with a known degree of error. This fact has made probability sampling indispensable for survey research, which has the express purpose of describing a population of subjects. The disadvantage of probability sampling is its expense. If the population is geographically widespread (e.g., adults in the United States), the expense of conducting face-to-face interviews or bringing a particular subset of the population to the laboratory may be prohibitive.

Subjects for laboratory experiments in psychology usually are selected by *convenience* (one method of nonprobability sampling). They often are volunteers recruited from introductory psychology classes, the library, or a dormitory. *Quota sampling* is a less frequently used nonprobability sampling strategy for selecting participants.

> In *quota sampling,* fixed numbers of specific categories of people (e.g., men and women, first and second borns) are selected for a study.

In clinical studies evaluating therapies for a specific disorder, *typical* or "textbook" *cases* of the disorder usually are selected and patients with dual diagnoses are excluded. *Critical cases* may be selected by case study researchers hoping to discover new insights about a disorder. When potential subjects are difficult to find (e.g., in studies of controlled drugs), the available subjects may be asked to give the names of other potential subjects, the *snowball sampling* procedure.

Such nonprobability sampling schemes share a common problem:

> Nonprobability sampling provides no way of determining the accuracy of generalizing results or even of specifying the groups to which the results can be generalized.

Consider a research project on memory that uses college freshmen at an Ivy League college as participants, randomly assigning these student volunteers to the conditions of the experiment. How should the results of such a study be generalized? Because the researchers may consider the processes they are investigating as basic, they may conclude that their results are universal, applying to all adults. But, in fact, there would be no evidence that the results actually would generalize beyond the narrow group of subjects tested in the study.

Probability Sampling

Techniques for probability sampling, the defining characteristic of modern survey research, improve surveys in the same ways that random assignment improves experiments. Both methods avoid systematic biases in selecting (or, in the case of the experiment, assigning) subjects, and both methods provide

TABLE 1 PROBABILITY SAMPLING METHODS

Type	Description
Simple random	Each member of the population has an equal probability of being selected.
Systematic	First subject is selected at random; the rest of the sample is selected from the list of population members at fixed intervals.
Stratified	The population is classified into subgroups and simple random samples of the desired size are selected from each subgroup.
Cluster	Subjects in the population are classified into clusters, which then are selected at random.
Multistage	The final sample is selected by means of two or more different sampling schemes done in order.

researchers with a way to calculate the potential error introduced by the sampling (or assignment).

The basic probability sampling schemes are listed in Table 1.

> In *simple random sampling*, the sample is selected so that each member of the population has an equal probability of being included.

Simple random sampling can be done by using a table of random numbers or a computer programmed to generate random numbers. In simple random sampling, each person in the population is assigned a code number and then numbers are selected using a random numbers table, or the computer generates numbers so that each member of the population has an equal chance of being selected. In random digit dialing, a popular form of simple random sampling, a computer dials telephone numbers selected at random for a certain area code and exchange.

Systematic sampling is an alternative to simple random sampling.

> In *systematic sampling*, the sample is selected from the list of population members by randomly selecting the first subject and then selecting the other members of the sample according to a prearranged scheme—by taking, say, every 5th, 10th, or 20th person on the list, until the sample is complete.

To select a sample of 100 from a population of 2,000, the first person would be chosen at random from the first 20 people on the population list. If the 11th person is selected, then the 31st, 51st, 71st, and so on, members also would be included. The advantage of this method over simple random sampling is that it is easier to do, and if the population list is in random order, systematic sampling is equivalent to simple random sampling.

Simple random sampling and systematic sampling give every member of the population an equal chance of being selected for the sample. This feature may not be desirable, however, if researchers want their samples to end up with set numbers of different categories of subjects (e.g., equal numbers of men and women or equal representation of particular age groups). Such control over the size of subgroups can be achieved with *stratified sampling.*

> In *stratified sampling,* the population is classified into subgroups and simple random samples of the desired size are taken separately from each subgroup.

In both simple random and stratified sampling, the members of the population are selected one at a time.

> In *cluster sampling,* the population is classified into subgroups (or clusters) and whole clusters of subjects are randomly selected.

In a cluster sampling of college dormitory residents, the students might be grouped by dormitory floors and a sample of floors selected by simple random sampling. Every student on a selected floor would be included in the sample. If the study used *multistage sampling,* after the initial selection of floors, a different sampling method would be used to select particular residents of each floor. The second stage might use simple random sampling or cluster sampling, say, clustering by rooms. Research on a large, geographically diverse population might involve several such stages.

Cluster and multistage sampling are done for economy, since they often are much easier to do than simple random sampling. Researchers also select these methods when the goals of the research require them to draw samples from a wide geographic region. But these gains in economy are purchased with a loss of accuracy. Cluster and multistage sampling require more subjects than simple random sampling to achieve the same level of accuracy.

Measuring Error

Perhaps you read the results of a *Newsweek* poll that reported that 49% (±4%) of Americans think that the government is withholding information about UFOs (*Newsweek,* 1996). The 49% figure is the percent of people answering this way *in the sample* of 769 adults responding to *Newsweek's* poll. The ±4% figure is a measure of the error in estimating the percent of voters in the population (all American adults) who hold this opinion *from the sample.* The error, 4%, is added and subtracted from 49% to give a range of possible values, 45% to 53%, with a set probability of including the population value. This range is called a *confidence interval, CI.* Typically, the size of the confidence interval is set so that the probability of including the population value is 95%; this was the case in the *Newsweek* poll.

The *Newsweek* poll estimated the percent of Americans who believe that the government is withholding information about UFOs. In general, the accuracy of such estimation depends on:

- The size of the sample, n; as the sample size increases, the error decreases.
- The size of the population, N_{pop}; as the population size increases, error increases.

- The population value (the true value) of the percent being estimated— extreme values, such as 99% or 1%, can be estimated with less error than middle values close to 50%. The value of 50% has the greatest error.

The impact of each of these factors on error is discussed in Box 5.

Modes of Administering the Survey

In 1994, researchers at the University of Chicago published the results of the most comprehensive survey of sexual practices ever done in the United States (Laumann, Gagnon, Michael, & Michaels, 1994). Unlike other well-known sex surveys (like the Kinsey report, the Janus report, and the Hite report), the Chicago survey used probability sampling, employing the same sampling methods as the GSS survey, which we discussed in Box 4. The Chicago survey involved intensive interviewing of 3,432 adults.

A critical design decision for these survey researchers was selecting the interviewing strategy. There are three general interviewing modes: *face-to-face interviews*, in which a trained interviewer asks the subject questions in person; *telephone interviews*, in which the interviewing is done by phone; and *self-administrating interviews*, in which the subject completes a paper-and-pencil form with no help from an interviewer. They decided on face-to-face interviews. We will discuss their reasons, because they highlight the general issues that researchers think about in selecting one mode over another.

The Chicago researchers considered the telephone survey first because it is convenient and less expensive than face-to-face interviews; there are no travel expenses and time is not wasted traveling between participants. Simple random sampling, with its high accuracy, also can be done with little effort by randomly dialing telephone numbers. (You could be called even if your telephone number is unlisted, because the computer can randomly pick your number!) Although telephone surveys are limited to people who have telephones, in the United States this includes about 93% of households (Kalton, 1983), resulting in little bias.

The problem with telephone interviews is that the method places restrictions on the length and complexity of the interview. Short simple interviews are perfect for the telephone, but experience shows that 45 minutes is the upper limit for a telephone interview (Laumann et al., 1994). Because the Chicago researchers needed a 90-minute interview, they eliminated the telephone method. In this case, the content of the questions also might have presented a problem, because respondents might be reluctant to give honest answers to intimate questions about their sexual practices over the phone.

Telephone surveys also frequently yield a lower *response rate*, the percent of participants contacted who complete the interview, than other methods. A French telephone sex survey, for example, managed only a 65.5% response rate compared to the 80% rate that the Chicago researchers were able to achieve with face-to-face interviewing (Laumann et al., 1994). (The increasing use of telemarketers may be raising people's resistance to participating in telephone surveys.)

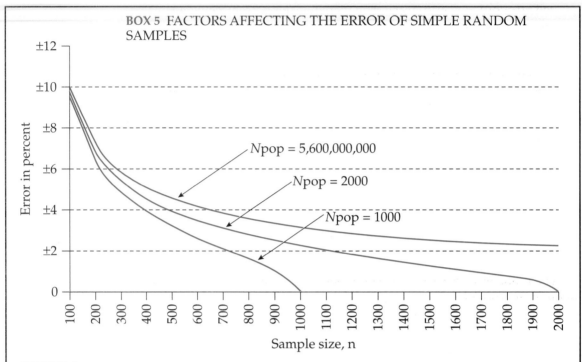

BOX 5 FACTORS AFFECTING THE ERROR OF SIMPLE RANDOM SAMPLES

FIGURE 4
Error for simple random samples as a function of the sample size, *n*, and the size of the population, N_{pop}.

Figure 4 shows the error in estimating population values from simple random samples for different sample sizes, *n*, and for three different-sized populations, N_{pop} = 1,000, 2,000, and a whopping 5,600,000,000, the population of the earth. For this graph, the population value was set at 50%, so these errors are the largest possible for the given *n* and *N*.

Notice, first, that when the sample size equals the population size (at $n = N_{pop} =$ 1,000 and at $n = N_{pop} =$ 2,000), there is no error. The graph also shows that an increase in the sample size of, say, 100, results in a greater reduction in error when the sample size is small than when it is large. As *n* becomes larger, the reduction in error achieved by increasing the sample size diminishes.

Finally, the graph shows, surprisingly, that the size of the population does not have much effect on accuracy. A sample of *n* = 500 drawn from a population of 1,000 has an error of ±3.2, but the same sample size drawn from a population of 5.6 billion has an error of only ±4.5. This result is critical for survey research because it means that relatively small samples can give accurate results even for huge populations.

Although simple random samples are used infrequently in survey research, the accuracy of such samples serves as a benchmark for evaluating other sampling schemes. Depending on the categories used in the stratification, stratified samples actually can have less error than simple random samples. Although the error associated with cluster and multistage samples is greater than the error for simple random samples, researchers still may choose these methods, considering their convenience to be worth the loss in accuracy. For example, the GSS database (see Box 4) uses stratified multistage sampling, even though this method requires about 1.5 times the sample size of a simple random sample to achieve the same accuracy (Davis & Smith, 1992).

Self-administered questionnaires also yield low rates of response, lower even than telephone surveys. (How many questionnaires that come in the mail do you answer?) In fact, the problem of response rates led the Chicago researchers to decide against the self-administered questionnaire for their survey. An additional problem with such questionnaires is that they may be too difficult for respondents to answer when the questions involve complicated and confusing *skip patterns* (e.g., answer questions 40–45 only if you answered "yes" to questions 38 and 39). When the interviewer can control the order of such complicated questions, there are fewer mistakes.

The Chicago researchers decided on face-to-face interviews to increase their response rates and because the questions they wanted respondents to answer were complicated. However, they did use self-administered questions for certain sections of their interview. For questions about income and very intimate sexual practices, the interviewer handed the respondents a self-administering form and asked them to put the completed questionnaire in a "privacy envelope." The interviewer never saw the participants' answers to these questions.

The problem with face-to-face interviewing is that it is the most expensive mode of questioning. The Chicago survey, for example, required 220 trained interviewers to conduct 90-minute interviews with 3,432 people. The expense could be justified in this case, however, because the results would contribute to developing public health strategies to fight AIDS.

The Wording of Questions

When well done, probability sampling is not a major source of error in surveys. Samuel Stouffer, one of the pioneers in the scientific use of surveys, discovered in his research that the

> error or bias attributable to sampling and to methods of questionnaire administration were relatively small as compared with other types of variation—especially variation attributable to different ways of wording questions. (Stouffer, 1950, in Payne, 1951, p. 5).

Slight changes in the wording of questions can result in major variations in people's answers, as Stanley Payne (1951) demonstrated in his book *The Art of Asking Questions.* Box 6 presents two of Payne's examples. The first shows the different responses he received to two questions that varied only in whether or not an alternative to the question ("or do you think layoffs are unavoidable?") was stated. Payne split his sample of subjects in half and presented each version to different halves. The results showed that 63% responded "yes" to version one, without the alternative, and only 35% answered "yes" to version two, with it—a 28% difference! In the second example, only one word was changed in the two versions of the question; the word "should" in version one was changed to "might" in version two. This variation resulted in a 19% difference in the percent responding "yes" to the question.

BOX 6 EFFECTS OF WORDING ON THE ANSWERS TO TWO QUESTIONS (FROM PAYNE, 1951)

Question 1:

Version 1: (No alternative is expressed.) Do you think most manufacturing companies that lay off workers during slack periods could arrange things to avoid layoffs and give steady work right through the year?

63% Yes   22% No   15% No opinion

Version 2: (Alternative expressed.) Do you think most manufacturing companies that lay off workers during slack periods could arrange things to avoid layoffs and give steady work right through the year, or do you think layoffs are unavoidable?

35% Yes   41% No   24% No opinion

Question 2:

Version 1: ("should") Do you think anything should be done to make it easier for people to pay doctor or hospital bills? 82% Yes

Version 2: ("might") Do you think anything might be done to make it easier for people to pay doctor or hospital bills? 63% Yes

---

Differences in people's responses to questions due to wording are much larger than errors due to sampling, and more worrisome. The sampling error can be measured but the effect of a specific wording cannot. In fact, there is no way for a researcher to predict the impact of alternative ways of stating questions. So researchers must rely on their experience, on the results of experiments comparing different wording, and on the advice of experts in writing their questions.

Before developing a questionnaire, it is a good idea to read what the experts have to say (see Payne, 1951; Schuman & Presser, 1981; Converse & Presser, 1986) and gain from their experience. In Chapter 12, we discuss suggestions from the experts on how to write good questions.

FINAL COMMENTS

This chapter began with the statement by Norbert Glenn, a field researcher, that "people who must have certitude, who cannot embrace conclusions tentatively" should not do social research. This quote highlights the major concern of field researchers, namely, how to deal with the lack of control that usually accompanies studies done outside of the laboratory. Actually, Glenn's advice applies to all researchers, because no research method, laboratory or otherwise, can claim certainty in its conclusions. In fact, the greater control that is possible in laboratory work is accompanied by increased doubt about whether the results will generalize beyond the restricted context of the research.

We can begin to reach certainty in drawing conclusions from research only when the results of many studies, using different methods, both field and laboratory, converge. Research on the health consequences of smoking is a well-known illustration of such convergence. The initial field studies on smoking (epidemiological research) were inconclusive and subject to multiple interpretations. In fact, R. A. Fisher, the developer of modern randomized experimental designs, concluded that the data did not implicate smoking as a cause of disease (Fisher, 1958, as cited in Gould, 1995). However, numerous studies conducted since the original investigations, employing widely different methods and subjects (e.g., experiments on animals and studies on people who have quit smoking) have led to the virtually certain conclusion that smoking causes disease. A similar convergence has been found for the relationship between watching violent television and subsequent aggression toward others (Eron et al., 1994).

Of course, the pace of moving toward certitude can be accelerated by improving individual studies. Such improvements are best achieved by designing and analyzing research results using methodological advances from all branches of science. In this book, we have presented many examples of how methods developed to study one type of problem have been applied with great success to other sorts of problems. Procedures developed for correlational research are used routinely in analyzing experimental data. Experimental designs developed for agriculture now are basic in psychology. Methods developed by ethologists observing animals in the wild now help to reduce error in studies of human interaction in the laboratory. Field studies to evaluate social programs and medical treatments use the $n = 1$ experimental designs invented by the behaviorists.

An interdisciplinary approach to research methodology cannot help but promote the kinds of cross-fertilization that we have described. Methods devised by researchers in other disciplines can provide an endless source of inspiration for innovation in psychology's methods. Researchers in other disciplines, likewise, have much to learn from psychologists.

*K*EY TERMS

True vs. quasi-experiments
Pretest-posttest one group design, O X O
Cross-sectional vs. longitudinal designs
Interrupted time-series design
Statistical regression
Interrupted time-series design with multiple replications
Interrupted time series with switching replications

Randomized control group design
Nonequivalent control group design
Interrupted time series with a nonequivalent no-treatment control group time series
Ethogram
Functional vs. empirical descriptions
Size of the behavioral unit
Blinding
Continuous sampling
Interobserver (or interrater) reliability

Intraobserver reliability
Acclimation and concealment
Unobtrusive measures
Archival data
Selective deposit and selective
  survival
Probability and nonprobability
  sampling
Population
Convenience sampling

Quota sampling
Typical, critical, and snowball
  sampling
Simple, systematic, stratified, cluster,
  and multistage sampling
Confidence interval
Face-to-face vs. telephone vs. self-
  administering interviews
Response rate
Skip pattern

KEY PEOPLE

Thomas D. Cook
Donald T. Campbell
Julian C. Stanley
H. Laurence Ross
Tannis Williams
Roger Bakeman and John Gottman

Jane Goodall
John Stuart Mill
Konrad Lorenz
Edward Laumann et al.
Samuel Stouffer
Stanley Payne

REVIEW QUESTIONS

1. Explain the limitations on the kinds of behavior that can be studied under laboratory conditions.

2. Diagram the pretest-posttest one group design.

3. Discuss the threats to internal validity of the O X O design. Use the Notel and Connecticut studies as examples to illustrate your points.

4. What two general methods are used to improve the O X O design?

5. How was the Notel study replicated with different measures and subgroups of subjects? What is the purpose of such replication?

6. Why did the Notel researchers replicate their longitudinal study with cross-sectional data?

7. Diagram the interrupted time-series design.

8. What was the purpose of the repeated pre-treatment observations in the Connecticut study?

9. How was statistical regression a problem in the Connecticut study?

10. Identify and describe the experimental design used in the Houston emergency room study.

11. Why are the control groups called "non-equivalent" in the non-equivalent control group design?

12. Describe the non-equivalent control groups in the Notel and Connecticut studies.

13. What percent of psychological studies use direct observation of behavior?

14. Distinguish between empirical and functional descriptions of behavior. Give examples.

15. Distinguish between molecular and molar descriptions of behavior. Give examples.

16. What observational bias did Rubin et al. find in their study of parents' perceptions of newborns?

17. How did Jane Goodall train her observers to separate fact from interpretation in their observations?

18. Identify three ways to reduce observer bias.

19. Distinguish between interobserver and intraobserver reliability.

20. Discuss four methods for reducing subject reactivity.

21. What unobtrusive measures did Suzuki et al. use in their study of termite fishing?

22. Distinguish among the following methods of nonprobability sampling:
    convenience,
    quota,
    snowball,
    typical case,
    critical case.

23. Distinguish among the following types of probability sampling:
    simple random,
    systematic,
    stratified,
    cluster,
    multistage.

24. What three factors affect the accuracy of a poll?

25. Why did the Chicago researchers decide to conduct face-to-face interviews in their survey of sexual behavior? Why did they use self-administering questions for certain parts of the survey?

26. What did Stouffer consider to be the major source of error in surveys?

27. What procedure did Payne use to study the effect of question wording on survey answers?

28. Under what conditions do the conclusions of social science research approach certainty?

11

Finding a Research Problem

❖

Asking the right question is more than half the work of science.
When we can understand how scientists do that, then we will
understand how to do science.

ROOT-BERNSTEIN

❖

PREPARING THE MIND
    The Literature Search
        Gradually narrow your focus
        Search from the present to the past
        Use all the resources available to you
    Collecting Your Own Observations
        "Bracket" preconceptions
        Entertain multiple hypotheses
        Make the familiar unfamiliar
        Make the unfamiliar familiar
        Be open to serendipity
EUREKA!—DISCOVERING IDEAS
    Use Theory to Generate Ideas
    Explore Analogies and Metaphors
    Keep Alert for Anomalies
    Look for Gaps in Knowledge
    Turn Assumptions on Their Heads
    Look for Patterns in Findings
    Try to Resolve Discrepancies
    Develop Skepticism about Findings, Methods, and
      Interpretations
    Improve Apparatus, Measures, and Procedures
    Focus on Practical Problems
FINAL THOUGHTS
KEY TERMS, KEY PEOPLE, REVIEW QUESTIONS

Being asked to conduct an original research project raises doubts and fears in most students. You may see yourself as about to enter "a vast uncharted region . . . with a good deal of mistrust in the appropriateness of [your] equipment," as John Lilly, the pioneering researcher on dolphin and whale communication we quoted in Chapter 1, put it. What kinds of research will make the grade? How can I find a good enough project? How can I come up with a question that hasn't been answered before? What if I can't think of a testable hypothesis? Fears such as these are common among students and not at all unusual even among seasoned research scientists. Janet Bavelas, a social psychologist, writes:

> Volumes could be written on the role of fear in research. . . . Fear stalks us from the beginning and continues throughout, until the results are in and checked. (Bavelas, 1987, p. 321)

Recognizing the inevitability of anxiety and frustration, and realizing that even professional researchers experience these emotions is helpful as you begin.

Starting a project is especially anxiety provoking. So naturally beginners are eager for any help they can get on how to come up with that all important question and that new and useful hypothesis. Unfortunately, discussions of scientific method by philosophers of science or in handbooks of research often are of little help. Most of these focus on the *later* stages of research when scientists attempt to *answer* research questions and *test* hypotheses. They rarely discuss how scientists come up with testable research questions or invent hypotheses to answer them.

Those accounts of the early phases of scientific research that are available aren't of much help to beginning researchers either. Typically they offer little how-to information. Instead, we find mystifying, perplexing, and discouraging stories of people of extraordinary genius (the Curies, Pasteurs, and Einsteins); of creative inspiration coming from "out of the blue," while the scientist is asleep, taking a bath, or relaxing under a tree; and tales of discoveries happened upon while the scientist worked on other problems. Although such stories do contain some truth—some scientists are brilliant, insights can seem to arrive from nowhere, and luck can be involved—historians of science, who study scientific discovery, believe that such irrational processes play a very small role in creativity.

Robert Weisberg (1986), for example, looked at how two important scientific discoveries came about: the Nobel Prize-winning discovery of the structure of the DNA molecule by the geneticists James Watson and Francis Crick and Charles Darwin's discovery of evolutionary theory. Weisberg concluded, based on his study of these scientists, that you don't have to be a person of extraordinary genius to do outstanding scientific work. Scientific discovery, Weisberg believes, involves the same kinds of rational and logical thought processes as day-to-day problem solving. So as you begin to think about your project, you can take courage from the findings of historians of science. Since we all solve problems on a daily basis, we all should be capable of asking significant research questions and formulating testable hypotheses.

Robert Root-Bernstein (1989), another historian of science, found that as a group innovative scientists are deeply curious about the problems they study. They need to be. A research project is a big undertaking; it involves time-consuming exploration into the work of other scientists and a substantial investment of the researcher's time and energy designing the study and collecting observations. It is their deep curiosity about the questions they seek to answer that sustains scientists through this process, even when progress seems far off and discouragement close at hand.

Research often is inspired by questions raised but unanswered by other scientists, by the desire to see whether a published result can be replicated, or because the researcher sees flaws in the design, measures, findings, or interpretations of other researchers. Students often become intrigued with problems suggested by their academic mentors or by working as a member of a research team. Working on a research project is a great way to develop ideas for further research, and once you get one idea you will find that others soon follow. Sometimes the enthusiasm of other scientists is the spark. It is exciting to imagine yourself resolving a controversy being debated in scientific journals and at professional conferences.

Like Weisberg and other historians of science, we are convinced that curiosity, careful thinking and hard work are much more important to developing good research questions and sound hypotheses than creative inspiration or luck. And, like the scientists Root-Bernstein studied, we believe that you will not go wrong if you follow the advice of Jonas Salk, inventor of the polio vaccine, and "do what makes your heart leap!" (Salk, in Root-Bernstein, 1989, p. 410). As you explore possibilities for research, pay attention to what excites you. At this stage of the research, your passion should be your guide, and on that subject you are the undisputed expert.

This chapter is designed to get you started on the sometimes frightening, sometimes frustrating, but always exciting process of developing an idea for research. It focuses, first, on how to become knowledgeable in a particular area of psychology and, second, on how to zero in on a specific research question and hypothesis to investigate.

PREPARING THE MIND

Once you decide on a general area of psychology to study, your first task will be to learn as much as you can about it. Innovative scientists agree with Pasteur's maxim that "in the fields of observation, chance favors only the prepared mind" (in Roberts, 1989, p. 244). On the basis of interviews she conducted with winners of the prestigious MacArthur Fellowship, a prize given for competence and creative potential in science and a variety of other fields, Denise Shekerjian concluded that to do creative work in any field requires you to "know—intellectually, or spiritually, or instinctively—what you're talking about" (Shekerjian, 1990, p. 59). Knowledge seems to be essential to creative work in any field.

There are two main ways to become expert in an area. The first is to learn what others have thought and done, by attending conferences, talking to professors, or searching the published literature by reading books, chapters, and journal articles. The second, which relies more on yourself, involves learning about a phenomenon by collecting observations yourself, for example, by carefully observing seating patterns in the student cafeteria, or looking for patterns in how good friends negotiate disagreements. We will discuss both of these general strategies to developing expertise in this chapter.

Whether you use one or both of these approaches, your goal at this stage will be to open yourself to the full range of data and possibilities. As Goleman and his coauthors put it:

> The first stage is preparation, when you immerse yourself in the problem, searching out any information that might be relevant. It's when you let your imagination roam free, open yourself to anything that is even vaguely relevant to the problem. The idea is to gather a broad range of data so that unusual and unlikely elements can begin to juxtapose themselves. Being receptive, being able to listen openly and well, is a crucial skill here. (Goleman, Kaufman, & Ray, 1992, p. 18)

A major obstacle to such receptivity that you will have to overcome is the tendency toward premature self-criticism. Janet Bavelas (1987), a social psychologist who has written about creativity in research, believes that there is a time to subject your ideas to critical scrutiny, but it is not when they are just beginning to surface and are most vulnerable. If you take care not to kill your hunches, Bavelas advises, and care for and feed them instead, after a while they will become strong enough to stand on their own. Then the time will be right for criticism.

Bavelas (1987) compiled a list of don'ts for students to follow to avoid killing their newborn ideas and observations. She advises: Don't dismiss ideas that you get, as though they didn't happen. Don't immediately find categories to put them in; putting new observations into old categories just reinforces the view that there is nothing new under the sun. Don't belittle them. Don't be practical or critical. Don't panic.

The Literature Search

As you begin to search the published literature, your thinking is likely to be relatively unfocused. You may only be able to define general topics of interest, like the determinants of self-esteem, or the effects of birth order on personality. As you familiarize yourself with the literature on these topics, you will be acquiring the raw materials you need to formulate a specific research question and hypothesis.

To be most useful in generating ideas, your review of the literature should be systematic. It will help to know the theories that have been advanced, the questions and controversies that have arisen, the types of research that have been done, and the findings that have been generated. The following strategies should help to make your search a thorough one.

Gradually narrow your focus. As we have said, your goal at this stage of your research should be to open yourself up to the widest possible range of ideas. To accomplish this, we recommend that you start by reading broad overviews of the theories, research, methods, and findings in a given area. Then gradually narrow your focus until you hit upon a research question that you want to explore.

One good place to start is with textbooks. First, think of the subfield within psychology of which your topic is a part (e.g., social psychology, personality, perception), then look at one or more texts on that topic. Texts in a particular area tend to cover the same general set of topics, focusing on the established theories and findings, the issues that have generated research, and the unresolved controversies. They usually include extensive bibliographies that you can use as a guide to the important readings on the topic of interest to you. If you don't have a text in that area, ask your professors for help in finding one. Professors often have many texts on the subjects that they teach.

If you have even the vaguest idea of what topic you would like to explore, *Psychological Abstracts, PsycINFO,* or *PsycLIT* will get you off to a good start. *Psychological Abstracts,* issued monthly by the American Psychological Association (APA), from 1927 to the present, contains summaries of published works in psychology and related disciplines. The bound volumes for each year contain subject and author indexes, and there are separately bound cumulative subject and author indexes, each covering several years. *PsycINFO, PsycLIT,* and other computer searches are another good place to start. Most libraries now enable students to conduct bibliographic searches using computers rather than printed indexes like the *Psychological Abstracts.*

PsycINFO is the on-line computer version of *Psychological Abstracts.* It contains citations and abstracts for the journal, book, chapter, and dissertation literature in psychology, for the years 1967 to the present. *PsycLIT* is a subset of *PsycINFO* covering the journal, book, and chapter literature and available on CD-ROM. Like *PsycINFO, PsycLIT* is cumulative, incorporating the contents of *Psychological Abstracts* since 1974. In addition, *PsycINFO* and *PsycLIT* have an optional historical database that includes references dating from 1887. The education literature, which covers many similar topics to those in psychology, can be searched with *ERIC.* If your library does not have access to these sources, it is well worth the trip to the nearest library that does. Box 1 discusses how to use these psychological sources.

Finding a review article can be invaluable as you begin. This special type of article, like a text, does some of the summarizing and integrating work for you. Its focus can be on theory, research, methods, or some combination of these. The *Annual Review of Psychology,* published yearly since 1950, summarizes recent developments in various subfields within psychology (Reed & Baxter, 1992). *Psychological Bulletin* focuses on evaluative and integrative reviews of research. *Psychological Review* covers articles presenting new theories or criticizing current theories. Articles in these journals usually contain comprehensive bibliographies that can be a great help in finding research studies on a topic. You also can find review articles in *PsycINFO/PsycLIT* by searching the *Thesaurus* term LITERATURE REVIEW.

BOX 1 USING *PSYCLIT, PSYCINFO,* AND *PSYCHOLOGICAL ABSTRACTS*

To use *PsycLIT, PsycINFO,* or *Psychological Abstracts,* first look for your subject category in the *Thesaurus of Psychological Index Terms* (APA, 1997). The thesaurus lists words and phrases in psychology that have been authorized by the APA for use in *Psychological Abstracts* (Reed & Baxter, 1992).

If you are using *Psychological Abstracts,* you will have to check for your search terms in each volume. Searching with a computer based system, like *PsycLIT* and *PsycINFO,* is easier.

A brief guide to *PsycLIT* is given in Box 2. The search words you type are used to scan all the references on the CD. If *PsycLIT* comes on more than one disc at your library, be sure to use all the discs to extend your search back to 1974. As the example of a journal record in Box 2 illustrates, each reference is divided into several fields, the title, author, author affiliation, and so on. These fields can be searched separately or together using the logical operations described in Box 2. Look at the search examples in the box to see how this is done. The exact form of search statements varies according to the search system being used. This one is for the Silver Platter system. The results of your search can be printed at the library or saved on a floppy disk.

If you use the right search terms, *PsycLIT, PsycINFO,* or *Psychological Abstracts* will provide you with a list of publications on the topic of interest to you. If you are having trouble finding research on your topic, it's possible that you have discovered an area that has not been studied; but maybe you just aren't using the right search terms. Check the thesaurus again for other possible search terms or ask the reference librarian for help. Librarians are up to date on a variety of different databases and search strategies that may be helpful to you.

The list of references that you get from *PsycINFO, PsycLIT,* or *Psychological Abstracts* will include books and chapters only for some years. *Psychological Abstracts* included abstracts of books and chapters from its beginning in 1927 up to 1980. It did not cover books or chapters from 1981 through 1991. Between 1987 and 1990, the American Psychological Association published a set of volumes called *PsycBOOKS,* which abstracted books and chapters. Beginning in 1992, *PsycLIT* and *Psychological Abstracts* once again included books and chapters. *PsycINFO* and *PsycLIT* provide access to books and book chapters published from 1987 to the present.

Spend time at this stage of your project; the leads you find will be well worth your effort. But be cautious because searches can be temperamental; for example, authors' names may be misspelled in the database, so if you search by author you may miss a critical study. Also, you need to know the conventions of the database and the search system. If you want to search for articles published in the *American Psychologist* on Silver Platter, for example, you have to use the search term *American-Psychologist;* the hyphen is critical. So try multiple searches to overcome any idiosyncrasies in how the articles are indexed.

BOX 2 PSYCLIT QUICK REFERENCE GUIDE

SILVERPLATTER®

QUICK REFERENCE GUIDE

To restart system	Press **F7 (Restart)**	**A phrase**	**Find:** well being
		A word root	**Find:** famil*
To select a database	Use arrow keys to highlight database	**Internal or limited truncation (one or no characters)**	**Find:** behavio?r;
	Press spacebar, then **Enter**		**Find:** norm?
List of commands	Press **F10,** then highlighted letter	**To combine concepts:**	
Database information	Press **F10,** then **G** for **Guide**	**Use AND to narrow search**	**Find:** symbolism and language
To use Thesaurus	Press **F10,** then **T** for **Thesaurus**	**Use OR to broaden search**	**Find:** wellness or health
To link chapters, books	Place cursor on <<SEE BOOKS>> or <<SEE CHAPTER>>	**Use NOT to narrow search**	**Find:** advertising not television
	Press **L** (for **Link**)	**Use WITH to restrict search to same field**	**Find:** crowd* with violence
To search authors	Press **F10,** then **I** for **Index** Type last name, then **Enter**	**Use NEAR to narrow search to number of words in proximity**	**Find:** computer near anxiety
To look for: A word	**Find:** hesitation		**Find:** expert near2 system?

The computer search will give only references to the research articles not the articles themselves. Getting the articles, which is necessary, may be more challenging. If your college library's journal collection is extensive, you will find most of the articles you need there. If it is smaller, your librarian can help you find the closest libraries that hold the journals you are looking for. You can have the papers or books sent to your library through interlibrary loan or go to the libraries to copy the articles yourself. If you photocopy the articles, be sure to include the references at the end of each article. The references are a valuable part of the paper because they are a list of relevant studies and theoretical papers that at least one researcher found helpful. Read the references, one by one, to get leads on other papers.

FIELD NAME	SAMPLE JOURNAL RECORD	SEARCH EXAMPLES
Title	TI: Effects of rock and roll music on mathematical, verbal, and reading comprehension performance.	rock with music in ti
Author	AU: Tucker,-Alexander; Bushman,-Brad-J.	tucker-alexander in au
Author Affiliation	IN: Iowa State U, US	iowa state in in
Journal Name	JN: Perceptual-and-Motor-Skills; 1991 Jun Vol 72 (3, Pt 1) 942	perceptual-and-motor-skills in jn
ISSN	IS: 00315125	00315125 in is
Language	LA: English	english in la
Publication Year	PY: 1991	1991 in py ; py=1989-1992
Abstract	AB: 151 undergraduates completed mathematics, verbal, and reading comprehension problems while listening to rock and roll music played at 80 db or in silence. The music decreased performance on math and verbal tests but not on reading comprehension. (PsycLIT Database Copyright 1992 American Psychological Assn, all rights reserved)	rock near1 roll in ab
Key Phrase	KP: rock & roll music; mathematics & verbal & reading comprehension performance; college students	mathematics with performance in kp
Descriptors	DE: ROCK-MUSIC; READING-COMPREHENSION; MATHEMATICAL-ABILITY; VERBAL-ABILITY; ADULTHOOD-	rock-music in de ; adulthood- in de
Classification Codes	CC: 2340; 23	2340 in cc ; 23 in cc
Population	PO: Human	human in po
Age Group	AG: Adult	adult in ag
Update	UD: 9201	9201 in ud
Accession Number	AN: 79-00362	79-00362 in an
Journal Code	JC: 1576	1576 in jc

Prepared by PsycINFO User Services, a department of the American Psychological Association.

Also, be sure to search the Internet, the information superhighway, fast becoming the eighth wonder of the world, for material related to your research topic. The Internet is by far the most diverse and dynamic of the new computer-based information sources. Information searching and retrieval on the Internet is made possible by networking a vast number of computers located all over the world. All the computers on this "World Wide Web" of networks can share information.

With an Internet connection, you can join live electronic conferences on academic topics, subscribe to electronic journals and newsletters, read scientific articles that are awaiting publication in print, access libraries, get shareware computer programs, view the collections of art galleries, listen to recordings of speeches and other events, watch live video, retrieve pictures taken from the Hubbell space telescope, publish your own electronic articles, and send E-mail (electronic mail) to other Internet subscribers world wide. *Every Student's Guide to the Internet* (Pitter et al., 1995) will get you started.

After you read various overviews (texts, books, chapters, review articles), you can follow your interests and begin reading more specialized theory and research papers. As you proceed, your ideas will become more and more focused. The more you read, the clearer you will be about which methods to use to test your ideas.

Search from the present to the past. We think the best strategy for reviewing the literature is to read up-to-date books and articles first. But don't consider your job done once you have looked up references from the last couple of years. Remember that the degree of confidence you have in the potential contribution of your research idea and the validity of your hypothesis will depend on how systematic your review of the literature has been.

Once you zero in on a topic of interest to you in the recent literature, follow up by reading the theory and research papers that led up to the modern work. In most cases, you will find that certain articles are referred to over and over again. When this happens, go back and read these frequently cited, and therefore influential, papers, chapters or books. Many researchers before you have considered them to be important.

From there you might follow up with a search using the *Social Science Citation Index (SSCI)*. *SSCI* lists alphabetically by author all the published works that cite a particular publication. Using *SSCI* will bring you up to date on research and theoretical developments that were inspired by the study that interests you. *SSCI*, first published in 1966, covers a wide range of journals in the social sciences.

Whatever the specifics of your search, eventually you will reach a point of diminishing returns when reading further yields little in the way of new information. Then you can stop, confident in the adequacy of your search.

Use all the resources available to you. In addition to reading, talk to professors and fellow students about your ideas. A professor often will be familiar with books, chapters, or articles that you might not find on your own or able to suggest resource persons to contact for leads. Also be sure to use the available library resources fully. Don't hesitate to ask the reference librarians for help; they are there to assist you and are well trained in the library skills that you need to acquire at this phase of your research.

Collecting Your Own Observations

The second approach to becoming well informed in a given area of psychology is making your own observations. This strategy can be an excellent follow-up to the literature review. Jean Piaget (1954) used it as he observed the development of intelligence in his two young children; so did Jane Goodall (1986) when she studied chimpanzees in the wild, and Erving Goffman (1959) as he collected information on "the presentation of self in everyday life" among the Shetland Islanders of Scotland.

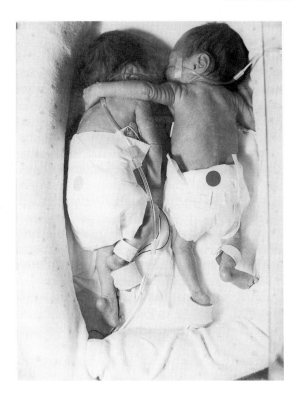

Twins Brielle and Kyrie snuggle together in their incubator.

Much of the advice on observing offered by scientists, who pride themselves on their ability to notice what others do not, has to do with getting rid of preconceptions, prejudices, and assumptions that can blind us to seeing what would be seen and understood with unobstructed vision. The following example highlights the importance of paying attention to what these scientists have to say.

It is standard practice in hospitals to isolate newborn premature babies in individual incubators to protect them from infection. When premature twin sisters Brielle and Kyrie, each weighing only about two pounds, were placed in their incubators, Kyrie was doing well but Brielle was having breathing problems, an accelerated heart rate, and was gaining weight slowly (Sheehan, 1995). When Brielle's heart rate suddenly became unstable and she started to change color, the attending nurse, Gayle Kasparian, tried the standard medical procedures—suctioning breathing passages and giving more oxygen, but Brielle didn't improve.

Then, as a last chance effort and ignoring established practice, Kasparian put Brielle into Kyrie's incubator where the tiny infants could snuggle together. Because Brielle's heart rate stabilized instantly, the sisters were allowed to stay together. Brielle started to gain weight and had no further heart rate problems. These dramatic and unexpected results led the hospital to begin scientific studies of "double bedding" in 1996. If the nurse who was watching the twins had not been able to go beyond the dictates of her training and experience, a young life might have been lost and a beneficial medical innovation missed.

"Bracket" preconceptions. Since training in one's discipline always leads to preconceptions, their potential blinding effects on researchers is a serious problem. Phenomenological researchers (see Chapter 2), who try to discover the essence of particular human experiences, often begin their studies by looking inward at their own perceptions of them. By reflecting on their own personal experiences, they hope to identify any preconceptions and biases that might color their receptivity to the experiences reported by their subjects. Once identified, they attempt to "set aside [these] theories, research presuppositions, ready-made interpretations, etc." in a process called "bracketing" (Ashworth, 1996, p. 1).

Karl Duncker (1945), a research psychologist, also devised an approach to reducing the impact of preconceptions in his research subjects. Duncker found that prior training with a complex solution in a problem-solving experiment could blind his subjects to easy and otherwise obvious solutions. In follow-up experiments, it became clear to Duncker that such blindness could be overcome by saying to subjects, "Don't be blind!" With this warning, subjects could overcome their expectations and see the simple solutions that they previously had missed.

A word to the wise should be enough. As you struggle to come up with a research question and hypothesis, think of Kasparian, Duncker, and the phenomenological researchers, and remind yourself periodically not to be blind. Or you might try the following strategy for minimizing the impact of biases, one that first was suggested by T. C. Chamberlin, a geologist, more than a century ago, and rediscovered by scientists three quarters of a century later.

Entertain multiple hypotheses. Chamberlin (1890/1965), like phenomenological researchers, was concerned with how scientists' preconceptions can unconsciously influence their observations and interpretations. He reasoned that if researchers can cultivate several potential explanations to account for a given phenomenon (the example he used was how the Great Lake basins were formed), they will be less likely to invest themselves in any particular one. As he put it, "with this method the dangers of parental affection for a favorite theory can be circumvented" (Chamberlin, 1890/1965, p. 754). Chamberlin believed that scientists who entertain multiple hypotheses will be less likely to selectively attend to data and less likely to offer interpretations distorted by their expectations and desires. Today Chamberlin's approach is routinely applied in investigative work outside of psychology.

When Trans World Airlines flight 800 mysteriously crashed in the summer of 1996, investigators looking for the cause of the crash considered several possible scenarios—pilot error, mechanical failure, explosive devices, and a missile fired from the ground or air. The investigators kept each of these possibilities in mind as they searched the wreckage for chemical traces of explosives, studied the physical damage to the plane, listened to the recording of the plane's last seconds, and examined reports of eyewitnesses.

Within psychology, D. B. Bromley (1986), an expert on case study methodology (see Chapter 2), also advises researchers to formulate and test multiple alternative hypotheses as they attempt to account for the data collected on a case. By being open to the full range of possible interpretations, he believes, the chances of arriving at a valid understanding increase. So follow Chamberlin's and Bromley's advice and consider many different hypotheses as you strive to understand unfamiliar and puzzling phenomena. Or try breaking free of preconceived ideas by adopting one of the following "tried-and-true" strategies of innovative scientists.

Make the familiar unfamiliar. Scientific observers recognized for their expertise advise beginning scientists to wonder about and question everything. Ask how, when, why, and what if in regard to the everyday happenings around you. Take nothing for granted. The biochemist Szent-Gyorgyi provides a model of this approach to observing familiar events:

> I like to see things simple, a bit infantile, without much sophistication, and to wonder about the simple things. People often fail to see that something is a miracle if they see it often. To me the greatest and most exciting miracles are what I see around me every day. (Szent-Gyorgyi, in Root-Bernstein, 1989, p. 32)

To foster this freshness of perspective in yourself, imagine how a child might view the phenomena you are observing. Think about what the child would notice and wonder about. Or try to adopt an outsider's perspective as you make your observations. Imagine that you are a being from another planet. What would an extraterrestrial focus on? How would the extraterrestrial describe the event and explain it to a fellow alien?

Make the unfamiliar familiar. Barbara McClintock, the Nobel Prize-winning geneticist, spent a lifetime in systematic research. The fact that she lived and breathed genetics was important in fostering the kind of intimate understanding that can spark innovation. But McClintock also developed imaginative abilities that allowed her to see things that were not visible to others. As she peered through the lens of her microscope at neurospora chromosomes, McClintock imagined she was a part of the microscopic world she observed:

> I found that the more I worked with them the bigger and bigger [they] got, and when I was really working with them I wasn't outside, I was down there. I was part of the system. I was right down there with them, and everything got big. I even was able to see the internal parts of the chromosomes. . . . It surprised me because I actually felt as if I were right down there and these were my friends.

> As you look at these things, they become part of you. And you forget yourself. The main thing is that you forget yourself. (McClintock, in Ferrucci, 1990, pp. 228–9)

Although McClintock had only her own resources as tools on these forays into the unknown, today technological advances allow any scientist to make the same kinds of up close and personal observations of microscopic material. Virtual reality headsets and motion sensors enable modern researchers to have the experience of walking on the surface of microscopic substances and studying the structure of their atoms at close range.

According to Root-Bernstein (1988), Alexander Fleming, the scientist who discovered penicillin, used a different approach to make the unfamiliar about microorganisms familiar. Like McClintock, he observed carefully and systematically. Although his peers threw out their cultures once an experiment was complete, Fleming saved his for weeks so that he could examine them regularly for any new and unusual developments. Fleming also played with his cultures. He painted pictures on petri dishes with different microorganisms so that he could watch images emerge in Technicolor as the cultures grew.

David Krech, a psychologist, found that a playful attitude helped him in his research as well:

> I play with my ideas, I live with them, and fantasize about them. I build them into a big, whole *megillah*, a systematic solution to all the problems of brain chemistry. In that way I keep them salient. (Krech, 1970, p. 62)

Be open to serendipity. Serendipity is a word that was coined by Horace Walpole in 1754 to refer to findings that researchers come across unexpectedly while trying to answer other questions (Roberts, 1989). Walpole had read a fairy tale about the three Princes of Serendip who were always happening upon discoveries they were not looking for.

Wilder Penfield, a neurologist and neurosurgeon, claims that such accidental discovery was involved in an important discovery he made as he "mapped" the cortex of an epileptic patient. Mapping involves probing different locations on the cortex with electrodes and noting the behavioral effects. During this painless procedure, a necessity prior to surgery on the brain, patients are awake and alert and can report on their experience.

> The first time I caused a patient to vocalize startled me much more than it did the patient. It came as a complete surprise. We had never caused vocalization. . . . And I remember the man on whom I used the electrode. He began to cry in a certain tone. I took the electrode away and he stopped instantly. I put it on again and he started, without knowing what I did. . . . The fact that it opened up one of the mechanisms that makes it possible for a man to talk, a control of vocalization upon the cortex, that was exciting. But, that was stumbling on something. (Penfield, 1970, p. 105–6)

There are plenty of other examples of serendipity in science. A breakdown in his apparatus for delivering reinforcements led B. F. Skinner to discover curves of extinction. Alexander Fleming's discovery of penicillin and Röntgen's discovery of X-rays were serendipitous. The events leading to these discoveries might have passed unnoticed by differently prepared minds.

EUREKA!—DISCOVERING IDEAS

As you read the literature and observe the world around you, you finally will reach the point when you must come up with a specific idea to research. You may or may not make a prediction, a hypothesis, about how the results will turn out. Some projects don't have clearly developed expectations—the researcher simply wonders "What would happen if?", or "How do scores on this measure relate to scores on this other measure?" In other cases, the researcher is able to come up with a hypothesis, a hunch that given certain conditions, certain other events or conditions will hold true as well. Whether your project has a hypothesis or not will depend on what is already known about the phenomena that you are interested in. Although you must know something to identify a research question, you must be even more knowledgeable to come up with a specific expectation of how the research will turn out.

Although we would like research ideas to come effortlessly from reading the research of others or from gazing at the world about us, this doesn't happen. Developing an idea almost always is a great deal of work. To make progress you must read and observe actively with a view to generating ideas. What follows are some suggestions for structuring your search. Keep them in mind as you think, read and observe.

Use Theory to Generate Ideas

One mark of a good theory is that it is heuristic, that is, that it inspires testable hypotheses. The approach to generating research ideas by deriving hypotheses from theory is called deductive reasoning.

Examples of deductive reasoning are easy to come by in psychology and this book is filled with them. In Chapter 1, for example, we discussed Mesmer's theory of animal magnetism and the commission's research evaluating that theory. The commissioners designed several experiments to test the conflicting predictions derived from their own psychological explanation of animal magnetism's effects and Mesmer's physical explanation of the same events. The prediction that Köhler made in his study of transposition (see Chapter 1) came from the Gestalt theory of learning. Köhler's research pitted this conception against Thorndike's S-R theory.

To apply this approach, first learn everything you can about a particular theory, like social learning theory (Bandura, 1971), Gestalt theory (Koffka, 1935), or Bem's self-perception theory (Bem, 1972). Then think about potential hypotheses based on the theory that might apply to your areas of interest. Consider whether established hypotheses based on that theory might be generalized to the phenomena of interest to you or whether you need to formulate a new hypothesis from the theory to account for the behaviors you plan to investigate.

Explore Analogies and Metaphors

Analogies and metaphors point to parallels between unfamiliar phenomena and more familiar objects and events. Biologists compare parts of the body to machines—the heart to a pump, the nervous system to an electrical system, the eye to a camera. The functioning of the brain often is compared to that of a computer. Thinking in terms of analogies like these can inspire hypotheses and inventions, as the following example illustrates.

Some of the technology that underlies modern cellular phones was patented half a century ago by Hedy Lamarr, a Viennese-born movie star of the 1930s and 1940s, then called "the most beautiful girl in the world" (Associated Press, 1997). In the 1930s, Lamarr's parents arranged a marriage for her to an Austrian armament manufacturer, with whom she attended business dinners and meetings at which weapon systems were discussed and filmed field tests watched. Curious from childhood about how things work, Lamarr listened and learned. When her husband's business dealings increasingly involved the Nazis, Lamarr left him and came to the United States.

When World War II began, Lamarr wanted to help in the war effort. Because of her experiences in Europe, her thoughts turned to weapon systems. She began to think about ways to get around the jamming that prevented the United States from using radio-controlled missiles against the Germans. One day, while fooling around at the piano, she and a musician friend, George Antheil, played a game. He began playing notes at one end of the piano and she echoed what he played at the other. She realized, "Hey, look, we're talking to each other, and we're changing all the time." Using this idea, they went on to invent a radio system for controlling torpedoes. It changed from one frequency to another at split-second intervals, so that the signal would control the torpedo but sound like random noise to anyone listening to it. They patented their "Secret Communication System," based on an analogy with their synchronized piano game, on August 11, 1942.

Analogies also suggest hypotheses in psychology. William Dement (1960), for example, found that subjects in his sleep experiments showed an unexpected consistency in the amount of their rapid eye movement (REM) sleep each night. This finding led Dement to hypothesize that dreaming, which is associated with REM sleep, might be a psychological need, analogous to the physical need people have for food or water. Dement then went on to test and confirm this hypothesis by depriving volunteers of REM sleep and studying the effects on their behavior.

Metaphors are figures of speech, based on analogies, that are applied to objects or events to which they do not literally apply. Models derived from studying physical disease, infection, and inoculation are applied to human behavior; for example, psychologists use terms like inoculation against stress and inoculation against attitude change to point to the ways in which small doses can build a kind of immunity to major assaults on the nervous system or attitudes.

Theodore Sarbin (1969/1982), a social psychologist, discussed how the metaphors we use have implications that direct our action and thought, including the ideas we develop and test in research. When we use terms like "mental illness," he argued, we extend models of physical disease to the mind (itself a metaphor), highlighting a narrow range of potential hypotheses about disturbed behavior and ignoring others. Because of the damaging consequences of the metaphor for the people to whom it is applied and the limited perspective it suggests to psychologists looking for the causes of misconduct, Sarbin called for the replacement of the "mental illness" metaphor.

In its place, Sarbin offered what he saw as a more appropriate and benign metaphor—"the transformation of social identity." In Sarbin's view, substituting this new metaphor for the old one would lead to a shift in the kinds of hypotheses that psychologists would entertain. Guided by the new metaphor, researchers would identify people whose attempts to establish viable social identities have been unsuccessful. With their help, they would study the "behavioral effects of prolonged degradation," and investigate other hypotheses about "the outcomes of upgrading social identities through commendation, promotion, and so on." In research inspired by the new metaphor, "the search for 'causes' will be in social systems, not in mythic internal entities" (Sarbin, 1969/1982, p. 147–8).

The examples we have presented in this section illustrate that when we apply analogies and metaphors to puzzling phenomena, what is known shapes our perceptions and thoughts about what is not known, suggesting hypotheses for research in the process. To find ideas for research, practice reasoning in analogies and critique common metaphors. As you work at understanding a new phenomenon, ask yourself what it is similar to. Let your imagination run wild as you generate ideas about other events that might be related to the ones you are interested in. Make connections.

Keep Alert for Anomalies

Oliver Sacks (1985), a neurologist, was asked to consult on a baffling case involving an accomplished professor of music who began to make absurd, even comical, perceptual errors in his everyday life. The man, whose eyesight was unimpaired, patted the top of parking-meters thinking they were children, couldn't distinguish between his foot and his shoe, and tried to pick up his wife's head, mistaking it for a hat. Sacks used the case to illustrate a complicated example of visual agnosia due to damage in the visual parts of the right hemisphere of the brain.

Anomalies are phenomena that make no sense given established thinking in a field. Sacks believes that understanding these rare events is critical to developing our understanding of brain functioning. In his words,

> Such cases constitute a radical challenge to one of the most entrenched axioms or assumptions of classical neurology—in particular, the notion that brain damage, any brain damage, reduces or removes the "abstract and categorical attitude." Here in the case of Dr. P, we see the very *opposite* of this. (Sacks, 1985, p. 5)

Like Sacks, researchers interested in psychological phenomena have spent their lives trying to understand anomalies.

Toward the close of the 19th century, Sigmund Freud, a young Viennese neurologist, struggled to understand the causes of his patients' unexplained symptoms, which included paralyses, visual and auditory disturbances, weakness, coughs, headaches, tics, and other bizarre phenomena. Freud invented psychoanalysis as a strategy for uncovering the psychological causes of such symptoms, which he believed were buried deep in the sufferers' unconscious minds. Later in his life Freud worked at understanding the causes of slips of the tongue, mysterious lapses of memory, dreams, and many psychological disorders, all puzzling anomalies.

Jean Piaget, perhaps the foremost developmental psychologist of the 20th century, like Freud, hit upon the idea of using anomalies to reveal the course of children's cognitive development. He devised ingenious tests showing that very young infants have no concept of the permanence of objects. He demonstrated the difficulties children experience in understanding that volume and number remain constant when objects change their shape or spatial arrangement. By studying anomalies of childhood reasoning, Piaget "provided the field with an entirely new vision of the nature of children, and of the what, when, and how of their cognitive growth" (Flavell, 1996, p. 200).

Life is full of puzzling and rare phenomena. So keep alert for them as you observe the world around you. When you find an anomaly, you also will have found a research question. If you come up with a tentative explanation, you will have invented a hypothesis.

Look for Gaps in Knowledge

Some of Oliver Sacks's work was inspired by his attempt to fill gaps in the published information on brain functioning. For instance, in his introduction to the case of the musician with visual agnosia, he wrote:

> Although right-hemisphere syndromes are as common as left-hemisphere syndromes—why should they not be?—we will find a thousand descriptions of left-hemisphere syndromes in the neurological and neuropsychological literature for every description of a right-hemisphere syndrome. It is as if such syndromes were somehow alien to the whole temper of neurology. (Sacks, 1985, p. 3)

Advances frequently are made by scientists who attempt to fill gaps in knowledge, and when such gaps are filled there is much excitement. One of the criticisms raised against Darwin's theory of evolution, for example, was the absence in the fossil record of the kinds of intermediate species that his theory predicted. When the *Archaeopteryx*, a so-called "missing link" between birds and reptiles, was discovered in 1861, Darwin's ideas gained in acceptance. The credibility of Darwin's theory continues to increase as the fossils of extinct transitional species are discovered in modern times. One of these, found in 1994 in Pakistan, is *Ambulocetus natans*, the swimming walking-whale, an intermediate

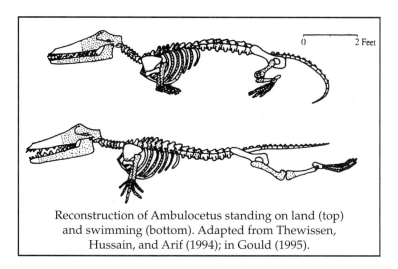

Reconstruction of Ambulocetus standing on land (top)
and swimming (bottom). Adapted from Thewissen,
Hussain, and Arif (1994); in Gould (1995).

form between land and water species with legs for walking on land and large feet and a flexible spine for swimming (Gould, 1995).

Gaps in knowledge regularly inspire research. In fact, many journal articles end by suggesting ideas for further research. As you read texts and review articles, ask yourself what questions remain to be answered, what controversies are not yet resolved, what types of research questions have been dismissed, ignored or overlooked. Root-Bernstein (1989) recommended searching old books for unanswered research questions or data overlooked or forgotten by modern researchers. In the following example, a desperate father found a treatment that saved his young son's life by doing just that (*Dateline NBC*, 1996).

Charlie was just one year old when he began to have epileptic seizures, which increased in frequency until he was having a hundred seizures a day. His doctors tried anticonvulsant drugs; none worked and their side effects, which were turning Charlie into "a zombie," were devastating. Because unchecked seizures can lead to brain damage, Charlie's doctors operated on his brain to stop the seizures, but their efforts were fruitless. The seizures did not stop.

Charlie's father, Jim Abrahams, then began attending medical lectures and reading everything he could find on how to treat epilepsy. One day he came upon a book, written by John Freeman of Johns Hopkins University in the 1920s, describing the ketogenic diet, a diet for epilepsy. The diet had been widely used, with great success, until the 1950s, when it was largely replaced by drug treatments. It consists of some protein, but mostly "lots of fat, bacon, butter and heavy whipping cream," all of which must be precisely measured for the diet to work (*Dateline NBC*, 1996, p. 19).

As soon as Charlie started on the diet, his seizures lessened. He was seizure free within two days. Since Charlie's father appeared on NBC's news magazine *Dateline*, fifty thousand people have requested and received copies of this new old diet for epilepsy.

Turn Assumptions on Their Heads

David Krech reported that he had been working for some time attempting to relate levels of enzyme activity in the brain to learning.

> But after about four years we just got bored with that problem. We quite deliberately reversed our thinking then. Instead of saying, "How do chemical differences in the brain affect learning," we asked the reverse problem, "How does learning affect brain chemistry." . . . Having asked that question, a whole new world opened up. (Krech, 1970, p. 63)

Krech went on to study the impact of enriching the environment of rats on their brain chemistry.

Since Krech made these remarks, whole new fields have developed to examine the complex interactions between biochemical and psychological processes. One of these is the field of psychoneuroimmunology, the study of the interactions between behavior and immunity (Maier, Watkins, & Fleshner, 1994). Researchers in this new field are discovering that psychological events, like stress and depression, alter immunity, a not too surprising finding. But they also are discovering that events in the immune system can modify behavior (e.g., changes in the immune system of animals can produce stress). Such studies have not been done with humans, but Maier et al. wonder whether the kinds of daily changes that occur in our immune systems might someday be shown to account for some of the unexplained mood swings most of us experience. Such hypotheses are sure to result in exciting new research in the years to come.

Krech's and Maier et al.'s remarks are testimony to the value of the strategy that Root-Bernstein (1989) calls "turning assumptions on their heads"—taking well-established findings and turning them around. Let's look at some examples of the many assumptions in psychology just waiting to be turned on their heads. You cannot take a course in child development without learning something about the effects of parents (usually mothers) on their children; but few researchers look at the ways that children's behaviors call out different responses in their parents. There are many claims made that pet ownership has a positive impact on people's health, but what is known about the impact of people presence on pets' health? Clearly, countless examples could be generated; use your imagination. As you learn about established ideas in the field, be inventive and practice turning assumptions on their heads.

Look for Patterns in Findings

Phenomenological researchers gather descriptions of people's experience which they analyze for patterns. A study by Ivana Guglietti-Kelly and Malcolm Westcott of "what shyness means to the shy person" (Guglietti-Kelly & Westcott, 1990, p. 150) is a good example of this approach to research. The researchers asked participants to describe a situation in which they felt shy, detailing what this experience was like. Once collected, the authors studied the descriptions for themes in how the subjects viewed their situation, themselves, and the activity of shyness.

On the basis of their analysis, the researchers formulated a description of the essence of shyness, which they asked their colleagues and the participants to read for missing elements. Incorporating their suggestions, they finally arrived at an "essential description of shyness" that captured the experiences of their subjects and was consistent with descriptions of shyness in the published literature.

> [Shyness is] an experience of separateness and aloneness in a social situation, which is precipitated by one's feelings of uncertainty about the ability to establish an identity and a rapport with others, fear of behaving inappropriately, and awareness of oneself as inhibited in the interaction. It is an uncomfortable state of vulnerability, which the individual seeks to escape. (Guglietti-Kelly & Westcott, 1990, p. 157)

Like this study, case studies, participant observation, and naturalistic observation attempt to find patterns in a wide array of data. So as you gather information about phenomena, from the literature or your own observations, look for patterns. And when you find them, don't take them for granted. Instead, ask how, why, when, and what if about the findings you discover. As you try to figure out the bases for the patterns, you will be generating research ideas using inductive reasoning.

Try to Resolve Discrepancies

Tiffany Field (1993) reported that discovering conflicting research reports on the effects of massage on premature infants inspired her own research. Some previous researchers had reported that massage led to weight gain, a desired outcome for preemies, but others did not find this. Field accounted for these conflicting findings by hypothesizing that the degree of pressure applied during massage is critical to reducing the stress of premature infants, that light stroking is aversive to them. She went on to do studies that confirmed this hypothesis.

Duane Rumbaugh (1993) recalls that an important finding about primate vision resulted from his attempts to understand discrepancies between the outcomes in his learning experiments for different species. Whereas most primates could learn his object discrimination tasks easily, gibbons and other tree-dwelling primates made little headway. Many experiments later, Rumbaugh concluded that tree-dwellers are at a disadvantage in his experiments because they attend to near visual stimuli rather than distant ones.

In Rumbaugh's experiments, the animals were required to peer through a Plexiglas divider to solve the problems. Instead of looking through the Plexiglas, though, the gibbons looked at the Plexiglas, studying its surface scratches and reflections, and paying no attention to the objects they were supposed to differentiate.

You can use Field and Rumbaugh as models in developing your research question. Like them, keep alert for conflicting findings. When you find discrepancies, generate hypotheses to explain them.

Develop Skepticism about Findings, Methods, and Interpretations

At the time that Barry Marshall began his research on ulcers, most scientists believed that they were caused by psychological stress. But in 1983 Marshall announced that bacteria living in the stomach lining caused people's peptic ulcers (as cited in Monmaney, 1993). Marshall had seen the bacteria in the stomach tissue of one after another of his ulcer patients (a pattern). Although researchers before Marshall also had observed the bacteria, they had not connected them with ulcers; they believed, following the accepted view, that bacteria could not survive in the stomach, a sterile environment.

Having observed the bacteria and faced with the disbelief of other researchers, Marshall experimented on himself. He knew that other researchers, who refused to believe what he had reported, would need experimental results to be convinced that he was correct. So Marshall drank a potent solution of the "ulcer bugs" to see what would happen. Two weeks later a biopsy of his stomach tissue revealed inflamed tissue containing high concentrations of the bacteria. His hypothesis confirmed, Marshall went on to show that antibiotics provide the most effective ulcer treatment. Marshall's bacterial hypothesis finally was accepted only when subsequent research demonstrated that the bacteria, later named *Helicobacter pylori*, could burrow into the stomach lining away from the stomach acids that would destroy them. (Incidentally, Marshall got better, and without medication. His immune system apparently was able to fight off the infection with no outside assistance.)

Maintaining a skeptical attitude, questioning the methods and findings of one's predecessors, is a potent source of research hypotheses. So, as you read research, think about possible problems in its design, measures, analysis, or the interpretation of its findings. Wonder about whether the research could be replicated. Might biases result from the particular apparatus or tasks used in the research? Might the results be specific to the particular subjects or situation tested?

Improve Apparatus, Measures, and Procedures

Katharine Payne was observing elephants in the zoo when she "repeatedly noticed a palpable throbbing in the air like distant thunder, yet all around me was silent" (Payne, 1989, p. 266). Sometime later she recalled singing in the choir as a child, standing in front of the biggest pipe of the church organ and, when the organist played bass notes, feeling vibrations similar to the ones she felt at the zoo. Going on a hunch that perhaps the vibrations she experienced were coming from the elephants (an analogy), Payne decided to tape-record them through many hours of seeming silence.

Electronic printouts of her recordings showed that she had recorded 400 calls, although only a third of them were audible to her. The printouts suggested that the elephants were communicating with one another by low-frequency sounds inaudible to the human ear. An improved measuring instrument (a recording rather than the human ear) and a device for revealing infrasound (the electronic printout) revealed a previously unknown world of animal sound.

Katherine Payne recording elephant sounds in Africa.

Payne continued her pioneering research on elephants in Kenya, Namibia, and Zimbabwe, where she and her colleagues conducted research to learn whether elephants use infrasound for long-distance communication. If so, many puzzling phenomena of elephant life, like how elephants get together when miles apart, would be explained. To test this hypothesis required sophisticated engineering and an ingenious and innovative method.

For one of their experiments, Payne and her colleagues recorded many hours of elephant calls, rich in infrasound. Later one researcher stationed himself in a van from which he later would play an infrasound call of his choosing over a loudspeaker. A second group of researchers, including Payne, were videotaping two male elephants at a water hole some distance from the van. These researchers did not know when the sound would be played, because it was inaudible to the human ear, nor which call the other researcher had selected. As they watched and waited, all of a sudden, the two elephants lifted their heads and spread their ears in unison; both then marched off together in the direction of the van. The broadcast sound had been the call of a female elephant ready to mate. The occupants of the van breathed a sigh of relief when the elephants continued on past the van. In later experiments, the researchers planned to track elephants with electronic collars and microphones to learn more about how they communicate.

The history of science is full of cases where new measuring techniques opened up frontiers for study or advanced our understanding of well-known phenomena. We now can observe how the brain functions with magnetic resonance imaging, as Elbert et al. (1995) did in their study of the cortical functioning of stringed instrument players (see Chapter 2). Researchers studying the communication of bees no longer have to paint distinctive dabs of paint on their backs and visually observe their comings and goings, as von Frisch did (see Chapter 3). They now can monitor the bees electronically by placing bar codes on them and using automatic scanning devices, like the ones at supermarkets. Data can be collected even when researchers are not available, opening up possibilities for research that were not available to von Frisch.

A bar-coded bee.

So as you read reports of research, consider the measures, apparatus, or procedures employed in them. Ask whether they might be replaced by measures with better reliability and validity (see Chapter 12, Planning the Study), instruments that might reveal different phenomena, or whether a refinement in procedure might lead to new findings. Like Payne, you may come up with a better measure, a better set of questions, or an improved observational technique.

Focus on Practical Problems

Psychologists always have been interested in addressing practical problems. Alfred Binet (1903) developed the first intelligence test to help school officials in France decide which students to keep in regular classes and which to educate in special classes. During World War II, Kurt Lewin collaborated with the anthropologist Margaret Mead to find ways to get people to eat plentiful and nutritious, but unpopular foods (e.g., turnips) when other more desired foods were in low supply (Hothersall, 1995). Inspired by observing the effects of different governments on their citizens, Lewin, Lippitt, and White (1939) conducted experiments to find out how authoritarian, democratic, and laissez-faire leadership styles affect children in groups. Countless studies have been done to assess therapeutic and educational techniques.

Tiffany Field's (1993) interest in premature infants began when her own child was born prematurely. As she witnessed the struggles of her newborn, she wondered how the stresses that premature babies suffer might be reduced. Her award-winning research, discussed earlier in the chapter, led to new understandings and practical recommendations for handling premature infants. Subsequent studies investigated the effects of massage on infants, looking at which preterm infants benefit most from massage, and examining the effects of massage on cocaine-exposed premature infants and on the infants of depressed adolescent girls. Field's subjects now include adults. Her study of the effects of massage therapy on adults' mental alertness is discussed in Chapter 13, Communicating Research, and reprinted in Appendix B.

Field points out that finding inspiration for research in one's own life, as she did, is by no means unique:

> If you conducted a survey among researchers you would find that nine out of ten are personally or socially concerned about the subject they are studying. Thus, the phrase, "research is me-search" appropriately describes this phenomenon. (Field, in Brannigan & Merrens, 1993, p. 3)

If your life is like everyone else's, it contains plenty of puzzles to be solved and phenomena to be curious about. So look around you. Think about recurrent problems that come up in college life—homesickness, making friends, getting along with roommates and others, issues concerned with eating, drinking, studying, grades. Are there ideas discussed in the literature that might be applied to understanding these problems? Might programs be developed to help students study more effectively, improve self-esteem, or alter attitudes toward different groups on campus? Use your imagination. Any number of programs might be instituted and evaluated.

*F*INAL THOUGHTS

We've focused in this chapter on the anxieties, the frustrations and the hard work associated with getting started in research. We wanted you to realize that your concerns as beginning researchers are not unique. But the picture we have painted is incomplete. In our eagerness to show you that some fear and frustration is to be expected, we've left out the joy and excitement that comes from finding the right problem or formulating a promising hypothesis.

To correct for this oversight, we now quote the last few lines of a poem, written by Root-Bernstein (1989, p. 420), entitled "How to Be a Maverick." Most of the poem summarizes Root-Bernstein's recommendations on how to develop the attitudes and lifestyles that foster scientific discovery. The poem ends with the following lines illustrating why discovery is well worth the price we pay for it:

> Do these things and you shall find
> surprises unexpected;
> Detours left which turn out right,
> old dogmas now corrected.
> So do us all a favor: Start thinking
> good thoughts now.
> Discovering and inventing: There's no
> better life, I vow!

So now, begin. Start keeping a research journal. Purchase a special notebook for the purpose, one that is convenient to carry around with you. In it, record ideas that you want to remember (they relate to what interests you) as well as things that strike you as personally relevant. The ideas that you put in your journal don't have to be momentous. Record any observations that you make or ideas that you encounter that strike you as especially fascinating, noteworthy, odd, disturbing, or puzzling. Use the journal to explore connections between ideas, to make notes on how an intriguing idea that you covered in your course on learning relates to the research you just read about in your personality, social psychology, or cognitive psychology courses.

Ideas are fleeting. For most of us, they go more quickly than they come. So capture your ideas as you get them by making a permanent record in your journal to mull over at your leisure later on. Whenever you are "struck" by an idea, jot it down for future reference. If you do this faithfully, you will end up with a list of ideas that could lead to a research project.

Before you know it, you are likely to see a pattern to your interests and soon you will be ready to focus on a particular area of study. And once you do, you may be pleasantly surprised. Many researchers find that as soon as they decide to work on a problem their world begins to change. Information and happenings related to their newfound interest are everywhere. Perhaps, like W. H. Murray, you will find:

> The moment one definitely commits oneself, then Providence moves too. All sorts of things occur to help one that would never otherwise have occurred. A whole stream of events issues from the decision; raising in one's favour all manner of unforeseen incidents and meetings and material assistance which no man could have dreamt would have come his way. (W. H. Murray, in Austin, 1977, p. 6)

KEY TERMS

Pasteur's maxim	*Social Science Citation Index*
Psychological Abstracts	Bracketing
PsycLIT	Multiple hypotheses
PsycINFO	Serendipity
ERIC	Analogy
Annual Review of Psychology	Metaphor
Psychological Bulletin	Anomalies
Psychological Review	"Turning assumptions on their heads"
The Internet	

KEY PEOPLE

Robert Weisberg	Karl Duncker
Robert S. Root-Bernstein	T. C. Chamberlin
Jonas Salk	Barbara McClintock
Janet Bavelas	Alexander Fleming
Gayle Kasparian	David Krech

Wilder Penfield
Hedy Lamarr
William Dement
Theodore Sarbin
Stephen J. Gould
Tiffany Field
Barry Marshall
Katharine Payne

Alfred Binet
Kurt Lewin
Oliver Sacks
Sigmund Freud
Jean Piaget
Ivana Guglietti-Kelly
Duane Rumbaugh

REVIEW QUESTIONS

1. What did Robert Weisberg conclude about the type of people who do outstanding scientific work?

2. What did Jonas Salk mean when he said "Do what makes your heart leap"?

3. Discuss the two general methods that are discussed in the chapter for preparing the mind to find a research problem.

4. What does Janet Bavelas say about how to nurture newborn ideas?

5. Distinguish among *PsycLIT, PsycINFO, Psychological Abstracts, ERIC,* and the *Social Science Citation Index.*

6. What preconception did Gayle Kasparian overcome in caring for premature twins Brielle and Kyrie?

7. What did Duncker's research show about the effect of prior training on problem solving?

8. What do phenomenological researchers do to overcome preconceptions that could bias their descriptions of experience?

9. How can entertaining multiple hypotheses help researchers overcome the effects of personal bias in their work?

10. What strategies can researchers use to develop fresh perspectives in viewing ordinary events?

11. How did Fleming's and Krech's attitudes prove helpful in their research?

12. Give examples of important scientific discoveries that were made by accident.

13. Give some examples of research that were generated from theory.

14. How did Hedy Lamarr use an analogy to discover a secret communication system?

15. According to Theodore Sarbin, what impact do psychologists' metaphors have on the kinds of research they do on mental disorders?

16. Explain why Oliver Sacks thinks that the anomaly of a man mistaking his wife's head for a hat is important theoretically?

17. What important lesson can we learn from the way Jim Abrahams found a cure for his son's seizures?

18. What is meant by "turning assumptions on their heads"? Give an example of how this strategy has led to research ideas?

19. Describe Guglietti-Kelly and Westcott's study of what shyness means to the shy person.

20. How did Tiffany Field's research on the effects of massage on premature infants and Duane Rumbaugh's research on primate learning resolve conflicting findings?

21. What experiment did Barry Marshall perform on himself to convince skeptics about the cause of ulcers?

22. How did Katharine Payne's innovations in measurement lead to important discoveries about elephant communication?

23. What did Tiffany Field mean by the phrase "research is me-search"?

12

Planning the Study

❖

To interrogate nature—that's where the fun is.

CARL SAGAN

❖

RECRUITING PARTICIPANTS
    Probability Sampling
    Convenience Sampling
ASSIGNING SUBJECTS TO GROUPS
DECIDING ON APPARATUS AND MEASURING
   INSTRUMENTS
    Instruments
    Self-report Measures
        Finding commercial tests
        Finding unpublished tests
CONSTRUCTING YOUR OWN QUESTIONNAIRE
    Open versus Closed Questions
    Closed Item Formats
    Use Standard English—Define Your Terms
EVALUATING PSYCHOLOGICAL MEASURES
    Reliability
    Validity
EVALUATING OBSERVATIONAL MEASURES
SPECIAL PROBLEMS OF CONTROL WITH HUMAN
   PARTICIPANTS
    The Hawthorne Effect
    Demand Characteristics and Experimenter Expectancies
    Controlling for Suggestion and Reactivity
        Holding events constant
        Randomization
        Statistical control

DEBRIEFING
APPLYING TO THE INSTITUTIONAL REVIEW BOARD
    Recruitment Procedures
    The Consent Form
    Procedures Involved in the Research
    Confidentiality
FINAL COMMENTS
KEY TERMS, KEY PEOPLE, REVIEW QUESTIONS

Congratulations! You've made it through the most anxiety-provoking and frustrating phase of the research. Most likely, you have a research question now, and possibly a hypothesis that "makes your heart leap." This and the knowledge you have gained in previous chapters will guide your selection of a research design. Although you still have many other decisions to make about how to proceed in your research, as we will see, the possibilities from which you will be choosing are more limited than they were earlier in the project.

Our goal in this chapter is to help you with the decision making that follows the selection of a design. We will try to anticipate questions you might have on how to recruit and assign participants to conditions; how to write a questionnaire; how to avoid special problems of control that can influence the results of research with human participants; how to write a consent form and apply to your campus institutional review board; and, finally, how to debrief participants at the end of your study.

RECRUITING PARTICIPANTS

Once you have decided on a research design, your first step will be to choose between the two basic methods for recruiting participants, probability sampling and convenience sampling, that were discussed in Chapter 10.

In probability sampling, subjects are selected at random from a population. Typically, this sampling is restricted to surveys, where the researcher wants to generalize the results of the sample to the entire population that was sampled. Probability sampling is time-consuming because all members of the population must be identified and listed, then potential participants must be randomly selected from this list and invited to be in the survey.

Probability sampling is a lot of work compared to convenience sampling, in which any available person is a potential participant. Convenience sampling, typically, is used for selecting subjects for experiments. Of course, the price of this ease of recruiting is that the results of the experiment cannot be generalized with a calculable error to any population.

Once you have decided on your sampling plan, you can implement it using one of the strategies to which we now turn.

BOX 1 COMPUTER PROGRAM FOR SIMPLE RANDOM SAMPLING

```
DIM S(30000) AS INTEGER
RANDOMIZE TIMER
CLS
INPUT "Enter the number of subjects in the sample:", N
INPUT "Enter the number of subjects in the population:", Npop
FOR i = 1 TO Npop
S(i) = i
NEXT i
C = Npop
FOR i = 1 TO N
Pick = INT(RND * C) + 1
LPRINT S(Pick)
   FOR j = Pick TO C - 1
   S(j) = S(j + 1)
   NEXT j
C = C - 1
NEXT i
END
```

To use the program, number the members of the population 1, 2, 3, etc., up to the total number; these numbers will serve to identify the selected sample. Then start the program, and enter the sample and population sizes. The program will print out the identification numbers of the selected sample. The same program can be used for stratified sampling by running the program separately for each stratum (see Chapter 10 for a discussion of these methods).

Probability Sampling

Chapter 6 described how to draw samples from a population by hand, a time-consuming and difficult process. However, probability sampling can be done more easily with a computer. Box 1 presents a computer program for simple random sampling along with instructions on using it. The program is written in Microsoft QuickBasic, the computer language that is distributed with the MS-DOS operating system for IBM-type computers. We have placed a version of this program, written in the Java programming language, on the Internet at the Website for this book (see the preface for the Web address).

Convenience Sampling

Convenience sampling is more common than probability sampling in student research. In fact, your college may have a ready-made convenience sample, a campus *subject pool*, available for you to use. At many schools, undergraduate majors in psychology are asked to participate in research as part of their course requirements. To avoid the ethical problem of coercing participation, students usually are allowed to choose which studies they will participate in, and offered alternative educational options (like serving as an observer in research or

attending a research presentation; McCord, 1991) if they do not wish to participate. Ask your faculty adviser if there is a subject pool at your school and how
it works.

There are alternative methods you can use if your college has no subject
pool. One way to recruit participants is to go to a class, where you will reach
many potential participants in one face-to-face meeting. Approach a sympathetic faculty member who teaches a large class and ask whether you can take
a few minutes at the beginning of class to recruit volunteers for your research.
Other methods of contacting volunteers include advertising in the school
newspaper, posting notices, asking friends and acquaintances to volunteer,
and asking for volunteers in the dining hall or dorms. Campus mailings or
telephone contacts are another possibility, but face-to-face recruiting usually
works best.

ASSIGNING SUBJECTS TO GROUPS

You will be conducting either an experiment or a correlational study. In a correlational study, the researcher does not set up the conditions of the study, but
rather observes the behavior of subjects in naturally occurring conditions. The
conditions either are chosen by the subjects themselves during the course of
their lives (as in the *Consumer Reports* evaluation of psychotherapy [1995], in
which people reported on their experiences with therapists of their choice), or
they are characteristics of the subjects themselves (as in Sulloway's [1996]
study of birth order and creativity). In an experiment, the researcher sets up
the conditions and decides which subjects will be observed in them. In the
Elkin et al. (1989) evaluation of psychotherapy, for example, the researchers
decided which type of therapy each participant received.

Ideally, the assignment of subjects to groups in an experiment should be
done randomly. In Chapter 6, we described how to randomly assign subjects to
conditions by hand, but the easiest method of randomizing subjects is by computer. Box 2 presents two QuickBasic programs for randomization, with and
without blocking (see chapter 6). Like the program for random sampling, these
programs can be run on the Internet (see the preface for the Web address).

DECIDING ON APPARATUS AND MEASURING INSTRUMENTS

Instruments

Special equipment may be needed to precisely control the stimuli you present
to subjects, to time their responses, or to record their behavior. The next step in
planning your research is to decide on the apparatus and measuring instruments that you will use.

Today we have measuring instruments for research never dreamed of by
psychology's pioneers—machines for magnetic resonance imaging, the lie detec-
tor, and audio and video recorders that allow researchers to record and play
back at different speeds, to name a few. Personal computers now replace many

BOX 2 COMPUTER PROGRAMS FOR RANDOM ASSIGNMENT

Program for randomization without blocks

```
DIM S(1000)
RANDOMIZE TIMER
CLS
INPUT "Enter the number of subjects per group:", N
INPUT "Enter the number of groups:", G
FOR i = 1 TO N * G
S(i) = i
NEXT i
C = N * G
K = N
L = 1
FOR i = 1 TO N * G
IF K = N THEN LPRINT "Group"; L: K = 0: L = L + 1
Pick = INT(RND * C) + 1
LPRINT S(Pick)
K = K + 1
  FOR j = Pick TO C - 1
  S(j) = S(j + 1)
  NEXT j
C = C - 1
NEXT i
END
```

Program for randomization with blocks

```
DIM S(50)
RANDOMIZE TIMER
CLS
INPUT "Enter the number of blocks:", B
INPUT "Enter the number of subjects per block:", S
FOR j = 1 TO B
LPRINT
LPRINT "Block "; j; ":";
C = S
FOR i = 1 TO S: S(i) = i: NEXT i
  FOR i = 1 TO S
  Pick = INT(RND * C) + 1
  LPRINT S(Pick);
    FOR k = Pick TO C - 1
    S(k) = S(k + 1)
    NEXT k
  C = C - 1
  NEXT i
NEXT j
END
```

To use the programs, number the subjects, 1, 2, 3, etc.; then start the program, enter the number of subjects and the number of conditions (or blocks). The computer will print a record of the numbers of the subjects it assigns to each condition.

of the instruments used by researchers in the past, and commercial software is available for conducting many types of experiments in perception, memory, and cognition (see Brooks/Cole Research Methods and Statistics Catalog, 1997).

Although B. F. Skinner (1959) had to personally design and build the first Skinner box to control the delivery of food pellets to his animal subjects (see Chapter 9), researchers today can purchase one. In fact, commercial firms now manufacture many of psychology's most commonly used instruments. Your psychology department may even own some of them. Unfortunately, scientific instruments are very expensive, a fact that may limit the kinds of measures available to you for your study.

You can get valuable information on the instruments to use in your research by reading the literature on the problem of interest to you. If any of the studies you discover used an apparatus specifically designed for the research, the published report usually will include a detailed diagram with measurements; if not, you may be able to get plans for the apparatus from the researcher.

Often the stimulus materials for research are verbal materials, (e.g., a description of an event, a story, pictures) that you can create yourself or get by writing to the originator. Don't be shy! Sharing is an agreed upon ethic among scientists, who want their work to be replicated and extended by others.

Self-report Measures

Because self-report paper-and-pencil measures are used for so many purposes in psychological research (e.g., assessing mood states, attitudes, abilities, and interests), most likely your study will include such a measure. If so, there are three general sources for you to explore: (1) publishing houses that sell commercial tests, (2) scientific journals that publish measures developed by researchers for their own studies, and (3) your own creativity.

Finding commercial tests. Some of the best measures are commercial. Usually extensive information is available on the reliability and validity of such measures. The Buros Institute of Mental Measurement at the University of Nebraska, Lincoln, provides excellent reference material on commercial tests. Box 3 discusses their publications, including the extensive information you will find at their Website on the Internet.

Commercial tests range in price from about twenty dollars for simple paper-and-pencil tests to several hundred dollars for intelligence tests and batteries of achievement and aptitude tests. If you want to use a commercial test in your study, most likely your professor will have to order it for you, or cosign the order form, because there are restrictions on who can purchase such measures. For example, The Psychological Corporation, one of the major test publishers, classifies tests into three categories according to the credentials required for purchasing them. The Wechsler intelligence scales, for instance, are Class C tests, which require a Ph.D. in psychology or education, or verification of required training or experience, to purchase them (The Psychological Corporation, 1997).

BOX 3 FINDING AND EVALUATING COMMERCIAL TESTS: THE BUROS INSTITUTE OF MENTAL MEASUREMENT

The Buros Institute, founded in 1939 by Oscar Buros, provides evaluative information on commercial tests and measurement issues for professionals. *The Mental Measurements Yearbook (MMY)*, published beginning in 1938, contains descriptive material on tests, reviews, and references. The volume now is issued on alternate years with *The Supplement to the Mental Measurements Yearbook.* Its companion volume, *Tests in Print*, is a bibliography of all commercial tests in print, and serves as an index for *MMY* reviews. These reference books should be available at your college library.

The Buros Institute's Website at the University of Nebraska, Lincoln, (www.unl.edu/buros) is a treasure-trove of information on tests. The site provides instructions on using *MMY* and *Tests in Print,* and offers several databases that can be searched from the Website for reviews of commercial tests, publishers, and unpublished tests.

The *Test Review Locator* lists the volumes of *MMY* and *Test Critiques,* a reference work on tests published by PRO-ED publishing company, that include reviews of particular tests. To use the *Locator,* you enter identifying information about the test. For example, if you enter "Beck" in the *Locator,* it shows that the *Beck Depression Inventory* was reviewed in the 11th *MMY* and in Volume II, 1985, of *Test Critiques.* Your library should have these volumes, so you can read the reviews. (If not, the institute has a fee based fax service for reviews.) The *Locator* also can be used to find tests you are not familiar with. If you enter "creativity," for example, the *Locator* lists reviews of creativity measures.

Students who wish to purchase a test from this publisher must send them a written request to use the test along with a letter from a faculty sponsor endorsing the student project. Because publishers' requirements vary, you should consult their catalogues to learn what they require. The addresses and telephone numbers of over 900 test publishers can be accessed using the *BUROS/ERIC Test Publisher Locator* at the Buros Institute Website (see Box 3 for the institute's address).

Finding unpublished tests. If you decide not to purchase a commercial test, you may find a suitable "unpublished test" in the psychological literature. Tests published in research articles are called "unpublished" to distinguish them from commercial tests. Box 4 provides information on a variety of directories and books on unpublished tests.

The primary sources for the directories and collections of tests presented in Box 4 were scientific journals, a source that you can explore yourself. In fact, your own search may turn up better possibilities than using the references in Box 4, because you can examine the latest journals using the unique search criteria most appropriate for your study. If you are able to find an unpublished test that you would like to use, the APA recommends that you contact its author to request permission. There is an excellent guide to finding commercial and noncommercial tests published by the APA at their Website (go to www.apa.org, then click on "Science Information"), which ends with this recommendation. Written permission is required for copyrighted tests.

BOX 4 FINDING AND EVALUATING UNPUBLISHED TESTS: DIRECTORIES AND DATABASES PROVIDING INFORMATION ABOUT MEASURES AND THEIR SOURCES

The APA's six volume *Directory of Unpublished Experimental Mental Measures* covers about 6,000 tests, published between 1970 and 1990 (Goldman, Saunders, & Busch, 1996; Goldman, Osborne, & Mitchell, 1996; Goldman & Mitchell, 1995). The entry for each test (covering topics from altruism to zygosity) includes its purpose, format, and reliability, as well as references to studies that have used it. The sixth volume includes a subject index for all the volumes. This series, started in 1974, supplements the *Mental Measurements Yearbooks,* by covering tests not commercially available. The volumes are intended to promote the use of promising unpublished tests, and to make tests available to student researchers who may not be able to afford commercial tests.

Carol Beere's two companion volumes, *Women and Women's Issues: A Handbook of Tests and Measures* (1979) and *Gender Roles: A Handbook of Tests and Measures* (1990), cover inventories related to women's issues and gender roles published between 1927 and 1988. Beere compiled these volumes to encourage gender-related research by making it easier for interested researchers to find quality measures. The latter volume, which covers 211 measures, provides a full description of each measure, as well as information on its reliability and validity, references to research that used it, and a bibliography of related articles.

The Buros Institute's Website (see Box 3) includes the Educational Testing Service (ETS)/*ERIC* test collection, which can be searched for information on over 10,000 tests. *Health and Psychosocial Instruments,* put out by Behavior Measurement Database Services (www.ovid.com), another extensive database on tests, covers over 15,000 tests. This database is available through libraries and on CD-ROM.

Reference works containing tests and inventories:

- Robinson et al.'s three volumes, *Measures of Political Attitudes* (Robinson, Rusk, & Head, 1973), *Measures of Occupational Attitudes and Occupational Characteristics* (Robinson, Athanasiou, & Head, 1973), and *Measures of Social Psychological Attitudes* (Robinson & Shaver, 1973), include a variety of inventories.

- *Measures for Clinical Practice: A Sourcebook* (2nd ed.): Vol. 1. *Couples, Families and Children,* and *Measures for Clinical Practice: A Sourcebook* (2nd ed.): Vol. 2. *Adults* (Fisher & Corcoran, 1994) are two handbooks containing scales for use in clinical practice with children, adults, and families.

- *Family Assessment: Inventories for Research and Practice* (McCubbin & Thompson, 1991) covers family assessment inventories.

- *Behavior Analysis Forms for Clinical Intervention* and *Behavior Analysis Forms for Clinical Intervention* (Vols. 1, 2) (Cautela, 1977, 1981) present forms for use in behavioral-clinical interventions.

- ETS has a collection of tests on microfiche that is available at libraries or directly from ETS. The ETS test collection is described at the Buros Website (see Box 3).

- *The Keirsey Temperament Sorter,* a measure of Jungian personality types, can be taken, scored, and interpreted at http://sunsite.unc.edu/jembin/mb.pl.

CONSTRUCTING YOUR OWN QUESTIONNAIRE

You may decide to write your own questionnaire rather than using one developed by someone else. With your own measure you can get at the precise distinctions you want to make. The tips from the experts that we offer in this section are designed to help you make decisions on the format and wording of your questions.

Open versus Closed Questions

Your first decision in developing your own questionnaire will be which of the two basic types of questions to use—*open-ended* or *closed*. Open-ended questions do not impose restrictions on participants' responses; closed questions do.

> *Open-ended questions* require participants to construct their own answers. *Closed questions* require them to choose answers from a list of options.

The following question is open-ended:

> What products do you think the Federal Drug Administration (FDA) should regulate?

Asked as a closed question, it might read:

> Please check the products you think the Federal Drug Administration (FDA) should regulate.
>
> ❏ prescription drugs
> ❏ herbal medicine
> ❏ cigarettes
> ❏ vitamins
> ❏ toothpaste

A combination question could be created by adding an open-ended alternative (e.g., "other _____") to this list. Questions of any of these types can be included in the same questionnaire.

Open-ended questions are necessary when the response alternatives are too numerous to list, for example, when participants are asked to report their occupations or majors. They also are useful in the early stages of research when investigators may be unsure of the range of possible answers to their questions. Because participants can answer open-ended questions in unanticipated ways, this format also affords researchers an opportunity to learn new things. In case studies, participant observation, and phenomenological studies, open-ended questions capture the richness of people's experience in ways that closed questions, with restricted response alternatives, cannot.

Once the variety of responses is understood, forced-choice questions offer researchers the advantages of standardizing the options from which respondents may choose and ease of item scoring. With open-ended questions, participants' answers may be ambiguous and they may not think of answers that are critical for the study, like the possibility of the FDA regulating cigarettes.

Closed Item Formats

Box 5 illustrates several common formats for closed questions as well as two unusual ones. For each of these, we give several examples of how the format would appear in test items. The items from commercial tests in the box are written in the same style as the items in the tests but are not the actual test items.

Formats 1 and 2, both variants of the agree-disagree, true-false format, are common in personality inventories. Format 2 is a variant of Format 1, which includes "don't know" or "not applicable" among the response alternatives.

Rating scales, the third format in Box 5, are useful for measuring the intensity of behaviors, opinions, or moods. This type of measure is called a Likert-type scale, after Rensis Likert, the scientist who introduced it for attitude measurement (Likert, 1932). Box 5 includes four-, seven-, and one-hundred-point scales for rating intensity. A typical questionnaire written in this format would include several questions on the same topic with the same rating alternatives. The scores on the separate items would be added to yield a total score.

BOX 5 QUESTION FORMATS FOR CLOSED ITEMS

Format 1. Agree-Disagree Items

Minnesota Multiphasic Personality Inventory-2[1] (MMPI-2), used for clinical diagnosis of patients.

   T   F   Sometimes I see myself brushing my teeth with the wrong hand.

Survey question on politics (Schuman & Presser, 1981).

   Do you agree or disagree that: Most men are better suited emotionally for politics than are most women.

   [ ] Agree   [ ] Disagree

Coopersmith Self-esteem Inventory[1].

   Like Me ❏   Unlike Me ❏   I do not worry too much about things.

Format 2. Agree-Disagree, with a "Don't Know" Alternative

Cattell 16 PF[1] (Primary Factors), a personality test which measures 16 basic personality traits.

   I worry too much about the future.

   a. Hardly ever
   b. ?
   c. Often

Strong Vocational Interest Blank[1], an interest inventory used in vocational counseling.

L: Like   I: Indifferent   D: Dislike

L I D   Riding a mountain bike down a steep hill

Format 3. Rating Scales

Hare Self-esteem Scale, a self-report measure for school age children (Hare, 1985).

a = Strongly disagree
b = Disagree
c = Agree
d = Strongly agree

_____ 1. I have at least as many friends as other people my age.

Beck Depression Inventory[1], a self-report measure of the severity of depression (Beck & Steer, 1987).

0 Tomorrow will be a good day.
1 I am not looking forward to tomorrow.
2 Nothing good will happen tomorrow.
3 Tomorrow will be as disappointing as every other day.

Bem Inventory[1], a measure of gender roles (Bem, 1978).
Indicate how true of you the following characteristic is:
good listener

1	2	3	4	5	6	7
Never or almost never true	Usually not true	Sometimes but infrequently true	Occasionally true	Often true	Usually true	Always or almost always true

Family Sense of Coherence Scale (Antonovsky & Sourani, 1988).

To what extent does it seem to you that family rules are clear?

1	2	3	4	5	6	7
The rules in the family are completely clear.						The rules aren't clear at all.

Semantic Differential, an instrument used to measure the meaning of abstract concepts (Osgood, Suci, & Tannenbaum, 1957).

My Spouse

Strong ___ : ___ : ___ : ___ : ___ : ___ : ___ Weak

BOX 5 CONTINUED

Mood Scales (Tuckman, 1988).

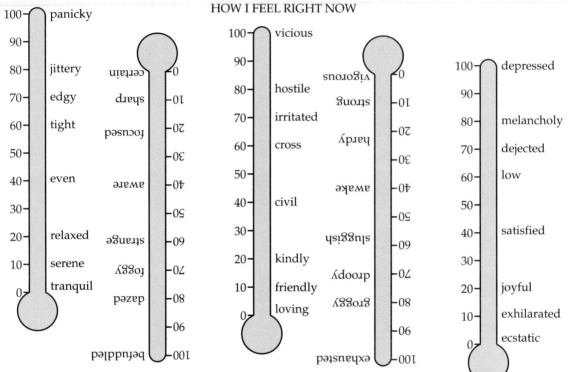

HOW I FEEL RIGHT NOW

There are five thermometers to measure your feelings. Mark a line on each one to show how "high" or "low" you feel. Each one measures a different feeling. Don't just mark them all the same. For two of them, you have to turn the paper over. Give your real, honest feeling. Don't just make something up.

Format 4. Forced Choice Question

Political survey question (Schuman & Presser, 1981).

Would you say that

❏ most men are better suited emotionally for politics than are most women,
❏ that men and women are equally suited,
❏ that women are better suited than men in this area?

Format 5. Rank Order Questions

The subject ranks the response alternatives according to their preference.
How important are each of the following in buying a new car?

Performance
Reliability
Style
Price
Size
Manufactured in US
Quality

Format 6. Magnitude Estimation (Lodge, 1981; in Converse & Presser, 1986)

I would like to ask your opinion about how serious YOU think certain crimes are. The first situation is, "A person steals a bicycle parked on the street." This has been given a score of 10 to show its seriousness. Use this situation to judge all others. For example, if you think a situation is 20 TIMES MORE serious than the bicycle theft, the number you tell me should be around 200, or if you think it is HALF AS SERIOUS, the number you tell me should be around 5, and so on.

COMPARED TO THE BICYCLE THEFT AT SCORE 10, HOW SERIOUS IS:

A parent beats his young child with his fists. The child requires hospitalization.

A person plants a bomb in a public building. The bomb explodes and 20 people are killed.

Format 7. Randomized Response

I would like to ask you whether you have ever used marijuana, but I don't want you to answer directly because it is illegal to use marijuana. So I will ask you to follow a procedure that will make it safe for you to answer. After you answer, no one will know if you have used marijuana or not, but from all the answers in the school I will be able to estimate the percent of students that have tried marijuana.

I want you to answer the question differently depending on the number you get from the number target. Hold your finger above the circle below, then shut your eyes and place your finger on the circle. Don't tell anyone the number you picked.

Now, if you got a **1, answer No** to the question.

If you got a **2, answer Yes** to the question.

If you got **3, 4, 5, or 6, then answer truthfully Yes or No** to the question:

   Have you tried marijuana?

   Answer: Yes No

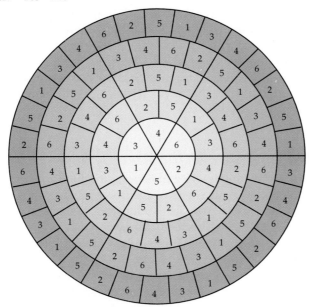

[1]This item and the other items in this box from commercial tests are written in the same style as the items on the tests but are not actual items from the tests.
[2]The number target is from Reaser, Hartsock, & Hoehn (1975).

Format 4, the forced-choice question, requires respondents to select their answers from several mutually exclusive alternatives covering all possible responses to the question. This format has the advantage of making all the response choices explicit, ensuring that respondents consider each alternative.

Rank-order questions, Format 5, require respondents to order a set of alternatives according to their preferences, a procedure that generates a great deal of information from a single question. Unfortunately, such rankings can be difficult to make, and consequently, unreliable.

The last two formats in Box 5, magnitude estimation and randomized response, are rare in psychological questionnaires, but both are worth considering for some applications.

Format 6, magnitude estimation, might seem impossible at first glance. However, in the example in Box 5, Lodge (1981) asked subjects to assign a number representing the seriousness of killing 20 people with a bomb, as well as other crimes, and they could do so! Magnitude estimation was popularized by S. S. Stevens, the psychophysicist who proposed the classification of scales discussed in Chapter 4.

The randomized response question, Format 7, is used to ensure the confidentiality of participants' answers to sensitive questions, like whether they have tried controlled drugs (Brown & Harding, 1973) or had premarital sex (Krotki & Fox, 1974). The question in Box 5, for example, asks respondents whether they have ever tried marijuana, an illegal drug. The way the question is asked prevents anyone from figuring out from the answer whether a particular subject has or has not tried the drug! But from the answers for the entire group of respondents, the researcher can estimate the *percent* of people in that group who have tried the drug. For this question, the estimate of the proportion of respondents trying marijuana is $(6 P_y-1)/4$, where P_y is the proportion of respondents answering yes. For example, if 100 people answer the question and 30 respond yes, then $(6 (\cdot 30) -1)/4 = .20$, or 20%, of the 100 people are estimated to have tried marijuana. Although Stanley Warner introduced this technique in 1965, the conditions that favor its use are still being studied (Fox & Tracy, 1986).

Use Standard English—Define Your Terms

To avoid misunderstandings, write questions in standard English, avoiding slang expressions and technical terms. Define terms that might be misinterpreted when they first occur. You also should replace any terms with a vague reference, such as "family," with specific phrases, such as "people living in the same household" or your "immediate family, including just your spouse and children"(Converse & Presser, 1986).

Once your first draft is complete, try it out on friends. Have them read each question out loud, then paraphrase the question and give their answers to it, explaining what they mean. With this procedure, you should be able to catch ambiguities in wording and discover ways to rewrite questions for greater clarity.

*E*VALUATING PSYCHOLOGICAL MEASURES

Regardless of the source of your measure (commercial, unpublished, or tailor-made), you will want it to be reliable and valid for your purpose. In this section, we discuss these properties of measures.

Reliability

The *reliability* of a measure is the degree to which repeated measurements of the same subjects under the same conditions yield consistent results.

Reliability is assessed by computing the correlation between the outcomes of two different administrations of a measure to the same group of subjects. A correlation coefficient of zero, $r = 0$, indicates a completely inconsistent measure; a correlation of one, $r = 1$, indicates perfect consistency; values between 0 and 1 indicate the degree of reliability.

First, consider a completely unreliable measure. Imagine that you "measure" a group of people by rolling two dice for each person, assigning them the sum of the two numbers as their scores. The possible values for this measure would range from 2 to 12. If you then "measured" the same people again several weeks later and compared the two sets of scores, you would find no consistency, that is, no reliability. The correlation between the two administrations of this "measure," most likely, would be close to zero.

The Wechsler Adult Intelligence Scale, WAIS-R, is at the other end of the reliability continuum from rolling dice. The WAIS-R manual reports that the correlation between two administrations of the test several weeks apart is $r = .95$ for 25–35-year-olds (Wechsler, 1981). When the same test is administered twice to assess reliability, as in this case, the result is called the *test-retest reliability* of the measure.

Test-retest reliability is determined by correlating the scores for two administrations of the same test to the same group of people.

Although test-retest is a common method of assessing reliability, it does have problems associated with memory and practice. If people remember questions from the first test, this knowledge can affect their scores on the retest.

To avoid such problems, methodologists have developed a procedure for assessing reliability using parallel forms of the same test. Parallel forms of a test are versions with different item content, but with the same type and difficulty level of items. Parallel forms of a vocabulary test, for example, would include different words of comparable difficulty. The item format (e.g., multiple choice, matching, etc.) would be the same for both forms.

Parallel-forms reliability is assessed by correlating the scores on parallel forms of the test administered to the same group of people at different times.

A disadvantage of using parallel forms is that, just as in test-retest reliability, subjects must be tested twice. In addition, the test developers have to construct alternative forms of the same test, which can be a difficult and time-consuming process. For these reasons, few tests are available in parallel forms.

These problems can be sidestepped, however, by using a clever procedure for determining reliability from the results of a single administration of a test. The subjects first take the test; then the items in the test are divided into halves, so that each half is a short version of the total scale. This creates, in effect, two short parallel forms of the same test. When the measures are psychological tests composed of a series of items, like the WAIS-R, this is easy to do. (With a weight or temperature scale, it is impossible.) Once half the items are assigned to scale "A" and the remaining items to scale "B," the two scales are scored separately, and the results correlated. The resulting correlation is the *split-half reliability*.

> The *split-half reliability* of a test is determined by dividing its items into two halves and correlating participants' scores on these parts. The test is administered only once, to one group of people.

For the WAIS-R, the split-half reliability for 20–24-year-olds is .94 (Wechsler, 1981). This reliability is for *half* the WAIS-R test. The reliability for the full test, because it is longer and should give a more consistent result than just half the test, is expected to be higher.

Researchers using the split-half method can estimate full-scale reliability by using the Spearman-Brown formula, which was developed for this purpose. Given the half-scale reliability, this formula computes an estimate of the full scale reliability, assuming that the full scale test is a direct extension of the half-scale test. For the WAIS-R, the formula gives a full-scale reliability of .97, an increase over the split-half reliability of .94. The Spearman-Brown formula is explained by Nunnally and Bernstein (1994) and in other texts on psychological testing.

The advantage of split-half reliability over the test-retest and parallel forms methods is that it requires only one administration of the test. The method also works well for measures that can vary markedly from day to day, like mood. However, the split-half reliability will depend on how the items in the full test are assigned to the two halves; different assignments result in different estimates of the full-scale reliability. This source of error can be overcome by using another method of assessing reliability, alpha reliability (see Nunnally & Bernstein, 1994).

> The *alpha reliability* of a scale is equal to the average of all the split-half reliabilities computed for every possible assignment of items to the two halves.

When the scale items have a true-false format, the alpha reliability sometimes is called the *KR-20 reliability*. There is a special formula for this case.

If you are not using a test with established reliability, you should plan your study so that you can compute the reliability of your test. Computing reliability will establish an important benchmark for your measure: If two versions of your test (the split halves) do not correlate with each other, it is unlikely that the scale will correlate with anything else. If the halves do correlate, the chances are better that the test will correlate with other measures.

Validity

The validity of a measure is concerned with its usefulness.

> A test is *valid* to the extent that inferences made from it are appropriate, meaningful, and useful. (Gregory, 1996, p. 107)

Research to evaluate the validity of measures falls into three general categories:

1. Studies on *criterion validity* investigate whether or not test scores predict future behavior or diagnose a present condition. For example, the publishers of the Scholastic Aptitude Test (SAT) claim that the test predicts college grades of students while they are still in high school. Validation here is straightforward. High school students who have taken the SAT are followed through college and their GPAs correlated with their SAT scores.

2. Studies on *content validity* investigate whether questions in a test are a fair and representative sample of the content they are supposed to examine. Experts in the content area of the test usually are involved in these studies.

3. Studies on *construct validity* investigate whether tests are good measures of the psychological concepts their authors claim they measure. For example, a construct validity study might investigate how people scoring high and low on a scale of extroversion behave socially.

A measure can be valid for one application but not for others. As Nunnally and Bernstein (1994), experts on validity, note, "One validates the *use* to which a measuring instrument is put rather than the instrument itself" (p. 84). This is an important idea to keep in mind as you evaluate possible measures for your own research. Pay particular attention to whether any measure you are considering has been shown to be valid for your specific purpose. To do so, look at how the measure has worked in research similar to your own.

EVALUATING OBSERVATIONAL MEASURES

Researchers assess the reliability of observations and tests using similar procedures. To evaluate the reliability of observations, researchers compare the ratings of different observers on the same set of subjects' behaviors.

> *Inter-observer* or *inter-rater reliability* is demonstrated by showing that observers agree in classifying subjects' behaviors.

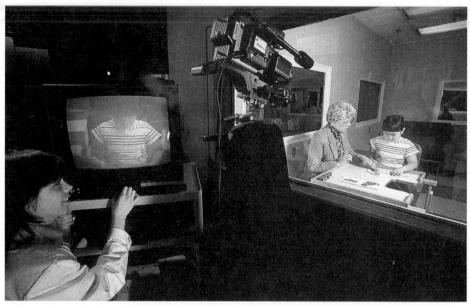

Videotaping a child's performance through a one-way mirror.

Good inter-observer reliability indicates that the observations are not idiosyncratic, that more than one observer can consistently apply the classification system.

The easiest way to determine inter-observer reliability is to videotape behaviors that are typical of how subjects will behave in the study. The tapes then can be used to train the observers and test for reliability.

Observers should be trained until they demonstrate a high level of agreement with the ratings of an experienced observer. Ninety percent agreement is a common criterion for training. For example, let's say you plan to have observers rate the violence in selected scenes from television shows on a four-point scale. The observers would be trained until their ratings match the ratings of an experienced observer for 90% of the scenes.

To determine reliability, set aside one tape from the videotaped sessions you use to train your observers. Have the observers independently categorize or rate the behaviors on the tape, then assess the extent of their agreement. If you cannot videotape, have two observers rate the same subjects' behaviors simultaneously.

Although correlation is used to establish the reliability of tests, this statistic is not used to assess inter-observer reliability. Recall from Chapter 5 that one reason for the correlation coefficient's popularity is that it allows researchers to compare measures with different units or scales (e.g., foot size and height, creativity and birth order). But in assessing the reliability of observations, we want to know the *exact agreement* of different observers, and the correlation coefficient does not indicate exact agreement.

For this reason, psychologists report inter-observer reliability either as the percent of exact agreement between observers, or by using a related statistic, Cohen's kappa. Percent agreement is calculated by tallying the number of times that two observers give the same rating to the same behaviors, then dividing by the number of ratings, and multiplying by 100, to convert to a percent. Cohen's *kappa* corrects the percent agreement for the possibility that observers could agree at a high level by chance alone. The calculation and interpretation of kappa is discussed in Cohen (1960) and Bakeman and Gottman (1986).

If the observation phase of your study goes on for a long time, you also should check for *intra-observer reliability.*

> *Intra-observer reliability* is the agreement in the ratings of the same observer at different times. Such reliability establishes that observers are consistent in their ratings over time.

Intra-observer reliability is checked by having the observer rate the same recorded behaviors at different times. If the results show insufficient agreement, the observer will have to be retrained.

In most studies, there is no issue about the validity of the observations. Observations often have a direct and immediate interpretation not typical of test scores. If a reliable observer records the occurrence of an event, such as the use of a tool by a chimpanzee, it is assumed that this is a valid observation. Research on the validity of observations usually is not necessary.

SPECIAL PROBLEMS OF CONTROL WITH HUMAN PARTICIPANTS

In previous chapters of this book, we have presented several examples of the special problems faced by researchers studying people. When they investigated Mesmer's animal magnetism, Franklin's commissioners discovered people who believed they had been cured by a treatment that later turned out to depend on suggestion. In Chapter 9, we saw that teachers who believed that facilitated communication would help their autistic clients express themselves began to control what their clients typed, without any awareness that they were doing so. In Chapter 10, we discussed the problem of subject reactivity, the possibility that being observed, per se, may alter subjects' behaviors in a study. In the next sections, we look more closely at such special problems and make recommendations on how you can control them in your own research.

The Hawthorne Effect

Social scientists began to recognize reactivity as a research problem early in this century when a study on worker productivity that began in the 1920s at the Hawthorne plant of the Western Electric Company, a telephone assembly factory, was published. The researchers (Roethlisberger & Dickson, 1939) wanted to measure workers' productivity, selecting the number of telephone relays assembled in a given unit of time as their measure. They decided to separate a small group of the plant's employees from the rest of the workforce, to enable them to record their behavior more accurately, to gain better control over extraneous events, and to prevent general disruption.

Workers in the relay assembly test room at the Hawthorne Works.

They first measured worker productivity in the regular shop, then in the new test room, and again when the company introduced a change in pay. Following this, the researchers introduced a series of improvements in the work situation, including changes in the length and number of rest periods, and in the length of the work week. At one point the workers even received a complimentary lunch during the morning break. Toward the end of the experiment, the original work conditions of no lunch and no rest periods were reinstated.

To their surprise, the authors reported that none of these changes was related in a one-to-one fashion to average hourly productivity, which continued to rise throughout the course of the study, even when the improvements were taken away. In fact, contrary to expectation, when the rest periods and complimentary lunches gradually were eliminated, total weekly output continued to increase, reaching an all-time high level when they were gone. On top of all this, the mental attitude of the workers improved.

The researchers concluded that their findings were a consequence of the special social circumstances created for workers in the experiment. Unlike regular shop workers, the employees in the test room were told of planned changes in the work situation in advance and asked about their opinions, fears, and concerns; they got rests and lunches not offered to regular employees, and they were allowed to talk as they worked; top management was interested in their progress; and their physical and mental well-being were concerns of the investigators. As a result, the researchers concluded, a cohesive social group had come into being, leading to the observed increases in motivation, productivity, and morale.

Roethlisberger and Dickson's interpretation of their results was challenged later by other investigators. Their reanalyses of the data collected at the Hawthorne works have shown that, in fact, productivity did not consistently increase throughout the study and the workers were not a cohesive group, happy with their special work conditions (Parsons, 1974; Bramel & Friend, 1981; and Rice, 1982). Nevertheless, psychologists continue to refer to the reactivity of people to the special treatment and attention they receive as research participants as the *Hawthorne effect.*

Demand Characteristics and Experimenter Expectancies

The special problems of studying people became the focus of research once again in 1962 when Martin Orne published one of the first papers to study the experiment as a social situation. Orne's research showed that people behave differently in experiments than they do in other situations. In experiments, they willingly perform dull, meaningless tasks for hours on end and engage in dangerous, even potentially lethal acts that they would never consider doing outside of an experiment (e.g., handling deadly snakes, or putting their fingers into corrosive acid). How, Orne wondered, could such seemingly bizarre behavior be explained? His answer focused on the attitudes we learn about science and scientists in this culture.

As a society, Orne argued, we hold scientists and their work in high esteem. We learn early that scientific research is essential, that it leads to important benefits. Because of these beliefs, participants come to experiments ready to assume the role of "good experimental subject," to put themselves in the experimenter's hands, much as a hypnotic subject might, ready to willingly perform tasks assigned to them, no matter how boring, uncomfortable, or painful they might be. They concoct purposes for meaningless tasks and trust that experimenters will not let harm befall them. To be "good subjects," they believe, they must cooperate, not "ruin the experiment," and help experimenters find what they are looking for. The experiment becomes a special problem-solving situation in which good subjects develop interpretations of researchers' purposes using any cues that might reveal this.

> The cues that suggest hypotheses to participants are called *demand characteristics* (Orne, 1962).

Demand characteristics are present in campus talk about the experiment, in details of the research setting, and even in the experimental design itself. If demand characteristics suggest particular behaviors to participants, and if they are motivated to comply, it follows that the effects of demand characteristics possibly might be mistaken for the effects of independent variables. To test this idea, Orne and Scheibe (1964) conducted an experiment to find out whether some of the effects usually attributed to sensory deprivation actually might result from demand characteristics.

The participants in sensory deprivation experiments usually are isolated in a testing room, where visual, auditory, and kinesthetic stimulation are severely reduced. Because sensory deprivation is disturbing and has been shown to result in disruption of intellectual functioning and in abnormal behavior, participants in such research are required to undergo physical examinations and sign release forms before they begin. During the experiment, participants may be asked to report any strange experiences they have; there may even be a "panic button" in the testing room for them to press should they become too uncomfortable to continue.

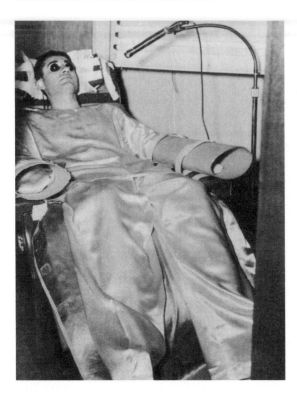

A participant in a standard sensory deprivation experiment.

Orne and Scheibe believed that some of the usual effects of sensory deprivation might be due to such special features of the experimental setting. To test this hypothesis, they created a "meaning deprivation" group whose members were exposed to such demand characteristics in the absence of sensory deprivation. Even though they would undergo no sensory deprivation, the people in this group were asked to report on their medical history and shown an "emergency tray" filled with drugs and medical paraphernalia that would be available in the test room for their safety. After this, the participants were taken to a "well-lighted cubicle containing 'food and water'," and given "an optional task" to keep them occupied for the four hours of the study. They received no other information about the purpose of the experiment. The people in the control group, who were treated identically to those in the "meaning deprivation" condition, were told that they were control subjects in a study of sensory deprivation. The results of the study supported Orne's hypothesis that participants' responses to demand characteristics can significantly affect research results.

Robert Rosenthal (1994), whose work complements Orne's, has argued that experimenters also unwittingly contribute to the invalidity of research by allowing their expectations to influence their findings. Rosenthal's research suggests that experimenters may inadvertently communicate their expectancies, or hypotheses, to research participants; if Orne is correct, they, in turn, use these cues to tell them how to behave in the study. In research on people, then, *experimenter expectancy effects* can be considered as one type of demand characteristic.

Rosenthal's first studies demonstrated that experimenters' expectations of how their subjects would rate photographs of people were related to the ratings they actually received (Rosenthal & Fode, 1961; as cited in Rosenthal, 1994). Since then, experimenter expectancy effects have been demonstrated in many types of research, including animal learning, person perception, and reaction time studies (Rosenthal, 1994).

Controlling for Suggestion and Reactivity

Demand characteristics, experimenter expectancy effects, and the Hawthorne effect can be controlled by using the same sorts of experimental techniques for control that we have discussed throughout this book, namely: (1) control by holding events constant, (2) randomization, and (3) statistical control.

Holding events constant. First, to the extent possible, researchers should take pains to give the same demand characteristics, as well as the same degree and kind of attention, to the experimental and control groups. Instructions to participants might be prerecorded on audio or videotape to avoid even unconscious bias. "No treatment" control groups, that receive no attention and, consequently, the expectation that their behavior will not change, should be avoided. Instead, control subjects should be given "rival treatments" that hold some promise of being effective and involve the same type of relationship with the experimenter as the experimental subjects have. In addition, whenever possible, experimenters, observers, and participants should be "blinded" as to the subjects' experimental conditions to eliminate differential effects of experimenter expectancies and demand characteristics on them.

Randomization. We have discussed the importance of randomly assigning subjects to experimental treatments many times in this book. If there are many observers or experimenters in a given study, they also should be randomly assigned to the conditions of the study. Such randomization will avoid any systematic bias that could arise if such people were assigned to observe and administer the treatments in the study in some other way.

Statistical control. If demand characteristics cannot be controlled, consider assessing the impact of these cues on the results by means of a postexperimental inquiry (Orne, 1962). You could interview the participants at the end of the experiment to find out whether they were aware of your hypothesis during the experiment (see the discussion of debriefing later in the chapter). If some were, you then could compare the experimental behaviors of those who were and were not aware of the actual hypothesis and correct for the effects of such knowledge by statistical methods.

Finally, for a given research topic, there may be no need for any special procedures for assessing the effects of demand characteristics or experimenter expectancies, because there may be no logical way that the presence of demand characteristics could explain the results (e.g., when participants report their sensory experiences in relation to slight variations in stimulation; in many learning experiments; in studies of infant behavior at various stages of development, etc.). In fact, Orne concluded:

> The need to concern oneself with these issues becomes more pronounced when investigating the effects of various interventions such as drugs, psychotherapy, hypnosis, sensory deprivation, conditioning of physiological responses, etc., on performance or experiential parameters . . . or . . . where attitude changes rather than performance changes are explored. (Orne, 1962, p. 156)

DEBRIEFING

The term *debriefing,* which originated in the military, has several meanings, all of which apply to how debriefing is used in research with human participants. According to the *Random House Unabridged Dictionary* (Flexner, 1993), the first two meanings of the verb "to debrief" are:

1. To interrogate (a soldier, astronaut) on return from a mission in order to assess the conduct and results of the mission.

2. To question formally and systematically in order to obtain useful intelligence or information.

One purpose of debriefing in research is to provide investigators with useful information on how participants understood the experiment's purpose and behaved during the experiment. In drug studies, for example, debriefing can tell researchers whether the participants complied with the recommended doses of drugs, or whether the people who received placebos guessed that their medication was inactive. This information on participants' expectations and behavior during the experiment can be used in analyzing the results.

The third dictionary definition of debriefing has to do with cautioning people involved in special operations against revealing privileged information to others.

3. To subject to prohibitions against revealing or discussing classified information, as upon separation from a position of military or political sensitivity.

This same sort of caution can be applied in the research setting. In a debriefing session, participants can be asked not to discuss the experiment with other potential subjects until the study is complete. This is important because prior information about the experimental procedures can affect how people behave in many studies. In fact, Marans (1988) advises experimenters to ask participants to sign a nondisclosure statement during the debriefing session and to take it home with them, as a reminder not to talk about the study until a later date.

The final meaning of the term "to debrief" originated in psychology:

4. *Psychol.* (after an experiment) to disclose to the subject the purpose of the experiment and any reasons for deception or manipulation.

The APA's ethical standards require researchers to debrief participants if they have been deceived in the research. Debriefing allows researchers to correct any misconceptions that they create as part of the study.

There is one final reason for debriefing that is not mentioned in the dictionary definition. Recall from Chapter 7 that the Belmont Report's principle of beneficence requires researchers to do everything possible to maximize the benefits people gain from their participation. One such benefit is educational. During the debriefing session, you can educate participants on the purpose of the research, current knowledge in the field related to the research question, and what you have learned from conducting the study. Such information will give subjects a sense of their role in advancing knowledge, something that most people will feel good about.

APPLYING TO THE INSTITUTIONAL REVIEW BOARD

Most likely, you will have to apply to the institutional review board (IRB) at your college to review the ethics of your proposed research before you begin collecting data. Even if your school does not have an IRB, you should be aware of the concerns of IRBs so that you can plan a study in conformity with accepted ethical practice.

The steps to take and the forms to complete for an IRB review will differ somewhat from school to school, so make sure you know the procedures at your college. If you plan to include people from another institution (e.g., a college, day care center, or clinic) in your research, you also will have to get approval from the IRB of that institution before proceeding. IRBs that review psychological research operate according to the ethical principles of the Belmont Report, federal and state law and regulations governing research with human subjects, and the APA ethical principles. So review the material in Chapter 7 and read the Belmont Report, reprinted in Appendix A, before completing the IRB application.

Recruitment Procedures

According to the Belmont Report's *principle of justice*, people from all walks of life should share equally in the burdens and benefits of research. Accordingly, you should invite as diverse a cross section of people to participate in your study as is permitted by your research design. In your application to the IRB, describe your sampling scheme (see Chapter 10) and how you plan to recruit participants. If you intend to use a probability sample, you should describe the sampling procedure. If your sampling will be done by convenience, describe where and how you will recruit participants. Provide enough detail so that the members of the IRB will be able to judge whether your research is equitable in its recruitment procedures.

The *principle of respect* requires that potential subjects in research decide for themselves whether to become involved, with full knowledge of what their participation will entail. Accordingly, your invitation to them must be straight-forward, describing the procedures, benefits, and risks, if any, as completely as possible. There must be no coercion of any sort, no threats of retaliation or loss for failure to participate, and no remuneration out of proportion to the require-ments of the study. To ensure compliance with this principle, the APA guide-lines require participants to sign a consent form prior to taking part in research.

The Consent Form

According to Joan Sieber, author of a book to guide students and IRBs through the review process, the consent form should describe the research and its pur-pose in simple, nonscientific language that is both friendly and respectful of potential participants. An appropriate consent form, in Sieber's view, should include the following points, reprinted from her book (Sieber, 1992, p. 35):

1. Identification of the researcher.

2. Explanation of the purpose of the study.

3. Request for participation, mentioning right to withdraw at any time with impunity.

4. Explanation of research method.

5. Duration of research participation.

6. A description of how confidentiality will be maintained.

7. Mention of the subject's right of refusal without penalty.

8. Mention of the right to withdraw own data at end of session.

9. Explanation of any risks.

10. Description of any feedback and benefits to subjects.

11. Information on how to contact the person designated to answer questions about subjects' rights or injuries.

12. Indication that subjects may keep a copy of the consent.

Remember that special precautions must be taken when potential participants include people who cannot be expected to give their informed consent (e.g., children, prisoners, and mentally disadvantaged people; see Chapter 7). Also, for certain types of research, you may ask the IRB to drop the requirement of informed consent, for example, when the research involves observing public behavior, when answering your questionnaire is tantamount to giving con-sent, and in extraordinary cases when consent would be impossible, like the emergency room study described in Chapter 10.

Box 6 reprints a sample consent form from Sieber's book that you can use as a model in writing your own. Remember to include a copy of the consent form in your application to the IRB.

BOX 6 SAMPLE CONSENT FORM (REPRINTED FROM SIEBER, 1992)

(Letterhead of the Researcher's Institution)

Dear Patient,

I am a psychologist who specializes in the study of taste perception. I am currently working with the staff of your department to see if we can learn ways to enhance your enjoyment of the food served to you here. We need your help in a new study on how sensitive people are to different tastes and which tastes they prefer. The results of this study may help doctors and dietitians, here and at other hospitals, plan diets to improve health, and may add to the understanding of taste perception.

In this study, we will find out how readily persons detect and identify sweet, sour, salty, and bitter tastes, and which tastes are preferred. This information will be analyzed in relation to some information that I am given by the staff physician from participants' medical records about their age, sex, smoking history, duration of lithium administration, and current lithium concentration. Persons participating in this study can expect to spend about 20 minutes on each of five different days. Participants will be asked to taste plain water and samples of water mixed with small amounts of some safe substances that normally are used to season food; they will be asked to answer some questions about how the samples taste and which ones they prefer. There is no foreseeable risk or discomfort. Participants may withdraw their data at the end of their participation if they decide that they didn't want to participate after all.

Participants' identity and personal information will be kept confidential (locked in a file cabinet to which I alone have access) and will be destroyed as soon as the study is completed. The results will be published in a scientific journal. After the study, all participants will be invited to a presentation on how taste perception works. Then each participant will be given the results of his taste test, and an opportunity to sample foods having both typical and increased amounts of the preferred tastes. We hope you will find this information useful to you in seasoning your food in the cafeteria.

Your participation in this study is strictly voluntary. You may withdraw your participation at any time. Your decision as to whether to participate will have no effect on any benefits you now receive or may need to receive in the future from any agency. For answers to questions pertaining to the research, research participants' rights, or in the event of a research-related injury, you may contact me directly, at 555-1212; Dr. John Smith, Director of Research, at 555-1313; or Dr. Mary Doe, Hospital Director, at 555-1414.

Sincerely yours,

Mary Jones, Research Psychologist

Please indicate your consent by signing a copy of this letter and returning it to me. The other copy is for you to keep.

I have read this letter and consent to participate

Signature:

Date:

Procedures Involved in the Research

The Belmont Report's *principle of beneficence* states that, if possible, participation in research should directly benefit subjects and, at a minimum, do them no harm. The research procedures must be described to the IRB in detail to allow the committee to assess the potential benefits and risks entailed. Its members must be able to decide whether any risks exist, whether these risks have been minimized, and whether less risky alternative procedures could be used.

The scheduling and content of the debriefing session also should be a part of your IRB application. The IRB will want to know whether the study involves deception and, if so, how misleading aspects of the study will be explained to participants. Remember, however, that the APA code of ethics for research specifies that "psychologists never deceive research participants about significant aspects that would affect their willingness to participate, such as physical risks, discomfort, or unpleasant emotional experiences" (APA, 1992, p. 1609).

Confidentiality

Finally, in your application to the IRB describe your plan for preserving the confidentiality of the data. The *principle of beneficence* requires that participants' data and records be kept confidential to avoid risks to them, when this is the wish of the participant, or when this is guaranteed by the researcher.

Whenever possible, the data should be recorded anonymously. This usually is possible if the data from a single participant are collected all at one time. If additional data have to be collected at a future time, some means of identifying participants will have to be recorded so that the data from different sessions can be collated. Individual records can be coded by identification number; if it is necessary to record names, the list of names and identification numbers can be stored in a secure place.

Researchers have devised ingenious strategies for preserving confidentiality in sensitive research. In some studies involving inflammatory information, the list of participants has been sent to a lawyer living in a foreign country who would be able to resist subpoenas from the U.S. government, thus protecting the confidentiality of the data even from a court order (Fox & Tracy, 1986)! Most likely, your study will not be this sensitive.

APA journals require that authors keep their data for five years and, when ethically permissible, share it with other researchers who may want to replicate the research or check its data analyses. After your study is complete, therefore, it is a good idea to record your data without identification in a shareable format.

FINAL COMMENTS

With the approval of your college's IRB, you finally are ready to do the study and analyze the data to find out what happened. If you do a qualitative rather than a quantitative study (e.g., a case study, participant observation study, or phenomenological research), the analysis will involve studying the records you collect to construct themes or patterns that are consistent with the observations. The analysis here will be challenging and your creativity will be an asset.

If your study is quantitative, the analysis will be more structured than in a qualitative study; in fact, we recommend that you plan the analysis in advance of doing the study. (Some IRBs may want information on your data analysis methods to judge whether they are adequate to answer the questions your study addresses.) If you are not good at statistical analysis, it will be worth your while to sit down with an expert to outline the analysis. In the process, you may discover that you need additional measures or different treatment groups.

You should do your data analysis on a computer; it is just too easy to make numerical mistakes computing by hand or with a calculator. (Remember, you will be sharing your results, and possibly your data, with other interested scientists, so your analysis should be error free.) Your college probably has one of the major commercial statistical packages, such as SPSS or SYSTAT. If not, you can download the program *Student Statistician* from the Website for this book (see the preface).

After the data analysis is complete, your final step will be to share your research with the scientific community. Researchers usually do this by giving presentations at scientific meetings and publishing articles in scientific journals. How this is done is the subject of the next, and final, chapter of this book.

KEY TERMS

Probability vs. convenience sampling
Subject pool
Random assignment with vs. without blocking
Self-report measures
Commercial vs. unpublished tests
The Buros Institute of Mental Measurement
Open-ended vs. closed questions
Formats for closed questions
Likert-type scale
Magnitude estimation
Randomized response question
Test-retest, parallel-forms, split-half, and alpha reliabilities
Spearman-Brown formula
KR-20 reliability

Criterion, content, and construct validities
Inter-observer and intra-observer reliability
Cohen's kappa
Hawthorne effect
Demand characteristics
Experimenter expectancy effects
Achieving control by holding events constant, randomization, and statistical control
Debriefing
Institutional Review Board (IRB)
Principle of justice
Principle of respect
Consent form
Principle of beneficence

KEY PEOPLE

Oscar Buros
Rensis Likert
Joan Sieber

F.J. Roethslisberger and W.J. Dickson
Martin Orne
Robert Rosenthal

REVIEW QUESTIONS

1. What is the difference between probability sampling and convenience sampling?

2. What ethical issues might be involved in having a campus subject pool? How might such issues be resolved?

3. What is the ideal method of assigning subjects to conditions in an experiment?

4. Name three major sources of psychological tests.

5. Explain how you would find a review of a particular commercial test.

6. What procedures must students follow to obtain commercial tests for research?

7. Explain how you would find an unpublished test of, say, self-esteem.

8. Distinguish between open-ended and closed questions.

9. What is a Likert-type scale?

10. Explain how a randomized response question ensures the confidentiality of respondents' answers to sensitive questions.

11. Distinguish between test-retest and parallel-forms reliability.

12. What is the relationship between split-half and alpha reliability?

13. Distinguish between the three general approaches to assessing the validity of measures?

14. Explain how researchers go about establishing inter-observer and intra-observer reliability in observational studies.

15. Explain why the correlation coefficient is not used to determine observer reliability.

16. Explain the "Hawthorne effect." Why is this a poor name for this effect?

17. Explain how demand characteristics account for the reaction of Orne's subjects to "meaning deprivation."

18. Identify and explain three strategies to control for suggestion and reactivity in research.

19. Give four reasons for debriefing subjects after an experiment.

20. How should the three principles of the Belmont Report shape what you write in your research proposal for the IRB?

13

Communicating Research

❖

It may seem strange that so many exceedingly intelligent persons
are wholeheartedly devoted to a profession in which the main
goal is to come up with creations with which their colleagues try
to find fault. At the same time, you may understand why great
minds find this endeavour fascinatingly challenging—to wrestle
from nature her secrets and formulate them in such simple and
comprehensible language that they are indisputable.

WILLIAM GARVEY

❖

THE LANGUAGE OF SCIENCE
CONTENTS AND ORGANIZATION OF PSYCHOLOGICAL
   RESEARCH REPORTS
      Title Page
      Abstract
      Introduction
           The research problem
           The literature review
           The rationale and design of the study
      Method
           Participants (or subjects)
           Apparatus/materials
           Procedure
      Results
           Organization
           Tables and figures
           Statistical analyses
      Discussion
      References
      Appendix, Author Note, Footnotes, Tables, and Figures

APA EDITORIAL STYLE
WRITING WITH "STYLE"
ORAL PRESENTATIONS
THE ETHICS OF SCIENTIFIC COMMUNICATION
FINAL THOUGHTS
KEY TERMS, KEY PEOPLE, REVIEW QUESTIONS

At this point, you probably have completed your study and are ready to write the report of your research. Unfortunately, many students don't look forward to this task, viewing it only as difficult busywork. If this is your experience, try thinking of the writing as an opportunity to rethink your project. Many researchers find that communicating their work to others helps them to develop a new perspective on it, a better understanding of how it fits with past research, and a clearer sense of its implications. Sometimes new ideas for research emerge in the process.

In this phase of your work, you move from being a solitary researcher in the cycle of discovery, to becoming a contributing member of the scientific community in the cycle of validation. In writing your report, you become part of a noble tradition, which Albert Einstein described as the most objective thing known to humankind. As we shall see, science as a community of scholars sharing discoveries and evaluating each other's work developed only a few hundred years ago. Yet in that short time, it has altered our understanding of the world and greatly enhanced the quality of our lives.

On November 28, 1660, a small group of British scientists and thinkers came together to establish the Royal Society of London for the Promotion of Natural Knowledge, or, more simply, the Royal Society. This band of revolutionaries had met many times before as the "Invisible College" (see Chapter 1), a group dedicated to rejecting knowledge based on authority and trusting "only the perpetually repeated observations of our own eyes and the careful weighings of our scales, . . . the answers experiments give us and no other answers!" (de Kruif, 1926/1954, p. 7). When political changes in Britain made secrecy unnecessary, its members asked the new king, Charles II, to formally recognize their group. He did so in 1662, creating the first officially sanctioned scientific society in the English speaking world.

The Royal Society's members wanted to make their pronouncements on scientific matters indisputable. Their method for doing so was to make scientists a community, one bound together by common rules of operation and by the exchange of scientific information—by communication. Henceforth, scientists were to keep the potential judgments of their peers in mind as they planned and carried out experiments; they were to "carry the eyes, and the imaginations of the whole company into the *Laboratory* with them" (Sprat, 1667/1958 p. 99). Once the research was complete, they were to report back to the group, demonstrating their methods and findings to them. For their part, the group would subject the scientist's claims to "critical, and reiterated scrutiny" (Sprat, 1667/1958 p. 99), pronouncing them demonstrated or not demonstrated. To be accepted as science, knowledge would have to be public and demonstrable. Seeing would be believing.

Another challenge was to make science progressive, especially in an age when knowledge was increasing at an unprecedented rate. The invention of the microscope and telescope had revealed unknown new worlds yet to be charted. Explorers visiting the New World had returned with previously unseen plant and animal species. How could the scientists of the Royal Society keep up with such discoveries? How could the public validation that had become the guiding credo of this new scientific community be assured?

Henry Oldenbourg, then secretary of the Royal Society, was put in charge of setting the agendas for the group's meetings. Oldenbourg decided to write to scientists all over England and Europe asking them about their work; he then translated their replies into Latin, English, and French, the languages that would allow the society's members to read them. In 1665, Oldenbourg started publishing the letters under the title *Philosophical Transactions: giving some Accompt* [Account] *of the Present Understandings, Studies, and Labours, of the Ingenious in many Considerable Parts of the World.* Oldenbourg had created the first scientific journal published in the English language (Roediger, 1987).

Before journals became popular, scientists published their research in books or individual pamphlets. But relying on books delayed the spread of knowledge because researchers had to accumulate enough findings to fill them before they could be published. Books also were expensive, so few people could afford them. Journals, by contrast, proved to be an efficient and timely way to disseminate the results of research, including single experiments and studies.

Despite the advantages of publishing in journals, at first few scientists submitted research reports to them, fearing that other scientists might claim their discoveries as their own. To quell such fears, when editors published reports they began to include the date on which they received them, giving scientists a means to establish the priority of their discoveries. Modern scientific journals have continued this practice for the same reason.

Because editors received few research reports in the early years, most were accepted uncritically, even when the findings they reported would strike most readers as fantastic. Roediger, for example, reports:

> In an early German journal, the *Miscellanea Curiosa,* an author wrote of a woman who vomited toads and another who vomited kittens. A different paper reported women who gave birth to animals of various sorts, including mice, frogs, crabs, and snakes. (Roediger, 1987, p. 226)

Because such reports damaged the credibility of science and its practitioners, *Philosophical Transactions* began to distinguish between papers that had been reviewed and approved and those that had not (Roediger, 1987). This practice evolved into modern peer review of scientific papers prior to publication. In this process, the editor of a journal, a recognized expert in the field, reads submitted papers to decide whether they warrant further review. If the decision is positive, two or more researchers are selected from among those working in the area covered by the paper to review it. These reviewers, along with the editor, exercise quality control over what is published in the journal. They look at whether the work contributes to scientific knowledge, addresses important problems, uses appropriate methods, and leads to sound conclusions.

As editors and reviewers began to function as gatekeepers for journals, their reputation and numbers grew rapidly. Today the journal is the prime vehicle for communicating research in psychology and other scientific disciplines, and the more thorough the peer review, the greater the journal's reputation and the esteem that comes from publishing in it.

Given the short history of psychology compared to other sciences, it is not surprising that psychology's first journal was published two centuries after *Philosophical Transactions* began. Alexander Bain, a 19th-century philosopher, a free-lance journalist, and a friend of John Stuart Mill, founded the journal *Mind,* in 1876 (Hothersall, 1995). Charles Darwin, Francis Galton, and many other distinguished scientists published in it. Other psychology journals soon followed, and today articles from 1,300 journals are reviewed each year in *PsycINFO, PsycLIT,* and *Psychological Abstracts* (see Chapter 11).

In Chapter 11, you learned how to use psychology journals as a source of information about research. In this chapter, we focus on how to write a research report in the style required for publishing in them. We also discuss the American Psychological Association's (APA's) ethical guidelines related to publishing, completing our discussion of the ethics of research. Let's begin by considering the goals of scientific writing and how the language of science helps to foster them.

*T*HE LANGUAGE OF SCIENCE

The members of the Royal Society wanted to dissociate themselves from the prescientific chemistry of the alchemists who sought ways to convert base metals into gold and to find the elixir of life. The alchemists conducted their studies in secret and wrote about them in private languages of their own invention. Such practices violated the basic tenet of the new science that discoveries be shared with and evaluated by other scientists.

The Royal Society wanted to ensure that scientific reports would be understandable to any trained scientist who read them. Scientific writing had to be clear—clear enough so that readers could follow the logic that led to the hypotheses and procedures; clear enough so that readers could replicate the research if they wished to or mentally imagine its procedures in a kind of armchair mental replication; and clear enough so that interested readers could evaluate a report's conclusions. Scientific reports also had to be accurate. As we shall discuss later in this chapter, accuracy is so fundamental to science that achieving it is considered to be a science writer's ethical responsibility.

In 1664, the society established a special committee for improving the English language. One of its members was Thomas Sprat, who later was commissioned by the society to write its history. One idea that the committee entertained, but rejected, was to create an artificial language that would be used by all scientists in reporting their research. The new language, once created, would enable its users to "describe precisely and exactly, without a trace of ambiguity, the object or concepts they wish to write about" (Walters, 1993, p. 241). Members of the Royal Society and others attempted to create such a language, but none of these languages proved practical. (Otherwise you might have studied the universal language, instead of French or Spanish, in high school!)

The committee required the members of the Royal Society to be clear, plain, and accurate in their scientific writing; but it soon became evident that the language of science also would have to be concise. The letters from scientists that the Royal Society received in its early days often were long rambling reports that had to be edited extensively for publication in the journal. Accordingly, Thomas Sprat, the society's historian and spokesperson, called on scientists to be extremely brief in their scientific reports. As he put it, scientists should describe "so many things, almost in an equal number of words" (Sprat, 1667/1958, p. 249). Today space still is limited in scientific journals and so must be used efficiently. So the Royal Society's recommendation that scientists report their research as briefly as possible continues to be a convention in science to this day.

CONTENTS AND ORGANIZATION OF PSYCHOLOGICAL RESEARCH REPORTS

In this section, we present an overview of the contents and organization of a research report, based on the guidelines established by the APA (1994) in its publication manual. This manual, which has been modified several times in the past, provides rules for researchers to follow in reporting their research. Like the rules of the Royal Society's special committee on language, these guidelines are intended to help researchers report clearly, accurately and concisely on what they did in their research, why they did it, what they found, and the conclusions to draw from it.

We begin with an overview of the contents of an APA style research report (see Box 1), including, in order: the Title page, Abstract, Introduction, Method, Results, Discussion, References, Appendix (when needed), Author note, Footnotes, Tables, Figure captions, and Figures. Because writing conventions are difficult to understand in the abstract, in Appendix B we also reprint an article by Tiffany Field and her coworkers (Field et al., 1996). We refer to the contents of this paper repeatedly in our presentation. Because the article is reprinted as a manuscript, you also can use it as a model in arranging and writing your own paper.

BOX 1 ORGANIZATION AND CONTENT OF THE RESEARCH REPORT

❏ The pages in the report should be arranged in the following order and, except for the figures, numbered consecutively, each with a manuscript page header (see Box 9 for directions on numbering and the page header).

❏ The title page, abstract, introduction, references, and the subsequent sections all begin on a new page.

Title page	Includes title, author's name and institutional affiliation, and a running head.
Abstract	A brief summary of the research report.
Body of paper	Includes the four major sections of the paper: introduction, method, results, and discussion, in that order.
References	A list of all references used in the report, arranged in alphabetical order by the first author's surname.
Appendix (optional)	Includes information too detailed or extensive to include in the body of the paper (e.g., questionnaires, large tables, instructions to participants, etc.).
Author note	Includes author's present address and affiliation; if different from the one on the title page; address to request further information; financial support, if any; acknowledgment of contributions of others to the research.
Footnotes	Content footnotes supplement information in the text. Copyright permission footnotes acknowledge permission to quote from copyrighted material.
Tables	Tables, labeled Table 1, Table 2, etc., each on a separate page.
Figure captions	Label figures Figure 1, Figure 2, etc., and give each an explanatory caption. List the captions together in order on this page.
Figures	Put each figure on a separate sheet with the figure number written on the back. No page numbers.

Title Page

As Box 1 illustrates, the title page includes the title, author's name and institutional affiliation, and a running head. The running head is an abbreviated title, no more than 50 characters long, that appears at the top of each page of a published article.

Although the title must be brief—ten to twelve words in length—it also must be informative, fully explaining the main features of the study. A good title captures the central idea of the research "simply and, if possible, with style" (APA, 1994, p. 7). The title should convey the problem or theoretical issue being investigated as well as the study's key variables. The title of the Field et al. paper, "Massage therapy reduces anxiety and enhances EEG patterns of alertness and math computations," unambiguously informs readers that the research examined the impact of massage therapy on anxiety and alertness, as measured by EEG (a physiological measure of brain arousal) and mathematical computations (a behavioral index of alertness).

Because there is so much research published, it is impossible for any scientist to read everything. So even dedicated psychologists must pick and choose which articles to read. The title must provide sufficient information so that readers can decide whether to read your abstract, which, in turn, must be complete and specific enough so that they know whether to read the complete report.

Abstract

Like the title, the abstract should accurately, completely, and concisely capture the essentials of the study. In 120 words (960 characters, including spaces) or less, the abstract informs readers of the problem investigated in the research, its method, results, conclusions, and implications. It makes sense to write the abstract after completing the full report, to ensure that it incorporates all necessary information. Because researchers today search the literature by computer, you also should take care to include key words in the abstract so that future computer searches using these terms will turn up your study.

As you read the Field et al. abstract, notice that although it fulfills all of the other requirements of an abstract, it exceeds the recommended word count. The added length was needed in this case because so many measures were used in the study. Because such exceptions to the APA requirements are sometimes unavoidable, the APA acknowledges that "authors should balance the rules of the *Publication Manual* with good judgment" (APA, 1994, p. xxiii) .

Introduction

The introduction begins on a new page, below the title of the paper which is repeated there, and requires no heading. Its purpose is to explain the nature of the research and why it was done. This section usually begins with a general statement of the research problem, reviews the literature, citing past research and theoretical papers on the problem, and ends with the specific questions or hypotheses that were tested in the study, along with the rationale for investigating them.

In writing the introduction, it is helpful to envision a particular sort of reader—one who is intelligent, well trained in psychology, but unfamiliar with the research tradition you are reporting. Your reader would know the language, general research techniques, and broad theoretical perspectives in the discipline, but would be unfamiliar with the specific problem under study or how past research is related to it.

The research problem. The introduction begins by focusing on the general topic that the research addressed and explaining its importance. Was the study aimed at testing a theoretical idea, resolving a practical problem, or addressing a methodological issue? Why should the reader be interested in learning about it?

Because even seasoned writers have trouble coming up with the first few sentences of a paper, Box 2 gives some examples of "leads" for the

BOX 2 **LEADS FOR THE INTRODUCTION**

Historical Roots of the Study's Focus

The Ayur-Veda, the earliest known medical text from India (around 1800 B.C.), lists massage along with diet and exercise as primary healing practices of that time. (Field, 1995, p. 105)

The National Institute of Mental Health (NIMH) (Rockville, Md) Treatment of Depression Collaborative Research Program was the first multisite coordinated study initiated by the NIMH in the field of psychotherapy. (Elkin et al., 1989, p. 971)

The Extent or Significance of a Practical Problem

Approximately 20,000 persons are murdered in the United States each year, making homicide the 11th leading cause of death and the 6th leading cause of the loss of potential years of life before age 65. (Sloan et al., 1988, p. 1256)

Pica, the ingestion of nonnutritive objects, is a specific form of self-injurious behavior that poses a significant health risk for a substantial number of persons with mental retardation. (Fisher et al., 1994, p. 447)

Statement of Major Idea That Will Be Extended, Amplified, Supported, or Challenged

One major advantage of living in a group is the opportunity provided to observe other group members find food. (Brown, 1986, p. 83)

Of the many kinds of tool-making and tool-using behaviors of chimpanzees, termite-fishing is one of the most widely distributed behaviors. (Suzuki et al., 1995, p. 219)

Definition of the Major Concept

Tourette Syndrome (TS) is a neurological disorder that is hypothesized to be of organic etiology; it consists of multiple motor and vocal tics. (Azrin & Peterson, 1990, p. 305)

A *sleeper effect* in persuasion is a delayed increase in the impact of a persuasive message. The term was first used by Hovland, Lumsdaine, and Sheffield (1949) to describe opinion change produced by the U.S. Army's *Why We Fight* films used during World War II. (Pratkanis, Greenwald, Leippe, & Baumgardner, 1988, p. 203)

Statement of Current Theories or Beliefs

> The most meaningful present-day theories of hypnosis interpret hypnotic phenomena along three major lines: (a) desire on the part of the subject to play the role of a hypnotized subject, (b) increase in suggestibility , and (c) a further less well-defined category that is called by White "an altered state of consciousness" and by others, "cortical inhibition," dissociation, etc. depending on their theoretical orientations. (Orne, 1959, p. 277)

> A little more than 10 years ago, Gentner (1982) came up with a set of cognitive and perceptual factors to explain "Why Nouns Are Learned Before Verbs," or at least why they are the predominant category in children's early lexicons. (Tardif, 1996, p. 492)

Case(s) Related to the Study's Purpose

> Recent detailed accounts in the public media about the suicide of three highly talented and gifted individuals dramatically draw our attention to the role of intense perfectionism in suicidal behavior. (Blatt, 1995, p. 1003)

Methodological Issue Addressed

> This study evaluates the validity of an innovative form of polygraph test, Reali's Positive Control Test, and compares it with a Control Question Test and a Guilty Knowledge Test in a laboratory model of field polygraph practice. (Forman & McCauley, 1987, p. 691)

introduction from published research papers. As you can see, their contents include definitions of the major concept to be explored, statements about the historical roots of the study's focus, major ideas that will be extended, amplified, supported, or challenged, and practical, theoretical, or methodological issues that will be addressed. Review these leads to see which might work for your project. A good lead will help capture your readers' interest from the outset.

Field et al.'s lead would fit in the category "extent or significance of a practical problem." They began by pointing to the increasing popularity of stress-management programs in the workplace and the lack of research evaluating them. They also noted the almost exclusive reliance on reactive measures, like "professional opinions" and survey studies, in studies assessing these programs. As we will see, their study used less reactive measures as well as self-report.

The literature review. After stating the research problem, the introduction shifts to a review of the literature. This review sets the stage for presenting the study, by citing past research and theoretical papers related to it. In their report, Field et al. reviewed recent studies on the stress-reducing benefits of massage therapy on HIV-positive men and adolescents with psychiatric problems. They concluded that massage reduces anxiety and depression, as measured by self-report, behavioral observations, salivary cortisol, norepinephrine levels, and enhanced immunity. They also reported that massage therapy was associated with increases in self-reported alertness in these studies and that research on the effects of *facial massage* has shown heightened alertness as measured by EEG, a physiological measure.

When referring to past publications in your literature review or elsewhere in the text of your paper, use the APA citation style. List the authors by their surnames only, separated by commas, followed by the year of publication in parentheses, as in the first example below. Use the same format for citing research or theoretical papers parenthetically, except that within parentheses replace the word *and* with the symbol *&*, as in the second example. Add the page number when quoting from a source, as in the third example. Examples:

    (1) Suzuki, Kuroda, and Nishihara (1995) found that
    (2) Research done in the Ndoki forest (Suzuki, Kuroda, & Nishihara, 1995) discovered that
    (3) The authors concluded: "We may now be in a position to say that chimpanzees can change and use the environment to their advantage by the use of tools" (Suzuki, Kuroda, & Nishihara, 1995, p. 234).

When a study has more than six authors, like the massage study, for example, cite only the first author's surname, followed by the Latin abbreviation *et al.* (meaning, *and others*) in place of the surnames of the remaining authors. Different rules for using *et al.* apply for citations following the first citation. Study Box 9, presented later in the chapter, for the specifics.

Because space is at a premium in journals, the literature review should be selective and logically ordered, presenting only those studies or theoretical papers that will help readers to better understand the research and why it was done. It should focus on similarities between the study and past research rather than on differences, as Murray Sidman, an experimental psychologist, explains:

> As a young graduate student, . . . I felt that my work had to be different, that it had to produce something new that would startle the world. Along these lines I once wrote a paper, describing some of my work, in which I emphasized how different my experiments were from anything else that had ever been done. One of my teachers, W. N. Schoenfeld, agreed that the data were very interesting. But he went on to add that I had written the paper from a peculiar point of view. I had emphasized the *differences* between my work and everyone else's. But science does not ordinarily advance that way. It is the job of science to find orderly relations among phenomena, not differences. It would have been more useful if I could have pointed out the similarities between my work and previous experiments. Although the task he set for me was not an easy one, I reached a new level of scientific maturity when I finally accepted his advice. (Sidman, 1960, p. 15)

The rationale and design of the study. The literature review leads to the rationale for the research, that is, the reasons for doing it. The rationale explains how the study contributes to answering the general questions or resolving the theoretical, methodological, or practical concerns raised early in the introduction. The introduction ends with the specific purpose of the study and its overall design, preparing readers for the detailed presentation of methods that follows in the next section of the report.

Because rationales, like leads, can be difficult to write, Box 3 reprints several, again, sampled from published research studies. As you can see in Box 3, the possible rationales for research are diverse, including improving designs or measures, investigating untested theories or phenomena, discovering new facts and procedures, replicating and extending research, and evaluating theories, procedures and measures.

BOX 3 **RATIONALES FOR THE INTRODUCTION**

Improvements in Research Design or Measures

To date, no study has been able to separate the effects of handgun control from differences among populations in terms of socioeconomic status, aggressive behavior, violent crime, and other factors. (Sloan et al., 1988, p. 1256)

The purpose of the present study was to further evaluate the effectiveness of the habit reversal method in reducing the multiple motor and vocal tics of TS by using a larger number of subjects and a controlled between-subjects experimental design. (Azrin & Peterson, 1990, p. 307)

Theory or Phenomenon Previously Untested, or Studied under Limited Conditions

Although most research on chimpanzee hunting has focused on the factors surrounding hunting success, little attention has been paid to the decision to undertake a hunt when prey are encountered. (Stanford, Wallis, Mpongo, & Goodall, 1994, p. 3)

Previous studies with controlled designs have examined the behavior of children immediately after a dietary challenge, but these studies have been criticized for their brief duration and laboratory settings. (Wolraich et al., 1994, p. 301)

Discovery

In the research presented here, we sought to identify a set of successful operations for obtaining a sleeper effect. (Pratkanis et al., 1988, p. 205)

The purpose of the present study was to give an empirical answer to this question by determining the physiological conditions in which lucid dreaming occurs. (LaBerge, Nagel, Dement, & Zarcone, 1981, p. 727)

Replication and Extension of Research with New Subjects or Improved Measures

There is little research on children's early vocabulary development in Mandarin. (Tardif, 1996, p. 496)

In the above studies subjects anecdotally reported enhanced alertness instead of the expected soporific effect following massage. The purpose of the present study was to investigate the effects of massage on alertness as measured by EEG and by speed and accuracy of performance on math computations. The only massage study in the literature that recorded EEG showed that *facial massage* was accompanied by decreased alpha and beta, a pattern that is inconsistent with drowsiness. (Field et al., 1996, p. 198)

Evaluation of Theories, Procedures, and Measures

The study had two major aims: (1) to test the feasibility and value of the collaborative clinical trial model (a model frequently used in the field of psychopharmacology) in the area of psychotherapy research and (2) to study, within this research model, the effectiveness of two specific forms of psychotherapy (cognitive behavior therapy [CBT] and interpersonal psychotherapy [IPT]) for treating nonbipolar, nonpsychotic depressed outpatients. (Elkin et al., 1989, p. 971)

Field et al. ended their introduction by explaining that their study substituted EEG and the speed and accuracy of mathematical computations for the anecdotal evidence of the effects of massage therapy offered by past researchers. They hypothesized that subjects who received massage therapy would demonstrate enhanced alertness (decreased alpha and beta brain waves and better performance on math computations) and less stress (as measured by anxiety, depression, and cortisol levels) than controls given relaxation therapy.

Method

As its name implies, the Method section presents the methodological details of the study. Although additional subsections can be added to increase clarity and simplicity, this section usually is divided into the three labeled subsections discussed below: Participants (or Subjects, if the research tested animals), Apparatus (or Materials), and Procedure. Provided that all necessary information is reported, other headings might be substituted for clarity or simplicity (as was done in the Field et al. study).

Participants (or subjects). This subsection includes the total number of subjects, as well as the number in each experimental group, their specific characteristics, and how they were recruited and assigned to conditions. Any special agreements with participants or payments made to them should be noted, as should the rates at which people declined to become involved or dropped out of the study.

Information on participants' major demographic characteristics (e.g., gender, education, and age) or other conditions pertinent to the research should be included. Use your judgment on which information to report. Religious affiliation might be important for some attitude surveys, for example, but it would not be relevant to a study of verbal learning. As a guideline, provide only information that will help in replicating the research or understanding the kinds of people to whom its results are likely to generalize.

Field et al. reported that they recruited participants from among the faculty and staff of the University of Miami School of Medicine. Their sex, education, income, extent of daily exercise, and answers to lifestyle questions—all relevant to the study's purposes and procedures—were assessed and reported, along with statistical analyses showing that the experimental and control groups were comparable prior to the treatment. The authors also described how they recruited participants (with advertising fliers) and assigned them to the experimental groups (randomization).

Because participants in research must be treated respectfully in the written report as well as in the conduct of the study itself, it is important to exercise care in selecting terms to refer to them. The *Publication Manual* points out that it is the responsibility of psychologists

> to avoid perpetuating demeaning attitudes and biased assumptions about people in their writings. Constructions that might imply bias against persons on the basis of gender, sexual orientation, racial or ethnic group, disability, or age should be avoided. Scientific writing should be free of implied or irrelevant evaluation of the group or groups being studied. (APA, 1994, p. 46)

To avoid bias in describing participants in research, the manual advises authors to choose reference terms that are "accurate, clear and free from bias," and "at the appropriate level of specificity" (APA, 1994, p. 47). For example, avoid using terms like *man* or *mankind* when referring to both men and women, selecting instead words like *people, humans, respondents, or men and women.* Similarly, instead of *he* or *his* (as in "we told each participant that he could quit whenever he wished," when both men and women participated), substitute plural nouns unspecific for gender (e.g., "we told the participants that they could quit at any time."). Rather than describing participants as *disabled,* explain that they had spinal cord injuries. Whenever possible, replace general terms, like *the elderly,* with more specific terms, like *participants aged 65–90.*

Since language often subtly conveys cultural biases, the *Publication Manual* recommends reading your written work carefully with an eye to detecting any implied evaluation. One was the manual suggests to do this is to read what you have written substituting your own group for the group or groups you are discussing, or, alternatively, imagining that you are a member of the group you are writing about and gauging your own reaction to your words. Better still, have representatives from the groups who take part in your study read your report and give you their reactions to it, and take account of their responses and preferences in deciding on its final wording.

The APA also recommends that, whenever possible, authors acknowledge the collaborative role that people play in research by choosing more active terms, like *participants* or *respondents*, to refer to them rather than the traditional but more passive term *subjects*. The participants' share in the research also is better recognized by using the active rather than the passive form of verbs (e.g., "the children answered several questions about . . . ." is active, "the children were interviewed" and "interviews were conducted with the children" are passive). Box 10, later in the chapter, includes additional examples of active and passive verbs.

When your research involves animals rather than people, report the total number of animals as well as the number in each experimental group. Also provide information on the animals' age, sex, weight, and general physiological condition, as well as other identifying information such as genus, species, and strain number. The name of the company that supplied the animals might also be helpful in replicating the research. Pertinent facts about how the animals were handled outside of the experimental setting also might be included for this reason.

Apparatus/materials. In this subsection, identify and describe the instruments and materials used in the research, including brand names and models, as well as the purposes to which they were put in the study. Again, some judgment is required here. The manufacturer of an instrument for measuring a complex physiological response, like EEG, usually would be reported; the brand name of an ordinary stopwatch or scale would not. In the report of the massage study, the authors provided information on the instruments they used to monitor EEG, as well as their settings, and all other information needed to duplicate their measures, including the computer software for analyzing EEG patterns. Their procedures for assessing participants' cortisol levels (a physiological measure of stress) were described in similar detail.

If equipment is specifically constructed for a study, detailed information on its design and measurements should be provided. Photographs or diagrams also might be included.

Similarly, the names and versions of psychological tests should be provided in this subsection, along with information on their reliability and validity. Observational schemes, like rating scales or category systems for recording behaviors, also should be identified and their measurement properties detailed. In their subsection entitled "Assessment Procedures," Field and her co-authors described both their long-term (e.g., the Life Events scale) and short-term measures (e.g., math computations). Their behavior rating scales also were carefully described, with accompanying statistics on validity and reliability. References were cited for each scale and measure so that interested readers would be able to learn more about them.

The amount of detail to report would depend on the measure. It would not be necessary to give the reliability or validity of widely used tests, since these would be generally acknowledged; but such information would be required for less popular measures. If tests were specifically developed for a study, they should be fully described, with documentation of their adequacy as measuring instruments.

Procedure. Although the procedure section should be as brief as possible, it should give enough information so that other researchers can replicate its essentials. Each step in the research, from the moment a subject's involvement began to when it ended, should be reported, including: instructions they were given, activities, events to which they were exposed, the timing of tasks, how the study ended, whether participants were paid for their involvement, and whether and how they were debriefed.

Field et al. provided enough information on the massage therapy so that other researchers could replicate it with the aid of a trained massage therapist. The purpose and treatment of the control group also were presented, as were the order and timing of the various assessments of participants during the study.

Results

The results section reports how the data were analyzed and the results of those analyses. Because this is the most technical section of the report, often filled with numbers and statistical terms, you may find it to be the hardest part of

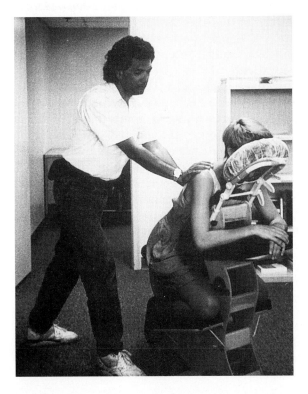

A participant in the Field et al. study receiving massage therapy.

the report to write in an interesting style. The challenge here is to present the technical material in a simple and engaging manner.

Box 4 presents the leads for the results sections of several published papers. If your study is straightforward and the measures are standard, well known procedures, you can begin this section with the study's most important findings. The first two entries in Box 4 begin in this way. However, as the other examples in the box show, often other leads are necessary to help readers interpret the findings that follow. For example, it might be necessary to include data on the characteristics and numbers of subjects who continued or dropped out of the experimental conditions, the nature and number of observations in naturalistic studies, or the reliability of measures. If the study involves an experimental manipulation, evidence may be provided demonstrating that it actually worked and to what degree.

Organization. Once such preliminaries have been covered, the findings must be presented in an organized format. There are three common ways to structure this presentation: (1) by time line, (2) by the type of dependent variable, and (3) by the importance of the results.

The time line organization is a natural for studies conducted in different phases. For example, Hentschel et al. (1993) organized the results of their study on the treatment of ulcers with antibiotics into two parts, under the headings Treatment Period and Follow-up Period.

When a study involves several dependent variables, the results often are organized into separate sections for each dependent variable or type of variable. In the report of their experiment on the effects of sugar on children, Wolraich et al. (1994) presented their results under separate headings for Behavioral and Cognitive Measures and Biochemical Tests. The Field et al. massage study also used this type of organization.

If your research involves a primary analysis, testing the hypotheses discussed in the introduction, and a secondary analysis suggested by these results, consider organizing the results section into primary and secondary analyses. Elkin et al. (1989) did this in their report of their study evaluating the effectiveness of different psychotherapies. Although the main analysis indicated no significant differences between the therapies, a secondary analysis, taking into account the severity of patients' depression, did show differential effects. The authors organized the results under three main headings: Patient Characteristics, Attrition, and Outcome Analyses; the last section was divided into two subsections, titled Pretreatment-Posttreatment Differences and Secondary Analyses.

A good organization with well-chosen headings can help readers to easily understand your results. Carefully constructed figures and tables also clarify the presentation.

Tables and figures. If your results involve only a few numbers, they can be presented in the text. But if the results are extensive and involve several groups and dependent measures, by all means, present them in a table. The

---

BOX 4 **LEADS FOR RESULTS SECTION**

REPORT OF MAIN QUANTITATIVE RESULTS

The effect of light treatment on the patients' Hamilton scale scores is shown in Figure 1 and Table 2. Mean (± SD) Hamilton scores before, during, and after bright light treatment for outpatients were 22.9 ± 5.4, 9.5 ± 4.4, and 16.4 ± 5.8, respectively ($p < .025$). (Rosenthal et al., 1985, p. 165)

The mean occurrence of each of the target behaviors across baseline, treatment and follow-up phases for the 12 role-play situations are presented in Table 1. (Frame, Matson, Sonis, Fialkov & Kazdin, 1982, p. 241)

ISSUES AFFECTING RESULTS

Description of Subjects and Dropout Rates

The characteristics of the 140 children who entered the study are shown in Table 1. The mean ages of the girls and the boys were similar, but the pubertal development of the girls was more advanced, as expected. (Johnston et al., 1992, p. 83)

Fifty-eight subjects were recruited for the study. Pilot studies of the first three subjects were used to refine the protocol; these children were therefore eliminated from the final analysis. Three subjects were eliminated because of poor compliance, as confirmed by the weekly urine tests for ascorbate and riboflavin; three withdrew before completing the study; and one (the youngest) was unable to complete the cognitive and behavioral assessments. (Wolraich et al., 1994, p. 303)

Nature and Number of Observations in Naturalistic Studies

A total of 364 pods were counted in 1991 and 395 in 1993, during the land-based surveys. The data sets for 1991 and 1993 were pooled for further analysis. (Brown & Corkeron, 1995, p. 167)

Excluding interjections and nonreferential onomatopoeia, the children in this sample produced a mean of 73.7 (SD = 30.28) wholly productive vocabulary types and 338.0 (SD = 251.77) vocabulary tokens in the 1-hr speech sample for which the following data were analyzed. (Tardif, 1996, p. 498)

Reliability of Observers

The agreement of judgments made by the examiner and blind judge for the three tests can be represented both as percent agreement and as the correlation between judgments (1 = innocent, 2 = inconclusive, 3 = deceptive). (Forman & McCauley, 1987, p. 693)

Base Line Conditions

At base line, the subjects ate their usual diets, which contained moderate amounts of fat (30.6 percent of energy), cholesterol (274 mg per day), and fiber (23.3 g per day) (Table 2). (Swain, Rouse, Curley, & Sacks, 1990, p. 149)

At base line, the use of psychoactive medication was comparable in the experimental and control nursing homes (Table 3). (Avorn et al., 1992, p. 170)

Field et al. study is a good example of the simplicity offered by well-laid-out tables. The major findings of this study were presented in two tables showing the means and standard deviations on the dependent measures for the conditions in the study. Table 2, in Appendix B, illustrates a common format for these tables.

The columns of the table correspond to the conditions of the study, massage therapy versus the control treatment, and within these two conditions, the pre- and posttreatment measures for the 1st and 10th days of the study. The rows give the results for the different dependent measures, depression, anxiety, math accuracy, etc. (The results for the EEG measures are in Table 3.) The means and standard deviations of the measures are included within the body of the table.

A separate statistical analysis was performed on each variable. The subscripts of the means in Table 2 indicate the results of these tests. Within a row, all the means with a common subscript, a, b, or c, are not statistically different from each other. The means with different subscripts are significantly different, at $p < .05$.

For example, look at the row for math computation accuracy. The means for the control condition vary from 60.0_a to 72.3_a, the higher the score the greater the accuracy. All the means for the control condition have the same subscript, a. This indicates that these means are not significantly different from each other, so there is no evidence that the accuracy scores for the subjects in the control group changed during the study. For the massage condition, the means start at 69.2_a and increase to 96.2_c by the end of the study. The subscripts a and c indicate that these means are significantly different. The subjects receiving massage increased their mean accuracy scores during the study to a level significantly higher than the levels in the control condition.

Once you know this code for reporting the results of statistical tests, the table is easy to read and clearly communicates the major findings of the study. Examples of other APA style tables are shown in Box 5.

Figures are a good alternative to presenting results in the text or tables when the amount of data is extensive or when the relationships are complex. Scatterplots showing the relationship between scores on two variables are common in psychological reports, as are histograms illustrating the distribution of scores on one variable, bar and line graphs of the means of treatment groups, and charts showing the sequence of events in an experiment. Box 5

BOX 5 APA FORMAT AND STYLE FOR TABLES AND FIGURES

Tables

❏ Table 1 below illustrates how to present descriptive statistics for two experimental groups. Note that type of therapy, the independent variable, is indicated in the first column; each row and column is labeled; and only horizontal lines are used to form the table.

❏ Table 2 shows results for a study with two independent variables.

Table 1

Hamilton Depression Scores at the Termination of Therapy

Therapy	M	SD	n
Cognitive	9.57	8.44	23
Prozac	10.41	9.39	20

Table 2

Hamilton Depression Scores for Severely and Moderately Depressed Patients at the Termination of Therapy

	Type of Therapy	
Symptoms	Prozac	Cognitive
Severe		
M	9.00	13.29
SD	4.09	3.91
n	15	14
Moderate		
M	12.21	8.87
SD	2.64	2.26
n	14	15

❏ Each table should be fully labeled. All tables (and figures) included in the paper must be referred to in the text; it should not be necessary to read the text to understand a table.

❏ Tables should be double-spaced. Capitalize only the first letter of major words in titles. Underline statistical symbols.

Figures

❏ Figures include graphs, charts, drawings, and photographs.

❏ Figures should be drawn 25% to 50% larger than their size will be in the published article; photographs should be 20% larger.

❏ Each figure should have a caption fully explaining the figure. It should not be necessary to read the text to understand a figure.

❏ Use the figures from published articles that are included in this book as guides in designing figures.

also gives information on the recommended APA format for figures. Edward Tufte's book *The visual presentation of quantitative information* (1983) and its sequel *Envisioning information* (1990) discuss how to construct figures with clarity and style.

Drawings and photographs also are useful for illustrating aspects of an experiment that are difficult to describe in the text, for example, the details of visual presentations, unique equipment, or involved spatial arrangements of the apparatus. Consider using a drawing or photograph when you think that readers will be unfamiliar with your materials and when realism and detail are essential. The apparatus used in the Held and Hein (1963) experiment on kittens, discussed in Chapter 6, is a good example of the value of pictures. This complex piece of equipment would be difficult to describe in words; the picture shown in Chapter 6 makes the equipment understandable.

Remember to refer to all tables and figures in the text, alerting your readers to the results revealed in them. Although the body of the results section is written in the past tense, because the study reports on research that is now complete use the present tense to refer to findings in tables or figures that are currently under discussion. For example, "Table 2 shows that the massage group . . ." (see Box 9: Past vs. present tense, later in the chapter). Tables and figures should be assigned independent and consecutive numbers.

Statistical analyses. When describing results statistically, include both measures of central tendency (means, medians) and measures of variability, such as the standard deviation or interquartile range. In reporting statistical analyses, note the test that you used, the value of the test statistic, the degrees of freedom, the alpha level, and the direction of the effect. Examples of how to do this are given in Box 6, under the heading Reporting Statistical Results. Assume that your readers understand how to interpret these statistics. Box 6 also shows how to abbreviate statistical symbols and units of measure as well as when to report numbers in words or figures.

The results section should contain all the results of the study. Do not save some results or stories of colorful behavior to add interest to the discussion. Readers should be able to find out everything that happened in your research by reading the results. Incidentally, describing the behavior of individual subjects is an excellent way to add interest to the results section and to illustrate reactions to the treatment, or other behavior, that would be lost in a straight quantitative presentation.

Discussion

The introduction evaluates and interprets research published in the literature; the discussion does the same for the study being reported, helping readers understand how the research answers the questions posed in the introduction.

BOX 6 APA GUIDELINES FOR ABBREVIATING STATISTICAL SYMBOLS AND PRESENTING NUMBERS AND RESULTS OF STATISTICAL ANALYSES

Statistical Symbols

❑ Abbreviate statistical terms as follows (underlining indicates that the symbol should be typeset in italics.)

Statistic	Abbreviation
Fisher's test statistic	F
Cohen's effect size	d
alpha level for statistical test	α
mean	M
standard deviation	SD
quartile	Q
statistic for t test	t
statistic for chi-square test	χ^2
Pearson correlation coefficient	r
number of subjects in subsample	n
total number of subjects in sample	N
nonsignificant	ns

Units of Measure

❑ Abbreviate units of measure when they follow numerical values (e.g., 10 cm); otherwise write out the unit. The metric system is used in APA papers; non-metric values also should be expressed as metric values (e.g., the box was 6 in. high (15.24 cm). Note that in. has a period, but some other units do not.

Unit of Measure	Abbreviation
ante meridiem	a.m.
centimeter	cm
degree Fahrenheit	° F
gram	g
hour	hr
inch	in.
kilometer	km
liter	L
post meridiem	p.m.
second	s

Numbers

❏ In general, write the words for numbers less than 10 (e.g., two stimuli); express numbers 10 or greater in figures (e.g., 14 trials). Some exceptions are numbers linked with a unit of measure or time, number of subjects, and mathematical functions which always are written in figures (e.g., 7 mg, 2 days, and a ratio of 2:1). Express summary statistics and test statistics to 2 digits more than the raw data (e.g., if the raw data are whole numbers, the mean is written with two decimal places). Use a zero before the decimal point for numbers less than one (0.54); but do not use the leading zero for probability values, proportions, or values of r, because these statistics cannot have a value greater than one (e.g., $p < .05$).

Reporting Statistical Results

❏ Report the alpha level for each statistical test. If the same level is used throughout the report, use a single statement like "The alpha level was .05 for all tests."

❏ In addition to alpha, for each test report the following: the value of the test statistic, the degrees of freedom, and the p value. If available, present the effect size. For example:

t-test: A t-test showed that the means on the self-esteem scale of the experimental ($M = 18.4$, $SD = 5.6$, $n = 12$) and control groups ($M = 5.35$, $SD = 3.3$, $n = 14$) were significantly different at the alpha level of .05 for a two-tailed test, $t(24) = 7.37$, $p = .000$.

F test, analysis of variance: Table 1 shows the means and standard deviations for the measure of creativity for the four instructional sets. There was a significant effect of set at the alpha level of .05, $F (3,44) = 3.40$, $MSE = 10.20$, $p = .03$.

Correlation coefficient: The correlation between maze learning scores for the two groups of matched subjects was $r = .92$ ($n = 44$, alpha level of .05 for a two-tailed test, $p = .000$), indicating that the basis for matching was excellent.

Chi-square: 80% of the cognitive therapy patients dropped out, compared to 90% drop out for patients in interpersonal therapy, and 70% for drug therapy. These dropout rates were significantly different, $\chi^2 (2, N = 150) = 6.25$, $p = .04$, with an alpha level of .05.

The discussion also evaluates the study's strengths and limitations to enable readers to better interpret its results.

As the "leads" in Box 7, reprinted from published studies, illustrate, the discussion often begins by summarizing the rationale and purpose of the research, giving its major results and conclusions, or commenting on their validity. Field et al. started their discussion by summarizing their findings and instructing readers on how to interpret them.

In addition to establishing whether the researchers' expectations were confirmed or disconfirmed, the discussion also considers how the findings fit with the results of past research. Are the findings similar to or different from the results reported by other investigators? in which ways? Field et al., for example, remarked that their finding of decreased depression for the massage group

---

BOX 7 **LEADS FOR THE DISCUSSION SECTION**

Summary of Rationale and Purpose of Study

Previous studies of the effectiveness of gun control have generally compared rates of homicide in nations with different approaches to the regulation of firearms. Unfortunately, the validity of these studies has been compromised by the large number of confounding factors that characterize national groups. (Sloan et al., 1988, p. 1259)

In this preliminary investigation, we evaluated the procedure known as empirically derived consequences for developing a treatment package for pica. (Fisher et al., 1994, p. 455)

Summary of Major Result, Conclusion, Finding

We can be fairly certain that chimpanzees of the Ndoki forest make and use two different types of tools in combination to fish for and feed on termites. (Suzuki et al., 1995, p. 227)

The results are consistent with our thesis that self-produced movement with its concurrent visual feedback is necessary for the development of visually-guided behavior. (Held & Hein, 1963, p. 875)

Validity of Results

The clinical and demographic features of the population described here were typical of seasonal affective disorder patients we have reported on elsewhere . (Rosenthal et al., 1985, p. 168)

Estimates of pod size collected from different observation platforms can differ within one study area. Data on pod sizes collected in this study are from a high land-based observation platform which is likely to give reasonably unbiased estimates. (Brown & Corkeron, 1995, p. 172)

---

was consistent with other massage studies. Similarly, the enhanced alertness (decreased alpha and beta brain waves) in the massage group did not surprise them, given prior research findings on the effects of facial massage.

The last major decision you will have to make in writing your report is how to end your discussion. The examples of "closes" from published research studies included in Box 8 illustrate a range of possibilities. As you can see there, your discussions might end by presenting the theoretical or practical implications of the research, offering qualifications of its results, or suggesting specific recommendations for future studies. Field et al. ended their paper by speculating on the causes of the massage therapy group's enhanced alertness and suggesting other dependent variables to add to future studies. They also pointed to the need for longer-term follow-up studies, with steady large doses of massage, and of documenting the cost-effectiveness of massage therapy.

BOX 8 **CLOSES FOR DISCUSSION SECTION**

Call for Action or Concern Based on Findings

Although our findings should be corroborated in other settings, our results suggest that a more restrictive approach to handgun control may decrease national homicide rates. (Sloan et al., 1988, p. 1261)

With the number of elderly patients in nursing homes projected to exceed 2 million by the end of this decade, such educational programs could enhance attempts to counter the overuse of psychoactive drugs in the vulnerable residents of these facilities. (Avorn et al., 1992, p. 172)

Speculative Hypotheses Explaining Findings

At present, it appears that the location of stands of fruit trees determine where chimpanzees travel, hence where they encounter and hunt colobus monkeys, but the explanation for why they hunt may lie more in social and reproductive rather than nutritional reasons. (Stanford et al., 1994, p. 17)

The present findings suggest that psychological influences play a major role in the maintenance, and perhaps the aetiology, of the disorder. (Azrin & Peterson, 1990, p. 317)

General Conclusion of the Study

We may now be in a position to say that chimpanzees can change and use the environment to their advantage by the use of tools. (Suzuki et al., 1995, p. 234)

These findings provide convincing evidence for a developmental process, in a least one higher mammal, which requires for its operation stimulus variation concurrent with and systematically dependent upon self-produced movement. (Held & Hein, 1963, p. 876)

Qualifications of the Major Result

It is important to note that pica was not eliminated completely with the introduction of treatment. (Fisher et al., 1994, p. 456)

Although multiple symptoms of the child's depression were successfully treated, the extent to which treatment eliminated the disorder remains unclear. (Frame et al., 1982, p. 242)

Suggestions/Plans for Future Research

Future publications reporting analyses of data obtained at 6-, 12- and 19-month follow-up evaluations will address these issues. (Elkin et al., 1989, p. 981)

References

The reference list, which comes at the end of the paper, links your research to previous work related to the same problem. Each study mentioned in the paper must appear among the references and each entry in the references must be referred to in the paper. (A bibliography includes works not cited in the text; a reference list does not.) Accuracy is essential, so be sure to photocopy the journal articles you use or carefully record references in your notes. The people who read your paper will use your references to find the articles, books, etc. that you cite.

The references should be listed in alphabetical order by the first author's surname. The APA *Publication Manual* specifies a precise format for reporting citations in the reference list. The general format is:

Author(s). (Year). Title. Publishing data.

Each reference ends with a period and is divided by periods into four major parts: (1) the author(s), (2) year of publication, (3) title, and (4) where, and, in the case of books or chapters in books, by whom, the work was published. Examples of the required format for a journal article, a book, and a chapter in a book, follow.

Journal article:

Suzuki, S., Kuroda, S., & Nishihara, T. (1995). Tool-set for termite-fishing by chimpanzees in the Ndoki forest, Congo. <u>Behaviour, 132,</u> 219–35.

Book:

Garvey, W. D. (1979). <u>Communication: The essence of science.</u> Elmsford, NY: Pergamon Press.

Chapter in a book:

Bem, D. J. (1972). Self-perception theory. In L. Berkowitz (Ed.), <u>Advances in experimental social psychology</u> (Vol. 6, pp. 1–62). New York: Academic Press.

Notice that:

- Each reference should be double-spaced, with the first line indented.
- Authors' surnames are presented first, followed by their initials.
- Authors' names are separated by commas and the symbol *&* is used rather than the word *and*.
- Only the first word of titles and subtitles is capitalized.
- The titles of books are underlined; the titles of articles are not.
- The name and volume number of journals are underlined.
- The publishing data for a journal article includes the name of the journal, its volume number, and the page numbers.

Calvin and Hobbes   by Bill Watterson

- The publishing data for a book is the publishing company and the city of its home office; the city is presented first, followed by a colon, then the name of the publishing company.
- References end with a period.

You can use the references in this book, which are presented in the APA format, as models. For unusual types of references that do not appear in this book or in the manuscript in the Appendix, consult the APA *Publication Manual,* which should be available at your library.

Appendix, Author Note, Footnotes, Tables, and Figures

As the overview in Box 1 shows, the references may be followed by an appendix, author note, footnotes, tables, figure captions, and figures. Box 1 describes the content and format of these sections. Although the Field et al. report had no figures or footnotes, it did include tables, which we already have discussed. The author note for the Field et al. paper illustrates the typical contents of this part of the report.

Most research articles, like the massage therapy study, do not include an appendix. However, your professor may require an appendix presenting your "raw" (unanalyzed) data, as well as other supporting information to show what you did in the study, for example, your questionnaires, instructions, debriefing questions, etc.

*A*PA EDITORIAL STYLE

So far, we have discussed the organization and contents of the research report and some of the APA's editorial style specifications. In this section, we complete our presentation of the how-tos of writing research papers according to the APA style. The rules for format and style published by the APA reflect the current writing practices of psychologists. Contrary to what you might think, the rules aren't there to frustrate you; they're meant to help. Using them creates uniformity of presentation in the psychological literature and so facilitates communication among researchers.

Box 9 shows the APA format for pages and headings, abbreviations, and the past and present tense of verbs. These rules of style, in conjunction with the guidelines we have presented already and the model manuscript, should provide you with the information you need to write a research report in the APA style.

The APA *Publication Manual* also makes recommendations to improve the readability of research reports. Although it used to be standard practice in psychology to write research reports in the passive voice and for authors to avoid

---

BOX 9 THE MECHANICS OF APA FORMAT AND STYLE

Page Setup

❏ Type text on 8½ by 11 inch white paper, with at least one-inch margins on all sides. Double-space all text (title page, abstract, the body of the paper, references, tables, figure captions, etc.), left justified with a ragged right edge.

❏ Number all pages consecutively in the upper right-hand corner, at least one inch from the right edge of the paper, in the space between the top edge of the paper and the first line of text. Figures are not numbered.

❏ Type a manuscript page header to identify pages should they become separated, at least five spaces to the left of the page number. The manuscript page header, which consists of the first two or three words of the title, should appear on each page of the manuscript. Only the first letters of the major words are capitalized.

❏ The running head, printed at the top of each page of a published article, is typed on the title page, flush with the left margin and below the manuscript page header, at least one inch from the top edge of the paper.

❏ Indent the first line of each paragraph. The single exception is the abstract, which is typed as a block. Each reference in the reference list is treated as a separate paragraph.

❏ All material that is to appear in italics in the published work is underlined in the manuscript.

Title, Author Affiliation, and Headings

❏ All information on the title page is centered, except for the running head, page number, and manuscript page header, as are all major headings in the paper. The title, which is repeated on the first page of the introduction, also is centered. All information on the title page, with the exception of the running head, and headings are typed in lowercase letters with the first letter of major words capitalized.

❏ Begin all parts of the paper except the introduction with its appropriate heading: Abstract, Method, Results, Discussion, References, Appendix, Author note, Footnotes, Figure captions. The introduction begins on a new page with the title of the paper centered at the top, and with no other heading.

❏ Use the formats below for papers with one, two, or three levels of headings.

❏

Method
[Center and capitalize]

<u>Participants</u> [Justify flush left, underline, and capitalize the first letter of major words.]
<u>Measures</u>
      <u>Rating scales</u> [Indent, underline, and capitalize the first word. End heading with a period. Continue text on the same line.].
      <u>Self-report scales.</u>
<u>Procedures</u>

Results

<u>Reliability Analysis</u>
<u>Comparative Analysis</u>

Discussion

Abbreviations

❏ Use abbreviations sparingly, only when they aid communication.
❏ Explain abbreviations when you first use them (e.g., Wechsler Adult Intelligence Scale (WAIS)), then use the abbreviation consistently.
❏ Do not start a sentence with a lowercase abbreviation.
❏ Use appropriate Latin abbreviations in the text of your paper if they are enclosed by parentheses; otherwise, use the corresponding English phrase. The abbreviation et al. is an exception. When citing a reference for the first time, use et al. to refer to authors after the first only if there are six or more authors. After the first citation, use et al. when the refernece has three or more authors. If the reference has two authors never use et al. A list of common abbreviations follows.

Meaning	Abbreviation
that is	i.e.,
for example	e.g.,
versus	vs.
compare	cf.
and so forth	etc.
namely	viz.,
and others	et al.

Past vs. Present Tense

❏ Use the past tense to refer to the research of other authors in the introduction and discussion sections (e.g., "Brown (1993) **found** that").
❏ Also describe procedures (in the method section) and report and discuss results (in the results section) in the past tense, for example, "The mean creativity score **was** 6.5."

❑ Use the present tense when discussing the results presented in your tables or figures, for example, "Table 1 **shows** that Instructional Set 1 results in higher creativity scores than the other three sets."

❑ Write the discussion in the present tense, for example, "The results **confirm** the prediction that. . . ."

at all costs referring to themselves using first-person pronouns, this is no longer the case. The most recent *Publication Manual* (APA, 1994) encourages authors to use the active voice and to refer to themselves when doing so promotes clarity.

Since it is not always easy to distinguish between active and passive verbs, Box 10 illustrates the differences between them. Although it is now acceptable to refer to yourself ("I met with subjects to debrief them"), you should do so sparingly. Too much discussion of you, and the emphasis shifts away from the research which should be the focus.

*W*RITING WITH "STYLE"

Clarity, accuracy, and conciseness are the bare bones of scientific communication. But one thing more is needed in good scientific writing. Your clear, accurate, and concise report should be written with what is sometimes called "style."

Georges Louis Buffon, an 18th-century French naturalist, who was recognized by the Academie Français for his excellent use of the French language,

---

BOX 10 ACTIVE VERSUS PASSIVE VOICE

❑ Passive verbs have a form of "to be" and a past participle; for example, "The data **were collected** in the waiting room."

❑ Use the active voice (any form but the passive) whenever possible, for example, "The patients filled out the questionnaire in the waiting room."

Passive Voice	Active Voice
The study **was designed** to test . . .	I designed the study to test. . . . (one author)
The film **was presented** to the children.	The children watched a 30-minute film
The means **are given** in Table 1.	Table 1 illustrates that the mean of Group A is. . . .
The stimuli **were chosen** to vary in color.	We chose the stimuli to vary in color. . . . (more than one author)
A t-test **was done** to compare. . . .	The t-test showed that the experimental group. . . . Or Using a t-test, we found a significant difference between the means. . . .

defined style as "the order and movement one puts into one's thoughts" (Shortland & Gregory, 1991, p. 53). To achieve style requires going beyond simply getting your ideas on paper to expressing them in a lively, engaging, and pleasing manner. According to Shortland and Gregory:

> Order is the structure you put on your paper. Movement is what carries the reader from one idea or event to the next. It is what ensures that the reader who picks up your article will see it through. (Shortland & Gregory, 1991, p. 53)

Let's look at structure, the first ingredient of writing with style. To some extent, following the APA format that we have outlined guarantees that your paper will have structure. So when we speak of structure here, we are thinking about the organization you impose on the material within each section of your paper. We hope that the suggestions that we have made so far have given you a good understanding of how to structure the separate sections of your paper. Beyond that, developing good structure in your writing involves careful thought about what you want to say and how you want to say it. Discussing your ideas with sympathetic professors and fellow students is a good way to figure out what you want to say.

One key to writing a well-structured paper is creating good transitions. Marsha Dutton, a professor of English, compares transitions in written work to the prongs on Lego blocks; both are involved in "holding together elements that might otherwise slide apart because of an absence of obvious connection" (Dutton, 1996, p. 16). She continues:

> Here's another metaphor for transitions: train passengers wishing to move from their seats to the dining car are grateful for the overlapping pieces of metal between cars that allow them to walk from one car to another rather than leaping across open space. Those metal gangplanks are transitions, keeping travelers from falling to the tracks below, just as your transitions keep readers from losing the train of your argument. (Dutton, 1996, p. 16)

With good transitions the links between ideas are apparent and each idea leads smoothly and logically to the next. The *Publication Manual* lists several sorts of transitional words that you should pay careful attention to as you write:

> time links (then, next, after, while, since), cause-effect links (therefore, consequently, as a result), addition links (in addition, moreover, furthermore, similarly), and contrast links (but, conversely, nevertheless, however, although, whereas). (APA, 1994, p. 24)

The second component of writing with style is movement. One way to make your writing lively is to follow the APA suggestion that, whenever possible, you use active rather than passive verbs. Another is careful editing. Your writing will be livelier if you work at making it easy to read. To do this, select the most basic words, remove all spelling errors, repetition and typos, and check for grammatical errors. A good way to spot awkward expressions, difficult-to-understand spots, and rough transitions is to read your report out loud. This also will alert you to overly long sentences and language that is too complex or artificial.

*O*RAL PRESENTATIONS

Before journals became popular, most scientists kept up with each others' work through correspondence (Garvey, 1979). Because there is an unavoidable delay between when research is done and when it is published, informal communication prior to publication still is the norm rather than the exception in science. In fact, Garvey reports that about 90% of the material published in scientific journals already has been communicated to other scientists informally through other means—in one-on-one meetings, at college colloquia where researchers present their work to faculty and students, and at local, state, regional, and national conferences. Groups of scientists working on similar problems (sometimes called "invisible colleges") keep up with each other's work by getting together regularly to discuss it, sometimes at conferences.

Although some scientists attend conferences primarily to meet with other scientists, most go to listen to presentations. In paper sessions, researchers give brief oral reports of research studies (usually 15 minutes or less). Such presenters receive requests for copies of their papers from interested parties who are unable to attend. In poster sessions, which are less formal than brief presentations, researchers display typed reports of their research. Those who attend can read the report and ask questions about it.

You may want to attend one of these conferences to get ideas, to keep up on the latest research, or even to present your study to other psychologists. Since it is easier to get a paper accepted for presentation at a professional conference than to publish it, conferences are a great way for young researchers to share their work, to get helpful feedback, and to test the waters to find out whether their work is likely to be accepted for publication.

For the most part, the format for presenting one's research at conferences is the same as it is for writing the study for publication. But an oral presentation cannot be as detailed as a written report; listeners cannot follow that much detail. So be selective in reporting your results. Present only indispensable information that your listeners need to understand your study, and concentrate on speaking in clear and simple language.

No matter how much we prepare, almost everyone other than the seasoned public speaker has some jitters about giving an oral presentation to peers. Because the anxiety of giving a talk stems from concerns that our work might be negatively evaluated, it is wise to avoid dwelling on this possibility. The best way we know to do this is to concentrate on the ideas you want to get across in your presentation. The more you focus on what your listeners need to know to understand your research, the more you will find your anxiety being replaced by positive energy, as the following excerpt from Richard Feynman's autobiography illustrates.

The excerpt describes an experience Feynman, now a Nobel Prize-winning physicist, had early in his scientific career. He had just learned that Albert Einstein and Wolfgang Pauli, in his words, "monster minds" of physics, were in the audience for the very first talk of his professional career:

> Then the time came to give the talk, and here are these *monster minds* in front of me, waiting! My first technical talk, and I have this audience! . . . they would put me through the wringer! I remember very clearly seeing my hands shaking as they were pulling out my notes from a brown envelope. But then a miracle occurred, as it has occurred again and again in my life, and it's lucky for me: the moment I start to talk about physics, and have to concentrate on what I'm explaining, nothing else occupies my mind—I'm completely immune to being nervous. So after I started to go, I just didn't know who was in the room. I was only explaining this idea, that's all. (Feynman, in Shortland & Gregory, 1991, p. 121)

In addition to following Feynman's principle, it also helps to rehearse by presenting your paper to your roommate, an encouraging friend, or the professor who sponsored your paper at the conference. If this is too difficult at first, rehearse with a tape recorder. Better still, present your paper to your dog. You'll get as much practice as you need, avoid negative feedback, and get tons of appreciation in the mix.

THE ETHICS OF SCIENTIFIC COMMUNICATION

In Chapter 7, we discussed the principles and code of conduct developed by the APA for human and animal research. We complete this presentation in this chapter by discussing the APA's six ethical standards for publishing and reviewing research (reprinted in Box 11).

In 1830, Charles Babbage, a British mathematician, developed a classification of dishonesty in reporting data that Morton Hunt believes "serious discussion of scientific fraud has not improved on" (Hunt, 1981, p. 50). Babbage categorized fraudulent data analysis into three types: "forging," or inventing and recording observations that actually never were collected; "trimming," or improving data by "clipping off little bits here and there which differ most in excess from the mean and in sticking them on to those which are too small," and "cooking," or selecting for analysis only those data which confirm one's hypotheses and discarding the rest (Babbage, in Hunt, 1981, pp. 46,50). Because such dishonesty is intolerable in science, the first of the APA's principles focuses on this.

Principle 6.21 in Box 11 specifies that it is unethical for psychologists to fabricate data or falsify results. If significant errors in published research are discovered, this principle requires psychologists to acknowledge these and publish corrections. It is the ethical responsibility of psychologists to prevent misinformation from contaminating scientific knowledge by deliberate falsification, the focus of the APA principle, or by carelessness in reporting or analyzing data. When scientists are accused of deliberate dishonesty, because of the seriousness of the offense, positions are lost and reputations ruined.

BOX 11 APA ETHICAL STANDARDS: COMMUNICATING AND REVIEWING RESEARCH

6.21 Reporting of Results

(a) Psychologists do not fabricate data or falsify results in their publications.

(b) If psychologists discover significant errors in their published data, they take reasonable steps to correct such errors in a correction, retraction, erratum, or other appropriate publication means.

6.22 Plagiarism

Psychologists do not present substantial portions or elements of another's work or data as their own, even if the other work or data source is cited occasionally.

6.23 Publication Credit

(a) Psychologists take responsibility and credit, including authorship credit, only for work they have actually performed or to which they have contributed.

(b) Principal authorship and other publication credits accurately reflect the relative scientific or professional contributions of the individuals involved, regardless of their relative status. Mere possession of an institutional position, such as Department Chair, does not justify authorship credit. Minor contributions to the research or to the writing for publications are appropriately acknowledged, such as in footnotes or in an introductory statement.

(c) A student is usually listed as principal author on any multiple-authored article that is substantially based on the student's dissertation or thesis.

6.24 Duplicate Publication of Data

Psychologists do not publish, as original data, data that have been previously published. This does not preclude republishing data when they are accompanied by proper acknowledgment.

6.25 Sharing Data

After research results are published, psychologists do not withhold the data on which their conclusions are based from other competent professionals who seek to verify the substantive claims through reanalysis and who intend to use such data only for that purpose, provided that the confidentiality of the participants can be protected and unless legal rights concerning proprietary data preclude their release.

6.26 Professional Reviewers

Psychologists who review material submitted for publication, grant, or other research proposal review respect the confidentiality of and the proprietary rights in such information of those who submitted it.

Scientific research builds on the contributions of scientists of the past who must be given credit for their work. Principles 6.22 and 6.23 in Box 11 have to do with giving credit where credit is due. Principle 6.22 states that it is unethical for psychologists to "present substantial portions or elements of another's work or data as their own, even if the other work or data source is cited occasionally." Always cite sources for ideas that helped to shape your own. Although excessive use of quotations is discouraged in scientific writing, when necessary, quote, citing the source of the quoted material.

Principle 6.23 explains how credit is assigned among coworkers in publishing. The order of the authors' names in published research should reflect the magnitude of their contributions, the first author having done the greatest amount, followed by the second, and so on. One's professional status alone should not influence the order of authorship. When students do the lion's share of the work, as in dissertations and theses, they should be listed as principal author.

Principles 6.24 and 6.25 focus on data. The first asserts that in research articles psychologists do not misrepresent data that has been published previously as original data. The next asserts that it is unethical to withhold data from other competent professionals who wish to verify results through reanalyses. The only exceptions are when the confidentiality of participants could not be preserved if the data were shared or when the law prohibits release of the data.

The final principle, 6.26, guides the work of peer reviewers. It states that it is the ethical responsibility of professional reviewers to "respect the confidentiality of and the proprietary rights" of those who submit work to them for review. Reviewers safeguard the ideas contained in research proposals, proposals for grants, and reports submitted for publication, thereby protecting the priority of the ideas within them and the reputations of researchers whose work is ill conceived.

FINAL THOUGHTS

With this discussion of ethics, we complete our presentation of the principles and mechanics of psychological report writing, thus ending our discussion of the cycles of scientific research that we introduced in the first chapter of this book. The cycle of discovery ends for any project when the data have been collected and analyzed. The cycle of validation begins with the scientific report and ends when other scientists read and respond to the research.

We began this chapter with a quote from William Garvey, who wondered why intelligent people would spend their lives working on creations that others try to find fault with. His answer was that it is "fascinatingly challenging—to wrestle from nature her secrets and formulate them in such simple and comprehensible language that they are indisputable." By now, you probably have experienced some of the excitement and challenge of designing and conducting research, and learning its results. You have yet to struggle with how to present your work clearly, accurately, and concisely to fellow researchers.

As you begin, let the excitement of making a contribution to science and of being a part of an honorable tradition, tracing back to the Royal Society and beyond, inspire you to put your best effort into this last phase of your research. We think you will find it well worth the effort. In the words of Shortland and Gregory:

> There is immense enjoyment to be had from communicating science. You have a fascinating piece of experience to convey and there is great personal pleasure to be had from conveying it well. Writing well, or communicating in any medium effectively, is as satisfying as any other important, stressful, difficult and tiring job well done. That, finally, is what is going to keep you going for hour after hour of rewriting, rehearsing and filing page after page in the rubbish basket, until you finally produce something of which you can be proud. (Shortland & Gregory, 1991, p. 11)

KEY TERMS

The Royal Society
Philosophical Transactions
Mind
APA *Publication Manual*
Abstract
Introduction
Literature review
Rationale
Method
Participants vs. subjects

Results
Discussion
Reference list
Citation
Transitions
Writing with style
Figure caption
Forging, trimming, and cooking
Plagiarism
Publication credit

KEY PEOPLE

Henry Oldenbourg
Alexander Bain
Charles Babbage

Tiffany Field
Murray Sidman

REVIEW QUESTIONS

1. What was the Royal Society's strategy for making valid pronouncements on scientific matters?
2. Why were journals advantageous for reporting scientific work?
3. Why did journal editors adopt a system of peer review of research articles?
4. What was psychology's first journal and when was it first published?
5. Why did the members of the Royal society want to dissociate themselves from the alchemists?
6. What are four characteristics of scientific writing?

7. List the major sections of an APA research report in the order in which they appear.
8. What information goes into the title of a research report?
9. What kinds of information about the study should be included in the abstract?
10. What are the three general sections of the introduction, in the order in which they usually appear?
11. What are the three most common subsections of the method section?
12. How can you avoid sexist language in a research report?
13. What level of detail should be given in the procedure section?
14. What information should you report on the statistical analysis you conducted on your data?
15. What are three different strategies for organizing the results section of a research paper?
16. Explain how subscripts are used in a table to present the results of statistical tests.
17. What tense is used to present the method and results? When is the present tense used to discuss results?
18. What is the purpose of the discussion?
19. How are most discussion sections organized?
20. What is the general format for reporting a citation in the reference list? What is the format for citing an article, chapter, or book within the text of your paper?
21. What are the correct abbreviations for: "that is," "for example," "and so forth," "and others," and "namely"?
22. What are transitions and what function do they serve?
23. Distinguish between passive and active verbs. What recommendations does the APA make on using these verb forms?
24. What are the two major components of writing "with style"?
25. What general lesson can we learn from Feynman's experience with public speaking?
26. Identify the different forms of dishonesty in reporting data that Charles Babbage described. What do the APA ethical guidelines have to say about these?
27. What is a psychologist's ethical responsibility with regard to sharing data with colleagues?

Appendix A

The Belmont Report

Ethical Principles and Guidelines for the Protection of Human Subjects of Research*

❖

DEPARTMENT OF HEALTH, EDUCATION, AND WELFARE

Office of the Secretary

Protection of Human Subjects

Belmont Report: Ethical Principles and Guidelines for the Protection of Human Subjects of Research, Report of the National Commission for the Protection of Human Subjects of Biomedical and Behavioral Research

AGENCY: Department of Health, Education, and Welfare.

ACTION: Notice of Report for Public Comment.

SUMMARY: On July 12, 1974, the National Research Act (Pub. L. 93–348) was signed into law, thereby creating the National Commission for the Protection of Human Subjects of Biomedical and Behavioral Research. One of the charges to the Commission was to identify the basic ethical principles that should underlie the conduct of biomedical and behavioral research involving human subjects and to develop guidelines which should be followed to assure that such research is conducted in accordance with those principles. In carrying out the above, the Commission was directed to consider: (i) the boundaries between biomedical and behavioral research and the accepted and routine practice of medicine, (ii) the role of assessment of risk-benefit criteria in the determination of the appropriateness of research involving

*By The National Commission for the Protection of Human Subjects of Biomedical and Behavioral Research, April 18, 1979.

human subjects, (iii) appropriate guidelines for the selection of human subjects for participation in such research and (iv) the nature and definition of informed consent in various research settings.

The Belmont Report attempts to summarize the basic ethical principles identified by the Commission in the course of its deliberations. It is the outgrowth of an intensive four-day period of discussions that were held in February 1976 at the Smithsonian Institution's Belmont Conference Center supplemented by the monthly deliberations of the Commission that were held over a period of nearly four years. It is a statement of basic ethical principles and guidelines that should assist in resolving the ethical problems that surround the conduct of research with human subjects. By publishing the Report in the **Federal Register,** and providing reprints upon request, the Secretary intends that it may be made readily available to scientists, members of Institutional Review Boards, and Federal employees. The two-volume Appendix, containing the lengthy reports of experts and specialists who assisted the Commission in fulfilling this part of its charge, is available as DHEW Publication No. (OS) 78–0013 and No. (OS) 78–0014, for sale by the Superintendent of Documents, U.S. Government Printing Office, Washington, D.C. 20402.

Unlike most other reports of the Commission, the Belmont Report does not make specific recommendations for administrative action by the Secretary of Health, Education, and Welfare. Rather, the Commission recommended that the Belmont Report be adopted in its entirety, as a statement of the Department's policy. The Department requests public comment on this recommendation.

National Commission for the Protection of Human Subjects of Biomedical and Behavioral Research

Members of the Commission

Kenneth John Ryan, M.D., Chairman, Chief of Staff, Boston Hospital for Women.

Joseph V. Brady, Ph.D., Professor of Behavioral Biology, Johns Hopkins University.

Robert E. Cooke, M.D., President, Medical College of Pennsylvania.

Dorothy I. Height, President, National Council of Negro Women, Inc.

Albert R. Jonsen, Ph.D., Associate Professor of Bioethics, University of California at San Francisco.

Patricia King, J.D., Associate Professor of Law, Georgetown University Law Center.

Karen Lebacqz, Ph.D., Associate Professor of Christian Ethics, Pacific School of Religion.

*David W. Louisell, J.D., Professor of Law, University of California at Berkeley.

Donald W. Seldin, M.D., Professor and Chairman, Department of Internal Medicine, University of Texas at Dallas.

*Deceased.

Eliot Stellar, Ph.D., Provost of the University and Professor of Physiological Psychology, University of Pennsylvania.

*Robert H. Turtle, LL.B., Attorney, VomBaur, Coburn, Simmons & Turtle, Washington, D.C.

Table of Contents

A. Boundaries Between Practice and Research
B. Basic Ethical Principles
    1. Respect for Persons
    2. Beneficence
    3. Justice
C. Applications
    1. Informed Consent
    2. Assessment of Risk and Benefits
    3. Selection of Subjects

Belmont Report

Ethical Principles and Guidelines for Research Involving Human Subjects

Scientific research has produced substantial social benefits. It has also posed some troubling ethical questions. Public attention was drawn to these questions by reported abuses of human subjects in biomedical experiments, especially during World War II. During the Nuremberg War Crime Trials, the Nuremberg code was drafted as a set of standards for judging physicians and scientists who had conducted biomedical experiments on concentration camp prisoners. This code became the prototype of many later codes[1] intended to assure that research involving human subjects would be carried out in an ethical manner.

The codes consist of rules, some general, others specific, that guide the investigators or the reviewers of research in their work. Such rules often are inadequate to cover complex situations; at times they come into conflict, and they are frequently difficult to interpret or apply. Broader ethical principles will provide a basis on which specific rules may be formulated, criticized and interpreted.

Three principles, or general prescriptive judgments, that are relevant to research involving human subjects are identified in this statement. Other principles may also be relevant. These three are comprehensive, however, and are stated at a level of generalization that should assist scientists, subjects, reviewers and interested citizens to understand the ethical issues inherent in research involving human subjects. These principles cannot always be applied so as to

---

*Deceased.

[1] Since 1945, various codes for the proper and responsible conduct of human experimentation in medical research have been adopted by different organizations. The best known of these codes are the Nuremberg Code of 1947, the Helsinki Declaration of 1964 (revised in 1975), and the 1971 Guidelines (codified into Federal Regulations in 1974) issued by the U.S. Department of Health, Education, and Welfare. Codes for the conduct of social and behavioral research have also been adopted, the best known being that of the American Psychological Association, published in 1973.

resolve beyond dispute particular ethical problems. The objective is to provide an analytical framework that will guide the resolution of ethical problems arising from research involving human subjects.

This statement consists of a distinction between research and practice, a discussion of the three basic ethical principles, and remarks about the application of these principles.

A. Boundaries Between Practice and Research

It is important to distinguish between biomedical and behavioral research, on the one hand, and the practice of accepted therapy on the other, in order to know what activities ought to undergo review for the protection of human subjects of research. The distinction between research and practice is blurred partly because both often occur together (as in research designed to evaluate a therapy) and partly because notable departures from standard practice are often called "experimental" when the terms "experimental" and "research" are not carefully defined.

For the most part, the term "practice" refers to interventions that are designed solely to enhance the well-being of an individual patient or client and that have a reasonable expectation of success. The purpose of medical or behavioral practice is to provide diagnosis, preventive treatment or therapy to particular individuals.[2] By contrast, the term "research" designates an activity designed to test an hypothesis, permit conclusions to be drawn, and thereby to develop or contribute to generalizable knowledge (expressed, for example, in theories, principles, and statements of relationships). Research is usually described in a formal protocol that sets forth an objective and a set of procedures designed to reach that objective.

When a clinician departs in a significant way from standard or accepted practice, the innovation does not, in and of itself, constitute research. The fact that a procedure is "experimental," in the sense of new, untested or different, does not automatically place it in the category of research. Radically new procedures of this description should, however, be made the object of formal research at an early stage in order to determine whether they are safe and effective. Thus, it is the responsibility of medical practice committees, for example, to insist that a major innovation be incorporated into a formal research project.[3]

[2]Although practice usually involves interventions designed solely to enhance the well-being of a particular individual, interventions are sometimes applied to one individual for the enhancement of the well-being of another (e.g., blood donation, skin grafts, organ transplants) or an intervention may have the dual purpose of enhancing the well-being of a particular individual, and, at the same time, providing some benefit to others (e.g., vaccination, which protects both the person who is vaccinated and society generally). The fact that some forms of practice have elements other than immediate benefit to the individual receiving an intervention, however, should not confuse the general distinction between research and practice. Even when a procedure applied in practice may benefit some other person, it remains an intervention designed to enhance the well-being of a particular individual or groups of individuals; thus, it is practice and need not be reviewed as research.

[3]Because the problems related to social experimentation may differ substantially from those of biomedical and behavioral research, the Commission specifically declines to make any policy determination regarding such research at this time. Rather, the Commission believes that the problem ought to be addressed by one of its successor bodies.

Research and practice may be carried on together when research is designed to evaluate the safety and efficacy of a therapy. This need not cause any confusion regarding whether or not the activity requires review; the general rule is that if there is any element of research in an activity, that activity should undergo review for the protection of human subjects.

B. Basic Ethical Principles

The expression "basic ethical principles" refers to those general judgments that serve as a basic justification for the many particular ethical prescriptions and evaluations of human actions. Three basic principles, among those generally accepted in our cultural tradition, are particularly relevant to the ethics of research involving human subjects: the principles of respect for persons, beneficence and justice.

1. *Respect for Persons.*—Respect for persons incorporates at least two ethical convictions: first, that individuals should be treated as autonomous agents, and second, that persons with diminished autonomy are entitled to protection. The principle of respect for persons thus divides into two separate moral requirements: the requirement to acknowledge autonomy and the requirement to protect those with diminished autonomy.

An autonomous person is an individual capable of deliberation about personal goals and of acting under the direction of such deliberation. To respect autonomy is to give weight to autonomous persons' considered opinions and choices while refraining from obstructing their actions unless they are clearly detrimental to others. To show lack of respect for an autonomous agent is to repudiate that person's considered judgments, to deny an individual the freedom to act on those considered judgments, or to withhold information necessary to make a considered judgment, when there are no compelling reasons to do so.

However, not every human being is capable of self-determination. The capacity for self-determination matures during an individual's life, and some individuals lose this capacity wholly or in part because of illness, mental disability, or circumstances that severely restrict liberty. Respect for the immature and the incapacitated may require protecting them as they mature or while they are incapacitated.

Some persons are in need of extensive protection, even to the point of excluding them from activities which may harm them; other persons require little protection beyond making sure they undertake activities freely and with awareness of possible adverse consequences. The extent of protection afforded should depend upon the risk of harm and the likelihood of benefit. The judgment that any individual lacks autonomy should be periodically reevaluated and will vary in different situations.

In most cases of research involving human subjects, respect for persons demands that subjects enter into the research voluntarily and with adequate information. In some situations, however, application of the principle is not obvious. The involvement of prisoners as subjects of research provides an instructive example. On the one hand, it would seem that the principle of respect for persons requires that prisoners not be deprived of the opportunity to volunteer for research. On the other hand, under prison conditions they may be subtly coerced or unduly influenced to engage in research activities for which they would not otherwise volunteer. Respect for persons would then dictate that prisoners be protected. Whether to allow prisoners to "volunteer" or to "protect" them presents a dilemma. Respecting persons, in most hard cases, is often a matter of balancing competing claims urged by the principle of respect itself.

2. *Beneficence.*—Persons are treated in an ethical manner not only by respecting their decisions and protecting them from harm, but also by making efforts to secure their well-being. Such treatment falls under the principle of beneficence. The term "beneficence" is often understood to cover acts of kindness or charity that go beyond strict obligation. In this document, beneficence is understood in a stronger sense, as an obligation. Two general rules have been formulated as complementary expressions of beneficent actions in this sense: (1) do not harm and (2) maximize possible benefits and minimize possible harms.

The Hippocratic maxim "do no harm" has long been a fundamental principle of medical ethics. Claude Bernard extended it to the realm of research, saying that one should not injure one person regardless of the benefits that might come to others. However, even avoiding harm requires learning what is harmful; and, in the process of obtaining this information, persons may be exposed to risk of harm. Further, the Hippocratic Oath requires physicians to benefit their patients "according to their best judgment." Learning what will in fact benefit may require exposing persons to risk. The problem posed by these imperatives is to decide when it is justifiable to seek certain benefits despite the risks involved, and when the benefits should be foregone because of the risks.

The obligations of beneficence affect both individual investigators and society at large, because they extend both to particular research projects and to the entire enterprise of research. In the case of particular projects, investigators and members of their institutions are obliged to give forethought to the maximization of benefits and the reduction of risk that might occur from the research investigation. In the case of scientific research in general, members of the larger society are obliged to recognize the longer term benefits and risks that may result from the improvement of knowledge and from the development of novel medical, psychotherapeutic, and social procedures.

The principle of beneficence often occupies a well-defined justifying role in many areas of research involving human subjects. An example is found in research involving children. Effective ways of treating childhood diseases and fostering healthy development are benefits that serve to justify research involving children—even when individual research subjects are not direct beneficiaries. Research also makes it possible to avoid the harm that may result from the application of previously accepted routine practices that on closer investigation turn out to be dangerous. But the role of the principle of beneficence is not always so unambiguous. A difficult ethical problem remains, for example, about research that presents more than minimal risk without immediate prospect of direct benefit to the children involved. Some have argued that such research is inadmissible, while others have pointed out that this limit would rule out much research promising great benefit to children in the future. Here again, as with all hard cases, the different claims covered by the principle of beneficence may come into conflict and force difficult choices.

3. *Justice.*—Who ought to receive the benefits of research and bear its burdens? This is a question of justice, in the sense of "fairness in distribution" or "what is deserved." An injustice occurs when some benefit to which a person is entitled is denied without good reason or when some burden is imposed unduly. Another way of conceiving the principle of justice is that equals ought to be treated equally. However, this statement requires explication. Who is equal and who is unequal? What considerations justify departure from equal distribution? Almost all commentators allow that distinctions based on experience, age, deprivation, competence, merit and position do sometimes constitute criteria justifying differential treatment for certain purposes. It is necessary, then, to explain in what respects people should be treated equally. There are several widely accepted formulations of just ways to distribute burdens and benefits. Each formulation mentions some relevant property on the basis of which burdens and benefits should be distributed. These formulations are (1) to each person an equal share, (2) to each person according to individual need, (3) to each person according to individual effort, (4) to each person according to societal contribution, and (5) to each person according to merit.

Questions of justice have long been associated with social practices such as punishment, taxation and political representation. Until recently these questions have not generally been associated with scientific research. However, they are foreshadowed even in the earliest reflections on the ethics of research involving human subjects. For example, during the 19th and early 20th centuries the burdens of serving as research subjects fell largely upon poor ward patients, while the benefits of improved medical care flowed primarily to private patients. Subsequently, the exploitation of unwilling prisoners as research subjects in Nazi concentration camps was condemned as a particularly flagrant injustice. In this country, in the 1940s, the Tuskegee syphilis study used disadvantaged, rural black men to study the untreated course of a disease that is by no means confined to that population. These subjects were deprived of demonstrably effective treatment in order not to interrupt the project, long after such treatment became generally available.

Against this historical background, it can be seen how conceptions of justice are relevant to research involving human subjects. For example, the selection of research subjects needs to be scrutinized in order to determine whether some classes (e.g., welfare patients, particular racial and ethnic minorities, or persons confined to institutions) are being systematically selected simply because of their easy availability, their compromised position, or their manipulability, rather than for reasons directly related to the problem being studied. Finally, whenever research supported by public funds leads to the development of therapeutic devices and procedures, justice demands both that these devices and procedures not provide advantages only to those who can afford them and that such research should not unduly involve persons from groups unlikely to be among the beneficiaries of subsequent applications of the research.

C. Applications

Applications of the general principles to the conduct of research leads to consideration of the following requirements: informed consent, risk/benefit assessment, and the selection of subjects of research.

1. *Informed Consent.*—Respect for persons requires that subjects, to the degree that they are capable, be given the opportunity to choose what shall or shall not happen to them. This opportunity is provided when adequate standards for informed consent are satisfied.

While the importance of informed consent is unquestioned, controversy prevails over the nature and possibility of an informed consent. Nonetheless, there is widespread agreement that the consent process can be analyzed as containing three elements: information, comprehension and voluntariness.

Information. Most codes of research establish specific items for disclosure intended to assure that subjects are given sufficient information. These items generally include: the research procedure, their purposes, risks and anticipated benefits, alternative procedures (where therapy is involved), and a statement offering the subject the opportunity to ask questions and to withdraw at any time from the research. Additional items have been proposed, including how subjects are selected, the person responsible for the research, etc.

However, a simple listing of items does not answer the question of what the standard should be for judging how much and what sort of information should be provided. One standard frequently invoked in medical practice, namely the information commonly provided by practitioners in the field or in the locale, is inadequate since research takes place precisely when a common understanding does not exist. Another standard, currently popular in malpractice law, requires the practitioner to reveal the information that reasonable persons would wish to know in order to make a decision regarding their care. This, too, seems insufficient since the research subject, being in essence a volunteer, may wish to know considerably more about risks gratuitously undertaken than do patients who deliver themselves into the hand of a clinician for needed care. It may be that a standard of "the reasonable volunteer" should be proposed: the extent and nature of information should be such that persons, knowing that the procedure is neither necessary for their care nor perhaps fully understood, can decide whether they wish to participate in the furthering of knowledge. Even when some direct benefit to them is anticipated, the subjects should understand clearly the range of risk and the voluntary nature of participation.

A special problem of consent arises where informing subjects of some pertinent aspect of the research is likely to impair the validity of the research. In many cases, it is sufficient to indicate to subjects that they are being invited to participate in research of which some features will not be revealed until the research is concluded. In all cases of research involving incomplete disclosure, such research is justified only if it is clear that (1) incomplete disclosure is truly necessary to accomplish the goals of the research, (2) there are no undisclosed risks to subjects that are more than minimal, and (3) there is an adequate plan for debriefing subjects, when appropriate, and for dissemination of research results to them. Information about risks should never be withheld for the purpose of eliciting the cooperation of subjects, and truthful answers should always be given to direct questions about the research. Care should be taken to distinguish cases in which disclosure would destroy or invalidate the research from cases in which disclosure would simply inconvenience the investigator.

Comprehension. The manner and context in which information is conveyed is as important as the information itself. For example, presenting information in a disorganized and rapid fashion, allowing too little time for consideration or curtailing opportunities for questioning, all may adversely affect a subject's ability to make an informed choice.

Because the subject's ability to understand is a function of intelligence, rationality, maturity and language, it is necessary to adapt the presentation of the information to the subject's capacities. Investigators are responsible for ascertaining that the subject has comprehended the information. While there is always an obligation to ascertain that the information about risk to subjects is complete and adequately comprehended, when the risks are more serious, that obligation increases. On occasion, it may be suitable to give some oral or written tests of comprehension.

Special provision may need to be made when comprehension is severely limited—for example, by conditions of immaturity or mental disability. Each class of subjects that one might consider as incompetent (e.g., infants and young children, mentally disabled patients, the terminally ill and the comatose) should be considered on its own terms. Even for these persons, however, respect requires giving them the opportunity to choose to the extent they are able, whether or not to participate in research. The objections of these subjects to involvement should be honored, unless the research entails providing them a therapy unavailable elsewhere. Respect for persons also requires seeking the permission of other parties in order to protect the subjects from harm. Such persons are thus respected both by acknowledging their own wishes and by the use of third parties to protect them from harm.

The third parties chosen should be those who are most likely to understand the incompetent subject's situation and to act in that person's best interest. The person authorized to act on behalf of the subject should be given an opportunity to observe the research as it proceeds in order to be able to withdraw the subject from the research, if such action appears in the subject's best interest.

Voluntariness. An agreement to participate in research constitutes a valid consent only if voluntarily given. This element of informed consent requires conditions free of coercion and undue influence. Coercion occurs when an overt threat of harm is intentionally presented by one person to another in order to obtain compliance. Undue influence, by contrast, occurs through an offer of an excessive, unwarranted, inappropriate or improper reward or other overture in order to obtain compliance. Also, inducements that would ordinarily be acceptable may become undue influences if the subject is especially vulnerable.

Unjustifiable pressures usually occur when persons in positions of authority or commanding influence—especially where possible sanctions are involved—urge a course of action for a subject. A continuum of such influencing factors exists, however, and it is impossible to state precisely where justifiable persuasion ends and undue influence begins. But undue influence would include actions such as manipulating a person's choice through the controlling influence of a close relative and threatening to withdraw health services to which an individual would otherwise be entitled.

2. *Assessment of Risks and Benefits.*—The assessment of risks and benefits requires a careful arrayal of relevant data, including, in some cases, alternative ways of obtaining the benefits sought in the research. Thus, the assessment presents both an opportunity and a responsibility to gather systematic and comprehensive information about proposed research. For the investigator, it is a means to examine whether the proposed research is properly designed. For a review committee, it is a method for determining whether the risks that will be presented to subjects are justified. For prospective subjects, the assessment will assist the determination whether or not to participate.

The Nature and Scope of Risks and Benefits. The requirement that research be justified on the basis of a favorable risk/benefit assessment bears a close relation to the principle of beneficence, just as the moral requirement that informed consent be obtained is derived primarily from the principle of respect for persons. The term "risk" refers to a possibility that harm may occur. However, when expressions such as "small risk" or "high risk" are used, they usually refer (often ambiguously) both to the chance (probability) of experiencing a harm and the severity (magnitude) of the envisioned harm.

The term "benefit" is used in the research context to refer to something of positive value related to health or welfare. Unlike "risk," "benefit" is not a term that expresses probabilities. Risk is properly contrasted to probability of benefits, and benefits are properly contrasted with harms rather than risks of harm. Accordingly, so-called risk/benefit assessments are concerned with the probabilities and magnitudes of possible harms and anticipated benefits. Many kinds of possible harms and benefits need to be taken into account. There are, for example, risks of psychological harm, physical harm, legal harm, social harm and economic harm and the corresponding benefits. While the most likely types of harms to research subjects are those of psychological or physical pain or injury, other possible kinds should not be overlooked.

Risks and benefits of research may affect the individual subjects, the families of the individual subjects, and society at large (or special groups of subjects in society). Previous codes and Federal regulations have required that risks to subjects be outweighed by the sum of both the anticipated benefit to the subject, if any, and the anticipated benefit to society in the form of knowledge to be gained from the research. In balancing these different elements, the risks and benefits affecting the immediate research subject will normally carry special weight. On the other hand, interests other than those of the subject may on some occasions be sufficient by themselves to justify the risks involved in the research, so long as the subjects' rights have been protected. Beneficence thus requires that we protect against risk of harm to subjects and also that we be concerned about the loss of the substantial benefits that might be gained from research.

The Systematic Assessment of Risks and Benefits. It is commonly said that benefits and risks must be "balanced" and shown to be "in a favorable ratio." The metaphorical character of these terms draws attention to the difficulty of making precise judgments. Only on rare occasions will quantitative techniques be available for the scrutiny of research protocols. However, the idea of systematic, nonarbitrary analysis of risks and benefits should be emulated insofar as possible. This ideal requires those making decisions about the justifiability of research to be thorough in the accumulation and assessment of information about all aspects of the research, and to consider alternatives systematically. This procedure renders the assessment of research more rigorous and precise, while making communication between review board members and investigators less subject to misinterpretation, misinformation and conflicting judgments. Thus, there should first be a determination of the validity of the presuppositions of the research; then the nature, probability and magnitude of risk should be distinguished with as much clarity as possible. The method of ascertaining risks should be explicit, especially where there is no alternative to the use of such vague categories as small or slight risk. It should also be determined whether an investigator's estimates of the probability of harm or benefits are reasonable, as judged by known facts or other available studies.

Finally, assessment of the justifiability of research should reflect at least the following considerations: (i) Brutal or inhumane treatment of human subjects is never morally justified. (ii) Risks should be reduced to those necessary to achieve the research objective. It should be determined whether it is in fact necessary to use human subjects at all. Risk can perhaps never be entirely eliminated, but it can often be reduced by careful attention to alternative procedures. (iii) When research involves significant risk of serious impairment, review committees should be extraordinarily insistent on the justification of the risk (looking usually to the likelihood of benefit to the subject—or, in some rare cases, to the manifest voluntariness of the participation). (iv) When vulnerable populations are involved in research, the appropriateness of involving them should itself be demonstrated. A number of variables go into such judgments, including the nature and degree of risk, the condition of the particular population involved, and the nature and level of the anticipated benefits. (v) Relevant risks and benefits must be thoroughly arrayed in documents and procedures used in the informed consent process.

3. *Selection of Subjects.*—Just as the principle of respect for persons finds expression in the requirements for consent, and the principle of beneficence in risk/benefit assessment, the principle of justice gives rise to moral requirements that there be fair procedures and outcomes in the selection of research subjects.

Justice is relevant to the selection of subjects of research at two levels: the social and the individual. Individual justice in the selection of subjects would require that researchers exhibit fairness: thus, they should not offer potentially beneficial research only to some patients who are in their favor or select only "undesirable" persons for risky research. Social justice requires that distinction be drawn between classes of subjects that ought, and ought not, to participate in any particular kind of research, based on the ability of members of that class to bear burdens and on the appropriateness of placing further burdens on already burdened persons. Thus, it can be considered a matter of social justice that there is an order of preference in the selection of classes of subjects (e.g., adults before children) and that some classes of potential subjects (e.g., the institutionalized mentally infirm or prisoners) may be involved as research subjects, if at all, only on certain conditions.

Injustice may appear in the selection of subjects, even if individual subjects are selected fairly by investigators and treated fairly in the course of research. Thus injustice arises from social, racial, sexual and cultural biases institutionalized in society. Thus, even if individual researchers are treating their research subjects fairly, and even if IRBs are taking care to assure that subjects are selected fairly within a particular institution, unjust social patterns may nevertheless appear in the overall distribution of the burdens and benefits of research. Although individual institutions or investigators may not be able to resolve a problem that is pervasive in their social setting, they can consider distributive justice in selecting research subjects.

Some populations, especially institutionalized ones, are already burdened in many ways by their infirmities and environments. When research is proposed that involves risks and does not include a therapeutic component, other less burdened classes of persons should be called upon first to accept these risks of research, except where the research is directly related to the specific conditions of the class involved. Also, even though public funds for research may often flow in the same directions as public funds for health care, it seems unfair that populations dependent on public health care constitute a pool of preferred research subjects if more advantaged populations are likely to be the recipients of the benefits.

One special instance of injustice results from the involvement of vulnerable subjects. Certain groups, such as racial minorities, the economically disadvantaged, the very sick, and the institutionalized may continually be sought as research subjects, owing to their ready availability in settings where research is conducted. Given their dependent status and their frequently compromised capacity for free consent, they should be protected against the danger of being involved in research solely for administrative convenience, or because they are easy to manipulate as a result of their illness or socioeconomic condition.

[FR Doc. 79–12065 Filed 4–17–79; 8:45 AM]

Appendix B

Massage Therapy   1

Running head: MASSAGE & ALERTNESS

Massage Therapy Reduces Anxiety and Enhances

EEG Pattern of Alertness and Math Computations

Tiffany Field, Gail Ironson, Frank Scafidi, Tom Nawrocki,

Alex Goncalves, and Iris Burman

Touch Research Institute,

University of Miami School of Medicine

Jeff Pickens

James Madison University

Nathan Fox

University of Maryland

Saul Schanberg and Cynthia Kuhn

Duke University Medical School

Massage Therapy   2

Abstract

Twenty-six adults were given a chair massage and 24 control group adults were asked to relax in the massage chair for 15 minutes, 2 times per week for 5 weeks. On the first and last days of the study they were monitored for EEG, before, during and after the sessions. In addition, before and after the sessions they performed math computations, they completed POMS Depression and State Anxiety Scales and they provided a saliva sample for cortisol. At the beginning of the sessions they completed Life Events, Job Stress and Chronic POMS Depression Scales. Group by repeated measures and post hoc analyses revealed the following: 1) frontal delta power increased for both groups, suggesting relaxation; 2) the massage group showed decreased frontal alpha and beta power (suggesting enhanced alertness); while the control group showed increased alpha and beta power; 3) the massage group showed increased speed and accuracy on math computations while the control group did not change; 4) anxiety levels were lower following the massage but not the control sessions, although mood state was less depressed following both the massage and control sessions; 5) salivary cortisol levels were lower following the massage but not the control sessions but only on the first day; and 6) at the end of the 5 week period depression scores were lower for both groups but job stress scores were lower only for the massage group.

Massage Therapy Reduces Anxiety and Enhances EEG Pattern
of Alertness and Math Computations

Despite the increasing popularity of stress-management
programs (Ivancevich, Matteson, Freedman, & Phillips, 1990)
very little evaluation research has been done. Most
evaluations are based on "professional opinions" and survey
studies rather than empirical studies. A recent study on
stress in HIV positive men suggested that those who were most
stressed gained most from a massage therapy intervention
(Ironson et al., 1996). Longterm (one month) effects
indicated immunological benefits including increased natural
killer cell number and natural killer cell cytotoxicity.
Massage therapy has also been noted to decrease anxiety and
depression as well as cortisol and norepinephrine levels and
improve sleep patterns in adolescents with psychiatric
problems (Field et al., 1992). Thus, massage is noted to
decrease anxiety and depression based on self-report,
behavior observations, salivary cortisol and urinary
norepinephrine levels and to enhance immune function.

In the above studies subjects anecdotally reported
enhanced alertness instead of the expected soporific effect
following massage. The purpose of the present study was to
investigate the effects of massage on alertness as measured
by EEG and by speed and accuracy of performance on math
computations. The only massage study in the literature that
recorded EEG patterns showed that <u>facial massage</u> was

accompanied by decreased alpha and beta, a pattern that is inconsistent with drowsiness (Jodo, Yamada, Hatayama, Abe, & Maruyama, 1988). The EEG alpha was expected to similarly decrease during the chair massage in this study and the behavioral measure of alertness, namely math computation performance, was expected to improve following massages. In addition, anxiety, depression and cortisol levels were expected to decrease as they did in the Field et al. (1992) study on disturbed adolescents and the Ironson et al. (1996) study on HIV men.

Method

Subjects

The subjects were 50 medical faculty and staff members (80% females, M age = 26). The subjects were well-educated (62% college graduate, 12% graduate school, 27% graduate degree). Income was less than $20,000 for 58%, $20-30,000 for 35% and greater than $30,000 for 8%. Forty-six percent of the sample exercised regularly, with moderate numbers exercising once per week (31%), to several times per week (27%), to daily (15%). Of the sample 50% had tried relaxation techniques, and 62% had received a massage prior to the study (62% rarely, 31% occasionally and 8% weekly). The subjects were recruited using advertising fliers at the medical school. They were randomly assigned to the massage and the relaxation control groups. Chi square analyses comparing the two groups on sex, education, income, and lifestyle questions (i.e., exercise and previous use of massage and relaxation) and a t test on age yielded no group differences (see Table 1).

Insert Table 1 about here

Therapy Procedures

Massage therapy. The massage therapy sessions were given by a professional massage therapist (different therapists each day) for 15 minutes a day, 2 days a week for 5 weeks, and the sessions were scheduled at noon each day. The subjects were seated fully clothed in a special massage chair, and a standard Swedish massage procedure (kneading of muscles) was used. The procedure consisted of long broad strokes with moderate pressure on the BACK: 1) compression to the back parallel to the spine from the shoulders to the base of the spine; 2) compression to the entire back adding some gentle rocking; 3) trapezius squeeze; 4) finger pressure around scapula and shoulder; 5) finger pressure along the length of the spine and back; and 6) circular strokes to the hips below the iliac crest. ARMS: 1) drop arms to the side. Knead arms from shoulder to lower arm; and 2) press down points on upper and lower arms. HANDS: 1) massage entire hands. Traction to the fingers; 2) press the fleshy part of the palm between the thumb and index finger for 15 to 20 seconds; and 3) traction of the arms both in lateral and superior directions (arm in line with the body). NECK: 1) kneading area of cervical vertebrae; 2) finger pressure along base of skull and along side of neck; 3) scalp massage; and 4) press down on trapezius, finger pressure and squeezing continuing down the arms.

Relaxation control group. The subjects were asked to relax by tightening and relaxing the same body parts as those that were massaged for the massage therapy group (and in the same sequence). The subjects were briefly shown by a research assistant how to tighten and release their muscles which they were told would help them relax. This group was included as a control for focusing on the body and for standardizing activity level during the assessment sessions (controlling movement artifact in the EEG measure).

Assessment Procedures

On the first and last day of the study the procedure was conducted in the following order: 1) the EEG cap was positioned on the subjects' head; 2) a saliva sample was taken for cortisol; 3) the subjects completed the three long-term measures including the Life Events, Job Stress and Chronic POMS Depression Scales; 4) the subjects completed the session baseline measures including the POMS Depression, State Anxiety and the math computations; and 5) immediately after the 15 minute massage/control sessions the subjects completed another math computation, the POMS Depression and State Anxiety Scale, and about 20 minutes after the end of the massage/control sessions they provided another saliva sample for cortisol.

Pre-post therapy session measures on first and last day. The following measures were used to assess the immediate effects of the massage on the first and last days of the study.

a) The Profile of Mood States (POMS; McNair, Lorr, & Droppelman, 1971). The POMS Scale is a 5-point adjective Likert rating scale asking the subject to describe how well an adjective describes his/her current feelings. The 14 items that comprise the depression factor were used. The scale has adequate internal consistency (r = .95; McNair & Lorr, 1964) and is an adequate measure of intervention effectiveness (Pugtach, Haskell, & McNair, 1969). A summary score is obtained by adding the weight of each item. This scale was used because positive mood state would be expected to affect alertness and performance on math computations and because massage therapy has been noted to improve mood state in stressed adolescents (Field et al., 1992).

b) The State Anxiety Inventory (STAI; Spielberger, Gorsuch, & Lushene, 1970). This is a 20 item scale which measures the transitory anxiety level in terms of severity (not at all to very much so). Characteristic items include "I feel tense," "I feel nervous" and "I feel relaxed." The STAI has adequate concurrent validity (Spielberger, 1972) and internal consistency (r = .83; Spielberger et al., 1970). In addition, the STAI state scores increase in response to situational stress and decline under relaxing conditions (Spielberger et al., 1970). A summary score is obtained by adding the weight of each item. This measure was included because state anxiety

Massage Therapy   8

is known to affect alertness and performance on cognitive tasks negatively and because state anxiety typically decreases following massage therapy (Field et al., 1992; Ironson et al., 1996).

c) <u>Salivary cortisol.</u> Saliva samples were collected and assayed for cortisol as a measure of stress that might be expected to affect alertness and performance on math computations. In addition, salivary cortisol levels decreased in at least two previous massage therapy studies (Field et al., 1992; Ironson et al., 1996). The samples were collected at the beginning of the therapy sessions and 20 minutes after the end of the sessions on the assessment days. Due to the 20 minute lag in cortisol change, saliva samples reflect responses to events occurring 20 minutes prior to collection. Salivary cortisol samples were obtained by having subjects place a cotton dental swab dipped in sugar-free lemonade crystals along their gumline for 30 seconds. The swab was placed in a syringe, and the saliva was squeezed into a microcentrifuge tube.

d) <u>Math computations.</u> Before the massage sessions a series of 7 numbers was given and after the massage a different series was given, and the subject was asked to add them. The time to complete the series and the correct/incorrect answer were recorded. This measure was used to determine the immediate effects of massage on a task that might be expected to be enhanced by alertness.

e) <u>EEG procedure.</u> EEG was considered the primary dependent variable in this study as the physiological measure of alertness. Although subjects have anecdotally reported heightened alertness in previous studies, no direct measures have been made of alertness. Although EEG alpha and beta were noted to decrease (suggesting heightened alertness) in a previous study (Jodo et al., 1988), face massage was used and no self-report or performance measures were included. EEG was recorded in the present study for 3 minute periods prior to, during and after the therapy sessions with the subjects' eyes closed. The EEG was recorded using a Lycra stretchable cap (manufactured by Electro-Cap, Inc.) that was positioned on the subject using the standard 10-20 system. Electrode gel was injected into the following sites: F3, F4, P3, P4 and Cz. Impedances were brought below 5K ohms, and the impedances of adjacent sites were brought within 500 ohms of each other. The EEG signals were amplified using a Grass Model 12 Neurodata Acquisition System with amplifiers set as follows: Low frequency filter: 1 Hz; High frequency filter: 100 Hz; Amplification: 20,000. The line frequency filter was on for all channels. The output from the amplifiers was directed to a Dell 325D PC fitted with an Analog Devices RTI-815 A/D board. The signal was sampled at a rate of 512 Hz and streamed to hard disk using data acquisition software (Snapstream HEM Data Corp.). Additional electrodes were positioned on the external canthus and the supraorbital position of one eye to record the subject's EOG, which was used to facilitate artifact scoring.

Massage Therapy 10

The first step involved the elimination of data which were unusable due to artifact from eye movements, muscle activity or technical difficulty. The artifact-free data were spectrally analyzed using a discrete Fourier transform with a Hanning window to yield power data for the following frequency bands: 1-4 Hz (Delta), 5-7 Hz (Theta), 8-12 Hz (Alpha), 13-20 Hz (Beta-low), 21-30 Hz (Beta-high). The EEG data were analyzed using an EEG analysis software package developed by James Long Company.

First day/last day measures.

a) Life Events Questionnaire. The Life Events Questionnaire comprises a list of 9 stressful events (e.g., death of mate or lover, major financial difficulties). The subject is asked to check which events have occurred in the last 4 weeks. The subject is then asked to rate how each event has affected his/her life from not at all to very stressful on a 4 point scale. This measure was included to ensure that the results of this study were not negatively affected by significant life events. The Cronbach's alpha (.71) for internal consistency was reasonable as was the test-retest reliability (.89).

b) Job Stress Yesterday Questionnaire. This questionnaire measures job stress experienced yesterday and consists of 31 words or phrases requiring two responses each. The first response is a word or phrase describing the job (e.g., hectic, hassled, comfortable, too little time to think or plan). Possible answers are YES, NO or ? (cannot decide). If the phrase does describe the job yesterday, the subject is then asked to rate on a 4 point scale how much it bothers him/her. This questionnaire was included as a self-report measure on job stress. Cronbach's alpha (.73) for internal consistency was reasonable as was the test-retest reliability (.87).

Results

Self-Report Data

Analyses of baseline measures yielded no group differences except that the control group had less job stress at baseline (higher scores are optimal). Data were subjected to repeated measures by group (massage/control) ANOVAS with session (presession/postsession) and phase (pretreatment/posttreatment) as the repeated measures. Post hoc Bonferroni corrected t tests were performed to assess the group by repeated measures interaction effects. A priori nonorthogonal contrasts were made because based on previous anecdotal reports by subjects and the facial massage EEG data (Jodo et al., 1988) we expected that the analyses would reveal enhanced alertness and performance. We also expected reduced anxiety, depression and cortisol levels following massage therapy based on previous massage studies (Field et al., 1992; Ironson et al., 1996). The analyses revealed the following (see Table 2): 1) a repeated measures effect revealed that the massage and relaxation control groups had significantly lower POMS depressed mood state scores following the first and last day sessions; 2) a repeated measures by group interaction effect revealed that the massage therapy group had significantly lower state anxiety scores after the first and the last day sessions than the relaxation control group; 3) no group differences or time changes were noted for the Life Events Scale; 4) for the Job Stress Scale, a significant repeated measures by group interaction effect was noted, suggesting a decrease in job stress (higher scores are optimal) but only for the massage therapy group; and 5) a repeated measures effect suggested that both groups showed a decrease in chronic depressed mood state.

Insert Table 2 about here

Saliva Cortisol Data

A repeated measures by group interaction effect revealed a decrease in salivary cortisol levels on the first day for the massage group and an increase on the last day for the relaxation control group.

Math Computations

Massage also facilitated performance on math computation tasks (see Table 2). Group by repeated measures interaction effects suggested that the massage therapy group performed better following the sessions on both the first and last days. The decreased time required to complete the math computation task was significantly greater for the massage

therapy group, and the decrease in the number of errors was
significantly greater for the massage therapy versus the
relaxation control group.

<u>EEG Data</u>

   Repeated measures ANOVAs with group as the between subjects
factor and pre-, during and postsession values as the repeated
measures were conducted on the frontal alpha, beta, delta and
theta values recorded before, during and after the massage/
control sessions. These group (massage/control) by trial
(before, during, after massage/control session) repeated
measures ANOVAs revealed the following (see Table 3 for
repeated measures and repeated measures by group interaction
effects and their F values): 1) a repeated measures effect
revealed that delta increased for both groups from pre- to
during the session, suggesting enhanced relaxation (see Table
3); 2) theta did not change for either group; 3) group by
repeated measures interaction effects suggested that: a) alpha
significantly decreased from pre- to during the massage and
from pre- to postmassage while alpha significantly increased
for the relaxation group from pre- to postmassage; and b) beta
significantly decreased for the massage group from pre- to
during and from pre- to postmassage, and the control group
significantly increased from pre- to postmassage.

Insert Table 3 about here

Massage Therapy   14

<u>Relations between EEG and Math Computation Measures</u>

Correlation analyses were performed for each of the groups to determine whether there was a relationship between the alpha and beta EEG measures and the math computation (speed and accuracy) variables. For the massage therapy group the number of problems correctly solved was correlated with the decrease in the natural log of alpha from the period pre- to during the massage ($r = .43$, $p < .05$), and the amount of time required to complete the computations was inversely related to the decrease in the natural log of beta from pre- to postmassage ($r = -.59$, $p < .001$).

Discussion

These data, like those of other studies on massage therapy, showed decreases in anxiety and stress hormones (cortisol) immediately after the sessions (Field et al., 1992; Ironson et al., 1996). And, both the massage therapy and relaxation therapy groups showed increased delta activity, suggesting that both therapies had a relaxation effect and temporary and more chronic shifts in mood state which may have related to their relaxation. The decrease in self-reported depression is consistent with other massage studies (Field et al., 1992; Ironson et al., 1996) as well as other relaxation studies (Platania-Solazzo et al., 1992).

Heightened alertness and enhanced performance on math computations occurred in the massage therapy group. The

massage sessions were characterized by an EEG pattern of
alertness. Although delta increased for both groups of
subjects, suggesting relaxation, the pattern of enhanced
alertness (decreased alpha and decreased beta) occurred in the
massage therapy group while a pattern of drowsiness (increased
alpha and increased beta) occurred in the relaxation control
group. The decreased alpha and decreased beta were not
surprising since at least one other study documented EEG alpha
decreases associated with facial massage (Jodo et al., 1988).
The correlation analysis further suggested that the accuracy
of the math computations and the decrease in pre- to during
massage EEG alpha were related. Although the alpha decrease
occurred during the massages it could have affected the state
of alertness for enhancing accuracy after the massage.
Further, the speed of performing the calculations and the
decrease in EEG beta pre- to postmassage were related. This
more contemporaneous relationship suggests that performance
speed may have been related to decreased beta.

The superior performance of the massage therapy group might
relate to the tactile and pressure stimulation. Tactile and
pressure stimulation, in addition to enhancing the EEG
patterns of alertness and math computations in this study,
have been noted to enhance parasympathetic activity (elevated
vagal tone) which is characteristic of a more relaxed, alert
state during which cognitive performance improves (Field et
al., 1992). Future research might add other measures such as

Massage Therapy   16

vagal activity and catecholamines to further understand the underlying mechanism for the massage therapy-enhanced alertness relationship.

In addition, a longer term follow-up would be important to assess the persistence of the effects. Presumably, like exercise, a steady dose of massage may be required. Larger doses may also be more effective and result in more clinically meaningful changes in mood state and cortisol than occurred in this study. Finally, the cost effectiveness of massage therapy would need to be documented for more widespread acceptance and adoption of the treatment.

Massage Therapy   17

References

Field, T., Morrow, C., Valdeon, C., Larson, S., Kuhn, C., & Schanberg, S. (1992). Massage reduces anxiety in child and adolescent psychiatric patients. *Journal of the American Academy of Child and Adolescent Psychiatry, 31,* 125-131.

Ironson, G., Field, T., Scafidi, F., Hashimoto, M., Kumar, M., Kumar, A., Price, A., Goncalves, A., Burman, I., Tetenman, C., Patarca, R., & Fletcher, M.A. (1996). Massage therapy is associated with enhancement of the immune system's cytotoxic capacity. *International Journal of Neuroscience, 84,* 205-217.

Ivancevich, J. M., Matteson, M. T., Freedman, S. M., & Phillips, J. S. (1990). Worksite stress management interventions. *American Psychologist, 45,* 252-261.

Jodo, E., Yamada, Y., Hatayama, T., Abe, T., & Maruyama, K. (1988). Effects of facial massage on the spontaneous EEG. *Tohoku Psycologica Folia, 47,* 8-15.

McNair, D. M., & Lorr, M. (1964). An analysis of mood in neurotics. *Journal of Abnormal and Social Psychology, 69,* 620-627.

McNair, D. M., Lorr, M., & Droppelman, L. F. (1971). *Profile of Mood States.* San Diego: Educational and Industrial Testing Service.

Platania-Solazzo, A., Field, T., Blank, J., Seligman, F., Kuhn, C., Schanberg, S., & Saab, P. (1992). Relaxation therapy reduces anxiety in child and adolescent psychiatry patients. *Acta Paedopsychiatrica, 55,* 115-120.

Massage Therapy   18

Pugtach, D., Haskell, D., & McNair, D. M. (1969).
Predictors and patterns of change associated with the course
of time-limited psychotherapy. Mimeo Report.

Spielberger, C. D., Gorsuch, R. L., & Lushene, R. E.
(1970). The State Trait Anxiety Inventory. Palo Alto, CA:
Consulting Psychologists Press.

Spielberger, C. D. (1972). Anxiety as an emotional state.
In C. D. Speilberger (Ed.), Anxiety: Current trends in theory
and research (vol. 1, pp. 23-49). New York: Academic Press.

Massage Therapy   19

Author Note

We would like to thank the subjects who participated and the researchers who helped with data collection and analyses. This research was supported by an NIMH Research Scientist Award (#MH00331), an NIMH Research Grant (#MH46586) to Tiffany Field and funding from Johnson and Johnson.

Correspondence concerning this article should be addressed to Tiffany Field, Ph.D., Touch Research Institute, University of Miami School of Medicine, P.O. Box 016820, Miami, Florida 33101.

Table 1

Means for Demographic Variables for Massage Therapy and Relaxation
Control Group Measures

Measures	Massage	Control	p
Age	26.4	26.2	NS
Gender (% female)	79.5	80.2	NS
Graduate degree (%)	26.8	28.0	NS
Income > $30,000 (%)	7.8	9.1	NS
Regular exercise (%)	47.3	45.4	NS
Tried relaxation (%)	49.2	51.0	NS
Tried massage (%)	64.1	60.9	NS

Table 2

Means for Massage Therapy and Relaxation Control Group Measures (SDs under means)

Measures	Massage Day 1 Pre	Massage Day 1 Post	Massage Day 10 Pre	Massage Day 10 Post	Control Day 1 Pre	Control Day 1 Post	Control Day 10 Pre	Control Day 10 Post	Effects*
POMS depression	1.5_a .4	$.6_b$[3] .2	1.4_a .4	$.5_b$[3] .3	2.1_a .6	$.9_b$[3] .3	1.7_a .5	$.8_b$[2] .3	S
State anxiety	37.0_a 11.3	30.0_b[4] 9.6	38.5_a 12.7	31.3_b[4] 10.5	38.0_a 13.2	37.0_a 12.9	37.0_a 13.9	5.2_a 11.4	SxG
Computation accuracy	69.2_a 20.9	89.2_b[2] 28.3	83.1_b 29.7	96.2_c[2] 31.0	60.0_a 24.0	68.2_a 20.7	70.8_a 26.3	72.3_a 25.9	SxG
Computation time	250.0_a 85.1	234.0_b[2] 72.3	232.5_b 75.9	210.9_c[1] 64.0	249.0_a 82.6	241.0_a 71.8	231.1_b 65.0	226.2_b 62.3	SxG
Salivary cortisol (ng)	2.1_a .5	1.6_b[2] .5	1.8_a .4	2.0_a .5	2.2_a .7	2.0_a .6	1.6_b .4	2.1_a[3] .6	SxG

(table continues)

Table 2

Means for Massage Therapy and Relaxation Control Group Measures (SDs under means)

	Day 1	Day 10	Day 1	Day 10	Effects
Life events	8.0_a	7.4_a	9.5_a	8.9_a	
Job stress*	38.7_a	44.0_b^1	47.0_b	46.0_b	PxG
Chronic POMS depression	4.5_a	3.8_b^1	5.1_a	3.6_b^1	P

$^1p < .05$, $^2p < .01$, $^3p < .005$, $^4p < .001$

*G = group (massage/control)

S = session (presession/postsession)

P = Phase (pretreatment posttreatment)

**higher score is optimal

Table 3

Natural log of raw power for Delta, Theta, Alpha, and Beta

Delta (1-4 Hz)

	Massage			Control		
	Pre	Dur	Post	Pre	Dur	Post
Mean	4.29	4.55	4.16	3.93	4.66	3.99
SD	.93	1.14	.81	.96	1.34	1.22

Pre v. Dur v. Post: Trial F = 6.32 p = .004

Pre v. Dur: Trial F = 8.07 p = .009

Theta (5-7 Hz)

	Massage			Control		
	Pre	Dur	Post	Pre	Dur	Post
Mean	3.02	2.71	3.02	2.92	3.25	3.00
SD	1.38	1.20	1.32	1.58	1.26	1.45

Alpha (8-12 Hz)

	Massage			Control		
	Pre	Dur	Post	Pre	Dur	Post
Mean	5.50	4.64	5.20	4.99	4.87	5.61
SD	1.58	1.30	1.67	1.01	1.41	1.32

Pre v. Dur v. Post: Trial F = 6.51 p = .003

Group by Trial F = 3.40 p = .04

Pre v. Dur: Trial F = 6.86 p = .02

Pre v. Post: Group by Trial F = 6.36 p = .02

(table continues)

Massage Therapy   24

Table 3

Natural log of raw power for Delta, Theta, Alpha, and Beta

Beta (13-30 Hz)

	Massage			Control		
	Pre	Dur	Post	Pre	Dur	Post
Mean	1.71	1.45	1.41	2.03	3.04	2.84
SD	1.81	2.14	1.95	1.50	1.44	1.49

Pre v. Dur v. Post: Trial F = 8.23 p = .001

Group by Trial F = 12.37 p = .000

Pre v. Dur: Trial F = 7.32 p = .01

Group by Trial F = 21.29 p = .000

Pre v. Post: Trial F = 13.68 p = .001

Group by Trial F = 5.20 p = .03

References

Allport, G. W. (1937). *Personality: A psychological interpretation.* New York: Holt.

Allport, G. W. (1965). *Letters from Jenny.* New York: Harcourt Brace.

Altmann, J. (1974). Observational study of behavior: Sampling methods. *Behaviour, 49,* 227–265.

American Psychological Association. (1952). Annual report of the policy and planning board of the American Psychological Association. *American Psychologist, 7,* 563–568.

American Psychological Association. (1982). *Ethical principles in the conduct of research with human participants.* Washington, DC: Author.

American Psychological Association. (1992). Ethical principles of psychologists and code of conduct. *American Psychologist, 47,* 1598–1616.

American Psychological Association. (1994). *Behavioral research with animals* (www.apa.org).

American Psychological Association. (1994). *Publication manual of the American Psychological Association* (4th ed.). Washington, DC: Author.

American Psychological Association. (1997). *Thesaurus of psychological index terms* (8th ed.). Washington, DC: Author.

Anastasi, A. (1988). *Psychological testing* (6th ed.). New York: Macmillan.

Antonovsky, A., & Sourani, T. (1988). Family sense of coherence and family adaptation. *Journal of Marriage and the Family, 50,* 79–92.

Ashworth, P. (1996). Presuppose nothing! The suspension of assumptions in phenomenological psychological methodology. *Journal of Phenomenological Psychology, 27,* 1–25.

Associated Press (1997, March 10). Lamarr saw the future 55 years ago. *Worcester Telegram & Gazette,* pp. A1, A4.

Associated Press (1997, May 2). Clinton to apologize for US syphilis study. *The Boston Globe,* p. A20.

Astor, G. (1983). *The disease detectives.* New York: Nal Books.

Austin, J. H. (1978). *Chase, chance, & creativity: The lucky art of novelty.* New York: Columbia University Press.

Avenoso, K. (1996, July 14). Erasing the passed: Prize-winning school beset by test-score scandal. *Boston Globe,* p. A1.

Avorn, J., Soumerai, S. B., Everitt, D. E., Ross-Degnan, D., Beers, M. H., Sherman, D., Salem-Schatz, S. R., &
Fields, D. (1992). A randomized trial of a program to reduce the use of psychoactive drugs in nursing homes. *The New England Journal of Medicine, 327,* 168–173.

Azrin, N. H., & Peterson, A. L. (1990). Treatment of Tourette syndrome by habit reversal: A waiting-list control group comparison. *Behavior Therapy, 21,* 305–318.

Bakeman, R., & Gottman, J. M. (1986). *Observing interaction: An introduction to sequential analysis.* New York: Cambridge University Press.

Bandura, A. (1971). *Social learning theory.* Morristown, NJ: General Learning Press.

Bandura, A., Ross, D., & Ross, S. A. (1963). Imitation of film-mediated aggressive models. *Journal of Abnormal and Social Psychology, 66,* 3–11.

Barlow, D. H., & Hersen, M. (1984). *Single case experimental designs: Strategies for studying behavior change* (2nd ed.). New York: Pergamon Press.

Bateson, P., & Young, M. (1981). Separation from the mother and the development of play in cats. *Animal Behaviour, 29,* 173–180.

Baumrind, D. (1964). Some thoughts on ethics of research: After reading Milgram's "Behavioral study of obedience" (1964). *American Psychologist, 19,* 421–423.

Bavelas, J. B. (1987). Permitting creativity in science. In D. N. Jackson & J. P. Rushton (Eds.), *Scientific excellence: Origins and assessment* (pp. 307–327). Newbury Park, CA: Sage.

Beck, A. T., & Steer, R. A. (1987). *Beck Depression Inventory manual.* San Antonio, TX: The Psychological Corporation.

Beecher, H. K. (1959). Generalization from pain of various types and diverse origins. *Science, 130,* 267–268.

Beecher, H. K. (1960). Increased stress and effectiveness of placebos and "active" drugs. *Science, 132,* 91–92.

Beecher, H. K. (1966). Ethics and clinical research. *The New England Journal of Medicine, 274,* 1354–1360.

Beere, C. A. (1979). *Women and women's issues: A handbook of tests and measures.* San Francisco: Jossey-Bass.

Beere, C. A. (1990). *Gender roles: A handbook of tests and measures.* New York: Greenwood Press.

Bem, D. J. (1972). Self-perception theory. In L. Berkowitz (Ed.), *Advances in experimental social psychology* (Vol. 6, pp. 1–62). New York: Academic Press.

Bem, S. (1978). *Bem Inventory.* Palo Alto, CA: Consulting Psychologists Press.

Bickell, W. H., Wall, M. J., Pepe, P. E., Martin, R. R., Ginger, V. F., Allen, M. K., & Mattox, K. L. (1994). Immediate versus delayed fluid resuscitation for hypotensive patients with penetrating torso injuries. *The New England Journal of Medicine, 331,* 1105–1109.

Binet, A. (1903). *L'Etude experimentale de l'intelligence* [The experimental study of intelligence]. Paris: Schleicher Fréres.

Blatt, S. J. (1995). The destructiveness of perfectionism. *American Psychologist, 50,* 1003–1020.

Bloch, G. J. (1980). *Mesmerism: A translation of the original medical and scientific writings of F. A. Mesmer, M. D.* Los Altos, CA: Kaufmann.

Boring, E. G. (1954). The nature and history of experimental control. *American Journal of Psychology, 67,* 573–589.

Bottorff, J. L., & Morse, J. M. (1994). Identifying types of attending: Patterns of nurses' work. *IMAGE: Journal of Nursing Scholarship, 26,* 53–60.

Bower, G. H., & Kihlstrom, J. F. (1995). Basic behavioral science research for mental health: A national investment. A report of the National Advisory Mental Health Council, Rockville, MD (1995). *American Psychologist, 50,* 485–495.

Box, J. F. (1978). *R. A. Fisher: The life of a scientist.* New York: Wiley.

Bramel, D., & Friend, R. (1981). Hawthorne, the myth of the docile worker, and class bias in psychology. *American Psychologist, 36,* 867–878.

Brandt, R. M. (1981). *Studying behavior in natural settings.* Lanham, MD: University Press of America.

Braucht, G. N., & Reichardt, C. S. (1993). A computerized approach to trickle-process, random assignment. *Evaluation Review, 17,* 79–90.

Bromley, D. B. (1986). *The case-study method in psychology and related disciplines.* New York: Wiley.

Brooks/Cole (1997). *Brooks/Cole research methods and statistics catalog.* Pacific Grove, CA: Brooks/Cole.

Brown, C. R. (1986). Cliff swallow colonies as information centers. *Science, 234,* 83–85.

Brown, G. H., & Harding, F. D. (1973). A comparison of methods of studying illicit drug usage. *HUMRO Technical Report 73-9.* Alexandria, VA: Human Resources Research Organization.

Brown, M., & Corkeron, P. (1995). Pod characteristics of migrating humpback whales (Megaptera novaeangliae) off the east Australian coast. *Behaviour, 132,* 163–179.

Campbell, D. T., & Stanley, J. C. (1963). *Experimental and quasi-experimental designs for research.* Chicago: Rand McNally.

Campbell, D. T., & Ross, H. L. (1968). The Connecticut crackdown on speeding: Time-series data in quasi-experimental analysis. *Law and Society Review, 3,* 33–53.

Cautela, J. R. (1977). *Behavior analysis forms for clinical intervention.* Champaign, IL: Research Press.

Cautela, J. R. (1981). *Behavior analysis forms for clinical intervention, Vol. 2.* Champaign, IL: Research Press.

Chamberlin, T. C. (1890/1965). The method of multiple working hypotheses. *Science, 148,* 754–759.

Clark, K. E. (1954). The APA study of psychologists. *American Psychologist, 9,* 117–120.

Cobb, N. J., Stevens-Long, J., & Goldstein, S. (1982). The influence of televised models on toy preference in children. *Sex Roles, 8,* 1075–1080.

Cohen, J. (1960). A coefficient of agreement for nominal scales. *Educational and Psychological Measurement, 20,* 37–46.

Cohen, J. (1988). *Statistical power analysis for the behavioral sciences* (2nd ed.). Hillsdale, NJ: Erlbaum.

Cohen, M. R., & Nagel, E. (1934). *An introduction to logic and scientific method.* New York: Harcourt.

Cohen, S., Tyrrell, D. A. J., & Smith, A. P. (1991). Psychological stress and susceptibility to the common cold. *The New England Journal of Medicine, 325,* 606–612.

Consumer Reports (1995). Mental health: Does therapy help? *60,* 734–739.

Consumer Reports (1996, July). The surprising truth about motor oils. *61,* 10–13.

Converse, J. M., & Presser, S. (1986). *Survey questions: Handcrafting the standardized questionnaire.* Sage University Paper series on Quantitative Applications in the Social Sciences, 07–063. Beverly Hills, CA: Sage.

Cook, T. D., & Campbell, D. T. (1979). *Quasi-experimentation: Design & analysis issues for field settings.* Chicago: Rand McNally.

Cowley, G. (1992, December 30). Can sunshine save your life? *Newsweek,* 56.

Cronbach, L. J. (1957). The two disciplines of scientific psychology. *American Psychologist, 12,* 671–684.

Darnton, R. (1968). *Mesmerism and the end of the enlightenment in France.* Cambridge, MA: Harvard University Press.

Darwin, C. (1859). *On the origin of species by means of natural selection, or, the preservation of favoured races in the struggle for life.* London: J. Murray.

Dateline NBC [Burrelle's Transcript]. (1996, March 22). New York: National Broadcasting Company.

Davis, J. A., & Smith, T. W. (1992). *The NORC General Social Survey: A user's guide.* Newbury Park, CA: Sage.

Dawkins, M. S., & Gosling, M. (Eds.) (1992). *Ethics in research on animal behaviour: Readings from "Animal Behaviour."* San Diego, CA: Academic Press.

de Kruif, P. (1926/1954). *Microbe hunters.* New York: Harcourt, Brace & World.

Delmolino, L. M., & Romanczyk, R. G. (1995, February). Facilitated communication: A critical review. *The Behavior Therapist,* 27–30.

Dement, W. (1960). The effect of dream deprivation. *Science, 131,* 1705–1707.

Denzin, N. K. (1970). *The research act: A theoretical introduction to sociological methods.* Chicago: Aldine Press.

Dewsbury, D. A. (1990). Early interactions between animal psychologists and animal activists and the founding of the APA Committee on Precautions in Animal Experimentation. *American Psychologist, 45,* 315–327.

Diener, E., & Crandall, R. (1978). *Ethics in social and behavioral research*. Chicago: University of Chicago Press.

DiIanni, D. (Writer, Producer, Director). (1993). *Nova: The Deadly Deception*. Princeton, NJ: Films for the Sciences and Humanities.

Duncker, K. (1945). On problem-solving. *Psychological Monographs, 58* (No. 5), pp. ix–113.

Dutton, M. (1996). *Literary analysis*. Unpublished manuscript, Hanover College, Hanover, IN.

Easthope, G. (1974). *A history of social research methods*. London: Longman.

Ebbinghaus, H. (1964). *Memory: A contribution to experimental psychology*. (H. A. Ruger & C. E. Bussenius, Trans.). New York: Dover. (Original work published 1885.)

Elbert, T., Pantev, C., Wienbruch, C., Rockstroh, B., & Taub, E. (1995). Increased cortical representation of the fingers of the left hand in string players. *Science, 270,* 305–307.

Elkin, I., Shea, T., Watkins, J. T., Imber, S. D., Sotsky, S. M., Collins, J. F., Glass, D. R., Pilkonis, P. A., Leber, W. R., Docherty, J. P., Fiester, S. J., & Parloff, M.B. (1989). National Institute of Mental Health treatment of depression collaborative research program. *Archives of General Psychiatry, 46,* 971–982.

Eron, L. D., Gentry, J. H., & Schlegal, P. (Eds.) (1994). *Reason to hope: A psychosocial perspective on violence and youth*. Washington, DC: American Psychological Association.

Ferrucci, P. (1990). *Inevitable grace*. Los Angeles: Tarcher.

Feychting, M., & Ahlbom, A. (1993). Magnetic fields and cancer in children residing near Swedish high-voltage power lines. *American Journal of Epidemiology, 138,* 467–482.

Feyerabend, P. (1975). *Against method: An outline of an anarchistic theory of knowledge*. London: Humanities Press.

Field, T. (1995). Massage therapy for infants and children. *Developmental and Behavioral Pediatrics, 16,* 105–111.

Field, T., Ironson, G., Scafidi, F., Nawrocki, T., Goncalves, A., Pickens, J., Fox, N., Schanberg, S., & Kuhn, C. (1996). Massage therapy reduces anxiety and enhances EEG patterns of alertness and math computations. *International Journal of Neuroscience, 86,* 197–205.

Field, T. M. (1993). The therapeutic effects of touch. In G. G. Brannigan & M. R. Merrens (Eds.), *The undaunted psychologist: Adventures in research* (pp. 3–11). New York: McGraw-Hill.

Fischer, J., & Corcoran, K. (1994). *Measures for clinical practice: A sourcebook* (2nd ed.): Vol. 1. *Couples, families and children*. New York: Free Press.

Fischer, J., & Corcoran, K. (1994). *Measures for clinical practice: A sourcebook* (2nd ed.): Vol. 2. *Adults*. New York: Free Press.

Fisher, R. A. (1926). The arrangement of field experiments. *Journal of Ministry of Agriculture, 33,* 503–513.

Fisher, R. A. (1935). *The design of experiments*. Edinburgh: Oliver & Boyd.

Fisher, R. A. (1958). Lung cancer and cigarettes? *Nature, 182,* 108.

Fisher, R. A., & Yates, F. (1953). *Statistical tables for biological, agricultural and medical research* (4th ed.). Edinburgh: Oliver & Boyd.

Fisher, W. W., Piazza, C. C., Bowman, L. G., Kurtz, P. F., Sherer, M. R., & Lachman, S. R. (1994). A preliminary evaluation of empirically derived consequences for the treatment of pica. *Journal of Applied Behavior Analysis, 27,* 447–457.

Flavell, J. H. (1996). Piaget's legacy. *Psychological Science, 7,* 200–203.

Fleiss, J. L., (1981). *Statistical methods for rates and proportions*. New York: Wiley.

Flexner, S. B. (Ed.) (1993). *Random House unabridged dictionary* (2nd ed.). New York: Random House.

Forman, R. F., & McCauley, C. (1987). Validity of the positive control polygraph test using the field practice model. *Journal of Applied Psychology, 71,* 691–698.

Fox, J. A., & Tracy, P. E. (1986). *Randomized response: A method for sensitive surveys*. Sage University Paper series on Quantitative Applications in the Social Sciences, 07–058. Beverly Hills, CA: Sage.

Frame, C., Matson, J. L., Sonis, W. A. Fialkov, M. J., & Kazdin, A. E. (1982). Behavioral treatment of depression in a prepubertal child. *Journal of Behavior Therapy and Experimental Psychiatry, 13,* 239–243.

Freud, S. (1957). Leonardo da Vinci and a memory of his childhood. In J. Strachey (Ed. and Trans.), *The standard edition of the complete psychological works of Sigmund Freud* (Vol. 11, pp. 63–137). London: Hogarth Press. (Original work published 1910)

Frezza, M., di Padova, C., Pozzato, G., Terpin, M., Baraona, E., & Lieber, C. S. (1990). The role of decreased gastric alcohol dehydrogenase activity and first-pass metabolism. *The New England Journal of Medicine, 322,* 95–99.

Fuchs, C. S., Stampfer, M. J., Colditz, G. A., Giovannucci, E. L., Manson, J. E., Kawachi, I., Hunter, D. J., Hankinson, S. E., Hennekens, C. H., Rosner, B., Speizer, F. E., & Willett, W. C. (1995). Alcohol consumption and mortality among women. *The New England Journal of Medicine, 332,* 1245–1250.

Galton, F. (1869). *Hereditary genius: An inquiry into its laws and consequences*. London: Macmillan.

Galton, F. (1874). *English men of science: Their nature and nurture*. London: Macmillan.

Galton, F. (1883). *Inquiries into human faculty and its development*. London: Macmillan.

Galton, F. (1886). Regression toward mediocrity in hereditary stature. *Royal Anthropological Institute of Great Britain and Ireland Journal, 15,* 246–263.

Galton, F. (1909). *Memories of my life* (3rd ed.). London: Methuen.

Garvey, W. D. (1979). *Communication: The essence of science*. Elmsford, NY: Pergamon Press.

Gee, P., Stephenson, D., & Wright, D. E. (1994). Temporal discrimination learning of operant feeding in goldfish. *Journal of the Experimental Analysis of Behavior, 62,* 1–13.

Gergen, K. J. (1973). Social psychology as history. *Journal of Personality and Social Psychology, 26,* 309–320.

Glenn, N. D. (1977). *Cohort Analysis.* Sage University Paper series on Quantitative Applications in the Social Sciences, 07–005. Beverly Hills, CA: Sage.

Goffman, E. (1959). *The presentation of self in everyday life.* Garden City, NJ: Doubleday.

Goldberg, L. R. (1981). Language and individual differences: The search for universals in personality lexicons. In L. Wheeler (Ed.), *Review of personality and social psychology* (pp. 141–165). Beverly Hills, CA: Sage.

Goldberg, L. R. (1993). The structure of phenotypic personality traits. *American Psychologist, 48,* 26–34.

Goldman, B. A., & Mitchell, D. F. (1995). *Directory of unpublished experimental mental measures* (Vol. 6). Washington, DC: American Psychological Association.

Goldman, B. A., Saunders, J. L., & Busch, J. C. (1996). *Directory of unpublished experimental mental measures* (Vols. 1–3). Washington, DC: American Psychological Association.

Goldman, B. A., Osborne, W. L., & Mitchell, D. F. (1996). *Directory of unpublished experimental mental measures* (Vols. 4–5). Washington, DC: American Psychological Association.

Goleman, D., Kaufman, P., & Ray, M. (1992). *The creative spirit: Companion to the PBS television series.* New York: Dutton.

Goodall, J. (1986). *The chimpanzees of Gombe: Patterns of behavior.* Cambridge, MA: Harvard University Press.

Goodall, J. (1987). A plea for the chimpanzees. *American Scientist, 75,* 574–577.

Gould, S. J. (1995). *Dinosaur in a haystack: Reflections on natural history.* New York: Harmony Books.

Gregory, R. J. (1996). *Psychological testing.* Needham Heights, MA: Allyn & Bacon.

Guglietti-Kelly, I., & Westcott, M. R. (1990). She's just shy: A phenomenological study of shyness. *Journal of Phenomenological Psychology, 21,* 150–164.

Hacking, I. (1984, November). Trial by number. *Science, 84,* 69–70.

Hall, C. H., & Kataria, S. (1992). Effects of two treatment techniques on delay and vigilance tasks with attention deficit hyperactive disorder (ADHD) children. *The Journal of Psychology, 126,* 17–25.

Hammond, A. (1984, November). Inside. *Science, 84,* 9.

Haney, C., Banks, C., & Zimbardo, P. (1973). A study of prisoners and guards in a simulated prison. In E. Aronson (Ed.), *Readings about the social animal* (7th ed., pp. 52–67). New York: Freeman.

Hare, B. R. (1985). *The HARE General and Area Specific (School, Peer, and Home) Self-esteem Scale.* Unpublished manuscript, Department of Sociology, SUNY Stony Brook, Stony Brook, NY.

Hathaway, S. R., & McKinley, J. C. (1989). MMPI-2. *Manual for administration and scoring.* Minneapolis, MN: University of Minnesota Press.

Heidbreder, E. (1961). *Seven psychologies.* New York: Appleton-Century-Crofts.

Held, R., & Hein, A. (1963). Movement-produced stimulation in the development of visually guided behavior. *Journal of Comparative and Physiological Psychology, 56,* 872–876.

Hempel, C. G. (1966). *Philosophy of natural science.* Englewood Cliffs, NJ: Prentice-Hall.

Henry, G. T. (1990). Practical sampling. Applied social research methods series (Vol. 21). Newbury Park, CA: Sage.

Hentschel, E., Brandstätter, G., Dragosics, B., Hirschl, A. M., Nemec, H., Schütze, K., Taufer, M., & Wurzer, H. (1993). Effect of ranitidine and amoxicillin plus metronidazole on the eradication of *Helicobacter pylori* and the recurrence of duodenal ulcer. *The New England Journal of Medicine, 328,* 308–311.

Holden, C. (1987). Animal regulations: So far, so good. *Science, 238,* 880–882.

Hothersall, D. (1995). *History of psychology* (3rd ed.). New York: McGraw-Hill.

Howes, D. H., & Solomon, R. L. (1950). A note on McGinnies' "Emotionality and perceptual defense." *Psychological Review, 57,* 229–234.

Humphreys, L. (1970). *Tearoom trade.* Chicago: Aldine Press.

Hunt, M. (1981, November 1). A fraud that shook the world of science. *New York Times Magazine,* 42–46, 50, 54, 58, 68, 70, 72, 74–75.

Jacobson, J. W., Mulick, J. A., & Schwartz, A. A. (1995). A history of facilitated communication. *American Psychologist, 50,* 750–765.

Jenkins, C. D., Zyzanski, S. J., & Rosenman, R. H. (1979). Coronary-prone behavior: One pattern or several? *Psychosomatic Medicine, 40,* 25–43.

Johnston, C. C., Jr., Miller, J. Z., Slemenda, C. W., Reister, T. K., Hui, S., Christian, J. C., & Peacock, M. (1992). Calcium supplementation and increases in bone mineral density in children. *The New England Journal of Medicine, 327,* 82–87.

Jones, T. W., Walter, P. B., Boulware, S. D., McCarthy, G., Sherwin, R. S., & Tamborlane, W. W. (1995). Enhanced adrenomedullary response and increased susceptibility to neuroglycopenia: Mechanisms underlying the adverse effects of sugar ingestion in healthy children. *The Journal of Pediatrics, 126,* 171–177.

Josselson, R. (1992). *The space between us: Exploring the dimensions of human relationships.* San Francisco: Jossey-Bass.

Joy, L. A., Kimball, M. M., & Zabrack, M. L. (1986). Television and children's aggressive behavior. In T. M. Williams (Ed.), *The impact of television: A natural experiment in three communities* (pp. 303–360). Orlando, FL: Academic Press.

Kalton, G. (1983). *Introduction to survey sampling.* Sage University Paper series on Quantitative Applications in the Social Sciences, 07–035. Beverly Hills, CA: Sage.

Katz, J. (1972). *Experimentation with human beings: The authority of the investigator, subject, professions, and state in the human experimentation process.* New York: Russell Sage Foundation.

Keith-Spiegel, P., & Koocher, G. P. (1985). *Ethics in psychology: Professional standards and cases.* New York: Random House.

Kelman, H. C. (1977). Privacy and research with human beings. *Journal of Social Issues, 33,* 169–195.

Kerr, J. S., Sherwood, N., & Hindmarch, I. (1991). Separate and combined effects of the social drugs on psychomotor performance. *Psychopharmacology, 104,* 113–119.

Kessler, R. C., McGonagle, K. A., Zhao, S., Nelson, C. B., Hughes, M., Eshleman, S., Wittchen, H., & Kendler, K. S. (1994). Lifetime and 12-month prevalence of DSM-III-R psychiatric disorders in the United States. *Archives of General Psychiatry, 51,* 8–19.

Kirk, R. E. (1982). *Experimental designs: Procedures for the behavioral sciences.* (2nd ed.). Monterey, CA: Brooks/Cole.

Klein, S. B. (1996). *Learning: Principles and applications* (3rd ed.). New York: McGraw-Hill.

Kneller, G. F. (1978). *Science as a human endeavor.* New York: Columbia University Press.

Koch, S. (Ed.). (1959–1963). *Psychology: A study of a science* (Vols. 1–6). New York: McGraw-Hill.

Koffka, K. (1935). *Principles of Gestalt psychology.* New York: Harcourt, Brace.

Koocher, G. P. (1977). Bathroom behavior and human dignity. *Journal of Personality and Social Psychology, 35,* 120–121.

Kor, E. M. (1992). Nazi experiments as viewed by a survivor of Mengele's experiments. In A. L. Caplan (Ed.), *When medicine went mad: Bioethics and the Holocaust* (pp. 3–8). Totowa, NJ: Humana Press.

Krech, D. (1970). Behavioral sciences. In S. Rosner & L. E. Abt (Eds.), *The creative experience* (pp. 59–70). New York: Grossman.

Krech, D. (1974). David Krech. In G. Lindzey (Ed.), *A history of psychology in autobiography* (Vol. 6, pp. 221–250). Englewood Cliffs, NJ: Prentice-Hall.

Krotki, K., & Fox, B. (1974). The randomized response technique, the interview, and the self-administered questionnaire: An empirical comparison of fertility reports. *Proceedings of the Social Statistics Section, American Statistical Association.*

Kuhn, T. S. (1970). *The structure of scientific revolutions* (2nd ed.). Chicago: University of Chicago Press.

LaBerge, S. P., Nagel, L. E., Dement, W. C., & Zarcone, V. P., Jr. (1981). Lucid dreaming verified by volitional communication during REM sleep. *Perceptual and Motor Skills, 52,* 727–732.

Laumann, E. O., Gagnon, J. H., Michael, R. T., & Michaels, S. (1994). *The social organization of sexuality: Sexual practices in the United States.* Chicago: University of Chicago Press.

Leahey, T. H. (1994). Operationism. In R. J. Corsini (Ed.), *Encyclopedia of Psychology* (2nd ed, Vol. 2, pp. 519–520). New York: John Wiley.

Lehner, P. N. (1979). *Handbook of ethological methods.* New York: Garland.

Leonard, W. H., & Clark, A. G. (1939). *Field plot technique.* Minneapolis, MN: Burgess.

Lewin, K., Lippitt, R., & White, R. K. (1939). Patterns of aggressive behavior in experimentally created "social climates." *Journal of Social Psychology, 10,* 271–299.

Lewontin, R. C. (1982). *Human diversity.* New York: Scientific American.

Liao, T. F. (1994). *Interpreting probability modes: Logit, Probit, and other generalized linear models.* Sage University Paper series on Quantitative Applications in the Social Sciences, 07-101. Thousand Oaks, CA: Sage.

Likert, R. (1932). A technique for the measurement of attitudes. *Archives of Psychology, No. 140.*

Lorenz, K. (1981). *The foundations of ethology.* New York: Springer-Verlag.

MacLeod, J. (1995). *Ain't no makin' it: Aspirations and attainment in a low-income neighborhood.* Boulder, CO: Westview.

Maier, S. F., Watkins, L. R., & Fleshner, M. (1994). Psychoneuroimmunology: The interface between behavior, brain, and immunity. *American Psychologist, 49,* 1004–1017.

Marans, D. G. (1988). Addressing research practitioner and subject needs: A debriefing-disclosure procedure. *American Psychologist, 43,* 826–828.

Marin, R. Alien Invasion (1996, July 8). *Newsweek,* 48–54.

Martin, P. R., & Bateson, P. (1993). *Measuring behaviour: An introductory guide* (2nd ed.). Cambridge: Cambridge University Press.

Masling, J. (1966). Role-related behavior of the subject and psychologist and its effects upon psychological data. *Nebraska Symposium on Motivation, 14,* 67–103.

McAdams, D. P. (1988). Biography, narrative, and lives: An introduction. *Journal of Personality, 56,* 1–18.

McCord, D. M. (1991). Ethics-sensitive management of the university human subject pool. *American Psychologist, 46,* 151.

McCrae, R. R., & John, O. P. (1992). An introduction to the five-factor model and its applications. *Journal of Personality, 60,* 175–215.

McCubbin, H. I., & Thompson, A. I. (Eds.) (1991). *Family assessment: Inventories for research and practice.* Madison, WI: University of Wisconsin Press.

McGinnies, E. (1949). Emotionality and perceptual defense. *Psychological Review, 56,* 244–251.

Medawar, P. B. (1979). *Advice to a young scientist.* New York: Harper.

Microsoft Encarta [Computer software]. (1994). Redmond, WA: Microsoft.

Middlemist, R. D., Knowles, E. S., & Matter, C. F. (1976). Personal space invasions in the lavatory: Suggestive evidence for arousal. *Journal of Personality and Social Psychology, 33,* 541–546.

Middlemist, R. D., Knowles, E. S., & Matter, C. F. (1977). What to do and what to report: A reply to Koocher. *Journal of Personality and Social Psychology, 35,* 122–124.

Milgram, S. (1963). Behavioral study of obedience. *Journal of Abnormal and Social Psychology, 67,* 371–378.

Milgram, S. (1964). Issues in the study of obedience: A reply to Baumrind. *American Psychologist, 19,* 848–852.

Mill, J. S. (1973). *A system of logic: Ratiocinative and inductive.* In J. M. Robson (Ed.), *Collected works of John Stuart Mill* (Vols. 7–8). Toronto: University of Toronto Press. (Original work published 1843.)

Miller, A. (1984). *For your own good: Hidden cruelty in child-rearing and the roots of violence.* New York: Farrar, Straus, Giroux.

Miller, N. E. (1985). The value of behavioral research on animals. *American Psychologist, 40*, 423–440.

Moberg, D. P., Piper, D. L., Wu, J., & Serlin, R. C. (1993). When total randomization is impossible: Nested randomized assignment. *Evaluation Review, 17*, 271–291.

Monmaney, T. (1993, September 20). Marshall's hunch. *The New Yorker, 69*, 64–72.

Morelli, G. (1983). Adolescent compulsion: A case study involving cognitive-behavioral treatment. *Psychological Reports, 53*, 519–522.

Murphy, L. L., Conoley, J. C., & Impara, J. C. (Eds.) (1994). *Tests in print IV*. Lincoln, NE: University of Nebraska Press.

National Commission for the Protection of Human Subjects of Biomedical and Behavioral Research (1979). *The Belmont Report: Ethical principles and guidelines for the protection of human subjects of research.* Washington, DC: U.S. Government Printing Office.

Neyman, J., & Pearson, E. S. (1933). On the problem of the most efficient tests of statistical hypotheses. *Transactions of the Royal Society of London (Series A), 231*, 289–337.

Novak, M. A., & Petto, A. J. (Eds.) (1991). *Through the looking glass: Issues of psychological well-being in captive nonhuman primates*. Washington, DC: American Psychological Association.

Nunnally, J. C., & Bernstein, I. H. (1994). *Psychometric theory*. New York: McGraw-Hill.

Office for Protection from Research Risks (1994). *Code of Federal Regulations 45CFR 46: Protection of Human Subjects*. Washington, DC: U.S. Government Printing Office.

Orlans, F. B. (1993). *In the name of science: Issues in responsible animal experimentation*. Oxford: Oxford University Press.

Orne, M. T. (1959). The nature of hypnosis: Artifact and essence. *Journal of Abnormal and Social Psychology, 58*, 277–299.

Orne, M. T. (1962). On the social psychology of the psychology experiment: With particular reference to demand characteristics and their implications. *American Psychologist, 17*, 776–783.

Orne, M. T., & Scheibe, K. E. (1964). The contribution of nondeprivation factors in the production of sensory deprivation effects: The psychology of the "panic button." *Journal of Abnormal and Social Psychology, 68*, 3–12.

Osgood, C. E., Suci, G. J., & Tannenbaum, P. H. (1957). *The measurement of meaning*. Urbana, IL: University of Illinois Press.

Palfreman, J. (Producer). (1993). *Frontline: Prisoners of silence* [Videotape]. Boston: WGBH Public Television.

Parsons, H. M. (1974). What happened at Hawthorne? *Science, 183*, 922–932.

Pavlov, I. P. (1960). *Conditioned reflexes* (rev. ed.) (G.V. Anrep, Trans. and Ed.). New York: Dover. (Original work published 1927)

Pavlov, I. P. (1928). *Lectures on conditioned reflexes* (W.H. Gantt, Trans.). New York: International.

Payne, K. (1989). Elephant talk. *National Geographic, 176*, 264–277.

Payne, S. L. (1951). *The art of asking questions*. Princeton, NJ: Princeton University Press.

Pearson, K. (1900). On the criterion that a given system of deviations from the probable in the case of a correlated system of variables is such that it can be reasonably supposed to have arisen from random sampling. *Philosophical Magazine (5th series), 50*, 157–175.

Pearson, K. (1914). *Life, letters, and labours of Francis Galton: Vol. I, Birth 1822 to marriage 1853*. Cambridge: Cambridge University Press.

Pearson, K. (1924). *Life, letters, and labours of Francis Galton. Vol. II, Researches of middle life*. Cambridge: Cambridge University Press.

Pearson, K. (1930). *Life, letters, and labours of Francis Galton. Vol. IIIa, Correlation, personal identification and eugenics*. Cambridge: Cambridge University Press.

Pearson, K. (1930). *Life, letters, and labours of Francis Galton. Vol. IIIb, Characterisation, especially by letters*. Cambridge: Cambridge University Press.

Penfield, W. (1970). Medical sciences. In S. Rosner & L. E. Abt (Eds.), *The creative experience* (pp. 103–113). New York: Grossman.

Pepler, D. J., & Craig, W. M. (1995). A peek behind the fence: Naturalistic observations of aggressive children with remote audiovisual recording. *Developmental Psychology, 31*, 548–553.

Pervin, L. A. (1996). *The science of personality*. New York: Wiley.

Piaget, J. (1952). Jean Piaget. In E. G. Boring, H. S. Langfeld, H. Werner, & R. M. Yerkes (Eds.), *A history of psychology in autobiography* (Vol. 4, pp. 237–256). Worcester, MA: Clark University Press.

Piaget, J. (1954). *The origins of intelligence in children*. New York: International Universities Press.

Pines, M. (1981, September). The civilizing of Genie. *Psychology Today, 15*, 28–34.

Pitter, K., Amato, S., Callahan, J., Kerr, N., Tilton, E., & Minato, R. (1995). *Every student's guide to the Internet*. New York: McGraw-Hill.

Polkinghorne, D. (1983). *Methodology for the human sciences: Systems of inquiry*. Albany, NY: State University of New York Press.

Polkinghorne, D. E. (1989). Phenomenological research methods. In R. S. Valle, & S. Halling (Eds.), *Existential-phenomenological perspectives in psychology: Exploring the breadth of human experience* (pp. 41–60). New York: Plenum Press.

Pool, R. (1993). Evidence for homosexuality gene. *Science, 261*, 291–292.

Pratkanis, A. R., Greenwald, A. G., Leippe, M. R., & Baumgardner, M. H. (1988). In search of reliable persuasion effects: III. The sleeper effect is dead. Long live the sleeper effect. *Journal of Personality and Social Psychology, 54*, 203–218.

Quetelet, M. A. (1849). *Letters on the theory of probabilities* (O. G. Downs, Trans.). London: Harles & Edwin Layton.

Rankin, N. O. (1986). Student Statistician [Computer software]. Worcester, MA: Author.

Reaser, J. M., Hartsock, S., & Hoehn, A. J. (1975). A test of the forced-alternative randomized response questionnaire technique. *HUMRO Technical Report 75-*

9. Alexandria, VA: Human Resources Research Organization.

Recht, L., Lew, R. A., & Schwartz, W. J. (1995). Baseball teams beaten by jet lag. *Nature, 377,* 583.

Reed, J. G., & Baxter, P. M. (1992). *Library use: A handbook for psychology* (2nd ed.). Washington, DC: American Psychological Association.

Report of Dr. Benjamin Franklin, and other commissioners, charged by the King of France, with the examination of the animal magnetism, as now practised at Paris. (1785). Translated from the French. With an Historical Introduction. London: J. Johnson.

Rice, B. (1982, February). The Hawthorne defect: Persistence of a flawed theory. *Psychology Today, 16,* 70, 72–74.

Roberts, R. M. (1989). *Serendipity: Accidental discoveries in science.* New York: Wiley.

Robinson, J. P., & Shaver, P. R. (1973). *Measures of social psychological attitudes.* Ann Arbor, MI: Institute for Social Research.

Robinson, J. P., Althanasiou, R., & Head, K. B. (1973). *Measures of occupational attitudes and occupational characteristics.* Ann Arbor, MI: Institute for Social Research.

Robinson, J. P., Rusk, J. G., & Head, K. B. (1973). *Measures of political attitudes.* Ann Arbor, MI: Institute for Social Research.

Robson, J. M. (1973). Textual introduction. In J. M. Robson (Ed.), *Collected works of John Stuart Mill* (Vol. 7, pp. xlix–cviii). Toronto: University of Toronto Press.

Roediger, H. L. III (1987). The role of journal editors in the scientific process. In D. N. Jackson & J. P. Rushton (Eds.), *Scientific excellence: Origins and assessment* (pp. 222–252). Newbury Park, CA: Sage.

Roethlisberger, F. J., & Dickson, W. J. (1939). *Management and the worker.* Cambridge, MA: Harvard University Press.

Root-Bernstein, R. S. (1988, May/June). Setting the stage for discovery: Breakthroughs depend on more than luck. *The Sciences,* 26–35.

Root-Bernstein, R. S. (1989). *Discovering.* Cambridge, MA: Harvard University Press.

Rosenthal, N. E., Sack, D. A., Carpenter, C. J., Parry, B. L., Mendelson, W. B., & Wehr, T. A. (1985). Antidepressant effects of light in seasonal affective disorder. *American Journal of Psychiatry, 142,* 163–170.

Rosenthal, R. (1984). *Meta-analytic procedures for social research.* Beverly Hills, CA: Sage.

Rosenthal, R. (1994). Interpersonal expectancy effects: A 30-year perspective. *Current Directions in Psychological Science, 3,* 176–179.

Rothman, K. J., & Michels, K. B. (1994). The continuing unethical use of placebo controls. *The New England Journal of Medicine, 331,* 394–398.

Roy, A. (1981). Specificity of risk factors for depression. *American Journal of Psychiatry, 138,* 959–961.

Rubin, J. Z., Provenzano, F. J., & Luria, Z. (1974). The eye of the beholder: Parents' views on sex of newborns. *American Journal of Orthopsychiatry, 44,* 512–519.

Rumbaugh, D. M. (1993). Learning about primates' learning, language, and cognition. In G. G. Brannigan

& M. R. Merrens (Eds.), *The undaunted psychologist: Adventures in research* (pp. 91–109). New York: McGraw-Hill.

Runyan, W. McK. (1982). In defense of the case study method. *American Journal of Orthopsychiatry, 52,* 440–446.

Runyan, W. McK. (1983). Idiographic goals and methods in the study of lives. *Journal of Personality, 51,* 413–437.

Runyan, W. McK. (1988). Progress in psychobiography. *Journal of Personality, 56,* 295–326.

Rush, A. J., Beck, A. T., Kovacs, M., & Hollon, S. (1977). Comparative efficacy of cognitive therapy and pharmacotherapy in the treatment of depressed outpatients. *Cognitive Therapy and Research, 1,* 17–37.

Ryan, T. A. (1959). Multiple comparisons in psychological research. *Psychological Bulletin, 56,* 26–47.

Sacks, O. (1985). *The man who mistook his wife for a hat and other clinical tales.* New York: Simon & Schuster.

Sarbin, T. R. (1982). The scientific status of the mental illness metaphor. In V. L. Allen & K. E. Scheibe (Eds.), *The social context of conduct: Psychological writings of Theodore Sarbin* (pp. 135–138). New York: Praeger.

Schreibman, L., & Koegel, R. L. (1975, March). Autism: A defeatable horror. *Psychology Today, 8,* 61–67.

Schuman H., & Presser, S. (1981). *Questions and answers in attitude surveys: Experiments on question form, wording, and context.* New York: Academic Press.

Seldes, G. (1972). *The great quotations.* New York: Bantom.

Seligman, M. E. P. (1995). The effectiveness of psychotherapy: The *Consumer Reports* study. *American Psychologist, 50,* 965–974.

Sheehan, N. (1995, November 19). Sisters kept close. *Worcester Telegram & Gazette,* p.A1.

Shekerjian, D. (1990). *Uncommon genius: How great ideas are born.* New York: Viking Press.

Shortland, M., & Gregory, J. (1991). *Communicating science: A handbook.* New York: Wiley.

Sidman, M. (1960). *Tactics of scientific research: Evaluating experimental data in Psychology.* New York: Basic Books.

Sieber, J. E. (1992). *Planning ethically responsible research: A guide for students and internal review boards.* Applied Social Research Methods Series (Vol. 31). Newbury Park, CA: Sage.

Sigall, H., & Ostrove, N. (1975). Effects of offender attractiveness and nature of the crime on juridic judgment. *Journal of Personality and Social Psychology, 31,* 410–414.

Singer, P. (1975). *Animal liberation.* New York: Avon Press.

Skinner, B. F. (1938). *The behavior of organisms.* New York: Appleton-Century-Crofts.

Skinner, B. F. (1956). A case study in scientific method. *American Psychologist, 11,* 221–233.

Skinner, B. F. (1959). A case history in scientific method. In S. Koch (Ed.), *Psychology: A study of a science: Vol. 2. General systematic formulations, learning, and special processes* (pp. 359–379). New York: McGraw-Hill.

Sloan, J. H., Kellermann, A. L., Reay, D. T., Ferris, J. A., Koepsell, T., Rivara, F. P., Rice, C., Gray, L., & LoGerfo, J. (1988). Handgun regulations, crime, assaults, and homicide. *The New England Journal of Medicine, 318,* 1256–1262.

Smith, T. W. (1988). *Timely artifacts: A review of measurement variation in the 1972–1988 GSS.* Chicago: National Opinion Research Center.

Sprat, T. (1667/1958). *History of the Royal Society.* (J. I. Cope & H. W. Jones (Eds.). London: Routledge & Kegan Paul.

Stanford, C. B., Wallis, J., Mpongo, E., & Goodall, J. (1994). Hunting decisions in wild chimpanzees. *Behaviour, 131,* 1–18.

Steering Committee of the Physicians Health Study Research Group (1988). Preliminary report: Findings from the aspirin component of the ongoing physicians' health study. *The New England Journal of Medicine, 318,* 262–264.

Stevens, S. S. (1946). On the theory of scales of measurement. *Science, 103,* 677–680.

Stewart, J. W., Quitkin, F. M., Terman, M., & Terman, J. S. (1990). Is seasonal affective disorder a variant of atypical depression? Differential response to light therapy. *Psychiatry Research, 33,* 121–128.

Stigler, S. M. (1986). *The history of statistics: The measurement of uncertainty before 1900.* Cambridge, MA: Harvard University Press.

Stillinger, J. (Ed.). (1969). *Autobiography of John Stuart Mill.* Boston: Houghton Mifflin.

Student (1908). The probable error of a mean. *Biometrika, 6,* 1–25.

Sulloway, F. J. (1996). *Born to rebel.* New York: McKay.

Suzuki, S., Kuroda, S., & Nishihara, T. (1995). Tool-set for termite-fishing by chimpanzees in the Ndoki forest, Congo. *Behaviour, 132,* 219–235.

Swain, J. F., Rouse, I. L., Curley, C. B., & Sacks, F. M. (1990). Comparison of the effects of oat bran and low-fiber wheat on serum lipoprotein levels and blood pressure. *The New England Journal of Medicine, 322,* 147–152.

Tardif, T. (1996). Nouns are not always learned before verbs: Evidence from mandarin speakers' early vocabularies. *Developmental Psychology, 32,* 492–504.

Tatar, M. M. (1978). *Spellbound: Studies on mesmerism and literature.* Princeton, NJ: Princeton University Press.

Terman, L. M., & Oden, M. H. (1947). *Genetic studies of genius: Vol. 4. The gifted child grows up.* Palo Alto, CA: Stanford University Press.

Terman, L. M., & Oden, M. H. (1959). *Genetic studies of genius: Vol. 5. The gifted child at mid-life.* Palo Alto, CA: Stanford University Press.

Thorndike, R. L. (1954). The psychological value systems of psychologists. *American Psychologist, 9,* 787–789.

The Psychological Corporation (1997). *Products for psychological assessment and intervention.* San Antonio, TX: Harcourt Brace.

Tuckman, B. W. (1988). The scaling of mood. *Educational and Psychological Measurement, 48,* 419–427.

Tufte, E. R. (1983). *The visual presentation of quantitative information.* Cheshire, CT: Graphics Press.

Tufte, E. R. (1990). *Envisioning information.* Cheshire, CT: Graphics Press.

Valenstein, E. S. (1986). *Great and desperate cures: The rise and decline of psychosurgery and other radical treatments for mental illness.* New York: Basic Books.

van Lawick-Goodall, J. (1971). *In the shadow of man.* Boston: Houghton Mifflin.

Veatch, R. M. (1989). Medical ethics: An introduction. In R.M. Veatch (Ed.), *Medical ethics* (pp. 1–26). Boston: Jones & Bartlett.

Veitch, J. A., Gifford, R., & Hine, D. W. (1991). Demand characteristics and full spectrum lighting effects on performance and mood. *Journal of Environmental Psychology, 11,* 87–95.

von Frisch, K. (1950). *Bees: Their vision, chemical senses, and language.* Ithaca, NY: Cornell University Press.

Walters, F. D. (1993). Scientific method and prose style in the early Royal Society. *Journal of Technical Writing and Communication, 23,* 239–258.

Ward, M. C. (1996). *A world full of women.* Needham Heights, MA: Allyn & Bacon.

Warner, S. L. (1965). Randomized response: A survey technique for eliminating evasive answer bias. *Journal of the American Statistical Association, 60,* 63–69.

Watson, J. B. (1928/1972). *Psychological care of infant and child.* New York: Arno Press.

Webb, E. J., Campbell, D. T., Schwartz, R. D., & Sechrest, L. (1966). *Unobtrusive measures: Nonreactive research in the social sciences.* Chicago: Rand McNally.

Webb, E. J., Campbell, D. T., Schwartz, R. D., Sechrest, L., & Grove, J. B. (1981). *Unobtrusive measures: Nonreactive research in the social sciences* (2nd ed.). Boston: Houghton-Mifflin.

Wechsler, D. (1981). *WAIS-R manual.* San Antonio, TX: The Psychological Corporation.

Wechsler, D. (1991). *Manual for the Wechsler Intelligence Scale for Children–III.* San Antonio, TX: The Psychological Corporation.

Weisberg, R. W. (1986). *Creativity: Genius and other myths.* New York: Freeman.

Willems, E. P. (1969). Planning a rationale for naturalistic research. In E. P. Willems, & H. L. Rausch (Eds.), *Naturalistic viewpoints in psychological research* (pp. 44–71). New York: Holt, Rinehart & Winston.

Williams, T. M. (Ed.) (1986). *The impact of television: A natural experiment in three communities.* New York: Academic Press.

Winch, W. H. (1908). The transfer of improvement in memory in school-children. *British Journal of Psychology, 2,* 284–293.

Winer, B. J., Brown, D. R., & Michels, K. M. (1991). *Statistical principles in experimental design* (3rd ed.). New York: McGraw-Hill.

Winter, D. G. (1996). *Personality: Analysis and interpretation of lives.* New York: McGraw-Hill.

Wissler, C. (1901). The correlation of mental and physical tests. *Psychological Review, Monograph Supplement 3* (No. 6).

Wolraich, M. L., Lindgren, S. D., Stumbo, P. J., Stegink, L. D., Appelbaum, M. I., & Kiritsy, M. C. (1994). Effects of diets high in sucrose or aspartame on the behavior and cognitive performance of children. *The New England Journal of Medicine, 330,* 301–307.

Yule, G. U. (1897). On the theory of correlation. *Journal of the Royal Statistical Society, 60,* 812–854.

Acknowledgments and Photo Credits

❖

Chapter 2 Figure 1, p. 39. Reprinted with permission from Elbert, T., Pantev, C., Wienbruch, C., Rockstroh, B., & Taub, E. (1995). Increased cortical representation of the fingers of the left hand in string players. *Science, 270,* 305–307. Copyright 1995 American Association for the Advancement of Science.

Table 1, p. 43. Reprinted with permission from *Nature,* Recht, L., Lew, R. A., & Schwartz, W. J. (1995). Baseball teams beaten by jet lag. *Nature, 377,* 583. Copyright 1995 Macmillan Magazines Limited.

Figure 2, p. 47. Reprinted with permission from Josselson, Ruthellen. (1992). *The Space Between Us: Exploring the Dimensions of Human Relationships,* p. 253. Copyright 1992 by Jossey-Bass Inc., Publishers.

Figure 3, p. 48. Figure titled "A Space for Describing Research Activities" from NATURALISTIC VIEWPOINTS IN PSYCHOLOGICAL RESEARCH by Edwin P. Willems and Harold L. Raush, copyright © 1969 by Holt, Rinehart and Winston, reproduced by permission of the publisher.

Figure 4, p. 50. From Runyan, William McKinley (1983). Idiographic goals and methods in the study of lives. *Journal of Personality, 51*:4 (December), figure 1, p. 416. Copyright 1983, Duke University Press. Reprinted with permission.

Figure 5, p. 52. Reproduced with permission of author and publisher from: Morelli, G. Adolescent compulsion: a case study involving cognitive-behavioral treatment. *Psychological Reports,* 1983, 53, 519–522. © Psychological Reports.

Chapter 3 Figure 3, p. 68. From Karl von Frisch (1950). *Bees: Their vision, chemical senses, and language.* Ithaca, NY: Cornell University Press. Used by permission of the publisher, Cornell University Press.

Chapter 4 Tables 2 and 3, pp. 89–90. Text from Microsoft® Encarta® Encyclopedia reproduced by permission from Microsoft Corporation. © 1994 Microsoft Corporation.

All rights reserved. Microsoft and Encarta are registered trademarks of Microsoft Corporation. Check out Encarta online at http://www.microsoft.com/encarta. For a limited time, the online edition of Encarta at http:///www.microsoft.com/encarta provides HTML links for online use of specific articles. Send your request to encweb@microsoft.com with the name of the article in the body of your message. Please include "Encarta Intro link" in the Subject line of your email.

Chapter 6 Figure 8, p. 136. From Joan Fisher Box (1978). *R. A. Fisher: The life of a scientist.* NY: Wiley. Copyright © 1978, John Wiley & Sons. Reprinted by permission of John Wiley & Sons, Inc.

Chapter 7 Boxes 3 and 4 170–73, 177. Reprinted from American Psychological Association. (1992). Ethical principles of psychologists and code of conduct, *American Psychologist, 47,* 1598–1616. Copyright © 1992 by the American Psychological Association. Reprinted with permission.

Chapter 8 Table 5 and Figures 3 and 4, p. 197. Reprinted from Jones, T. W., Walter, P. B., Boulware, S. D., McCarthy, G., Sherwin, R. S., & Tamborlane, W. W. (1995). Enhanced adrenomedullary response and increased susceptibility to neuroglycopenia: Mechanisms underlying the adverse effects of sugar ingestion in healthy children. *The Journal of Pediatrics, 126,* 171–177. By permission of Mosby-Year Book, Inc.

Chapter 9 Table 1, p. 209. From Rosenthal, N. E., Sack, D. A., Carpenter, C. J., Parry, B. L., Mendelson, W. B., & Wehr, T. A. Antidepressant effects of light in seasonal affective disorder. *American Journal of Psychiatry, 142,* 163–170, 1985. Copyright 1985, the American Psychiatric Association. Reprinted by permission.

Figure 1, p. 210. Reprinted with permission from Martin, P. R., & Bateson, P. (1993). *Measuring behaviour: An introductory guide (2nd ed.).* Cambridge: Cambridge University Press.

Figure 3, p. 219. Reprinted with permission of author and publisher from Gee, P., Stephenson, D., and Wright, D. E. (1994). Temporal Discrimination Learning of Operant Feeding in Goldfish. *Journal of the Experimental Analysis of Behavior, 62*, 1–13. Copyright 1994 by the Society for the Experimental Analysis of Behavior, Inc.

Figure 4, p. 222. Reprinted from *Journal of Behavior Therapy and Experimental Psychiatry*, Volume 13, Frame, C., Matson, J. L., Sonis, W. A., Fialkov, M. J., and Kazdin, A. E., Behavioral treatment of depression in a prepubertal child, 239–243, Copyright 1982, with kind permission from Elsevier Science Ltd, The Boulevard, Langford Lane, Kidlington 0X5 1GB, UK.

Chapter 10 Figures 1 and 2, pp. 233, 236. Reprinted from Campbell, D. T., & Ross, H. L. (1968). The Connecticut crackdown on speeding: Time-series data in quasi-experimental analysis, *Law and Society Review, 3*, 33–53. Reprinted by permission of the Law and Society Association.

Figure 3, p. 238. Reprinted with permission of author and publisher from Williams, T. M., (Ed.) (1986). *The impact of television: A natural experiment in three communities.* New York: Academic Press.

Box 2, p. 241. Reprinted by permission of the publisher from THE CHIMPANZEES OF GOMBE: PATTERNS OF BEHAVIOR by Jane Goodall, Cambridge, Mass.: Harvard University Press, Copyright © 1986 by the Presidents and Fellows of Harvard College.

Box 3, p. 242. Reprinted with permission of author and publisher from Williams, T. M., (Ed.) (1986). *The impact of television: A natural experiment in three communities.* New York: Academic Press.

Box 6, p. 256. Payne, S. L.; THE ART OF ASKING QUESTIONS. Copyright © 1951 by Princeton University Press. Reprinted by permission of Princeton University Press.

Chapter 11 Poem, p. 283. "How to Be a Maverick," reprinted in part from Root-Bernstein, R. S. (1989) *Discovering.* Cambridge, MA: Harvard University Press, by permission of Robert S. Root-Bernstein.

Chapter 12 Box 5, p. 296–99. The number target was reprinted from Fox, J. A., & Tracy, P. E. *Randomized Response: A Method for Sensitive Surveys.* Sage University Paper series on Quantitative Applications in the So-cial Sciences, 07-058, p. 29, copyright © 1986 by Sage Publications. Reprinted by Permission of Sage Publications, Inc.

Box 5, p. 296–99. The magnitude estimation question was reprinted from Converse, J. M., & Presser, S. *Survey questions: Handcrafting the standardized questionnaire.* Sage University Paper series on Quantitative Applications in the Social Sciences, 07-063, pp. 29–30, copyright © 1986 by Sage Publications. Reprinted by Permission of Sage Publications, Inc.

Box 5, p. 296–99. Mood thermometers reprinted from Tuckman, B. W. The scaling of mood. *Educational and Psychological Measurement, 48*, 419–427, copyright © 1988 by Sage Publications. Reprinted by Permission of Sage Publications, Inc.

The information on consent forms was reprinted from Sieber, J. E. (1992). *Planning ethically responsible research: A guide for students and Internal Review Boards.* Applied Social Research Methods Series. (Vol. 31), p. 35, copyright © 1988 by Sage Publications. Reprinted by Permission of Sage Publications, Inc.

Box 6, p. 313. Reprinted from Sieber, J. E. (1992). *Planning ethically responsible research: A guide for students and Internal Review Boards.* Applied Social Research Methods Series, (Vol. 31), pp. 36–37, copyright © 1988 by Sage Publications. Reprinted by Permission of Sage Publications, Inc.

Chapter 13 Boxes 7 and 10, pp. 339 and 345. Adapted from the American Psychological Association. (1994). *Publication manual of the American Psychological Association* (4th ed.). Washington, DC:L APA Copyright © 1994 by the American Psychological Association. Adapted with permission.

Box 11, p. 349. Reprinted from American Psychological Association. (1992). Ethical principles of psychologists and code of conduct, *American Psychologist, 47*, 1598–1616. Copyright © 1992 by the American Psychological Association. Reprinted with permission.

Appendix B P. B-1. Manuscript of Field, T., Ironson, G., Scafidi, F., Nawrocki, T., Goncalves, A., Pickens, J., Fox, N., Schanberg, S. & Kuhn, C. Massage therapy reduces anxiety and enhances EEG patterns of alertness and math computations. Reproduced from *International Journal of Neuroscience*, 1996, Vol. 86, pp. 197–205 with permission of Gordon and Breach Science Publishers.

Photo Credits

p. 11, Wolfgang Köhler Papers, American Philosophical Society, Philadelphia PA.
p. 20, Corbis-Bettmann.
p. 22, Corbis-Bettmann.
p. 26, Bibliothèque Nationale, Paris.
p. 31, UPI/Corbis-Bettmann.
p. 38, © Gilda Schiff-Zirinsy/Photo Researchers.
p. 66, Nina Leen, LIFE Magazine © Time Inc.
p. 69, © Scotts Miracle-Gro Products, Inc.
p. 94, The Granger Collection, New York.
p. 59, Corbis-Bettmann.
p. 95, Courtesy of Cambridge University Press.

p. 115, The Granger Collection, New York.

p. 139, Forestry Commission.

p. 145, Courtesy of Dr. Alan Hein, MIT.

p. 158, Courtesy American Medical Association Archives.

p. 65, ©1965 by Stanley Milgram. From the film OBEDI-ENCE, distributed by Penn State, Media Sales.

p. 212, UPI/Corbis-Bettmann.

p. 213, Courtesy of B. F. Skinner Foundation.

p. 218, © 1994 Dr. Philip Gee.

p. 240, Reproduced by permission of the publisher from *The Chimpanzees of Gombe* by Jane Goodall. Harvard University Press Cambridge MA. © 1986 by the President and Fellows of Harvard College (After D. Bygott).

p. 246, © Gérard Lacz/Animals Animals.

p. 269, Courtesy of the Worcester Telegram & Gazette/ Chris Christo.

p. 282, © 1997 Scott Camazine & Sue Trainor.

p. 281, Courtesy of Katharine B. Payne, Cornell.

p. 277, Reprinted with permission from *Science*, vol. 263, 14 January 1994. © 1997 American Association for the Advancement of Science.

p. 308, Meredith Corporation.

p. 331, Courtesy of Dr. Tiffany Field.

p. 306, Property of AT&T Archives. Reprinted with permission of AT&T.

p. 304, © Richard T. Nowitz/Photo Researchers.

Indexes

---❖---

Name Index

A

Abrahams, Jim, 277
Adler, Alfred, 125
Allport, Gordon, 49–50
Anastasi, Anne, 15–16
Antheil, George, 274

B

Babbage, Charles, 349
Bain, Alexander, 320
Bakeman, Roger, 237–238
Bavelas, Janet, 263
Beecher, Henry, 35, 165
Beere, Carol, 294
Bentham, Jeremy, 59–60
Bernard, Claude, 175
Bertillon, Alphonse, 115–116
Binet, Alfred, 282
Bridgeman, Percy, 15
Bromley, D. B., 271
Buros, Oscar, 293

C

Campbell, Donald T., 75–78, 206, 230, 231
Chamberlin, T. C., 270
Clark, Kenneth, 36
Cohen, Jacob, 149, 152
Cohen, Sheldon, 84–87
Cook, Thomas D., 76, 231
Cronbach, Lee, 34, 36, 40

D

Darwin, Charles, 5, 92, 276–277
Dement, William, 274
Duncker, Karl, 270

E

Ebbinghaus, Hermann, 51, 207
Elbert, Thomas, 37–38
Elkin, Irene, 147

F

Feyerabend, Paul, 8–9
Feynman, Richard, 347
Fisher, Ronald A., 16–17
    designs in psychology, 140–143
    and factorial design, 185
    randomized experimental designs of, 129–140
Fisher Box, Joan, 185
Fleming, Alexander, 272
Franklin, Benjamin, 21
Freud, Sigmund, 53, 276

G

Galton, Sir Francis
    invention of correlational analysis, 109–118
    invention of norm-based measurement,
        91–95, 98–101
Gauss, Carl, 97, 99
Goffman, Erving, 268–269
Goldman, Bert, 294
Goodall, Jane, 30, 48, 239
Gosset, William, 137
Gottman, John, 237–238
Guglietti-Kelly, Ivana, 278–279

H

Hein, Alan, 144–145
Held, Richard, 144–145
Hempel, Carl, 7–8, 33
Humphreys, Laud, 166

J

Jones, T. W., 196–198
Josselson, Ruthellen, 46–47

K

Kasparian, Gayle, 269–270
Kessler, Ronald, 30–32, 38–39
Kneller, George, 3, 5
Koch, Sigmund, 35
Köhler, Wolfgang, 9, 10, 11, 12, 13, 14, 17
Krech, David, 272, 278
Kuhn, Thomas, 8, 9

L

Lamarr, Hedy, 274
Laumann, Edward, 253
Lineman, Eduard, 43
Likert, Rensis, 296
Lilly, Antoinette, 2
Lilly, John, 2
Lorenz, Konrad, 242, 245

M

McClintock, Barbara, 271–272
MacLeod, Jay, 44–45
Magendie, Françoise, 175
Marshall, Barry, 280
Mesmer, Anton, 18–26
Milgram, Stanley, 164
Mill, James, and Bentham, 59–60
Mill, John Stuart, 58–60
  and event analysis, 239
  Mill's methods, 60–79
    applications of, 75–79
    limitations of, 72–75
    main research steps, 61–62
    observing and controlling events, 60–70
    research designs
      method of agreement, 70
      method of concomitant variation, 67–68
      method of difference, 63–64
Miller, Alice, 54
Mitchell, David, 294
Morelli, George, 51

N

Neyman, Jersey, 147

O

Oldenbourg, Henry, 319
Orne, Martin, 307–308

P

Pavlov, Ivan, 7, 79, 207
Payne, Katharine, 280–281
Payne, Stanley, 255
Pearson, Egon, 147
Pearson, Karl, 101–105, 118
Penfield, Wilder, 272
Piaget, Jean, 3, 8, 84, 276

Q

Quetelet, M. A., 95, 97–99

R

Recht, Lawrence, 43
Root-Bernstein, Robert S., 262, 277, 278
  poem by, 283
Rosenthal, Robert, 308–309
Ross, H. Laurence, 230
Rush, A. J., 143
Rumbaugh, Duane, 279
Runyan, William, 50

S

Sacks, Oliver, 275, 276
Salk, Jonas, 262
Sarbin, Theodore, 275
Shane, Harold, 205
Shekerjian, Denise, 262
Sidman, Murray, 208
Sieber, Joan, 312
Singer, Peter, 175–176
Skinner, B.F., 7, 8, 47–48, 79, 207–208
  ABAB design of, 211–215
Stanley, Julian C., 75–78, 206, 230, 231
Stevens, S. S., 15, 87
Stouffer, Samuel, 255
Sulloway, Frank, 9

T

Terman, Lewis, 40
Thorndike, Edward, 9, 10, 12, 13
Thorndike, Robert, 36

V

Von Frisch, Karl, 66–68

W

Watson, John, 207
Wechsler, David, 118
Weisberg, Robert, 261
Westcott, Malcolm, 278–279
Willems, Edwin, 32–33, 47
    two-dimensional descriptive space, 32, 41, 47–48

Williams, Tannis, 231
Wolraich, Mark, 145

Y

Yule, George, 119, 120, 122

Z

Zimbardo, Philip, 166
    prison experiment, 166

Subject Index

———— ❖ ————

A

ABAB design, 213–215
ABABCBC design, 216
Abstract section, of research report, 323
Acclimation, and subject reactivity, 245
Aggregate measures, 99–101
Alpha (α) level, in statistical test, 104–105
Alpha reliability, 302
Alternating treatment design, 216–219
American Psychological Association; *see* APA
Analogies, hypotheses from, 274–275
Analysis of covariance (ANCOVA), 201
Analysis of variance, 190
Animal learning, hypotheses of, 9–12
Animal magnetism; *see* Mesmer's theory of animal magnetism
Animal research ethics, 175–176
   Animal Welfare Act of 1985, 176–178
   APA Code of Conduct, 177–178
Animal Welfare Act of 1985, 176–178
Annual Review of Psychology, 264
Anomalies, research questions about, 275–276
Antecedent conditions, research classification and control of, 33–40
APA
   ethics of scientific communication, 347, 349
   finding self-measurement test sources, 292–294
APA Code of Conduct for Research
   on animals, 177–178
   on humans, 170–174
APA *Publication Manual,* overview, 321–344
Apparatus, and test design, 14
Appendix section, of research report, 342
Archival data, definition and problems of, 247–249
Archival research, definition and examples, 42–43
Assignment, of subjects to groups, 290

Assumptions
   statistics and violation of, 152
   "turning assumptions on their heads," 278
ATD; *see* Alternating treatment design
Author note, in research report, 342

B

Bar chart, 196–197
Baseline phase, of Skinner's experiment, 213–214
Behavioral criterion, 216
Behavioral units, and natural observation, 239, 241–242
Belmont Report, 166–168
Bertillonage, 115–116
Between-subjects design, 75, 77–79
   and factorial design, 186–187, 190–193
Blinding, and observer bias control, 243
Block randomization, 217
Bracketing, of preconceptions, 270
Buros Institute of Mental Measurement, 292–293

C

Carry-over effects, threat of, 77
Case study, 51–53
Causal hypotheses, 34, 37–38
Causal relationships, 123–124; *see also* Laws of causation
Changing criterion design, 216
Closed question, 295, 300
Cluster sampling, 252
Code of federal regulation for the protection of human species, 168–170
Cohen's kappa, 304
Commercial tests, sources of, 292–293
Common cause, and correlation, 123
Common correlates, between variables, 125–126

411

Comorbidity, survey of, 30–32
Completely randomized design, 138
 in psychological research, 140–141
  cognitive therapy study, 143
Concealment strategy, and subject reactivity, 245
Confidence interval (CI), 252–253
Confounded study, 65
Consent form, for research participants, 312
Construct validity, 74–75, 303
Content validity, 303
Continuous sampling, and observer bias
      control, 243–244
Control, experimental; see Experimental control
Control group design, 77
 no treatment control groups, 309
 with random asssignment of subjects, 207–208
  limitations of, 208–211
Controlling for rival hypotheses, 14, 61, 64
Convenience sampling, 288, 289–290
Correlation
 and causality, 123–124
 by chance, 124–125
 and common correlates, 125–126
 and correlation coefficient, 115–118
 by custom, 125
 graph of, 112–114
 importance of, 109
 and prediction: method of least squares, 119–122
Correlation coefficient (r), 115–118
Correlators, 36
Counterbalancing, and treatment order, 193–194
Creativity, in science, 8
Criterion validity, 303
Critical sampling, 250
Cross-sectional studies, 39–40
 using OXO design, 231, 232
Crucial experiment, 12
Cumulative records, of kymograph
      recordings, 212
Curvilinear relationship, of correlation, 120–121
Cycle of discovery, 5, 318
 for Mesmer's theory, 18–21
Cycle of validation, 5, 17, 318
 for Mesmer's theory, 21–26

D

Data
 confidentiality of, 314, 349
 definition of, 16

Data analysis, 314–315; see also Statistical analysis
      of data
 conclusions from, 16–17
 fraudulent, 349
 and general linear model, 200–201
Debriefing, of research partcipants, 310–311
Deduction, 10
Deductive reasoning, 10–11
 and hypotheses generation, 273
Degrees of freedom (df), in analysis
      of variance, 199
Demand characteristics, 307–309
 controlling for, 309–310
Dependent variables, definition, 71
Direct causation, and correlation, 123–124
Discussion section, of research report, 338–339
Double blind study, 65

E

Empirical descriptions, of observed
      behaviors, 239–241
Empirical evidence, and scientific method, 4
Empirical sciences, definition of, 4
Empiricism, John Stuart Mill and, 58–60
Error; see Measure of error
Error rate problem, 152–153
Ethics of research
 animal studies, 175–178
  Animal Welfare Act of 1985, 176–178
  APA Code of Conduct, 177–178
 APA Code of Conduct, 170–174
 Belmont Report, 166–168
 code of federal regulations for protection
      of human subjects, 168–170
 debriefing research participants, 311
 Golden Rule and, 179
 need for legislative change, 165–166
 Nurenberg Code, 159–161
  informed consent, 162–163
  risk/benefit analysis, 163–164
 Tuskegee syphilis study, 157–159, 162
Ethics of scientific communication, APA
      guidelines, 347, 349
Ethnography, 44
Ethogram, 239
Eugenics, 91
 regression analysis and, 114–115
Event analysis, 61–62, 239, 241
Events, now called variables, 71–72

Evidence
    and scientific method, 3–4
    rules of, 4–5
Experiment
    vs. passive observational study, 13–14,
        33–34, 36–37
    single-case; *see* Single-case experiment
    subject assignment in, 290
Experimental control
    definition of, 64–65
    for suggestion and reactivity, 309–310
Experimental treatments; *see* Treatments
Experimenter expectancy effects, 308–309
    controlling for, 309–310
Experimenters, 36–37
Exploratory research, 33
External validity, 73–74, 75
    of factorial design, 199–200
    maximizing in single-case design, 224–225
    and sampling techniques, 249, 250
Extinction phase, of Skinner's
        experiment, 213–214

F

Face-to-face interviews, 253, 255
Facilitated communication, single-case
        test of, 204–206
Factor, independent variable as, 186
Factor analysis, 49
Factorial design, 185–186
    advantages of, 199–200
    and analysis of variance, 190
    assigning subjects to treatments, 186–187
    between and within-subject designs, 190–194
        number of factors, 198–199
        subject factors, 194–198
    comparisons between conditions, 187
    definition of, 186
    Factor A main effect, 189
    Factor B main effect, 189–190
    interaction between Factors A and B, 187–188
Field experiment
    definition of, 35, 230
    need for, 229–230
Field experiment designs
    and nonequivalent control groups, 235–237
    OXO design, 230–232
    OXO design with different measures and
        subgroups, 232
    OXO design with repeated measures, time-series
        designs, 232–235
Field research, 35
Field studies, 35
Figure captions, in reseach report, 342
Figures, in research report, 342
Five-factor model, 49
Footnotes, in research report, 342
F test, 188–190
Functional descriptions, of observed
        behaviors, 239, 241–242

G

Gaussian distribution; *see* Normal distribution
Generalizable results, 13
General linear model (GLM), 200–201

H

Hawthorne effect, 305–306
Histogram, 97
History, threat of, 76
Hypotheses
    correlational tests of, 37–40
    definition, 9–10
    designing test of, 10–16
        controlling for rival, 14, 61, 64–65
    drawing conclusions, 16–17
    multiple, 270–271
    null; *see* Null hypothesis
    of research participants; *see* Demand
        characteristics
Hypothesis testing, 9, 10
Hypothesis testing research, 9, 10

I

Idiographic research
    case study as, 51–53
    life-narratives as, 54
    vs. nomothetic, 49–50
    psychobiography as, 53–54
    single-case experiment as, 51
Independent variables
    definition of, 71
    factors as, 186
Inductive reasoning, 7–8
Informed consent, principle of, 162–163
Innovation, in science, 8

Instability, threat of, 153
Institutional Animal Care and Use Committee
        (IACUC), 176
Institutional Review Board (IRB), 168
    applying to, 311–314
Instrumentation, threat of, 76–77
Instruments, research
    availability of, 290, 292
    sources of, 292–294
Intelligence, Galton's measurements of, 92–101
Interactions, factorial, 183–185, 187–188; see also
        Factorial designs; F test
Internal validity, 72–73, 75
    and single-case design, 224–225
Internet, 267–268
Interobserver (or interrater) reliability, 244, 303–305
    Cohen's kappa and, 304
Interrupted time-series design, 232–234
    with multiple replications, 234–235
    with nonequivalent no-treatment control group
        time series, 236
    with switching replications, 235
Interval scales, 88–89
Interviews, types of, 253–255
Intraobserver reliability, 244, 303, 305
Introduction section, of research report, 323–328
The Invisible College, 4

K

KR-20 reliability, 302
Kymograph, 212

L

Laboratory research, 34–35
Latin square design, 139–140
    application in psychology, 142–143
        children's high sugar diet study, 145–146
Laws of causation
    Mill's definition, 61
    Mill's methods for proving, 60–61, 62
        method of agreement, 69–70
        method of concomitant variation, 65–69
        method of difference, 62–64
Least squares method; see Method of least squares
Levels, in factorial design, 185–186
Linear relationship, of correlation, 119–120
Life-narrative, 54
Likert-type scale, 296

Line chart, 196–197
Literature review, in research report, 325–326
Longitudinal studies, 39–40
    and OXO design, 231

M

Magnitude estimation, 298
Main effect, of factor, 189–190
Manipulation, of conditions/events, 14–15, 33–40
Maturation, threat of, 76
Mean, 98
Measure of error, 130–133
    in completely randomized design, 138
    in Latin square design, 138–140
    in randomized blocks design, 133–138
Measurement scale properties; see Scale
        properties
Measurement scale types; see Scale types
Measures, in psychological research
    Galton's scaling method, 100–101
    importance of, 83–84
    normal distribution and, 95, 97–100
    norm-based, 91–93
        and correlation coefficient, 118
    percentiles and, 93–95, 98
    scales of, 87–90
    standard, 90–91
    statistical; see Statistical tests
    variety of, 14–16, 84–87
        nonreactive, 85–86
        reactive, 85–86
Median, 94
Mesmer's theory of animal magnetism, 18–26
Meta-analysis, 225
Metaphor, hypotheses generation
        from, 274–275
Method section, of research report, 328
Method of agreement, 69–70
Method of concomitant variation, 65–69
Method of difference, 62–65
    randomized design and, 130–133
Method of least squares, 119–122
Milgram's obediance study, 164
Mill's methods, 60–79
    applications of, 75–79
    limitations of, 72–75
    main research steps, 61–62
    observing and controlling events, 60–70
    research designs

method of agreement, 70
method of concomitant
    variation, 67–68
method of difference, 63–64
Mind, 320
Mixed design, 192
Mortality, threat of, 78–79
Multiple baseline design, 220–221, 223, 224
Multiple correlation coefficient, 121
Multiple hypotheses, openess to, 270–271
Multiple measures, of variables, 86
Multistage sampling, 252

N

National Comorbidity Survey, 30–32
Natural experiment, 35
Naturalistic observation, 33
    behavioral units selection, 239, 241–242
    minimizing observer bias, 242–244
    observer reliability and, 244
    and psychological research, 237–239
    subject reactivity reduction techniques, 244–249
Naturalistic research, 47–49
Nominal scale, 90
Nomothetic research, 49–50
Nonequivalent control group design, 232, 235–237
Non-normal distribution, 101–105
Nonprobability sampling, 249–250
Nonreactive measures, 85–86
Normal distribution, 95, 97–98
    percentiles and, 98
    of human characteristics, 99–100
Norm-based measurement, 91, 109
    beginnings of, 91–93
    and correlation coefficient, 118
Null hypothesis, 135–137
Nuremberg Code, 159–161
Nuremberg trials, 159–160

O

Observational studies, 13–14, 16, 33–34, 237–238
    psychologists' preferences for, 36–37
    testing causal hypotheses, 37–38
    testing coexistence hypotheses, 37–38
    testing hypotheses about sequence, 39–40
Observer reliability, 244, 303–305
Open-ended questions, 295–296
Operational definition, of concepts, 14–15

Operationism, 14–15
Oral presentations, of scientific work, 346–347
Order effects, and treatments, 193–194
Ordinal scales, 89–90
OXO single-case design, 206–208
    advantages of, 208–211

P

Parallel-forms reliability, 301
Partial causation, and correlation, 124
Participant observation, 43–46
Participants, human
    control problems in research, 305–310
        demand characteristics, 307–309
        Hawthorne effect, 305–306
        suggestion and reactivity, 309–310
    vs. subjects, 328
Passive observational study, 13, 33
Pasteur's maxim, 262
Pearson correlation coefficient (r), 118–120
Pearson's chi-square (X^2) test, 103–105
Peer reviewers, ethics of, 349
Percentiles, 93–95
Personality, structure of and five-factor
    model, 49
Phenomenological research, 46–47
Phenylketonuria (PKU), 183
Philosophical Transactions, 319–320
Pilot study, 150
Placebo treatment, 25, 65
Plagiarism, 348
Population, 42
Power; *see* Statistical power
Pretest-posttest one group design (OXO),
    modifications of, 230–237
Principal of beneficence, 167
    and data confidentiality, 314
    and subject debriefing, 311, 314
Principal of informed consent, 162–163
Principal of justice, 167–168
    and subject recruitment, 311
Principal of respect, 167
    and participant consent, 312
Probability sampling
    computer aided, 288–289
    in surveys, 42
Progress, and scientific method, 6
Psychobiography, 53–54
Psychological Abstracts, 264

Psychological Bulletin, 264
Psychological Review, 264
PsycINFO, 264
PsycLIT, 264
Publication credit, 348

Q

Qualitative variables, 71–72
Quantitative variables, 71–72
Quasi-experiments; *see* Field experiments
Questionnaire, construction of, 295–300
Question, closed, 295, 300
Question, open-ended, 295–296
Question, randomized response, 300
Question, rank order, 300
Question formats, closed item, 296, 300
Quota sampling, 250

R

Random assignment, of experimenters, 309
Random assignment, of subjects, 80, 290
    computerized, 290
    vs. systematic assignment, 191, 309
    with blocking, 133–134, 141–142
        and ATDs, 216–217
    without blocking, 140–141
Randomized blocks design, 133–138, 141
    determining measure of error, 134–135
    and null hypothesis, 135–137
    in perceptual development study, 144–145
    randomization in, 133–134
    replication in, 133, 216–217
    and *t* test, 137–138
Randomized control group design, 232
    field studies applications, 235–237
    limitations of, 208–211
Randomized experiments, 80
Randomized response question, 300
Randomized test, 137, 138
Ratio scales, 88
Reactive measures, 85–86
References list, of research report, 339, 341
Regression, discovery of, 109–111
Regression coefficient (r), 111, 114
Regression line, 112–114
Regression to the mean, 110–111, 114
Reliability, of observational measures, 244
    determining, 303–305

Reliability, of psychological measures,
    15–16, 301–302
    alpha, 302
    KR-20, 302
    parallel-forms, 301
    split-half, 302
    test-retest, 301
Replicated results, 4, 5–6, 137
Replication
    in randomized blocks design, 133
    in single-case design, 215–224
        multiple baseline, 220–221, 223, 224
        sequential, 215–219
        simultaneous, 215,219–220
Report writing; *see* Research report
Research
    interests of psychologists, 35–40
    value of multiple methods of, 40, 54
Research, classification of
    experimental vs. observational, 33–34
    idiographic vs. nomothetic, 49–50
    laboratory vs. field, 34–35
    natural experiment, 35
    naturalistic, 47–49
    passive observational, 41
    Willems's, 32, 33, 41, 47–48
Research communication, 317–350
    ethics of, 347–349
    and language of science, 320–321
    psychological report writing, 321–342
        APA editorial style, 342–344
        writing with style, 344–346
    oral presentations, 346–347
Research designs; *see also* specfic designs
    deciding on, 13–14
    need for diversity of, 54
    and psychologist's interests, 35–37
    and Willems's classification, 32, 33–48
Research problems identification
    difficulty of, 261–262
    in scientific research process, 6
    techniques, 262–284
        analogies and metaphors, 274–275
        anomalies, 275–276
        collecting observations, 268–272
        developing subject expertise, 262–263
        filling knowledge gaps, 276–277
        generating ideas from theory, 273
        improving current practices, 280–282
        journalizing ideas, 283–284

literature search, 263–268
patterns analysis, 278–279
practical problem solving, 282–283
resolving discrepancies, 279
skepticism, 280
turning assumptions on their heads, 278
Research report, APA editorial style for, 342, 344
Research report, organization and contents of APA
 style, 321–342
 abstract, 323
 appendix, 342
 author note, 342
 discussion, 338–339
 Field et al. manuscript, A1–A13
 figures, 342
 footnotes, 342
 introduction, 323
 literature review, 325–326
 rationale and study design, 326, 328
 research problem, 323, 325
 method, 328
 apparatus/measures, 329–330
 participants (or subjects), 328–329
 procedure, 329
 references, 339, 341
 results, 330–331
  organization of, 331, 333
  statistical analyses, 336
  tables and figures, 333–334
 tables, 342
 title page, 322
Response rates, and surveys, 253, 255
Results
 communication of; see
  Research communication
 definition of, 16
 generalization of, 13
 reaching conclusions from, 17
 replication of, 4, 5–6
Results section, of research report, 330–331
Royal Commission, 21
 refutation of Mesmer's theory, 21–26
Royal Society, scientific communication
 and, 318–319

S

Sampling, types, 249–252
Scale, Likert-type, 296
Scale properties, 87–88

Scales, standard vs. norm-based
 measurement, 90–91
Scale types, and properties, 87–90
Scatter, 113
Scatterplot, 112–114
Science
 appeal of, 2–3
 distinguishing features of, 3–6
 and innovation, 7–9
 serendipity in, 272
Scientific communication
 and community of scientists, 17–18
 ethics of, 347–349
 language of, 320–321
 research report; see Research report
Scientific community, 5
 research evaluation by, 17–18
Scientific method; see Scientific research process
Scientific research process, 6–18
 designing test for hypothesis, 10–16
  apparatus, manipulations, and
   measures, 14–16
 drawing conclusions, 16–17
 evaluation by scientific community, 17–18
 hypotheses generation, 9–10
 observation to explanation, 6–9
 research problem identification, 6
Selection, threat of, 78–79
Selective deposit, of archival data, 247–249
Selective survival, of archival data, 247–249
Self-administering interviews, 253, 255
Self-report measures, sources for, 292–294
Sequential replication design, 215–219
Serendipity, in science, 272
Skewed distributions, 102
Significance, level of, 137
Significance probability (p), 104, 136
Simple random sampling, 251, 252
Simultaneous replication design, 215, 219–220
Single-case (n=1) experiment, 51, 205
 advantages of, 208–211
 facilitated communication test as, 204–206
 and OXO design, 206–208
 principles of design and analysis, 223–226
 replication in modern
  multiple baseline, 220–221, 223, 224
  sequential, 215, 219
  simultaneous, 215, 219–220
 Skinner's basic, 211–215
Skewed distributions, 102–105

Skinner box, 212
Skip pattern, and questonnaires, 255
Snowball sampling, 250
Social Science Citation Index, 268
Speciesism, 175–176
Spearman-Brown formula, 302
Split-half reliability, 302
Standard deviation, 98
Standard scales, vs. norm-based, 90–91
Standardized mean difference (d), 148–149
Statistical analysis of data, 314–315
    reporting, 336
Statistical conclusion validity, 152–153
Statistical control, 79, 80
    in human experiments, 309
    and method of least squares, 121–122
Statistical power
    low power and conclusion validity, 152
    strategies for increasing, 150–151
    and treatment size effect, 148–150
    Type I and Type II errors, 146–148
Statistical regression, as threat in study, 234
Statistical significance, 136–137
Statistical test, 101–105
Stratified sampling, 252
Stress, and disease resistance, 84–87
Student, 137
Study, well-controlled vs. confounded, 64–65
Subject assignment, to groups, 290
Subject factors, and factorial designs, 191, 194–199
Subject pool, availability of, 289–290
Subject reactivity, reduction strategies for, 244–249
Subject recruitment, probability and convenience
        sampling, 288–290
Subjects
    in factorial design, 191
    experiment power and number of, 146–151
    vs. participants, 328
    in psychological research, 12–13
    selection in surveys, 41–42
Summary statistics, limitations of, 208–210
Summary table, for analysis of variance, 190
Survey research
    design of, 41–42
    error measurement, 252–253
    modes of administering, 253, 255
    question wording, 255–256
    sampling procedures, 249–252
Systematic assignment, vs. random, 191, 290, 309
Systematic sampling, 251–252

T

Tables, in research report, 342
Tachistoscope, 73
Telephone interviews, 253, 255
Testing, threat of, 76–77
Test-retest reliability, 301
Tests
    beginnings of norm-based, 91–101
    commercial vs. unpublished, 292–293
    statistical, 101–105
Tests in Print IV, 84
Theory, in scientific method, 6–8, 16–17
Threat of carry-over effects, 77
Threat of history, 76
    in single-case design, 224–225
Threat of instability, 153
Threat of instrumentation, 76–77
    in single-case design, 225
Threat of maturation, 76
    in single-case design, 224–225
Threat of mortality, 78–79
Threat of selection, 78–79
Threat of testing, 76–77
    in single-case design, 225
Title page, in research report, 322
Transitions, in writing, 345–346
Treatment effect size, and statistical
        research, 148–150
    estimating effect size, 150
Treatment phase, in Skinner's experiment, 213–214
Treatments, experimental
    in factorial design, 185–187
        assigning subjects to, 186–187
        number of, 185–186
True experiments, 230
t test, 137–138
"Turning assumptions on their heads," 278
Tuskegee syphilis study, 157–159, 162
"The Two Disciplines of Scientific
        Psychology," 36–37
Type I errors, 146–147
    and error rate problem, 152–153
Type II errors, 147

U

Uncontrolled variables
    dealing with, 79–80, 200–201
        Fisher's approach to, 129, 130–140

Unpublished tests, sources of, 293
Unobtrusive measures, and naturalistic
　　observation, 245–247
Utilitarianism, 59–60

V

Validity, of psychological measures, 16, 302–303
　　demand characteristics and experimenter
　　　　expectancies, 307–310
　　of statistical conclusions, 152–153
Variable(s)
　　correlation of, 115–118
　　　　and causal relationships, 123–124
　　　　and noncausal relationships, 124–126
　　dealing with uncontrolled, 79–80
　　　　Fisher's approach to, 129, 130–140
　　definition of, 71
　　dependent; *see* Dependent variables
　　independence of, 115–116
　　independent; *see* Independent variables
　　interactions; *see* Factorial designs
　　measurement of, 84
　　Mill's terminology for, 71, 72

quantitative vs. qualitative, 71–72
　　statistical control of, 121–122
Variance, analysis of, 190
Varying the circumstances, 62

W

Well controlled study, 64
Wichita jury study, 166
Willems's two-dimensional descriptive
　　space, 32, 41, 47–48
Within-subjects design, 75, 76–77
　　and factorial design, 193–194
　　with virtually total control, 79
Writing with style, 344–346

Y

Yoked control designs, 144

Z

Zimbardo's prison experiment, 166
z scores, 116–117